Shaping the Environment: Science, Technology, and Society

Lynchburg College Symposium Readings

Third Edition

2009

Volume VIII

Shaping the Environment: Science, Technology, and Society

Edited by

David O. Freier, PhD

Library of Congress Control Number: 2009907050
ISBN: Hardcover 978-1-4415-4898-6
Softcover 978-1-4415-4897-9

This book was printed in the United States of America.

To order additional copies of this book, contact:
Xlibris Corporation
1-888-795-4274
www.Xlibris.com
Orders@Xlibris.com
23037

Contents

Acknowledgements

We gratefully acknowledge the following permissions to reprint material used in this text:

From *PRIORITIES IN BIOMEDICAL ETHICS.* © 1981 James F. Childress. Used by permission of Westminster John Knox Press.

Pages 123-136 from THE ECOLOGY OF COMMERCE: A DECLARATION OF SUSTAINABILITY by PAUL HAWKEN. Copyright © 1993 by Paul Hawken. Reprinted by permission of HarperCollins Publishers.

BRAVE NEW WORLD by ALDOUS HUXLEY, copyright 1932, 1960 by Aldous Huxley. Reprinted by permission of HarperCollins Publishers.

A Sand County Almanac (1966) by Leopold, Aldo. By permission of Oxford University Press, Inc.

Odum, W.E. (1982, October). Environmental Degradation and the Tyranny of Small Decisions. *BioScience, 32*(9), 728-729. Used by permission.

From ISHMAEL by Daniel Quinn, copyright © 1992 by Daniel Quinn. Used by permission of Bantam Books, a division of Random House, Inc.

"A Country of Illusion", "First Causes", from CADILLAC DESERT, REVISED AND UPDATED by Marc P. Reisner, copyright © 1986, 1993 by Marc R. Reisner. Used by permission of Viking Penguin, a division of Penguin Group (USA) Inc.

From THE IMPACT OF SCIENCE ON SOCIETY by Bertrand Russell. Copyright © 1951. Columbia University Press. Reprinted by Permission of the publisher.

From SMALL IS BEAUTIFUL: ECONOMICS AS IF PEOPLE MATTERED by E. F. SHUMACHER. Copyright © 1973 by E. F. Schumacher. Reprinted by permission of HarperCollins Publishers.

The Lives of a Cell. New York: The Viking Press. 3-5, 11-15, 91-95, copyright © 1972 by The Massachusetts Medical Society, "On Societies as Organisms", copyright © 1971 by The Massachusetts Medical Society, from THE LIVES OF A CELL by Lewis Thomas. Used by permission of Viking Penguin, a division of Penguin Group (USA) Inc.

J. D. Watson and F. H. C. Crick, "The Molecular Structure of Nucleic Acids: A Structure for Deoxyribose Nucleic Acid." Reprinted by permission of Macmillan LTD.

A special thanks goes to Professor Nina Salmon for agreeing to copyedit this volume. The editors further acknowledge with thanks the dedicated work of Rachel Moore ('08), Elizabeth Childress ('12), and Catherine Eagle, administrative assistant for their editorial assistance.

Lynchburg College Symposium Readings Senior Symposium and the LCSR Program

The ten-volume series, Lynchburg College Symposium Readings, has been developed by Lynchburg College faculty for use in the Senior Symposium and the Lynchburg College Symposium Readings Program (SS/LCSR). Each volume presents primary source material organized around interdisciplinary, liberal arts themes.

In 1976, the College developed the Senior Symposium as a two-hour, interdisciplinary course, required of all graduating seniors. On Mondays, students in all sections of the course come together for public lectures, given by invited guest speakers. On Wednesdays, Symposium students meet in their sections for student-led discussions and presentations on associated readings from the LCSR series. The course requires students, who have spent their later college years in narrowing the scope of their studies, to expand their fields of vision within a discussion group composed of and led by their peers. Students can apply analytical and problem-solving capabilities learned in their major fields of study to issues raised by guest speakers and classical readings.

This approach works against convention in higher education, which typically emphasizes the gradual exclusion of subject areas outside of a student's major field. But Senior Symposium leads students, poised for graduation, into their post-college intellectual responsibilities. They gain experience in taking their liberal education into real world problems, using it to address contemporary problems thoughtfully and critically. In order to do this successfully, students must abandon their habitual posture as docile receptors of authoritative information for a much more skeptical attitude toward opinion, proof, reasoning, and authoritative experience. The effort to think constructively through a variety of conflicting opinions—on a weekly basis—prepares them well for the mature, independent, well-reasoned points of view expected of educated adults.

The LCSR Program's primary goals are to foster an appreciation of the connection between basic skills and interdisciplinary knowledge, and to promote greater cross-disciplinary communication among faculty and students. General education core courses or courses that serve other program requirements may be classified as "LCSR," as long as they fulfill certain speaking and writing activities connected to LCSR readings. The effect of the program has been to help create the atmosphere of a residential academic community; shared learning creates a climate in which teaching and learning take root more forcefully.

Since its inception, the SS/LCSR Program has helped create opportunities for faculty interaction across the disciplines in "pre-service" and "in-service" workshops. Each May, the LCSR Program sponsors a four-day pre-service workshop to which all new full-time and part-time faculty members are invited. Participants receive individual sets of the Lynchburg College Symposium Readings, which they make their own by using them during the workshop in exercises designed to promote familiarity with a wide variety of the readings. The goals of the workshop are several: for those unfamiliar with the program, to begin planning an LCSR course; for new faculty, to become acquainted with those they have not met and get to know their acquaintances better; for other faculty of various experiential levels, to share their pedagogical successes; for new teachers, to ask questions about teaching, about the College, and about the students in an informal setting; for experienced teachers to re-visit some of their assumptions, pedagogies, and strategies; to inspire strong scholarship, creative teaching, risk-taking, and confidence among all participants.

Another opportunity comes with the "in-service" workshops, which occur each month during the school year. The LCSR Program sponsors luncheons and dinners at which faculty teaching in the program give informal presentations on their use of specific teaching strategies or reading selections. Attendance is voluntary, but many try to be present for every session. For those involved in the LCSR program, teaching has become what Lee Schulman, President of the Carnegie Foundation, calls "community property."

On the Lynchburg College campus, there is evidence of a systematic change in teaching effectiveness as well as sustained faculty commitment to the program. By the 2002-2003 academic year, nearly two-thirds of all full-time faculty members and more than half of all part-time faculty members had completed the workshop at some time during their time at Lynchburg College. In any given semester, roughly ten to fifteen percent of the total class enrollments are in LCSR courses, not counting the required Senior Symposium. An important feature of this program is that participation is voluntary on the part of the faculty and, except for the required Senior Symposium, on the part of students. The program's influence quietly pervades the campus community, improving teaching and scholarship. Many see the LCSR Program as the College's premier academic program.

The Senior Symposium/LCSR program publishes *Agora*, an in-house journal that features the best of student writings responding to LCSR texts. The journal selections by students must integrate classical ideas and issues with contemporary ones. Faculty may also submit writings that address innovative teaching strategies. The journal takes its title from the marketplace at the heart of classical Athens, where much of Athenian public life was carried on: mercantile exchange, performance, political debate, athletic contests, and the public worship of deities all took place within the hustle and bustle of the Athenian agora. Similarly, the journal seeks to be a marketplace for compelling ideas and issues. Faculty members and students serve together on the editorial committee.

Since 1976, the Senior Symposium and the LCSR Program have affected the academic community both within and beyond the Lynchburg College campus. In 1991, Professor Richard Marius from Harvard University's writing center in reviewing the program favorably said, "I have seldom in my life been so impressed by an innovation in college education. I suppose the highest compliment that I could pay to the program was that I wished I could teach in it." Also in 1991, Professor Donald Boileau of George Mason University's Communication Studies department wrote, "what I discovered was a sound program that not only enriches the education of students at Lynchburg College, but what I hope can be a model for many other colleges and universities throughout our country." In spring 2003, in an article titled, "Whither the Great Books," Dr. William Casement described the LCSR program as the "most fully organized version" of the recent growth of great-books programs that employ an "across-the-disciplines structure." According to him, this approach perhaps encourages the use of the great books across the curriculum, which can be less isolating than even interdisciplinary programs. The Senior Symposium and LCSR Programs have received national acclaim in such publications as Loren Pope's *Colleges That Change Lives* and Charles Sykes and Brad Miner's *The National Review of College Guide, America's 50 Top Liberal Arts Schools.*

Shaping the Environment: Science, Technology, and Society is the eighth of the third edition of the Lynchburg College Symposium Readings series. The first edition, published in the early 1980s, included several selections also printed in the third edition. We gratefully acknowledge the work of Dr. Julius Sigler, Vice President for Academic Affairs and Dean of the College who edited the first and second editions of this volume. The Senior Symposium was the creation of Dr. James Huston, Dean of the College, *Emeritus* (1972-1984). With Dr. Michael Santos, professor of history, he co-founded the LCSR program. Dean Huston served as the first series editor, and with Dr. Julius Sigler, co-edited the second series. All three remain committed to the program today, and for this we are grateful.

Peggy Pittas, PhD
Series Managing Editor
Katherine Gray, PhD

Introduction

> It is interesting to contemplate an entangled bank, clothed with many plants of many kinds, with birds singing on the bushes, with various insects flitting about, and with worms crawling through the damp earth, and to reflect that these elaborately constructed forms, so different from each other, and dependent on each other in so complex a manner, have all been produced by laws acting around us. These laws, taken in the largest sense, being Growth with Reproduction; Inheritance which is almost implied by reproduction; Variability from the indirect and direct action of the external conditions of life, and from use and disuse; a Ratio of Increase so high as to lead to a Struggle for Life, and as a consequence to Natural Selection, entailing Divergence of Character and the Extinction of less-improved forms. Thus, from the war of nature, from famine and death, the most exalted object which we are capable of conceiving, namely, the production of the higher animals, directly follows. There is grandeur in this view of life, with its several powers, having been originally breathed into new forms or into one; and that, whilst this planet has gone cycling on according to the fixed law of gravity, from so simple a beginning endless forms most beautiful and most wonderful have been, and are being, evolved.[1]

The contents of this volume provide a wide introduction to ideas that continue to provide substantive points of discussion both within scientific fields and amongst the lay public. As Charles Darwin wrote above in his final paragraph from *Origin of Species*, his ideas and those contained within many of the works within this volume contain a grandeur or at the least a significance which in many instances continue to be part of the public discussion of science. These ideas range from the foundational, such as Darwin's natural selection, to the more philosophical and radical ideas put forth by Paul Feyerabend in *Science in a Free Society*. The readers of the selections included in this volume are encouraged to begin with the ideas here and to seek out and expand their investigations from the introductions provided within.

The first unit in the volume is science, with an emphasis on the biological sciences. It opens with Darwin's chapter on natural selection, where he elaborates upon the details of his proposed mechanism for descent with modification and, in his smooth and Victorian style, provides a long series of evidence and support for this idea. This is followed by the work of scientist Louis Agassiz, one of Darwin's main opponents within the United States, but who was noted for his work in the area of natural history. Best known for his extensive work on the effects of glaciers, Agassiz lectured extensively throughout the United States. Vannevar Bush provides insight into the nature of science in a public context, where he considers the rapidly expanding importance of science to national issues that held true when written at the end of World War II and which remain true today. Slipping back into the biological realm, Lewis Thomas provides an elegant view of the cellular basis of life, a principal concept of the biological sciences that grew to full strength during the 20th century. Finally Feyerabend offers a counterpoint to the modern methods of science, arguing from a relativistic point of view, that modern science has become as dogmatic as religion, and in some ways could be considered a religion of its own.

The second unit of this volume, *Technology*, opens with the only true technical work of science included within this volume, the brief, but concise description by James Watson and Francis Crick on their proposed structure of the molecular composition of deoxyribonucleic acid, or DNA. It fronts a section of five works where the remaining excerpts are all from pieces of fiction. In the pursuit of technology, as well as the world of fiction, the door (or as some have said, Pandora's Box) opened by Watson and Crick has led to the continuing development of molecular science but has proved an equally fruitful realm for authors of science fiction. In this line of fiction, Aldous Huxley questions man's use of technology through his fictional future. Similar issues arise in the classic work of H.G. Wells *The Time Machine*. As science rapidly produces new technologies, it is imperative that we consider how these technologies will be used to the benefit of humankind and the planet we inhabit. Swift, in *Gulliver's Travels*, provides a sharp critique about the use and advances of science, that could be considered a cautionary tale, or one where the lay skeptics hold back the progress of science due to their lack of understanding of the methods of science. Technology closes with another iconic tale, that of Shelley's *Frankenstein*. This much popularized work that began as a ghost story has evolved into the story of man's misuse of science, to his own detriment.

The third unit focuses upon more recent works regarding issues of the environment. It leads off with two short sections from Leopold's *A Sand County Almanac*, a work of both scientific and poetic value. Leopold was among the earliest to consider the breadth of the environment and its importance to man. Not included in this volume but found in previous editions, but of equal and foundational importance are the words of Rachel Carson in *Silent Spring*. Her opening chapter entitled "A Fable for Tomorrow" paints a picture of the idyllic American landscape with rolling hills, orchards, birds, insects and the numerous and diverse forms of life that can be found in such an environment. This idyllic scene is spoiled by the sudden blight that erodes this environment, with Carson ending her opening statement with a brief but ominous set of words;

No witchcraft, no enemy action had silenced the rebirth of new life in this stricken world. The people had done it themselves.[2]

This self-imposed affliction of damage to the environment is reflected in the remaining four selections in the environment section. Hawken discusses the concept of sustainability in the corporate world, which places his ideas well ahead of business approaches that are only now beginning to be adapted for use in the business world. Daniel Quinn in *Ishmael* provides a fictional framework for examination of global issues and problems with the overtones of the nature of the society involved, those he characterizes as "Leavers" and "Takers". In *Cadillac Desert* Marc Reisner explores the history of water use and apportionment across the American west, from its foundations in the 19th century, through the political manipulations of the early and mid 20th centuries, to a final glimmer of hope just beginning when his work was first published in 1986. This section concludes with a reprise of T. R. Malthus' *The Principle of Population* from the first edition. Issues of human overpopulation, food source production, and a concern that overpopulation could lead to serious shortages of foods for everyone are again issues in the forefront of contemporary conversations on the environment.

The final unit circles back around to issues that have been raised throughout the volume, with a focus on society. Bertrand Russell discuses the role and impact of science within society by looking back historically from his vantage of the 1950's. A briefer, but no less significant work is that of the ecologist William E. Odum in his *Environmental Degradation and the Tyranny of Small Decisions*. This piece could easily have been included within the environment section of the volume, but fits even better within the society segment. Even though he wrote on the importance of every individual's role in decision making and its effect on the environment, his comments readily transfer to how we examine the role of science in society. The well-known work of Garrett Hardin's *The Tragedy of the Commons* reflects his ideas on societal use of resources, and of course science and technology are clearly important resources of any society. The economist E.F. Schumacher brings his unique merger of European and Asian concepts to bear on a wide range of subjects, including the use of land, the human impact of technology, nuclear power, and what he calls "Buddhist Economics". The final piece is by James F. Childress a professor of ethics and religious studies. He reflects upon bioethics, and the role of such biotechnology in current society.

The readings contained within this volume span a wide range of disciplines, but all have some bearing, either direct or indirect, upon the sciences. They should prove useful in areas such as the life and environmental sciences, but also to those in the humanities, the health sciences, business, and other areas of academic pursuit. This collection is but the most current of works upon which modern science is built. As current and future science produces new ideas, these works will be supplanted by new and no less significant ideas. John A. Moore in his outstanding work, *Science as a Way of Knowing*, clearly lays out the importance of an understanding of science, and in particular biology, to all persons:

> Very difficult decisions will have to be made if we are to have a sustainable human society in a sustainable environment. Many of those decisions will require extensive knowledge of biology. We have reached the point in history, therefore, when biological knowledge is the *sine qua non* for a viable human future. Such knowledge will be especially necessary for the leaders of society—in government, industry, business, and education—but the tough decisions will have to be supported by an informed electorate. A critical subset of society will have to understand the nature of life, the interactions of

> living creatures with their environment, and the strengths and limitations of the data and procedures of science itself. The acquisition of biological knowledge, for so long a luxury except for those in agriculture and the health sciences, has now become a necessity for all.[3]

Those who continue to learn from the ever more rapid pace of scientific discovery will be the ones who provide the answers we need to ensure a future for ourselves and our planet.

Works Cited:

1. Darwin, Charles. (1859). *The Origin of Species by Means of Natural Selection.* London, Penguin Book Group. 459-460.
2. Carson, Rachel. (1962). *Silent Spring.* Boston: Houghton Mifflin Company. 3
3. Moore, John A. (1993). *Science as a Way of Knowing.* Cambridge, MA; Harvard University Press. 4

David O. Freier, PhD

Section I

WHAT IS SCIENCE?

What is science? This appears to be a simple question, but this simple question has provided a wide ranging set of answers that continue to provoke heated discussion within the fields of practicing scientists, and by those whose areas of expertise include philosophy, politics, and religion.

In truth, there is no one simple answer to this question but rather a set of answers which continue to be refined through practice and discussion. The foundations of modern science are built upon the ideas of Francis Bacon, Isaac Newton, and Rene Descartes, but their earliest principles have been extended and expanded far beyond their original thinking. In his work *This Is Biology* the preeminent twentieth century evolutionary biologist Ernst Mayr devotes a chapter to the question, "What is Science?" He writes;

> A number of factors account for the difficulties philosophers have encountered in agreeing upon a definition of science. One of them is that science is both an activity (that which scientists do) and a body of knowledge (that which scientists know). [25]

His may be the most apt description of what science is. It is a way of viewing and acting upon the world around oneself, the activity of science. At the same time it is also a collected body of knowledge that one can draw upon to answer a question, or to aid in refining the specifics of the question being asked. True scientists do not practice a specialty, but rather they seek out the proper questions by reviewing what is already known and then use their acumen as scientists to push forward the boundaries of knowledge. They seek answers to their questions by the practice of science.

In this section each of the selections was written by scientists and authors who found the available scientific knowledge lacking in some significant way. Their thoughts, investigations, and ideas moved these boundaries forward. For some, the change did not proceed as expected, although in many cases, their ideas remain at the forefront of today's scientific understanding. Students should use these ideas to build upon their own understanding and continue to advance the practice and the body of knowledge that is science.

SOURCES:

Mayr, Ernst. (1997). *This Is Biology. The Science of the Living World.* The Belknap Press of Harvard University Press.

Moore, John A. (1993). *Science As a Way of Knowing. The Foundations of Modern Biology.* Harvard University Press.

Charles Darwin

1809-1882

The Origin of Species

1892

Charles Darwin may have been the last great polymath of the biological sciences. The pre-eminent naturalist of his day, his youth was spent hunting rather than concentrating on his education. He attended seminary at Cambridge but moved to the University of Edinburgh where he planned to follow his father into the field of medicine. However, he soon realized his interest in geology and spent much of his time perfecting his naturalist's skills under the tutelage of the geologist, Professor Adam Sedgwick. In 1831, his father allowed young Charles to join the voyage of the H.M.S. Beagle as the companion to the ship's captain, Robert FitzRoy.

During that voyage Darwin became the ship's naturalist and began to collect and develop his ideas on life and its evolution. The many collecting excursions throughout the islands of the Atlantic and Pacific, most notably the Galapagos Islands, and his forays deep into South America, provided the raw material for making connections between his collected specimens and the examples of life with which he had grown up. His reading of Charles Lyell's first volume on *Principles of Geology* during the voyage provided him with the idea of slow change over time. Upon his return to England, Darwin read Malthus. In response he wrote, " . . . [I] happened to read for amusement Malthus on *Population*, and being well prepared to appreciate the struggle for existence which everywhere goes on from long-continued observation of the habits of animals and plants, it at once struck me that under these circumstances favourable variations would tend to be preserved and unfavourable ones to be destroyed." (Darwin, 1886, p. 42-43).This observation provided the two key elements for an explanation of the evolution of life on earth, slow change over time and competition for resource between individuals in a population.

In 1859, he published *On the Origin of Species by Means of Natural Selection*, which he called his abstract to his arguments in favor of his ideas about the evolution of life on earth. The section included here is his principal description of the theory of natural selection. The simplicity of Darwin's idea of natural selection, prompted his friend Thomas Henry Huxley to have said, "Why didn't I think of that?" Natural selection in its essence is a simple concept, yet has profound implications for the structure of all fields of biology, and thus has remained at the foundation of modern biological study.

SOURCES:

Darwin, Francis (Ed.) (1892). *The Autobiography of Charles Darwin and Selected Letters.*
New York: Dover Publications Inc.

Hellman, Hal. (1998.) *Great Feuds in Science. Ten of the Liveliest Disputes Ever.* New York: John Wiley & Sons Inc.

SELECTION FROM:

Darwin, Charles. (1886). *The Origin of Species by Means of Natural Selection, or the Preservation of Favored Races in the Struggle for Life.* New York: D. Appleton and Company. 62-105.

CHAPTER IV

NATURAL SELECTION; OR THE SURVIVAL OF THE FITTEST.

Natural Selection—its power compared with man's selection—its power on characters of trifling importance—its power at all ages and on both sexes—Sexual Selection—On the generality of intercrosses between individuals of the same species—Circumstances favourable and unfavourable to the results of Natural Selection, namely, intercrossing, isolation, number of individuals—Slow action—Extinction caused by Natural Selection—Divergence of Character, related to the diversity of inhabitants of any small area, and to naturalisation—Action of Natural Selection, through Divergence of Character, and Extinction, on the descendants from a common parent—Explains the grouping of all organic beings—Advance in organisation—Low forms preserved—Convergence of character—Indefinite multiplication of species—Summary.

How will the struggle for existence, briefly discussed in the last chapter, act in regard to variation? Can the principle of selection, which we have seen is so potent in the hands of man, apply under nature? I think we shall see that it can act most efficiently. Let the endless number of slight variations and individual differences occurring in our domestic productions, and, in a lesser degree, in those under nature, be borne in mind; as well as the strength of the hereditary tendency. Under domestication, it may be truly said that the whole organisation becomes in some degree plastic. But the variability, which we almost universally meet with in our domestic productions, is not directly produced, as Hooker and Asa Gray have well remarked, by man; he can neither originate varieties, nor prevent their occurrence; he can only preserve and accumulate such as do occur. Unintentionally he exposes organic beings to new and changing conditions of life, and variability ensues; but similar changes of conditions might and do occur under nature. Let it also be borne in mind how infinitely complex and close-fitting are the mutual relations of all organic beings to each other and to their physical conditions of life; and consequently what infinitely varied diversities of structure might be of use to each being under changing conditions of life. Can it, then, be thought improbable, seeing that variations useful to man have undoubtedly occurred, that other variations useful in some way to each being in the great and complex battle of life, should occur in the course of many successive generations? If such do occur, can we doubt (remembering that many more individuals are born than can possibly survive) that individuals having any advantage, however slight, over others, would have the best chance of surviving and of procreating their kind? On the other hand, we may feel sure that any variation in the least degree injurious would be rigidly destroyed. This preservation of favourable individual differences and variations, and the destruction of those which are injurious, I have called Natural Selection, or the Survival of the Fittest. Variations neither useful nor injurious would not be affected by natural selection, and would be left either a fluctuating element, as perhaps we see in certain polymorphic species, or would ultimately become fixed, owing to the nature of the organism and the nature of the conditions.

Several writers have misapprehended or objected to the term Natural Selection. Some have even imagined that natural selection induces variability, whereas it implies only the preservation of such variations as arise and are beneficial to the being under its conditions of life. No one objects to agriculturists speaking of the potent effects of man's selection; and in this case the individual differences given by nature, which man for some object selects, must of necessity first occur. Others have objected that the term selection implies conscious choice in the animals which become modified; and it has even been urged that, as plants have no volition, natural selection is not applicable to them! In the literal sense of the word, no doubt, natural selection is a false term; but who ever objected to chemists speaking of the elective affinities of the various elements?—and yet an acid cannot strictly be said to elect the base with which it in preference combines. It has been said that I speak of natural selection as an active power or Deity; but who objects to an author speaking of the attraction of gravity as ruling the movements of the planets? Every one knows what is meant and is implied by such metaphorical expressions; and they are almost necessary for brevity. So again it is difficult to avoid personifying the word Nature; but I mean by Nature, only the aggregate action and product of many natural laws, and by laws the sequence of events as ascertained by us. With a little familiarity such superficial objections will be forgotten.

We shall best understand the probable course of natural selection by taking the case of a country undergoing some slight physical change, for instance, of climate. The proportional numbers of its inhabitants will almost immediately undergo a change, and some species will probably become extinct. We may conclude, from what we have seen of the intimate and complex manner in which the inhabitants of each country are bound together, that any change in the numerical proportions of the inhabitants, independently of the change of climate itself, would seriously affect the others. If the country were open on its borders, new forms would certainly immigrate, and this would likewise seriously disturb the relations of some of the former inhabitants. Let it be remembered how powerful the influence of a single introduced tree or mammal has been shown to be. But in the case of an island, or of a country partly surrounded by barriers, into which new and better adapted forms could not freely enter, we should then have places in the economy of nature which would assuredly be better filled up, if some of the original inhabitants were in some manner modified; for, had the area been open to immigration, these same places would have been seized on by intruders. In such cases, slight modifications, which in any way favoured the individuals of any species, by better adapting them to their altered conditions, would tend to be preserved; and natural selection would have free scope for the work of improvement.

We have good reason to believe, as shown in the first chapter, that changes in the conditions of life give a tendency to increased variability; and in the foregoing cases the conditions have changed, and this would manifestly be favorable to natural selection, by affording a better chance of the occurrence of profitable variations. Unless such occur, natural selection can do nothing. Under the term of "variations," it must never be forgotten that mere individual differences are included. As man can produce a great result with his domestic animals and plants by adding up in any given direction individual differences, so could natural selection, but far more easily from having incomparably longer time for action nor do I believe that any great physical change, as of climate, or any unusual degree of isolation, to check immigration, is necessary in order that new and unoccupied places should be left, for natural selection to fill up by improving some of the varying inhabitants. For as all the inhabitants of each country are struggling together with nicely balanced forces, extremely slight modifications in the structure or habits of one species would often give it an advantage over others; and still further modifications of the same kind would often still further increase the advantage, as long as the species continued under the same conditions of life and profited by similar means of subsistence and defence. No country can be named in which all the native inhabitants are now so perfectly adapted to each other and to the physical conditions under which they live, that none of them could be still better adapted or improved; for in all countries, the natives have been so far conquered by naturalised productions, that they have allowed some foreigners to take firm possession of the land. And as foreigners have thus in every country beaten some of the natives, we may safely conclude that the natives might have been modified with advantage, so as to have better resisted the intruders.

As man can produce, and certainly has produced, a great result by his methodical and unconscious means of selection, what may not natural selection effect? Man can act only on external and visible characters: Nature, if I may be allowed to personify the natural preservation or survival of the fittest, cares nothing for appearances, except in so far as they are useful to any being. She can act on every internal organ, on every shade of constitutional difference, on the whole machinery of life. Man selects only for his own good: Nature only for that of the being which she tends. Every selected character is fully exercised by her, as is implied by the fact of their selection. Man keeps the natives of many climates in the same country; he seldom exercises each selected character in some peculiar and fitting manner; he feeds a long and a short beaked pigeon on the same food; he does not exercise a long-backed or long-legged quadruped in any peculiar manner; he exposes sheep with long and short wool to the same climate. He does not allow the most vigorous males to struggle for the females. He does not rigidly destroy all inferior animals, but protects during each varying season, as far as lies in his power, all his productions. He often begins his selection by some half-monstrous form; or at least by some modification prominent enough to catch the eye or to be plainly useful to him. Under nature, the slightest differences of structure or constitution may well turn the nicely balanced scale in the struggle for life, and so be preserved. How fleeting are the wishes and efforts of man! how short his time! and consequently how poor will be his results, compared with those accumulated by Nature during whole geological periods? Can we wonder, then, that Nature's productions should be far "truer" in character than man's productions; that they should be infinitely better adapted to the most complex conditions of life, and should plainly bear the stamp of far higher workmanship?

It may metaphorically be said that natural selection is daily and hourly scrutinising, throughout the world, the slightest variations; rejecting those that are bad, preserving and adding up all that are good; silently and insensibly working, *whenever and wherever opportunity offers*, at the improvement of each organic being in relation to its organic and inorganic conditions of life. We see nothing of these slow changes in progress, until the hand of time has marked the lapse of ages, and then so imperfect is our view into long-past geological ages, that we see only that the forms of life are now different from what they formerly were.

In order that any great amount of modification should be effected in a species, a variety, when once formed must again, perhaps after a long interval of time, vary or present individual differences of the same favourable nature as before; and these must be again preserved, and so onwards step by step. Seeing that individual differences of the same kind perpetually recur, this can hardly be considered as an unwarrantable assumption. But whether it is true, we can judge only by seeing how far the hypothesis accords with and explains the general phenomena of nature. On the other hand, the ordinary belief that the amount of possible variation is a strictly limited quantity is likewise a simple assumption.

Although natural selection can act only through and for the good of each being, yet characters and structures, which we are apt to consider as of very trifling importance, may thus be acted on. When we see leaf-eating insects green, and bark-feeders mottled-grey; the alpine ptarmigan white in winter, the red grouse the colour of heather, we must believe that these tints are of service to these birds and insects in preserving them from danger. Grouse, if not destroyed at some period of their lives, would increase in countless numbers; they are known to suffer largely from birds of prey; and hawks are guided by eyesight to their prey—so much so, that on parts of the Continent persons are warned not to keep white pigeons, as being the most liable to destruction. Hence natural selection might be effective in giving the proper colour to each kind of grouse, and in keeping that colour, when once acquired, true and constant. Nor ought we to think that the occasional destruction of an animal of any particular colour would produce little effect: we should remember how essential it is in a flock of white sheep to destroy a lamb with the faintest trace of black. We have seen how the colour of the hogs, which feed on the "paint root" in Virginia, determines whether they shall live or die. In plants, the down on the fruit and the colour of the flesh are considered by botanists as characters of the most trifling importance, yet we hear from an excellent horticulturist, Downing, that in the United States smooth-skinned fruits suffer far more from a beetle, a Curculio, than those with down; that purple plums suffer far more from a certain disease than yellow plums, whereas another disease attacks yellow-fleshed peaches far more than those with other coloured flesh. If, with all the aids of art, these slight differences make a great difference in cultivating the several varieties, assuredly, in a state of nature, where the trees would have to struggle with other trees and with a host of enemies, such differences would effectually settle which variety, whether a smooth or downy, a yellow or purple fleshed fruit, should succeed.

In looking at many small points of difference between species, which, as far as our ignorance permits us to judge, seem quite unimportant, we must not forget that climate, food, &c., have no doubt produced some direct effect. It is also necessary to bear in mind that, owing to the law of correlation, when one part varies, and the variations are accumulated through natural selection, other modifications, often of the most unexpected nature, will ensue.

As we see that those variations which, under domestication appear at any particular period of life, tend to reappear in the offspring at the same period;—for instance, in the shape, size, and flavour of the seeds of the many varieties of our culinary and agricultural plants; in the caterpillar and cocoon stages of the varieties of the silkworm; in the eggs of poultry, and in the colour of the down of their chickens; in the horns of our sheep and cattle when nearly adult;—so in a state of nature, natural selection will be enabled to act on and modify organic beings at any age, by the accumulation of variations profitable at that age, and by their inheritance at a corresponding age. If it profit a plant to have its seeds more and more widely disseminated by the wind, I can see no greater difficulty in this being effected through natural selection, than in the cotton-planter increasing and improving by selection the down in the pods on his cotton-trees. Natural selection may modify and adapt the larva of an insect to a score of contingencies, wholly different from those which concern the mature insect; and these modifications may affect, through correlation, the structure of the adult. So, conversely, modifications in the adult may affect the structure of the larva; but in all cases natural selection will ensure that they shall not be injurious: for if they were so, the species would become extinct.

Natural selection will modify the structure of the young in relation to the parent, and of the parent in relation to the young. In social animals it will adapt the structure of each individual for the benefit of the whole community; if the community profits by the selected change. What natural selection cannot do, is to modify the structure of one species, without giving it any advantage, for the good of another species; and though statements to this effect may be found in works of natural history, I cannot find one case which will bear investigation. A structure used only once in an animal's life, if of high importance to it, might be modified to any extent by natural selection; for instance, the great jaws possessed by certain insects, used exclusively for opening the cocoon—or the hard tip to the beak of unhatched birds, used for breaking the egg. It has been asserted, that of the best short-beaked tumbler-pigeons a greater number perish in the egg than are able to get out of it; so that fanciers assist in the act of hatching. Now, if nature had to make the beak of a full-grown pigeon very short for the bird's own advantage, the process of modification would be very slow, and there would be simultaneously the most rigorous selection of all the young birds within the egg, which had the most powerful and hardest beaks, for all with weak beaks would inevitably perish; or, more delicate and more easily broken shells might be selected, the thickness of the shell being known to vary like every other structure.

It may be well here to remark that with all beings there must be much fortuitous destruction, which can have little or no influence on the course of natural selection. For instance a vast number of eggs or seeds are annually devoured, and these could be modified through natural selection only if they varied in some manner which protected them from their enemies. Yet many of these eggs or seeds would perhaps, if not destroyed, have yielded individuals better adapted to their conditions of life than any of those which happened to survive. So again a vast number of mature animals and plants, whether or not they be the best adapted to their conditions, must be annually destroyed by accidental causes, which would not be in the least degree mitigated by certain changes of structure or constitution which would in other ways be beneficial to the species. But let the destruction of the adults be ever so heavy, if the number which can exist in any district be not wholly kept down by such causes,—or again let the destruction of eggs or seeds be so great that only a hundredth or a thousandth part are developed,—yet of those which do survive, the best adapted individuals, supposing that there is any variability in a favourable direction, will tend to propagate their kind in larger numbers than the less well adapted. If the numbers be wholly kept down by the causes just indicated, as will often have been the case, natural selection will be powerless in certain beneficial directions; but this is no valid objection to its efficiency at other times and in other ways; for we are far from having any reason to suppose that many species ever undergo modification and improvement at the same time in the same area.

Sexual Selection

Inasmuch as peculiarities often appear under domestication in one sex and become hereditarily attached to that sex, so no doubt it will be under nature. Thus it is rendered possible for the two sexes to be modified through natural selection in relation to different habits of life, as is sometimes the case; or for one sex to be modified in relation to the other sex, as commonly occurs. This leads me to say a few words on what I have called Sexual Selection. This form of selection depends, not on a struggle for existence in relation to other organic beings or to external conditions, but on a struggle between the individuals of one sex, generally the males, for the possession of the other sex. The result is not death to the unsuccessful competitor, but few or no offspring. Sexual selection is, therefore, less rigorous than natural selection. Generally, the most vigorous males, those which are best fitted for their places in nature, will leave most progeny. But in many cases, victory depends not so much on general vigour, as on having special weapons, confined to the male sex. A hornless stag or spurless cock would have a poor chance of leaving numerous offspring. Sexual selection, by always allowing the victor to breed, might surely give indomitable courage, length to the spur, and strength to the wing to strike in the spurred leg, in nearly the same manner as does the brutal cockfighter by the careful selection of his best cocks. How low in the scale of nature the law of battle descends, I know not; male alligators have been described as fighting, bellowing, and whirling round, like Indians in a war-dance, for the possession of the females; male salmons have been observed fighting all day long; male stag-beetles sometimes bear wounds from the huge mandibles of other males; the males of certain hymenopterous insects have been frequently seen by that inimitable observer M. Fabre, fighting for a particular female who sits by, an apparently unconcerned beholder of the struggle, and then retires with the conqueror. The war is, perhaps, severest between the males of polygamous animals, and these seem oftenest provided with special weapons. The males of carnivorous animals are already well armed; though to them and to others, special means of defence may be given through means of sexual selection, as the mane of the lion, and the hooked jaw to the male salmon; for the shield may be as important for victory, as the sword or spear.

Amongst birds, the contest is often of a more peaceful character. All those who have attended to the subject, believe that there is the severest rivalry between the males of many species to attract, by singing, the females. The rock-thrush of Guiana, birds of paradise, and some others, congregate; and successive males display with the most elaborate care, and show off in the best manner, their gorgeous plumage; they likewise perform strange antics before the females, which, standing by as spectators, at last choose the most attractive partner. Those who have closely attended to birds in confinement well know that they often take individual preferences and dislikes; thus Sir R. Heron has described how a pied peacock was eminently attractive to all his hen birds. I cannot here enter on the necessary details; but if man can in a short time give beauty and an elegant carriage to his bantams, according to his standard of beauty, I can see no good reason to doubt that female birds, by selecting, during thousands of generations, the most melodious or beautiful males, according to their standard of beauty, might produce a marked effect. Some well-known laws, with respect to the plumage of male and female birds, in comparison with the plumage of the young, can partly be explained through the action of sexual selection on variations occurring at different ages, and transmitted to the males alone or to both sexes at corresponding ages; but I have not space here to enter on this subject.

Thus it is, as I believe, that when the males and females of any animal have the same general habits of life, but differ in structure, colour, or ornament, such differences have been mainly caused by sexual selection: that is, by individual males having had, in successive generations, some slight advantage over other males, in their weapons, means of defence, or charms, which they have transmitted to their male offspring alone. Yet, I would not wish to attribute all sexual differences to this agency for we see in our domestic animals peculiarities arising and becoming attached to the male sex, which apparently have not been augmented through selection by man. The tuft of hair on the breast of the wild turkey cock cannot be of any use, and it is doubtful whether it can be ornamental in the eyes of the female bird;—indeed, had the tuft appeared under domestication, it would have been called a monstrosity.

Illustrations of the Action of Natural Selection, or the Survival of the Fittest.

In order to make it clear how, as I believe, natural selection acts, I must beg permission to give one or two imaginary illustrations. Let us take the case of a wolf, which preys on various animals, securing some by craft, some by strength, and some by fleetness; and let us suppose that the fleetest prey, a deer for instance, had from any change in the country increased in numbers, or that other prey had decreased in numbers, during that season of the year when the wolf was hardest pressed for food. Under such circumstances the swiftest and slimmest wolves would have the best chance of surviving and so be preserved or selected,—provided always that they retained strength to master their prey at this or some other period of the year, when they were compelled to prey on other animals. I can see no more reason to doubt that this would be the result, than that man should be able to improve the fleetness of his greyhounds by careful and methodical selection, or by that kind of unconscious selection which follows from each man trying to keep the best dogs without any thought of modifying the breed. I may add, that, according to Mr. Pierce, there are two varieties of the wolf inhabiting the Catskill Mountains in the United States, one with a light greyhound-like form, which pursues deer, and the other more bulky, with shorter legs, which more frequently attacks the shepherd's flocks.

It should be observed that, in the above illustration, I speak of the slimmest individual wolves, and not of any single strongly-marked variation having been preserved. In former editions of this work I sometimes spoke as if this latter alternative had frequently occurred. I saw the great importance of individual differences, and this led me fully to discuss the results of unconscious selection by man, which depends on the preservation of all the more or less valuable individuals, and on the destruction of the worst. I saw, also, that the preservation in a state of nature of any occasional deviation of structure, such as a monstrosity, would be a rare event; and that, if at first preserved, it would generally be lost by subsequent intercrossing with ordinary individuals. Nevertheless, until reading an able and valuable article in the 'North British Review' (1867), I did not appreciate how rarely single variations, whether slight or strongly-marked, could be perpetuated. The author takes the case of a pair of animals, producing during their lifetime two hundred offspring, of which, from various causes of destruction, only two on an average survive to pro-create their kind. This is rather an extreme estimate for most of the higher animals, but by no means so for many of the lower organisms. He then shows that if a single individual were born, which varied in some manner, giving it twice as good a chance of life as that of the other individuals, yet the chances would be strongly against its survival. Supposing it to survive and to breed, and that half its young inherited the favourable variation; still, as the Reviewer goes on to show, the young would have only a slightly better chance of surviving and breeding; and this chance would go on decreasing in the succeeding generations. The justice of these remarks cannot, I think, be disputed. If, for instance, a bird of some kind could procure its food more easily by having its beak curved, and if one were born with its beak strongly curved, and which consequently flourished, nevertheless there would be a very poor chance of this one individual perpetuating its kind to the exclusion of the common form; but there can hardly be a doubt, judging by what we see taking place under domestication, that this result would follow from the preservation during many generations of a large number of individuals with more or less strongly curved beaks, and from the destruction of a still larger number with the straightest beaks.

It should not, however, be overlooked that certain rather strongly marked variations, which no one would rank as mere individual differences, frequently recur owing to a similar organisation being similarly acted on,—of which fact numerous instances could be given with our domestic productions. In such cases, if the varying individual did not actually transmit to its offspring its newly-acquired character, it would undoubtedly transmit to them, as long as the existing conditions remained the same, a still stronger tendency to vary in the same manner. There can also be little doubt that the tendency to vary in the same manner has often been so strong that all the individuals of the same species have been similarly modified without the aid of any form of selection. Or only a third, fifth, or tenth part of the individuals may have been thus affected, of which fact several instances could be given. Thus Graba estimates that about one-fifth of the guillemots in the Faroe Islands consist of a variety so well marked, that it was formerly ranked as a distinct species under the name of Uria lacrymans. In cases of this kind, if the variation were of a beneficial nature, the original form would soon be supplanted by the modified form, through the survival of the fittest.

To the effects of intercrossing in eliminating variations of all kinds, I shall have to recur; but it may be here remarked that most animals and plants keep to their proper homes, and do not needlessly wander about; we see this even with migratory birds, which almost always return to the same spot. Consequently each newly formed variety would generally be at first local, as seems to be the common rule with varieties in a state of nature; so that similarly modified individuals would soon exist in a small body together, and would often breed together. If the new variety were successful in its battle for life, it would slowly spread from a central district, competing with and conquering the unchanged individuals on the margins of an ever-increasing circle.

It may be worthwhile to give another and more complex illustration of the action of natural selection. Certain plants excrete sweet juice, apparently for the sake of eliminating something injurious from the sap: this is effected, for instance, by glands at the base of the stipules in some Leguminosæ, and at the backs of the leaves of the common laurel. This juice, though small in quantity, is greedily sought by insects; but their visits do not in any way benefit the plant. Now, let us suppose that the juice or nectar was excreted from the inside of the flowers of a certain number of plants of any species. Insects in seeking the nectar would get dusted with pollen, and would often transport it from one flower to another. The flowers of two distinct individuals of the same species would thus get crossed; and the act of crossing, as can be fully proved, gives rise to vigorous seedlings, which consequently would have the best chance of flourishing and surviving. The plants which produced flowers with the largest glands or nectaries, excreting most nectar, would oftenest be visited by insects, and would oftenest be crossed; and so in the long run would gain the upper hand and form a local variety. The flowers, also, which had their stamens and pistils placed, in relation to the size and habits of the particular insect which visited them, so as to favour in any degree the transportal of the pollen, would likewise be favoured. We might have taken the case of insects visiting flowers for the sake of collecting pollen instead of nectar; and as pollen is formed for the sole purpose of fertilisation, its destruction appears to be a simple loss to the plant; yet if a little pollen were carried, at first occasionally and then habitually, by the pollen-devouring insects from flower to flower, and a cross thus effected, although nine-tenths of the pollen were destroyed, it might still be a great gain to the plant to be thus robbed; and the individuals which produced more and more pollen, and had larger anthers, would be selected.

When our plant, by the above process long continued, had been rendered highly attractive to insects, they would, unintentionally on their part, regularly carry pollen from flower to flower; and that they do this effectually, I could easily show by many striking facts. I will give only one, as likewise illustrating one step in the separation of the sexes of plants. Some holly-trees bear only male flowers, which have four stamens producing a rather small quantity of pollen, and a rudimentary pistil; other holly trees bear only female flowers; these have a full-sized pistil, and four stamens with shrivelled anthers, in which not a grain of pollen can be detected. Having found a female tree exactly sixty yards from a male tree, I put the stigmas of twenty flowers, taken from different branches, under the microscope, and on all, without exception, there were a few pollen-grains, and on some a profusion. As the wind had set for several days from the female to the male tree, the pollen could not thus have been carried. The weather had been cold and boisterous, and therefore not favourable to bees, nevertheless every female flower which I examined had been effectually fertilised by the bees, which had flown from tree to tree in search of nectar. But to return to our imaginary case: as soon as the plant had been rendered so highly attractive to insects that pollen was regularly carried from flower to flower, another process might commence. No naturalist doubts the advantage of what has been called the "physiological division of labour;" hence we may believe that it would be advantageous to a plant to produce stamens alone in one flower or on one whole plant, and pistils alone in another flower or on another plant. In plants under culture and placed under new conditions of life, sometimes the male organs and sometimes the female organs become more or less impotent; now if we suppose this to occur in ever so slight a degree under nature, then, as pollen is already carried regularly from flower to flower, and as a more complete separation of the sexes of our plant would be advantageous on the principle of the division of labour, individuals with this tendency more and more increased, would be continually favoured or selected, until at last a complete separation of the sexes might be effected. It would take up too much space to show the various steps, through dimorphism and other means, by which the separation of the sexes in plants of various kinds is apparently now in progress; but I may add that some of the species of holly in North America, are, according to Asa Gray, in an exactly intermediate condition, or, as he expresses it, are more or less diœciously polygamous.

Let us now turn to the nectar-feeding insects; we may suppose the plant, of which we have been slowly increasing the nectar by continued selection, to be a common plant; and that certain insects depended in main part on its nectar for food. I could give many facts showing how anxious bees are to save time: for instance, their habit of cutting holes and sucking the nectar at the bases of certain flowers, which with a very little more trouble, they can enter by the mouth. Bearing such facts in mind, it may be believed that under certain circumstances individual differences in the curvature or length of the proboscis, &c., too slight to be appreciated by us, might profit a bee or other insect, so that certain individuals would be able to obtain their food more quickly than others; and thus the communities to which they belonged would flourish and throw off many swarms inheriting the same peculiarities. The tubes of the corolla of the common red and incarnate clovers (Trifolium pratense and incarnatum) do not on a hasty glance appear to differ in length; yet the hive bee-can easily suck the nectar out of the incarnate clover, but not out of the common red clover, which is visited by humble-bees alone; so that whole fields of the red clover offer in vain an abundant supply of precious nectar to the hive bee. That this nectar is much liked by the hive-bee is certain; for I have repeatedly seen, but only in the autumn, many hive-bees sucking the flowers through holes bitten in the base of the tube by humble-bees. The difference in the length of the corolla in the two kinds of clover, which determines the visits of the hive-bee, must be very trifling; for I have been assured that when red clover has been mown, the flowers of the second crop are somewhat smaller, and that these are visited by many hive-bees. I do not know whether this statement is accurate; nor whether another published statement can be trusted, namely, that the Ligurian bee, which is generally considered a mere variety of the common hive-bee, and which freely crosses with it, is able to reach and suck the nectar of the red clover. Thus, in a country where this kind of clover abounded, it might be a great advantage to the hive-bee to have a slightly longer or differently constructed proboscis. On the other hand, as the fertility of this clover absolutely depends on bees visiting the flowers, if humble bees were to become rare in any country, it might be a great advantage to the plant to have a shorter or more deeply divided corolla, so that the hive-bees should be enabled to suck its flowers. Thus I can understand how a flower and a bee might slowly become, either simultaneously or one after the other, modified and adapted to each other in the most perfect manner, by the continued preservation of all the individuals which presented slight deviations of structure mutually favourable to each other.

I am well aware that this doctrine of natural selection, exemplified in the above imaginary instances, is open to the same objections which were first urged against Sir Charles Lyell's noble views on "the modern changes of the earth, as illustrative of geology;" but we now seldom hear the agencies which we see still at work, spoken of as trifling or insignificant, when used in explaining the excavation of the deepest valleys or the formation of long lines of inland cliffs. Natural selection acts only by the preservation and accumulation of small inherited modifications, each profitable to the preserved being; and as modern geology has almost banished such views as the excavation of a great valley by a single diluvial wave, so will natural selection banish the belief of the continued creation of new organic beings, or of any great and sudden modification in their structure.

[* * *]

Circumstances favourable for the production of new forms through Natural Selection.

This is an extremely intricate subject. A great amount of variability, under which term individual differences are always included, will evidently be favourable. A large number of individuals, by giving a better chance within any given period for the appearance of profitable variations, will compensate for a lesser amount of variability in each individual and is, I believe, a highly important element of success. Though Nature grants long periods of time for the work of natural selection, she does not grant an indefinite period; for as all organic beings are striving to seize on each place in the economy of nature, if any one species does not become modified and improved in a corresponding degree with its competitors, it will be exterminated. Unless favourable variations be inherited by some at least of the offspring, nothing can be effected by natural selection. The tendency to reversion may often check or prevent the work; but as this tendency has not prevented man from forming by selection numerous domestic races, why should it prevail against natural selection?

In the case of methodical selection, a breeder selects for some definite object, and if the individuals be allowed freely to intercross, his work will completely fail. But when many men, without intending to alter the breed, have a nearly common standard of perfection, and all try to procure and breed from the best animals, improvement surely but slowly follows from this unconscious process of selection, notwithstanding that there is no separation of selected individuals. Thus it will be under nature; for within a confined area, with some place in the natural polity not perfectly occupied, all the individuals varying in the right direction, though in different degrees, will tend to be preserved. But if the area be large, its several districts will almost certainly present different conditions of life; and then, if the same species undergoes modification in different districts, the newly-formed varieties will intercross on the confines of each. But we shall see in the sixth chapter that intermediate varieties, inhabiting intermediate districts, will in the long run generally be supplanted by one of the adjoining varieties. Intercrossing will chiefly affect those animals which unite for each birth and wander much, and which do not breed at a very quick rate. Hence with animals of this nature, for instance, birds, varieties will generally be confined to separated countries; and this I find to be the case. With hermaphrodite organisms which cross only occasionally, and likewise with animals which unite for each birth, but which wander little and can increase at a rapid rate, a new and improved variety might be quickly formed on any one spot, and might there maintain itself in a body and afterwards spread, so that the individuals of the new variety would chiefly cross together. On this principle, nurserymen always prefer saving seed from a large body of plants, as the chance of intercrossing is thus lessened.

Even with animals which unite for each birth, and which do not propagate rapidly, we must not assume that free intercrossing would always eliminate the effects of natural selection; for I can bring forward a considerable body of facts showing that within the same area, two varieties of the same animal may long remain distinct, from haunting different stations, from breeding at slightly different seasons, or from the individuals of each variety preferring to pair together.

Intercrossing plays a very important part in nature by keeping the individuals of the same species, or of the same variety, true and uniform in character. It will obviously thus act far more efficiently with those animals which unite for each birth; but, as already stated, we have reason to believe that occasional intercrosses take place with all animals and plants. Even if these take place only at long intervals of time, the young thus produced will gain so much in vigour and fertility over the offspring from long-continued self-fertilisation, that they will have a better chance of surviving and propagating their kind; and thus in the long run the influence of crosses, even at rare intervals, will be great. With respect to organic beings extremely low in the scale, which do not propagate sexually, nor conjugate, and which cannot possibly intercross, uniformity of character can be retained by them under the same conditions of life, only through the principle of inheritance, and through natural selection which will destroy any individuals departing from the proper type. If the conditions of life change and the form undergoes modification, uniformity of character can be given to the modified offspring, solely by natural selection preserving similar favourable variations.

Isolation, also, is an important element in the modification of species through natural selection. In a confined or isolated area, if not very large, the organic and inorganic conditions of life will generally be almost uniform; so that natural selection will tend to modify all the varying individuals of the same species in the same manner. Intercrossing with the inhabitants of the surrounding districts will, also, be thus prevented. Moritz Wagner has lately published an interesting essay on this subject, and has shown that the service rendered by isolation in preventing crosses between newly-formed varieties is probably greater even than I supposed. But from reasons already assigned I can by no means agree with this naturalist, that migration and isolation are necessary elements for the formation of new species. The importance of isolation is likewise great in preventing, after any physical change in the conditions such as of climate, elevation of the land, &c., the immigration of better adapted organisms; and thus new places in the natural economy of the district will be left open to be filled up by the modification of the old inhabitants. Lastly, isolation will give time for a new variety to be improved at a slow rate; and this may sometimes be of much importance. If, however, an isolated area be very small, either from being surrounded by barriers, or from having very peculiar physical conditions, the total number of the inhabitants will be small; and this will retard the production of new species through natural selection, by decreasing the chances of favourable variations arising.

The mere lapse of time by itself does nothing, either for or against natural selection. I state this because it has been erroneously asserted that the element of time has been assumed by me to play an all-important part in modifying species, as if all the forms of life were necessarily undergoing change through some innate law. Lapse of time is only so far important, and its importance in this respect is great, that it gives a better chance of beneficial variations arising and of their being selected, accumulated, and fixed. It likewise tends to increase the direct action of the physical conditions of life, in relation to the constitution of each organism.

If we turn to nature to test the truth of these remarks, and look at any small isolated area, such as an oceanic island, although the number of species inhabiting it is small, as we shall see in our chapter on Geographical Distribution; yet of these species a very large proportion are endemic,—that is, have been produced there, and nowhere else in the world. Hence an oceanic island at first sight seems to have been highly favourable for the production of new species. But we may thus deceive ourselves, for to ascertain whether a small isolated area, or a large open area like a continent, has been most favourable for the production of new organic forms, we ought to make the comparison within equal times; and this we are incapable of doing.

Although isolation is of great importance in the production of new species, on the whole I am inclined to believe that largeness of area is still more important, especially for the production of species which shall prove capable of enduring for a long period, and of spreading widely. Throughout a great and open area, not only will there be a better chance of favourable variations, arising from the large number of individuals of the same species there supported, but the conditions of life are much more complex from the large number of already existing species; and if some of these many species become modified and improved, others will have to be improved in a corresponding degree, or they will be exterminated. Each new form, also, as soon as it has been much improved, will be able to spread over the open and continuous area, and will thus come into competition with many other forms. Moreover, great areas, though now continuous, will often, owing to former oscillations of level, have existed in a broken condition; so that the good effects of isolation will generally, to a certain extent, have concurred. Finally, I conclude that, although small isolated areas have been in some respects highly favourable for the production of new species, yet that the course of modification will generally have been more rapid on large areas; and what is more important, that the new forms produced on large areas, which already have been victorious over many competitors, will be those that will spread most widely, and will give rise to the greatest number of new varieties and species. They will thus play a more important part in the changing history of the organic world.

In accordance with this view, we can, perhaps, understand some facts which will be again alluded to in our chapter on Geographical Distribution; for instance, the fact of the productions of the smaller continent of Australia now yielding before those of the larger Europæo-Asiatic area. Thus, also, it is that continental productions have everywhere become so largely naturalised on islands. On a small island, the race for life will have been less severe, and there will have been less modification and less extermination. Hence, we can understand how it is that the flora of Madeira, according to Oswald Heer, resembles to a certain extent the extinct tertiary flora of Europe. All fresh-water basins, taken together, make a small area compared with that of the sea or of the land. Consequently, the competition between fresh-water productions will have been less severe than elsewhere; new forms will have been then more slowly produced, and old forms more slowly exterminated. And it is in fresh-water basins that we find seven genera of Ganoid fishes, remnants of a once preponderant order: and in fresh water we find some of the most anomalous forms now known in the world as the Ornithorhynchus[1] and Lepidosiren, which, like fossils, connect to a certain extent orders at present widely sundered in the natural scale. These anomalous forms may be called living fossils; they have endured to the present day, from having inhabited a confined area, and from having been exposed to less varied, and therefore less severe, competition.

To sum up, as far as the extreme intricacy of the subject permits, the circumstances favourable and unfavourable for the production of new species through natural selection. I conclude that for terrestrial productions a large continental area, which has undergone many oscillations of level, will have been the most favourable for the production of many new forms of life, fitted to endure for a long time and to spread widely. Whilst the area existed as a continent, the inhabitants will have been numerous in individuals and kinds, and will have been subjected

---

1 Ornithorhynchus is another name for a platypus.

to severe competition. When converted by subsidence into large separate islands, there will still have existed many individuals of the same species on each island: intercrossing on the confines of the range of each new species will have been checked: after physical changes of any kind, immigration will have been prevented, so that new places in the polity of each island will have had to be filled up by the modification of the old inhabitants; and time will have been allowed for the varieties in each to become well modified and perfected. When, by renewed elevation, the islands were reconverted into a continental area, there will again have been very severe competition: the most favoured or improved varieties will have been enabled to spread: there will have been much extinction of the less improved forms, and the relative proportional numbers of the various inhabitants of the reunited continent will again have been changed; and again there will have been a fair field for natural selection to improve still further the inhabitants, and thus to produce new species.

That natural selection generally acts with extreme slowness I fully admit. It can act only when there are places in the natural polity of a district which can be better occupied by the modification of some of its existing inhabitants. The occurrence of such places will often depend on physical changes, which generally take place very slowly, and on the immigration of better adapted forms being prevented. As some few of the old inhabitants become modified, the mutual relations of others will often be disturbed; and this will create new places, ready to be filled up by better adapted forms; but all this will take place very slowly. Although all the individuals of the same species differ in some slight degree from each other, it would often be long before differences of the right nature in various parts of the organisation might occur. The result would often be greatly retarded by free intercrossing. Many will exclaim that these several causes are amply sufficient to neutralise the power of natural selection. I do not believe so. But I do believe that natural selection will generally act very slowly, only at long intervals of time, and only on a few of the inhabitants of the same region. I further believe that these slow, intermittent results accord well with what geology tells us of the rate and manner at which the inhabitants of the world have changed.

Slow though the process of selection may be, if feeble man can do much by artificial selection, I can see no limit to the amount of change, to the beauty and complexity of the coadaptations between all organic beings, one with another and with their physical conditions of life, which may have been affected in the long course of time through nature's power of selection, that is by the survival of the fittest.

Extinction caused by Natural Selection

This subject will be more fully discussed in our chapter on Geology; but it must here be alluded to from being intimately connected with natural selection. Natural selection acts solely through the preservation of variations in some way advantageous, which consequently endure. Owing to the high geometrical rate of increase of all organic beings, each area is already fully stocked with inhabitants; and it follows from this, that as the favoured forms increase in number, so, generally, will the less favoured decrease and become rare. Rarity, as geology tells us, is the precursor to extinction. We can see that any form which is represented by few individuals will run a good chance of utter extinction, during great fluctuations in the nature of the seasons, or from a temporary increase in the number of its enemies. But we may go further than this; for, as new forms are produced, unless we admit that specific forms can go on indefinitely increasing in number, many old forms must become extinct. That the number of specific forms has not indefinitely increased, geology plainly tells us; and we shall presently attempt to show why it is that the number of species throughout the world has not become immeasurably great.

We have seen that the species which are most numerous in individuals have the best chance of producing favourable variations within any given period. We have evidence of this, in the facts stated in the second chapter, showing that it is the common and diffused or dominant species which offer the greatest number of recorded varieties. Hence, rare species will be less quickly modified or improved within any given period; they will consequently be beaten in the race for life by the modified and improved descendants of the commoner species.

From these several considerations I think it inevitably follows, that as new species in the course of time are formed through natural selection, others will become rarer and rarer, and finally extinct. The forms which stand in closest competition with those undergoing modification and improvement, will naturally suffer most. And we have seen in the chapter on the Struggle for Existence, that it is the most closely-allied forms,—varieties of the same species, and species of the same genus or of related genera,—which, from having nearly the same structure, constitution, and habits, generally come into the severest competition with each other; consequently, each new variety or species, during the progress of its formation, will generally press hardest on its nearest kindred, and tend to exterminate them. We see the same process of extermination amongst our domesticated productions, through the selection of improved forms by man. Many curious instances could be given showing how quickly new breeds of cattle, sheep, and other animals, and varieties of flowers, take the place of older and inferior kinds. In Yorkshire, it is historically known that the ancient black cattle were displaced by the long-horns, and that these "were swept away by the short-horns" (I quote the words of an agricultural writer) "as if by some murderous pestilence."

[* * *]

On the Degree to which Organisation tends to advance.

Natural Selection acts exclusively by the preservation and accumulation of variations, which are beneficial under the organic and inorganic conditions to which each creature is exposed at all periods of life. The ultimate result is that each creature tends to become more and more improved in relation to its conditions. This improvement inevitably leads to the gradual advancement of the organisation of the greater number of living beings throughout the world. But here we enter on a very intricate subject, for naturalists have not defined to each other's satisfaction what is meant by an advance in organisation. Amongst the vertebrata the degree of intellect and an approach in structure to man clearly come into play. It might be thought that the amount of change which the various parts and organs pass through in their development from the embryo to maturity would suffice as a standard of comparison; but there are cases, as with certain parasitic crustaceans, in which several parts of the structure become less perfect, so that the mature animal cannot be called higher than its larva. Von Baer's standard seems the most widely applicable and the best, namely, the amount of differentiation of the parts of the same organic being, in the adult state, as I should be inclined to add, and their specialisation for different functions; or, as Milne Edwards would express it, the completeness of the division of physiological labour. But we shall see how obscure this subject is if we look, for instance, to fishes, amongst which some naturalists rank those as highest which, like the sharks, approach nearest to amphibians; whilst other naturalists range the common bony or teleostean fishes as the highest, inasmuch as they are most strictly fish-like, and differ most from the other vertebrate classes. We see still more plainly the obscurity of the subject by turning to plants, amongst which the standard of intellect is of course quite excluded; and here some botanists rank those plants as highest which have every organ, as sepals, petals, stamens, and pistils, fully developed in each flower; whereas other botanists, probably with more truth, look at the plants which have their several organs much modified and reduced in number, as the highest.

If we take as the standard of high organisation, the amount of differentiation and specialisation of the several organs in each being when adult (and this will include the advancement of the brain for intellectual purposes), natural selection clearly leads towards this standard: for all physiologists admit that the specialisation of organs, inasmuch as in this state they perform their functions better, is an advantage to each being; and hence the accumulation of variations tending towards specialisation is within the scope of natural selection. On the other hand, we can see, bearing in mind that all organic beings are striving to increase at a high ratio and to seize on every unoccupied or less well occupied place in the economy of nature, that it is quite possible for natural selection gradually to fit a being to a situation in which several organs would be superfluous or useless: in such cases there would be retrogression in the scale of organisation. Whether organisation on the whole has actually advanced from the remotest geological periods to the present day will be more conveniently discussed in our chapter on Geological Succession.

But it may be objected that if all organic beings thus tend to rise in the scale, how is it that throughout the world a multitude of the lowest forms still exist; and how is it that in each great class some forms are far more highly developed than others? Why have not the more highly developed forms everywhere supplanted and exterminated the lower? Lamarck, who believed in an innate and inevitable tendency towards perfection in all organic beings, seems to have felt this difficulty so strongly, that he was led to suppose that new and simple forms are continually being produced by spontaneous generation. Science has not as yet proved the truth of this belief, whatever the future may reveal. On our theory the continued existence of lowly organisms offers no difficulty; for natural selection, or the survival of the fittest, does not necessarily include progressive development—it only takes advantage of such variations as arise and are beneficial to each creature under its complex relations of life. And it may be asked what advantage, as far as we can see, would it be to an infusorian animalcule—to an intestinal worm—or even to an earth-worm, to be highly organised. If it were no advantage, these forms would be left, by natural selection, unimproved or but little improved, and might remain for indefinite ages in their present lowly condition. And geology tells us that some of the lowest forms, as the infusoria and rhizopods, have remained for an enormous period in nearly their present state. But to suppose that most of the many now existing low forms have not in the least advanced since the first dawn of life would be extremely rash; for every naturalist who has dissected some of the beings now ranked as very low in the scale, must have been struck with their really wondrous and beautiful organisation.

Nearly the same remarks are applicable if we look to the different grades of organisation within the same great group; for instance, in the Vertebrata, to the co-existence of mammals and fish—amongst mammalia, to the co-existence of man and the ornithorhynchus—amongst fishes, to the coexistence of the shark and the lancelet (Amphioxus), which latter fish in the extreme simplicity of its structure approaches the invertebrate classes. But mammals and fish hardly come into competition with each other; the advancement of the whole class of mammals, or of certain members in this class, to the highest grade, would not lead to their taking the place of fishes. Physiologists believe that the brain must be bathed by warm blood to be highly active, and this requires aërial respiration; so that warm-blooded mammals when inhabiting the water lie under a disadvantage in having to come continually to the surface to breathe. With fishes, members of the shark family would not tend to supplant the lancelet; for the lancelet, as I hear from Fritz Müller, has as sole companion and competitor on the barren sandy shore of South Brazil, an anomalous annelid. The three lowest orders of mammals, namely, marsupials, edentata, and rodents, co-exist in South America in the same region with numerous monkeys, and probably interfere little with each other. Although organisation, on the whole, may have advanced and be still advancing throughout the world, yet the scale will always present many degrees of perfection; for the high advancement of certain whole classes, or of certain members of each class, does not at all necessarily lead to the extinction of those groups with which they do not enter into close competition. In some cases, as we shall hereafter see, lowly organised forms appear to have been preserved to the present day, from inhabiting confined or peculiar stations, where they have been subjected to less severe competition, and where their scanty numbers have retarded the chance of favorable variations arising.

Finally, I believe that many lowly organised forms now exist throughout the world, from various causes. In some cases variations or individual differences of a favorable nature may never have arisen for natural selection to act on and accumulate. In no case, probably, has time sufficed for the utmost possible amount of development. In some few cases there has been what we must call retrogression of organisation. But the main cause lies in the fact that under very simple conditions of life a high organisation would be of no service,—possibly would be of actual disservice, as being of a more delicate nature, and more liable to be put out of order and injured.

Looking to the first dawn of life, when all organic beings, as we may believe, presented the simplest structure, how, it has been asked, could the first steps in the advancement or differentiation of parts have arisen? Mr. Herbert Spencer would probably answer that, as soon as simple unicellular organism came by growth or division to be compounded of several cells, or became attached to any supporting surface, his law "that homologous units of any order became differentiated in proportion as their relations to incident forces became different" would come into action. But as we have no facts to guide us, speculation on the subject is almost useless. It is, however, an error to suppose that there would be no struggle for existence, and, consequently, no natural selection, until many forms had been produced: variations in a single species inhabiting an isolated station might be beneficial, and thus the whole mass of individuals might be modified, or two distinct forms might arise. But, as I remarked towards the close of the Introduction, no one ought to feel surprise at much remaining as yet unexplained on the origin of species, if we make due allowance for our profound ignorance on the mutual relations of the inhabitants of the world at the present time, and still more so during past ages.

Convergence of Character.

Mr. H. C. Watson thinks that I have overrated the importance of divergence of character (in which, however, he apparently believes), and that convergence, as it may be called, has likewise played a part. If two species, belonging to two distinct though allied genera, had both produced a large number of new and divergent forms, it is conceivable that these might approach each other so closely that they would have all to be classed under the same genus; and thus the descendants of two distinct genera would converge into one. But it would in most cases be extremely rash to attribute to convergence a close and general similarity of structure in the modified descendants of widely distinct forms. The shape of a crystal is determined solely by the molecular forces, and it is not surprising that dissimilar substances should sometimes assume the same form; but with organic beings we should bear in mind that the form of each depends on an infinitude of complex relations, namely on the variations which have arisen, these being due to causes far too intricate to be followed out,—on the nature of the variations which have been preserved or selected, and this depends on the surrounding physical conditions, and in a still higher degree on the surrounding organisms with which each being has come into competition,—and lastly, on inheritance (in itself a fluctuating element) from innumerable progenitors, all of which have had their forms determined through equally complex relations. It is incredible that the descendants of two organisms, which had originally differed in a marked manner, should ever afterwards converge so closely as to lead to a near approach to identity throughout their whole organisation. If this had occurred, we should meet with the same form, independently of genetic connection, recurring in widely separated geological formations; and the balance of evidence is opposed to any such an admission.

Mr. Watson has also objected that the continued action of natural selection, together with divergence of character, would tend to make an indefinite number of specific forms. As far as mere inorganic conditions are concerned, it seems probable that a sufficient number of species would soon become adapted to all considerable diversities of heat, moisture, &c.; but I fully admit that the mutual relations of organic beings are more important; and as the number of species in any country goes on increasing, the organic conditions of life must become more and more complex. Consequently there seems at first sight no limit to the amount of profitable diversification of structure, and therefore no limit to the number of species which might be produced. We do not know that even the most prolific area is fully stocked with specific forms: at the Cape of Good Hope and in Australia, which support such an astonishing number of species, many European plants have become naturalised. But geology shows us, that from an early part of the tertiary period the number of species of shells, and that from the middle part of this same period the number of mammals, has not greatly or at all increased. What then checks an indefinite increase in the number of species? The amount of life (I do not mean the number of specific forms) supported on an area must have a limit, depending so largely as it does on physical conditions; therefore, if an area be inhabited by very many species, each or nearly each species will be represented by few individuals; and such species will be liable to extermination from accidental fluctuations in the nature of the seasons or in the number of their enemies. The process of extermination in such cases would be rapid, whereas the production of new species must always be slow. Imagine the extreme case of as many species as individuals in England, and the first severe winter or very dry summer would exterminate thousands on thousands of species. Rare species, and each species will become rare if the number of species in any country becomes indefinitely increased, will, on the principle often explained, present within a given period few favorable variations; consequently, the process of giving birth to new specific forms would thus be retarded. When any species becomes very rare, close interbreeding will help to exterminate it; authors have thought that this comes into play in accounting for the deterioration of the Aurochs in Lithuania, of Red Deer in Scotland, and of Bears in Norway, &c. Lastly, and this I am inclined to think is the most important element, a dominant species, which has already beaten many competitors in its own home, will tend to spread and supplant many others. Alph. de Candolle has shown that those species which spread widely, tend generally to spread *very* widely; consequently, they will tend to supplant and exterminate several species in several areas, and thus check the inordinate increase of specific forms throughout the world. Dr. Hooker has recently shown that in the S.E. corner of Australia, where, apparently, there are many invaders from different quarters of the globe, the endemic Australian species have been greatly reduced in number. How much weight to attribute to these several considerations I will not pretend to say; but conjointly they must limit in each country the tendency to an indefinite augmentation of specific forms.

Summary of Chapter.

If under changing conditions of life organic beings present individual differences in almost every part of their structure, and this cannot be disputed; if there be, owing to their geometrical rate of increase, a severe struggle for life at some age, season, or year, and this certainly cannot be disputed; then, considering the infinite complexity of the relations of all organic beings to each other and to their conditions of life, causing an infinite diversity in structure, constitution, and habits, to be advantageous to them, it would be a most extraordinary fact if no variations had ever occurred useful to each being's own welfare, in the same manner as so many variations have occurred useful to man. But if variations useful to any organic being ever do occur, assuredly individuals thus characterised will have the best chance of being preserved in the struggle for life; and from the strong principle of inheritance, these will tend to produce offspring similarly characterised. This principle of preservation, or the survival of the fittest, I have called Natural Selection. It leads to the improvement of each creature in relation to its organic and inorganic conditions of life; and consequently, in most cases, to what must be regarded as an advance in organisation. Nevertheless, low and simple forms will long endure if well fitted for their simple conditions of life.

Natural selection, on the principle of qualities being inherited at corresponding ages, can modify the egg, seed, or young, as easily as the adult. Amongst many animals, sexual selection will have given its aid to ordinary selection, by assuring to the most vigorous and best adapted males the greatest number of offspring. Sexual selection will also give characters useful to the males alone, in their struggles or rivalry with other males; and these characters will be transmitted to one sex or to both sexes, according to the form of inheritance which prevails.

Whether natural selection has really thus acted in adapting the various forms of life to their several conditions and stations, must be judged by the general tenor and balance of evidence given in the following chapters. But we have already seen how it entails extinction; and how largely extinction has acted in the world's history, geology plainly declares. Natural selection, also, leads to divergence of character; for the more organic beings diverge in structure, habits, and constitution, by so much the more can a large number be supported on the area,—of which we see proof by looking to the inhabitants of any small spot, and to the productions naturalised in foreign lands. Therefore, during the modification of the descendants of any one species, and during the incessant struggle of all species to increase in numbers, the more diversified the descendants become, the better will be their chance of success in the battle for life. Thus the small differences distinguishing varieties of the same species, steadily tend to increase, till they equal the greater differences between species of the same genus, or even of distinct genera.

We have seen that it is the common, the widely diffused and widely ranging species, belonging to the larger genera within each class, which vary most; and these tend to transmit to their modified offspring that superiority which now makes them dominant in their own countries. Natural selection, as has just been remarked, leads to divergence of character and to much extinction of the less improved and intermediate forms of life. On these principles, the nature of the affinities, and the generally well-defined distinctions between the innumerable organic beings in each class throughout the world, may be explained. It is a truly wonderful fact—the wonder of which we are apt to overlook from familiarity—that all animals and all plants throughout all time and space should be related to each other in groups, subordinate to groups, in the manner which we everywhere behold—namely, varieties of the same specie most closely related, species of the same genus less closely and unequally related, forming sections and sub-genera, species of distinct genera much less closely related, and genera related in different degrees, forming sub-families, families, orders, sub-classes, and classes. The several subordinate groups in any class cannot be ranked in a single file, but seem clustered round points, and these round other points, and so on in almost endless cycles. If species had been independently created, no explanation would have been possible of this kind of classification; but it is explained through inheritance and the complex action of natural selection, entailing extinction and divergence of character, as we have seen illustrated in the diagram.

The affinities of all the beings of the same class have sometimes been represented by a great tree. I believe this simile largely speaks the truth. The green and budding twigs may represent existing species; and those produced during former years may represent the long succession of extinct species. At each period of growth all the growing twigs have tried to branch out on all sides, and to overtop and kill the surrounding twigs and branches, in the same manner as species and groups of species have at all times overmastered other species in the great battle for life. The limbs divided into great branches, and these into lesser and lesser branches, were themselves once, when the tree was young, budding twigs; and this connection of the former and present buds, by ramifying branches, may well represent the classification of all extinct and living species in groups subordinate to groups. Of the many twigs which flourished when the tree was a mere bush, only two or three, now grown into great branches, yet survive and bear the other branches; so with the species which lived during long-past geological periods, very few have left living and modified descendants. From the first growth of the tree, many a limb and branch has decayed and dropped off; and these fallen branches of various sizes may represent those whole orders, families, and genera which have now no living representatives, and which are known to us only in a fossil state. As we here and there see a thin straggling branch springing from a fork low down in a tree, and which by some chance has been favoured and is still alive on its summit, so we occasionally see an animal like the Ornithorhynchus or Lepidosiren, which in some small degree connects by its affinities two large branches of life, and which has apparently been saved from fatal competition by having inhabited a protected station. As buds give rise by growth to fresh buds, and these, if vigorous, branch out and overtop on all sides many a feebler branch, so by generation I believe it has been with the great Tree of Life, which fills with its dead and broken branches the crust of the earth, and covers the surface with its ever-branching and beautiful ramifications.

Louis Agassiz

1807-1873

Methods of Study in Natural History

1863

The life and career of Louis Agassiz poses a study in contrasts. Born in the French-speaking region of Switzerland, he studied under the great French natural scientist Georges Cuvier. He considered himself the intellectual heir of Cuvier, and many of his later positions on controversial concepts stemmed from this heritage, including his support for Cuvier's geological catastrophism and classification of animals. After a thirteen-year professorship at the Lyceum in Switzerland, he came to the United States in 1846 for a lecture tour and in 1848, he accepted a position at Harvard where he established the Harvard Museum of Comparative Zoology in 1859. This was the same year in which Charles Darwin first published *The Origin of Species*. He became the most noted public American scientist of the nineteenth century and one of the most vocal critics of Darwin's theory of evolution.

His achievements include a detailed analysis of the succession of fossil fishes over geological time including their development within the egg. He is considered the father of glaciology, as his hobby was the study of glaciers and their geologic effects. Philosophically he was trained in the school of *Naturphilosophie*, a German Romantic philosophy exploring metaphysical connections within the study of living things. This coupled with his intellectual training under Cuvier led him to be a devout proponent of creationism, and strongly opposed to Darwin's idea of natural selection. The ideas and success of Agassiz provided a juxtaposition as his work on fossils supported Darwinian natural selection, but his scientific philosophy in the line of Cuvier opposed those same ideas. The majority of his students at Harvard fled the institution at the completion of their graduate training because of this philosophical difference of opinion, and many of them became the founders of significant biological departments across the United States during the latter half of the nineteenth century.

The selection below includes two Chapters of Agassiz's philosophical views on investigation of natural history, first a general discussion and critique of Aristotelian methods, and then a more specific one dealing with nomenclature and classification of organisms.

1. What are the philosophical connections between Agassiz and the scientists he both critiques and discusses, Aristotle, Lamarck, Cuvier and Baer?
2. Do Agassiz's positions still work well today in the era of reductionist biology, especially considering the practice of molecular and genomic sciences?

Sources:

University of California Museum of Paleontology. *Louis Agassiz.* Retrieved July 20, 2007, from www.ucmp.berkeley.edu/history/agassiz.html.

Gould, Stephen Jay. (1992). *Bully for Brontosaurus. Reflections in Natural History.* W.W. Norton, New York.

Selection from:

Agassiz, Louis. (1863). *Methods of Study in Natural History.* Boston: Ticknor and Fields Reprinted Arno Press 1970. 1-29.

CHAPTER I.

GENERAL SKETCH OF THE EARLY PROGRESS IN NATURAL HISTORY

IT is my intention, in this series of papers, to give the history of the progress in Natural History from the beginning,—to show how men first approached Nature,—how the facts of Natural History have been accumulated, and how these facts have been converted into science. In so doing, I shall present the methods followed in Natural History on a wider scale and with broader generalizations than if I limited myself to the study as it exists to-day. The history of humanity, in its efforts to understand the Creation, resembles the development of any individual mind engaged in the same direction. It has its infancy, with the first recognition of surrounding objects; and, indeed, the early observers seem to us like children in their first attempts to understand the world in which they live. But these efforts, that appear childish to us now, were the first steps in that field of knowledge which is so extensive that all our progress seems only to show us how much is left to do.

Aristotle is the representative of the learning of antiquity in Natural Science. The great mind of Greece in his day, and a leader in all the intellectual culture of his time, he was especially a naturalist, and his work on Natural History is a record not only of his own investigations, but of all preceding study in this department. It is evident that even then much had been done, and, in allusion to certain peculiarities of the human frame, which he does not describe in full, he refers his readers to familiar works, saying, that illustrations in point may be found in anatomical text-books.[1]

Strange that in Aristotle's day, two thousand years ago, such books should have been in general use, and that in our time we are still in want of elementary text-books of Natural History, having special reference to the animals of our own country, and adapted to the use of schools. One fact in Aristotle's "History of Animals" is very striking, and makes it difficult for us to understand much of its contents. It never occurs to him that a time may come when the Greek language—the language of all culture and science in his time—would not be the language of all cultivated men. He took, therefore, little pains to characterize the animals he alludes to, otherwise than by their current names; and of his descriptions of their habits and peculiarities, much is lost upon us from their local character and expression. There is also a total absence of systematic form, of any classification or framework to express the divisions of the animal kingdom into larger or lesser groups. His only divisions are genera and species: classes, orders, and families, as we understand them now, are quite foreign to the Greek conception of the animal kingdom. Fishes and birds, for instance, they considered as genera, and their different representatives as species. They grouped together quadrupeds also, in contradistinction to animals with legs and wings, and they distinguished those that bring

[1] See Aristotle's Zoölogy, Book I., Chapter XIV.

forth living young from those that lay eggs. But though a system of Nature was not familiar even to their great philosopher, and Aristotle had not arrived at the idea of a classification on general principles, he yet stimulated a search into the closer affinities among animals by the differences he pointed out. He divided the animal kingdom into two groups, which he called *Enaima* and *Anaima*, or animals with blood and animals without blood. We must remember, however, that by the word *blood* he designated only the red fluid circulating in the higher animals; whereas a fluid akin to blood exists in all animals, variously colored in some, but colorless in a large number of others.

After Aristotle, a long period elapsed without any addition to the information he left us. Rome and the Middle Ages gave us nothing, and even Pliny added hardly a fact to those that Aristotle recorded. And though the great naturalists of the sixteenth century gave a new impulse to this study, their investigations were chiefly directed towards a minute acquaintance with the animals they had an opportunity of observing, mingled with commentaries upon the ancients. Systematic Zoölogy was but little advanced by their efforts.

We must come down to the last century, to Linnæus, before we find the history taken up where Aristotle had left it, and some of his suggestions carried out with new freshness and vigor. Aristotle had already distinguished between genera and species; Linnæus took hold of this idea, and gave special names to other groups of different weight and value. Besides species and genera, he gives us orders and classes,—considering classes the most comprehensive, then orders, then genera, then species He did not, however, represent these groups as distinguished by their nature, but only by their range; they were still to him, as genera and species had been to Aristotle, only larger or smaller groups, not founded upon and limited by different categories of structure. He divided the animal kingdom into six classes, which I give here, as we shall have occasion to compare them with other classifications:—*Mammalia, Birds, Reptiles, Fishes, Insects,* and *Worms.*

That this classification should have expressed all that was known, in the last century, of the most general relations among animals, only shows how difficult it is to generalize on such a subject; nor should we expect to find it an easy task, when we remember the vast number of species (about a quarter of a million) already noticed by naturalists. Linnæus succeeded, however, in finding a common character on which to unite most of his classes; but his definition of the class of Mammalia, that group to which we ourselves belong, remained very imperfect. Indeed, in the earlier editions of his classification, he does not apply the name of Mammalia to this class, but calls the higher animals *Quadrupedia*, characterizing them as the animals with four legs and covered with fur or hair, that bring forth living young and nurse them with milk. In thus admitting external features as class characters, he excluded many animals which by their mode of reproduction, as well as by their respiration and circulation, belong to this class as much as the Quadrupeds,—as, for instance, all the Cetaceans (Whales, Porpoises, and the like), which, though they have not legs, nor are their bodies covered with hair or fur, yet bring forth living young, nurse them with milk, are warm-blooded and air-breathing. As more was learned of these animals, there arose serious discussion and criticism among contemporary naturalists respecting the classification of Linnæus, all of which led to a clearer insight into the true relations among animals. Linnæus himself, in his last edition of the "Systema Naturæ," shows us what important progress he had made since he first announced his views; for he there substitutes for the name of *Quadrupedia* that of *Mammalia*, including among them the Whales, which he characterizes as air-breathing, warm-blooded, and bringing forth living young which they nurse with milk. Thus the very deficiencies of his classification stimulated naturalists to new criticism and investigation into the true limits of classes, and led to the recognition of one most important principle,—that such groups are founded, not on external appearance, but on internal structure, and that internal structure, therefore, is the thing to be studied. The group of Quadrupeds was not the only defective one in this classification of Linnæus; his class of Worms, also, was most heterogeneous, for he included among them Shell-Fishes, Slugs, Star-Fishes, Sea-Urchins, Corals, and other animals that bear no relation whatever to the class of Worms as now defined.

But whatever its defects, the classification of Linnæus was the first attempt at grouping animals together according to certain common structural characters. His followers and pupils engaged at once in a scrutiny of the differences and similarities among animals, which soon led to a great increase in the number of classes; instead of six, there were presently nine, twelve, and more. But till Cuvier's time there was no great principle of classification. Facts were accumulated and more or less systematized, but they were not yet arranged according to law; the principle was still wanting by which to generalize them and give meaning and vitality to the whole. It was Cuvier who found the key. He himself tells us how he first began, in his investigations upon the internal organization of animals, to use his dissections with reference to finding the true relations between animals, and how ever after his knowledge of anatomy assisted him in his classifications, while his classifications threw new light again on his anatomical investigations,—each science thus helping to fertilize the other. He was not one of those superficial observers who are in haste to announce every new fact that they chance to find, and his first paper[2] specially devoted to classification gave to the world the ripe fruit of years of study. This was followed by his great work, "Le Règne Animal." He said that animals were united in their most comprehensive groups, not on special characters, but on different *plans of structure*,—moulds, he called them, in which all animals had been cast. He tells us this in such admirable language, that I must, to do justice to his thought, give it in his own words:—

> "Si l'on considère le règne animal d'après les principes que nous venons de poser en se débarrassant des préjugés établis sur les divisions anciennement admises, en n'ayant égard qu'à l'organisation et à la nature des animaux, et non pas à leur grandeur, à leur utilité, au plus ou moins de connaissance que nous en avons, ni à toutes les autres circonstances accessoires, on trouvera qu'il existe quatre formes principales, quatre plans généraux, si l'on peut s'exprimer ainsi, d'après lesquels tous les animaux semblent avoir été modelés, et dont les divisions ultérieures, de quelque titre que les naturalistes les aient décorées, ne sont que des modifications assez légères, fondées sur le développement ou l'addition de quelques parties, qui ne changent rien à l'essence du plan."[3]

The value of this principle was soon tested by its application to facts already known, and it was found that animals whose affinities had been

---

2 "Sur un nouveau rapprochement à établir entre les Clases qui composent le Règne Animal."—*Ann. Mus.*, Vol. XIX.

3 If we consider the animal kingdom according to the principles advanced above,—freeing ourselves at the same time from prejudices founded on previously established divisions, and looking at animals only with reference to their nature and organization, excluding their size, their utility, our greater or less familiarity with them, and all other accessory circumstances,—we shall find that there exist four principle forms, four general plans, if we may so express it, in accordance with which all animals seem to have been modeled, and the ulterior divisions of which, by whatever title naturalists may have dignified them, are only comparatively light modifications, founded on the development or the addition of some parts not affecting the essential elements of the plan.

questionable before were now at once referred to their true relations with other animals by ascertaining whether they were build on one or another of these plans. Of such plans or structural conceptions Cuvier found in the whole animal kingdom only four, which he called *Vertebrates, Mollusks, Articulates*, and *Radiates.*

With this new principle as the basis of investigation, it was no longer enough for the naturalist to know a certain amount of features characteristic of a certain number of animals,—he must penetrate deep enough into their organization to find the secret of their internal structure. Till he can do this, he is like the traveller in a strange city, who looks on the exterior of edifices entirely new to him, but knows nothing of the plan of their internal architecture. To be able to read in the finished structure the plan on which the whole is built is now essential to every naturalist.

Each of these plans may be stated in the most general terms. In the *Vertebrates* there is a vertebral column terminating in a prominent head; this column has an arch above and an arch below, forming a double internal cavity. The parts are symmetrically arranged on either side of the longitudinal axis of the body. In the *Mollusks,* also, the parts are arranged according to a bilateral symmetry on either side of the body, but the body has but one cavity, and is a soft, concentrated mass, without a distinct individualization of parts. In the *Articulates* there is but one cavity, and the parts are here again arranged on either side of the longitudinal axis, but in these animals the whole body is divided from end to end into transverse rings or joints movable upon each other. In the *Radiates* we lose sight of the bilateral symmetry so prevalent in the other three, except as a very subordinate element of structure; the plan of this lowest type is an organic sphere, in which all parts bear definite relations to a vertical axis.

It is not upon any special features, then, that these largest divisions of the animal kingdom are based, but simply upon the general structural idea. Striking as this statement was, it was coldly received at first by contemporary naturalists: they could hardly grasp Cuvier's wide generalizations, and perhaps there was also some jealousy of the grandeur of his views. Whatever the cause, his principle of classification was not fully appreciated; but it opened a new road for study, and gave us the key-note to the natural affinities among animals. Lamarck, his contemporary, not recognizing the truth of this principle, distributed the animal kingdom into two great divisions, which he calls *Vertebrates* and *Invertebrates.* Ehrenberg also, at a later period, announced another division under two head,—those with a continuous solid nervous centre, and those with merely scattered nervous swellings.[4] But there was no real progress in either of these latter classifications, so far as the primary divisions are concerned; for they correspond to the old division of Aristotle, under the head of animals with or without blood, the *Enaima* and *Anaima*.

This coincidence between systems based on different foundations may teach us that every structural combination includes certain inherent necessities which will bring animals together on whatever set of features we try to classify them; so that the division of Aristotle, founded on the circulating fluids, or that of Lamarck, founded on the absence or presence of a backbone, or that of Ehrenberg, founded on the differences of the nervous system, covers the same ground. Lamarck attempted also to make the faculties of animals a basis for division among them. But our knowledge of the psychology of animals is still too imperfect to justify any such use of it. His divisions into Apathetic, Sensitive, and Intelligent animals are entirely theoretical. He places, for instance, Fishes and Reptiles among the Intelligent animals, as distinguished from Crustacea and Insects, which he refers to the second division. But one would be puzzled to say how the former manifest more intelligence than the latter, or why the latter should be placed among the Sensitive animals. Again, some of the animals that he calls Apathetic have been proved by later investigators to show an affection and care for their young, seemingly quite inconsistent with the epithet he has applied to them. In fact, we know so little of the faculties of animals that any classification based upon our present information about them must be very imperfect.

Many modifications of Cuvier's great divisions have been attempted; but though some improvements have been made in the details of his classification, all departures from its great fundamental principle are errors, and do but lead us away from the recognition of the true affinities among animals. Some naturalists, for instance, have divided off a part of the Radiate and Articulates, insisting upon some special feature of structure, and mistaking these for the more important and general characteristics of their respective plans. Subsequent investigations have shown these would-be improvements to be retrograde movements, only proving more clearly that Cuvier detected in his four plans all the great

4 For more details upon the systems of Zoölogy see Agassiz's Essay on Classification in his "Contributions to the Natural History of the United States," Vol. I.; also printed separately.

structural ideas on which the vast variety of animals is founded. This result is of greater importance than may at first appear. Upon it depends the question, whether all such classifications represent merely individual impressions and opinions of men, or whether there is really something in Nature that presses upon us certain divisions among animals, certain affinities, certain limitations, founded upon essential principles of organization. Are our systems the inventions of naturalists, or only their reading of the Book of Nature? and can that book have more than one reading? If these classifications are not mere inventions, if they are not an attempt to classify for our own convenience the objects we study, then they are thoughts which, whether we detect them or not, are expressed in Nature,—then Nature is the work of thought, the production of intelligence, carried out according to plan, therefore premeditated,—and in our study of natural objects we are approaching the thoughts of the Creator, reading his conceptions, interpreting a system that is his and not ours.

All the divergence from the simplicity and grandeur of the division of the animal kingdom first recognized by Cuvier arises from an inability to distinguish between the essential features of a plan and its various modes of execution. We allow the details to shut out the plan itself, which exists quite independent of special forms. I hope we shall find a meaning in all these plans that will prove them to be the parts of one great conception and the work of one Mind.

CHAPTER II.

NOMENCLATURE AND CLASSIFICATION.

PROCEEDING upon the view that there is a close analogy between the way in which every individual student penetrates into Nature and the progress of science as a whole in the history of humanity, I continue my sketch of the successive steps that have led to our present state of knowledge. I began with Aristotle, and showed that this great philosopher, though he prepared a digest of all the knowledge belonging to his time, yet did not feel the necessity of any system or of any scientific language differing from the common mode of expression of his day. He presents his information as a man with his eyes open narrates in a familiar style what he sees. As civilization spread and science had its representatives in other countries besides Greece, it became indispensable to have a common scientific language, a technical nomenclature, combining many objects under common names, and enabling every naturalist to express the results of his observations readily and simply in a manner intelligible to all other students of Natural History.

Linnæus devised such a system, and to him we owe a most simple and comprehensive scientific mode of designating animals and plants. It may at first seem no advantage to give up the common names of the vernacular and adopt the unfamiliar ones, but a word of explanation will make the object clear. Perceiving, for instance, the close relations between certain members of the larger groups, Linnæus gave to them names that should be common to all, and which are called generic names,—as we speak of Ducks, when we would designate in one word the Mallard, the Widgeon, the Canvas-Back, etc.; but to these generic names he added qualifying epithets, called specific names, to indicate the different kinds in each group. For example, the Lion, the Tiger, the Panther, the Domestic Cat constitute such a natural group, which Linnæus called *Felis*, Cat, indicating the whole genus; but the species he designates as *Felis catus*, the Domestic Cat,—*Felis leo*, the Lion,—*Felis tigris*, the Tiger,—*Felis panthera*, the Panther. So he called all the Dogs *Canis*; but for the different kinds we have *Canis familiaris,* the Domestic Dog,—*Canis* lupus, the Wolf—*Canis vulpes*, the Fox, etc.

In some families of the vegetable kingdom we can appreciate better application of this nomenclature, because we have something corresponding to it in the vernacular. We have, for instance, one name for all the Oaks, but we call the different kinds Swamp Oak, Red Oak, White Oak, Chestnut Oak, etc. So Linnæus in his botanical nomenclature, called all the Oaks by the generic name *Quercus*, (characterizing them by their fruit, the acorn, common to all,) and qualified them as *Quercus bicolor, Quercus rubra, Quercus alba, Quercus castanea*, etc., etc. His nomenclature, being so easy of application, became at once exceedingly popular, and made him the great scientific legislator of his century. He insisted on Latin names, because, if every naturalist should use his own language, it must lead to great confusion, and this Latin nomenclature of double significance was adopted by all. Another advantage of this binominal Latin nomenclature consists in preventing the confusion frequently arising from the use of the same name to designate different animals in different parts of the world,—as, for instance, the name of Robin, used in America to designate a bird of the Thrush family, which is entirely different form the Robin of the Old World, one of the warblers,—or of different names for the same animal, as Perch or Chogset or Burgall for our Cunner. Nothing is more to be deprecated than an over-appreciation of technicalities, valuing the name more highly than the thing; but some knowledge of this scientific nomenclature is necessary to every student of Nature.

While Linnæus pointed out classes, orders, genera, and species, other naturalists had detected other divisions among animals, called families. Lamarck, who had been a distinguished botanist before he began his study of the animal kingdom, brought to his zoölogical researches his previous methods of investigation. Families in the vegetable kingdom had long been distinguished by French botanists; and one cannot examine the groups they call by this name, without perceiving, that, though they bring them together and describe them according to other characters, they have been unconsciously led to unite them from the general similarity of their port and bearing. Take, for instance, the families of Pines, Oaks, Beeches, Maples, etc., and you feel at once, that, besides the common characters given in the technical descriptions of these different groups of trees, there is also a general resemblance among them together, even if we knew nothing of the special features of their structure. By an instinctive recognition of this family likeness between plants, botanists have been led to seek for structural characters on which to unite them, and the groups so founded generally correspond with the combinations suggested by their appearance.

By a like process Lamarck combined animals into families. His method was adopted by French naturalists generally, and found favor especially with Cuvier, who was particularly successful in limiting families among animals, and in naming them happily, generally selecting names expressive of the features on which the groups were founded, or borrowing them from familiar animals. Much, indeed, depends upon the pleasant sound and the significance of a name; for an idea reaches the mind more easily when well expressed, and Cuvier's names were both simple and significant. His descriptions are also remarkable for their graphic precision,—giving all that is essential, omitting all that is merely accessory. He has given us the keynote to his progress in his own expressive language:—

> "Je dus donc, et cette obligation me prit un temps considérable, je dus faire marcher de front l'anatomie et la zoologie, les dissections et le classement; chercher dans mes premières remarques sur l'organisation des distributions meilleures; m'en servir pour arriver à des remarques nouvelles; employer encore ces remarques à perfectionner

> les distributions; faire sortir enfin de cette fécondation mutuelle des deux sciences, l'une par l'autre, un système zoologique propre à servir d'introducteur et de guide dans le champ de l'anatomie, et un corps de doctrine anatomiue propre à servir de développement et d'explication au système zoologique."[5]

It is deeply to be lamented that so many naturalists have entirely overlooked this significant advice of Cuvier's, with respect to combining zoölogical and anatomical studies in order to arrive at a clearer perception of the true affinities among animals. To sum it up in one word, he tells us that the secret of his method is "comparison,"—ever comparing and comparing throughout the enormous range of his knowledge of the organization of animals, and found upon the differences as well as the similarities those broad generalizations under which he has included all animal structures. And this method, so prolific in his hands, has also a lesson for us all. In this country there is a growing interest in the study of Nature; but while there exist hundreds of elementary works illustrating the native animals of Europe, there are few such books here to satisfy the demand for information respecting the animals of our land and water. We are thus forced to turn more and more to our own investigations and less to authority; and the true method of obtaining independent knowledge is this very method of Cuvier's,—comparison.

Let us make the most common application of it to natural objects. Suppose we see together a Dog, a Cat, a Bear, a Horse, a Cow, and a Deer. The first feature that strikes us as common to any two of them is the horn in the Cow and Deer. But how shall we associate either of the others with these? We examine the teeth, and find those of the Dog, the Cat, and the Bear sharp and cutting, while those of the Cow, the Deer, and the Horse have flat surfaces, adapted to grinding and chewing, rather than cutting and tearing. We compare these features of their structure with the habits

---

5 "I therefore felt myself obliged, and this obligation cost me no little time, to make my studies in anatomy and zoölogy, dissection and classification, keep pace with each other; to seek in my earlier investigations upon organization a better distribution of groups; to employ these again as a means of perfecting my classification; to arrive, in short, by this mutual fecundation of the two sciences at a zoölogical system which might serve as a pioneer and guide in the field of anatomy, and an anatomical method which would aid in the development and explanation of the zoölogical system."

of these animals, and find that the first are carnivorous, that they seize and tear their prey, while the others are herbivorous or grazing animals, living only on vegetable substances, which they chew and grind. We compare further the Horse and Cow, and find that the Horse has front teeth both in the upper and lower jaw, while the Cow has them only in the lower; and going still further, and comparing the internal with the external features, we find this arrangement of the teeth in direct relation to the different structure of the stomach in the two animals,—the Cow having a stomach with four pouches, adapted to a mode of digestion by which the food is prepared for the second mastication, while the Horse has a simple stomach. Comparing the Cow and the Deer, we find that the digestive apparatus is the same in both; but though they both have horns, in the Cow the horn is hollow, and remains through life firmly attached to the bone, while in the Deer it is solid and is shed every year. With these facts before us, we cannot hesitate to place the Dog, the Cat, and the Bear in one division, as carnivorous animals, and the other three in another division as herbivorous animals,—and looking a little further, we perceive, that, in common with the Cow and the Deer, the Goat and the Sheep have cloven feet, and that they are all ruminants, while the Horse has a single hoof, does not ruminate, and must therefore be separated from them, even though, like them, he is herbivorous.

This is but the simplest illustration, taken from the most familiar objects, of this comparative method; but the same process is equally applicable to the most intricate problems in animal structures, and will give us the clew to all true affinities between animals. The education of a naturalist now consists chiefly in learning how to compare. If he have any power of generalization, when he has collected his facts, this habit of mental comparison will lead him up to principles, and to the great laws of combination. It must not discourage us, that the process is a slow and laborious one, and the results of one lifetime after all very small. It might seem invidious, were I to show here how small is the sum total of the work accomplished even by the great exceptional men, whose names are known throughout the civilized world. But I may at least be permitted to speak disparagingly of my own efforts, and to sum up in the fewest words the result of my life's work. I have devoted my whole life to the study of Nature, and yet a single sentence may express all that I have done. I have shown that there is a correspondence between the succession of Fishes in geological times and the different stages of their growth in the egg,—this is all. It chanced to be a result that was found to apply to other groups and has led to other conclusions of a like nature. But, such as it is, it has been reached by this system of comparison, which, though I speak of it now in its application to the study of Natural History, is equally important in every other branch of knowledge. By the same process the most mature results of scientific research in Philology, in Ethnology, and in Physical Science are reached. And let me say that the community should foster the purely intellectual efforts of scientific men as carefully as they do their elementary schools and their practical institutions, generally considered so much more useful and important to the public. For from what other source shall we derive the higher results that are gradually woven into the practical resources of our life, except from the researches of those very men who study science, not for its uses, but for its truth? It is this that gives it its noblest interest: it must be for truth's sake, and not even for the sake of its usefulness to humanity, that the scientific man studies Nature. The application of science to the useful arts requires other abilities, other qualities, other tools than his; and therefore I say that the man of science who follows his studies into their practical application is false to his calling. The practical man stands ever ready to take up the work where the scientific man leaves it, and to adapt it to the material wants and uses of daily life.

The publication of Cuvier's proposition, that the animal kingdom is built on four plans, however imperfectly understood and appreciated at first, created, nevertheless, an extraordinary excitement throughout the scientific world. All naturalists proceeded to test it, and some among them soon recognized in it a great scientific truth,—while others, who thought more of making themselves prominent than of advancing science, proposed poor amendments, that were sure to be rejected on further investigations. Some of these criticisms and additions, however, were truly improvements, and touched upon points overlooked by Cuvier. Blainville, especially, took up the element of form among animals,—whether divided on two sides, whether radiated, whether irregular, etc. He, however, made the mistake of giving very elaborate names to animals already known under simpler ones. Why, for instance, call all animals with parts radiating in every direction *Actinomorpha* or *Actinozoaria*, when they had received the significant name of *Radiates*? It seemed to be a new system, when in fact it was only a new name. Ehrenberg, likewise, made an important distinction, when he united the animals according to the difference in their nervous systems; but he also encumbered the nomenclature unnecessarily, when he added to the names *Anaima* and *Enaima* of Aristotle those of *Myeloneura* and *Ganglioneura*.

But it is not my object to give all the classifications of different authors here, and I will therefore pass over many noted ones, as those of Burmeister, Milne-Edwards, Siebold and Stannius, Owen, Leuckart, Vogt, Van Beneden, and others, and proceed to give some account of one investigator who did as much for the progress of Zoölogy as Cuvier, though he is comparatively little known among us.

Karl Ernst von Baer proposed a classification based, like Cuvier's, upon plan; but he recognized what Cuvier failed to perceive,—namely, the importance of distinguishing between type (by which he means exactly what Cuvier means by plan) and complication of structure,—in other words, between plan and the execution of the plan. He recognized four types, which correspond exactly to Cuvier's four plans, though he calls them by different names. Let us compare them.

Cuvier.	*Baer.*
Radiates,	Peripheric,
Mollusks,	Massive,
Articulates,	Longitudinal,
Vertebrates.	Doubly Symmetrical.

Though perhaps less felicitous, the names of Baer express the same ideas as those of Cuvier. By the *Peripheric* type he signified those animals in which all parts converge from the periphery or circumference of the animal to its centre. Cuvier only reverses this definition in this name of *Radiates*, signifying the animals in which all parts radiate from the centre to the circumference. By *Massive*, Baer indicated those animals in which the body is undivided, soft and concentrated, without a very distinct individualization of parts,—exactly the animals included by Cuvier under his name of *Mollusks*, or soft-bodied animals. In his selection of the epithet *Longitudinal*, Baer was less fortunate; for all animals have a longitudinal diameter, and this word was not, therefore, sufficiently special. Yet his *Longitudinal* type answers exactly to Cuvier's *Articulates*,—animals in which all parts are arranged in a succession of articulated joints along a longitudinal axis. Cuvier has expressed this jointed structure in the name *Articulates*; whereas Baer, in his name of *Longitudinal*, referred only to the arrangement of joints in longitudinal succession, in a continuous string, as it were, one after another, indicating thus the prevalence of length as the predominant diameter of the body. For the *Doubly Symmetrical* type his name is the better of the two; since Cuvier's name of *Vertebrates* alludes only to the backbone,—while Baer, who is an embryologist, signified in his their mode of growth also. He knew what Cuvier did not know, when he first proposed his classification, that in its first formation the germ of the Vertebrate divides in two folds; one turning up above the backbone, to form and enclose all the sensitive organs,—the spinal marrow, the organs of sense, all those organs by which life is expressed; the other turning down below the backbone, and enclosing all those organs by which life is maintains,—the organs of digestion, of respiration, or circulation, of reproduction, etc. So there is in this type not only an equal division of parts on either side, but also a division above and below, making thus a double symmetry in the plan, expressed by Baer in the name he gave it. Baer was perfectly original in his conception of these four types, for his paper was published in the very same year with that of Cuvier. But even in Germany, his native land, his ideas were not fully appreciated: strange that it should be so,—for, had his countrymen recognized his genius, they might have earlier claimed him as the compeer of the great French naturalist.

Baer also founded the science of Embryology, under the guidance of his teacher, Döllinger. His researches in this direction showed him that animals were not only built on four plans, but that they grew according to four modes of development. The Vertebrate arises from the egg differently from the Articulate,—the Articulate differently from the Mollusk,—the Mollusk differently from the Radiate. Cuvier only showed us the four plans as they exist in the adult; Baer went a step further, and showed us the four plans in the process of formation.

But his greatest scientific achievement is perhaps the discovery that all animals originate from eggs, and that all these eggs are at first identical in substance and structure. The wonderful and untiring research condensed into this simple statement, that all animals arise from eggs, and that all those eggs are identical in the beginning, may well excite our admiration. This egg consists of an outer envelope, the vitelline membrane, containing a fluid more or less dense, and variously colored, the yolk; within this is a second envelope, the so-called germinative vesicle, containing a somewhat different and more transparent fluid, and in the fluid of this second envelope float one or more so-called germinative specks. At this stage of their growth all eggs are microscopically small, yet each one has such tenacity of its individual principle of life that no egg was ever known to swerve from the pattern of the parent animals that gave it birth.

Vannevar Bush

1890-1974

Science: The Endless Frontier

1945

Born in Chelsea, Massachusetts to a Universalist minister and his wife, Vannevar Bush was a sickly child, spending long periods of time bed-ridden. A talented student growing up, with an aptitude for math, his academic success empowered his desire to do things independently. Bush earned his doctorate in engineering from MIT, was an assistant professor at Tufts University, and conducted research at MIT on the earliest analog computers. In 1931 he completed the first ever differential analyzer—a machine to solve differential equations. In 1937 he became President of the Carnegie Institution, and during World War II, he was appointed the Director of the Office of Scientific Research and Development (OSRD) by President Franklin D. Roosevelt.

In his capacity as the Director of OSRD, and aware that the country was unprepared for the needs of the military during World War II, Bush's efforts during and after the war led to a change in the way basic research was conducted in the United States. The changes included the government support of basic research financially, and the creation of federal structures to direct and support specific research aims that would benefit the development of science and technology for the citizens of the United States. Some of his ideas predicted the internet information age though he died in 1974 before any of this current technology had even been developed.

Science: The Endless Frontier was written in 1945 and served as an outline showing how basic science research could be developed and supported. His efforts led to the creation of the National Science Foundation (NSF) in 1950, securing Bush's goal of a union of science and government, though this union was not as vigorous as he had hoped.

1. Compare the current state of basic science research and applied scientific research. How would have Bush viewed the recent changes in these areas as far as U.S. government involvement?
2. Should government and scientific research be connected? Are there moral or ethical problems created by these links?

SOURCE:

Griffin, Scott. (2000). *Internet Pioneers.* Retrieved July 23, 2007, from http://www.ibiblio.org/pioneers/bush.html

SELECTION FROM:

Bush, Vannevar. (1945). *Science: The Endless Frontier.* Washington, D.C.: National Science Foundation. Reprinted July 1960. 5-12, 17-22, 31-34.

SUMMARY OF THE REPORT

Scientific Progress is Essential

Progress in the war against disease depends upon a flow of new scientific knowledge. New products, new industries, and more jobs require continuous additions to knowledge of the laws of nature, and the application of that knowledge to practical purposes. Similarly, our defense against aggression demands new knowledge so that we can develop new and improved weapons. This essential, new knowledge can be obtained only through basic scientific research.

Science can be effective in the national welfare only as a member of a team, whether the conditions be peace or war. But without scientific progress no amount of achievement in other directions can insure our health, prosperity, and security as a nation in the modern world.

For The War Against Disease

We have taken great strides in the war against disease. The death rate for all diseases in the Army, including overseas forces, has been reduced from 14.1 per thousand in the last war to 0.6 per thousand in this war. In the last 40 years life expectancy has increased from 49 to 65 years, largely as a consequence of the reduction in the death rates of infants and children. But we are far from the goal. The annual deaths from one or two diseases far exceed the total number of American lives lost in battle during this war. A large fraction of these deaths in our civilian population cut short the useful lives of our citizens. Approximately 7,000,000 persons in the United States are mentally ill and their care costs the public over $175,000,000 a year. Clearly much illness remains for which adequate means of prevention and cure are not yet known.

The responsibility for basic research in medicine and the underlying sciences, so essential to progress in the war against disease, falls primarily upon the medical schools and universities. Yet we find that the traditional sources of support for medical research in the medical schools and universities, largely endowment income, foundation grants, and private donations, are diminishing and there is no immediate prospect of a change in this trend. Meanwhile, the cost of medical research has been rising. If we are to maintain the progress in medicine which has marked the last 25 years, the Government should extend financial support to basic medical research in the medical schools and in universities.

For Our National Security

The bitter and dangerous battle against the U-boat was a battle of scientific techniques—and our margin of success was dangerously small. The new eyes which radar has supplied can sometimes be blinded by new scientific developments. V-2 was countered only by capture of the launching sites.

We cannot again rely on our allies to hold off the enemy while we struggle to catch up. There must be more—and more adequate—military research in peacetime. It is essential that the civilian scientists continue in peacetime some portion of those contributions to national security which they have made so effectively during the war. This can best be done through a civilian-controlled organization with close liaison with the Army and Navy, but with funds direct from Congress, and the clear power to initiate military research which will supplement and strengthen that carried on directly under the control of the Army and Navy.

And for the Public Welfare

One of our hopes is that after the war there will be full employment. To reach that goal the full creative and productive energies of the American people must be released. To create more jobs we must make new and better and cheaper products. We want plenty of new, vigorous enterprises. But new products and processes are not born full-grown. They are founded on new principles and new conceptions which in turn result from basic scientific research. Basic scientific research is scientific capital. Moreover, we cannot any longer depend upon Europe as a major source of this scientific capital. Clearly, more and better scientific research is one essential to the achievement of our goal of full employment.

How do we increase this scientific capital? First, we must have plenty of men and women trained in science, for upon them depends both the creation of new knowledge and its application to practical purposes. Second, we must strengthen the centers of basic research which are principally the colleges, universities, and research institutes. These institutions provide the environment which is most conducive to the creation of new scientific knowledge and least under pressure for immediate, tangible results. With some notable exceptions, most research in industry and in Government involves application of existing scientific knowledge to practical problems. It is only the colleges, universities, and a few research institutes that devote most of their research efforts to expanding the frontiers of knowledge.

Expenditures for scientific research by industry and Government increased from $140,000,000 in 1930 to $309,000,000 in 1940. Those for the colleges and universities increased from $20,000,000 to $31,000.000, while those for research institutes declined from $5,200,000 to $4,500,000 during the same period. If the colleges, universities, and research institutes are to meet the rapidly increasing demands of industry and Government for new scientific knowledge, their basic research should be strengthened by use of public funds.

For science to serve as a powerful factor in our national welfare, applied research both in Government and in industry must be vigorous. To improve the quality of scientific research within the Government, steps should be taken to modify the procedures for recruiting, classifying, and compensating scientific personnel in order to reduce the present handicap of governmental scientific bureaus in competing with industry and the universities for top-grade scientific talent. To provide coordination of the common scientific activities of these governmental agencies as to policies and budgets, a permanent Science Advisory Board should be created to advise the executive and legislative branches of Government on these matters.

The most important ways in which the Government can promote industrial research are to increase the flow of new scientific knowledge through support of basic research, and to aid in the development of scientific talent. In addition, the Government should provide suitable incentives to industry to conduct research (*a*) by clarification of present uncertainties in the Internal Revenue Code in regard to the deductibility of research and development expenditures as current charges against net income, and (*b*) by strengthening the patent system so as to eliminate uncertainties which now bear heavily on small industries and so as to prevent abuses which reflect discredit upon a basically sound system. In addition, ways should be found to cause the benefits of basic research to reach industries which do not now utilize new scientific knowledge.

We Must Renew Our Scientific Talent

The responsibility for the creation of new scientific knowledge—and for most of its application—rests on that small body of men and women who understand the fundamental laws of nature and are skilled in the techniques of scientific research. We shall have rapid or slow advance on any scientific frontier depending on the number of highly qualified and trained scientists exploring it.

The deficit of science and technology students who, but for the war, would have received bachelor's degrees is about 150,000. It is estimated that the deficit of those obtaining advanced degrees in these fields will amount in 1955 to about 17,000—for it takes at least 6 years from college entry to achieve a doctor's degree or its equivalent in science or engineering. The real ceiling on our productivity of new scientific knowledge and its application in the war against disease, and the development of new products and new industries, is the number of trained scientists available.

The training of a scientist is a long and expensive process. Studies clearly show that there are talented individuals in every part of the population, but with few exceptions, those without the means of buying higher education go without it. If ability, and not the circumstance of family fortune, determines who shall receive higher education in science, then we shall be assured of constantly improving quality at every level of scientific activity. The Government should provide a reasonable number of undergraduate scholarships and graduate fellowships in order to develop scientific talent in American youth. The plans should be designed to attract into science only that proportion of youthful talent appropriate to the needs of science in relation to the other needs of the Nation for high abilities.

Including Those in Uniform

The most immediate prospect of making up the deficit in scientific personnel is to develop the scientific talent in the generation now in uniform. Even if we should start now to train the current crop of high-school graduates none would complete graduate studies before 1951. The Armed Services should comb their records for men who, prior to or during the war, have given evidence of talent for science, and make prompt arrangements, consistent with current discharge plans, for ordering those who remain in uniform, as soon as militarily possible, to duty at institutions here and overseas where they can continue their scientific education. Moreover, the Services should see that those who study overseas have the benefit of the latest scientific information resulting from research during the war.

The Lid Must Be Lifted

While most of the war research has involved the application of existing scientific knowledge to the problems of war, rather than basic research, there has been accumulated a vast amount of information relating to the application of science to particular problems. Much of this can be used by industry. It is also needed for teaching in the colleges and universities here and in the Armed Forces Institutes overseas. Some of this information must remain secret, but most of it should be made public as soon as there is ground for belief that the enemy will not be able to turn it against us in this war. To select that portion which should be made public, to coordinate its release, and definitely to encourage its publication, a Board composed of Army, Navy, and civilian scientific members should be promptly established.

A Program for Action

The Government should accept new responsibilities for promoting the flow of new scientific knowledge and the development of scientific talent in our youth. These responsibilities are the proper concern of the

Government, for they vitally affect our health, our jobs, and our national security. It is in keeping also with basic United States policy that the Government should foster the opening of new frontiers and this is the modern way to do it. For many years the Government has wisely supported research in the agricultural colleges and the benefits have been great. The time has come when such support should be extended to other fields.

The effective discharge of these new responsibilities will require the full attention of some over-all agency devoted to that purpose. There is not now in the permanent governmental structure receiving its funds from Congress an agency adapted to supplementing the support of basic research in the colleges, universities, and research institutes, both in medicine and the natural sciences, adapted to supporting research on new weapons for both Services, or adapted to administering a program of science scholarships and fellowships.

Therefore I recommend that a new agency for these purposes be established. Such an agency should be composed of persons of broad interest and experience, having an understanding of the peculiarities of scientific research and scientific education. It should have stability of funds so that long-range programs may be undertaken. It should recognize that freedom of inquiry must be preserved and should leave internal control of policy, personnel and the method and scope of research to the institutions in which it is carried on. It should be fully responsible to the President and through him to the Congress for its program.

Early action on these recommendations is imperative if this Nation is to meet the challenge of science in the crucial years ahead. On the wisdom with which we bring science to bear in the war against disease, in the creation of new industries, and in the strengthening of our Armed Forces depends in large measure our future as a nation.

Part One

INTRODUCTION

Scientific Progress Is Essential

We all know how much the new drug, penicillin, has meant to our grievously wounded men on the grim battlefronts of this war—the countless lives it has saved—the incalculable suffering which its use has prevented. Science and the great practical genius of this Nation made this achievement possible.

Some of us know the vital role which radar has played in bringing the Allied Nations to victory over Nazi Germany and in driving the Japanese steadily back from their island bastions. Again it was painstaking scientific research over many years that made radar possible.

What we often forget are the millions of pay envelopes on a peacetime Saturday night which are filled because new products and new industries have provided jobs for countless Americans. Science made that possible, too.

In 1939 millions of people were employed in industries which did not even exist at the close of the last war—radio, air conditioning, rayon and other synthetic fibers, and plastics are examples of the products of these industries. But these things do not mark the end of progress—they are but the beginning if we make full use of our scientific resources. New manufacturing industries can be started and many older industries greatly strengthened and expanded if we continue to study nature's laws and apply new knowledge to practical purposes.

Great advances in agriculture are also based upon scientific research. Plants which are more resistant to disease and are adapted to short growing seasons, the prevention and cure of livestock diseases, the control of our insect enemies, better fertilizers, and improved agricultural practices, all stem from painstaking scientific research.

Advances in science when put to practical use mean more jobs, higher wages, shorter hours, more abundant crops, more leisure for recreation, for study, for learning how to live without the deadening drudgery which has been the burden of the common man for ages past. Advances in science will also bring higher standards of living, will lead to the prevention or cure of diseases, will promote conservation of our limited national resources, and will assure means of defense against aggression. But to achieve these objectives—to secure a high level of employment, to maintain a position of world leadership, the flow of new scientific knowledge must be both continuous and substantial.

Our population increased from 75 million to 130 million between 1900 and 1940. In some countries comparable increases have been accompanied by famine. In this country, the increase has been accompanied by more abundant food supply, better living. more leisure, longer life, and better health. This is, largely, the product of three factors—the free play of initiative of a vigorous people under democracy, the heritage of great national wealth, and the advance of science and its application.

Science, by itself, provides no panacea for individual, social, and economic ills. It can be effective in the national welfare only as a member of a team, whether the conditions be peace or war. But without scientific progress no amount of achievement in other directions can insure our health, prosperity, and security as a nation in the modern world.

Science Is a Proper Concern of Government

It has been basic United States policy that Government should foster the opening of new frontiers. It opened the seas to clipper ships and furnished land for pioneers. Although these frontiers have more or less disappeared, the frontier of science remains. It is in keeping with the American tradition—one which has made the United States great—that new frontiers shall be made accessible for development by all American citizens.

Moreover, since health, well-being, and security are proper concerns of Government, scientific progress is, and must be, of vital interest to Government. Without scientific progress the national health would deteriorate; without scientific progress we could not hope for improvement in our standard of living or for an increased number of jobs for our citizens; and without scientific progress we could not have maintained our liberties against tyranny.

Government Relations to Science—Past and Future

From early days the Government has taken an active interest in scientific matters. During the nineteenth century the Coast and Geodetic Survey, the Naval Observatory, the Department of Agriculture, and the Geological Survey were established. Through the Land Grant College Acts the Government has supported research in state institutions for more than 80 years on a gradually increasing scale. Since 1900 a large number of scientific agencies have been established within the Federal Government, until in 1939 they numbered more than 40.

Much of the scientific research done by Government agencies is intermediate in character between the two types of work commonly referred to as basic and applied research. Almost all Government scientific work has ultimate practical objectives but, in many fields of broad national concern, it commonly involves long-term investigation of a fundamental nature. Generally speaking, the scientific agencies of Government are not so concerned with immediate practical objectives as are the laboratories of industry nor, on the other hand, are they as free to explore any natural phenomena without regard to possible economic applications as are the educational and private research institutions. Government scientific agencies have splendid records of achievement, but they are limited in function.

We have no national policy for science. The Government has only begun to utilize science in the nation's welfare. There is no body within the Government charged with formulating or executing a national science policy. There are no standing committees of the Congress devoted to this important subject. Science has been in the wings. It should be brought to the center of the stage—for in it lies much of our hope for the future.

There are areas of science in which the public interest is acute but which are likely to be cultivated inadequately if left without more support than will come from private sources. These areas—such as research on military problems, agriculture, housing, public health, certain medical research, and research involving expensive capital facilities beyond the capacity of private institutions—should be advanced by active Government support. To date, with the exception of the intensive war research conducted by the Office of Scientific Research and Development, such support has been meager and intermittent.

For reasons presented in this report we are entering a period when science needs and deserves increased support from public funds.

Freedom of Inquiry Must Be Preserved

The publicly and privately supported colleges, universities, and research institutes are the centers of basic research. They are the wellsprings of knowledge and understanding. As long as they are vigorous and healthy and their scientists are free to pursue the truth wherever it may lead, there will be a flow of new scientific knowledge to those who can apply it to practical problems in Government, in industry, or elsewhere.

Many of the lessons learned in the war-time application of science under Government can be profitably applied in peace. The Government is peculiarly fitted to perform certain functions, such as the coordination and support of broad programs on problems of great national importance. But we must proceed with caution in carrying over the methods which work in wartime to the very different conditions of peace. We must remove the rigid controls which we have had to impose, and recover freedom of inquiry and that healthy competitive scientific spirit so necessary for expansion of the frontiers of scientific knowledge.

Scientific progress on a broad front results from the free play of free intellects, working on subjects of their own choice, in the manner dictated by their curiosity for exploration of the unknown. Freedom of inquiry must be preserved under any plan for Government support of science in accordance with the Five Fundamentals listed on page 32.

The study of the momentous questions presented in President Roosevelt's letter has been made by able committees working diligently. This report presents conclusions and recommendations based upon the studies of these committees which appear in full as the appendices. Only in the creation of one over-all mechanism rather than several does this report depart from the specific recommendations in regard to the single mechanism and have found this plan thoroughly acceptable.

Part Three

SCIENCE AND THE PUBLIC WELFARE

Relation to National Security

In this war it has become clear beyond all doubt that scientific research is absolutely essential to national security. The bitter and dangerous battle against the U-boat was a battle of scientific techniques—and our margin of success was dangerously small. The new eyes which radar supplied to our fighting forces quickly evoked the development of scientific countermeasures which could often blind them. This again represents the ever continuing battle of techniques. The V-1 attack on London was finally defeated by three devices developed during this war and used superbly in the field. V-2 was countered only by capture of the launching sites.

The Secretaries of War and Navy recently stated in a joint letter to the National Academy of Sciences:

This war emphasizes three facts of supreme importance to national security: (1) Powerful new tactics of defense and offense are developed around new weapons created by scientific and engineering research: (2) the competitive time element in developing those weapons and tactics may be decisive; (3) war is increasingly total war, in which the armed services must be supplemented by active participation of every element of civilian population.

To insure continued preparedness along farsighted technical lines, the research scientists of the country must be called upon to continue in peacetime some substantial portion of those types of contribution to national security which they have made so effectively during the stress of the present war.

[* * *]

There must be more—and more adequate—military research during peacetime. We cannot again rely on our allies to hold off the enemy while we struggle to catch up. Further, it is clear that only the Government can undertake military research; for it must be carried on in secret, much of it has no commercial value, and it is expensive. The obligation of Government to support research on military problems is inescapable.

Modern war requires the use of the most advanced scientific techniques. Many of the leaders in the development of radar are scientists who before the war had been exploring the nucleus of the atom. While there must be increased emphasis on science in the future training of officers for both the Army and Navy, such men cannot be expected to be specialists in scientific research. Therefore, a professional partnership between the officers in the Services and civilian scientists is needed.

The Army and Navy should continue to carry on research and development on the improvement of current weapons. For many years the National Advisory Committee for Aeronautics has supplemented the work of the Army and Navy by conducting basic research on the problems of flight. There should now be permanent civilian activity to supplement the research work of the Services in other scientific fields so as to carry out in time of peace some part of the activities of the emergency wartime Office of Scientific Research and Development.

Military preparedness requires a permanent independent, civilian-controlled organization, having close liaison with the Army and Navy, but with funds directly from Congress and with the clear power to initiate military research which will supplement and strengthen that carried on directly under the control of the Army and Navy.

Science and Jobs

One of our hopes is that after the war there will be full employment, and that the production of goods and services will serve to raise our standard of living. We do not know yet how we shall reach that goal, but it is certain that it can be achieved only by releasing the full creative and productive energies of the American people.

Surely we will not get there by standing still, merely by making the same things we made before and selling them at the same or higher prices. We will not get ahead in international trade unless we offer new and more attractive and cheaper products.

Where will these new products come from? How will we find ways to make better products at lower cost? The answer is clear. There must be a stream of new scientific knowledge to turn the wheels of private and public enterprise. There must be plenty of men and women trained in science and technology for upon them depend both the creation of new knowledge and its application to practical purposes.

More and better scientific research is essential to the achievement of our goal of full employment.

The Importance of Basic Research

Basic research is performed without thought of practical ends. It results in general knowledge and an understanding of nature and its laws. This general knowledge provides the means of answering a large number of important practical problems, though it may not give a complete specific answer to any one of them. The function of applied research is to provide such complete answers. The scientist doing basic research may not be at all interested in the practical applications of his work, yet the further progress of industrial development would eventually stagnate if basic scientific research were long neglected.

One of the peculiarities of basic science is the variety of paths which lead to productive advance. Many of the most important discoveries have come as a result of experiments undertaken with very different purposes in mind. Statistically, it is certain that important and highly useful discoveries will result from some fraction of the undertakings in basic science; but the results of one particular investigation cannot be predicted with accuracy.

Basic research leads to new knowledge. It provides scientific capital. It creates the fund from which the practical applications of knowledge must be drawn. New products and new processes do not appear full-grown. They are founded on new principles and new conceptions, which in turn are painstakingly developed by research in the purest realms of science.

Today, it is truer than ever that basic research is the pacemaker of technological progress. In the nineteenth century, Yankee mechanical ingenuity, building largely upon the basic discoveries of European scientists, could greatly advance the technical arts. Now the situation is different.

A nation which depends upon others for its new basic scientific knowledge will be slow in its industrial progress and weak in its competitive position in world trade, regardless of its mechanical skill.

Centers of Basic Research

Publicly and privately supported colleges and universities and the endowed research institutes must furnish both the new scientific knowledge and the trained research workers. These institutions are uniquely qualified by tradition and by their special characteristics to carry on basic research. They are charged with the responsibility of conserving the knowledge accumulated by the past, imparting that knowledge to students, and contributing new knowledge of all kinds. It is chiefly in these institutions that scientists may work in an atmosphere which is relatively free from the adverse pressure of contention, prejudice, or commercial necessity. At their best they provide the scientific worker with a strong sense of solidarity and security, as well as a substantial degree of personal intellectual freedom. All of these factors are of great importance in the development of new knowledge, since much of new knowledge is certain to arouse opposition because of its tendency to challenge current beliefs or practice.

Industry is generally inhibited by preconceived goals, by its own clearly defined standards, and by the constant pressure of commercial necessity. Satisfactory progress in basic science seldom occurs under conditions prevailing in the normal industrial laboratory. There are some notable exceptions, it is true, but even in such cases it is rarely possible to match the universities in respect to the freedom which is so important to scientific discovery.

To serve effectively as the centers of basic research these institutions must be strong and healthy. They must attract our best scientists as teachers and investigators. They must offer research opportunities and sufficient compensation to enable them to compete with industry and government for the cream of scientific talent.

During the past 25 years there has been a great increase in industrial research involving the application of scientific knowledge to a multitude of practical purposes—thus providing new products, new industries, new investment opportunities, and millions of jobs. During the same period research within Government—again largely applied research—has also been greatly expanded. In the decade from 1930 to 1940 expenditures for industrial research increased from $116,000,000 to $240,000,000 and those for scientific research in Government rose from $24,000,000 to $69,000,000. During the same period expenditures for scientific research in the colleges and universities increased from $20,000,000 to $31,000,000, while those in the endowed research institutes declined from $5,200,000 to $4,500,000. These are the best estimates available. The figures have been taken from a variety of sources and arbitrary definitions have necessarily been applied, but it is believed that they may be accepted as indicating the following trends:

(a) Expenditures for scientific research by industry and Government—almost entirely applied research—have more than doubled between 1930 and 1940. Whereas in 1930 they were six times as large as the research expenditures of the colleges, universities, and research institutes, by 1940 they were nearly ten times as large.
(b) While expenditures for scientific research in the colleges and universities increased by one-half during this period, those for the endowed research institutes have slowly declined.

If the colleges, universities and research institutes are to meet the rapidly increasing demands of industry and Government for new scientific knowledge, their basic research should be strengthened by use of public funds.

Research Within the Government

Although there are some notable exceptions, most research conducted within governmental laboratories is of an applied nature. This has always been true and is likely to remain so. Hence Government, like industry, is dependent upon the colleges, universities, and research institutes to expand the basic scientific frontiers and to furnish trained scientific investigators.

Research within the Government represents an important part of our total research activity and needs to be strengthened and expanded after the war. Such expansion should be directed to fields of inquiry and service which are of public importance and are not adequately carried on by private organizations.

The most important single factor in scientific and technical work is the quality of personnel employed. The procedures currently followed within the Government for recruiting, classifying and compensating such personnel place the Government under a severe handicap in competing with industry and the universities for first-class scientific talent. Steps should be taken to reduce that handicap.

In the Government the arrangement whereby the numerous scientific agencies form parts of large departments has both advantages and disadvantages. But the present pattern is firmly established and there is much to be said for it. There is, however, a very real need for some measure of coordination of the common scientific activities of these agencies, both as to policies and budgets, and at present no such means exist.

A permanent Science Advisory Board should be created to consult with these scientific bureaus and to advise the executive and legislative branches of Government as to the policies and budgets of Government agencies engaged in scientific research.

This board should be composed of disinterested scientists who have no connection with the affairs of any Government agency.

Industrial Research

The simplest and most effective way in which the Government can strengthen industrial research is to support basic research and to develop scientific talent.

The benefits of basic research do not reach all industries equally or at the same speed. Some small enterprises never receive any of the benefits. It has been suggested that the benefits might be better utilized if "research clinics" for such enterprises were to be established. Businessmen would thus be able to make more use of research than they now do. This proposal is certainly worthy of further study.

One of the most important factors affecting the amount of industrial research is the income-tax law. Government action in respect to this subject will affect the rate of technical progress in industry. Uncertainties as to the attitude of the Bureau of Internal Revenue regarding the deduction of research and development expenses are a deterrent to research expenditure. These uncertainties arise from lack of clarity of the tax law as to the proper treatment of such costs.

The Internal Revenue Code should be amended to remove present uncertainties in regard to the deductibility of research and development expenditures as current charges against net income.

Research is also affected by the patent laws. They stimulate new invention and they make it possible for new industries to be built around new devices or new processes. These industries generate new jobs and new products, all of which contribute to the welfare and the strength of the country.

Yet, uncertainties in the operation of the patent laws have impaired the ability of small industries to translate new ideas into processes and products of value to the Nation. These uncertainties are, in part, attributable to the difficulties and expense incident to the operation of the patent system as it presently exists. These uncertainties are also attributable to the existence of certain abuses which have appeared in the use of patents. The abuses should be corrected. They have led to extravagantly critical attacks which tend to discredit a basically sound system.

It is important that the patent system continue to serve the country in the manner intended by the Constitution, for it has been a vital element in the industrial vigor which has distinguished this Nation.

The National Patent Planning Commission has reported on this subject. In addition, a detailed study, with recommendations concerning the extent to which modifications should be made in our patent laws is currently being made under the leadership of the Secretary of Commerce. It is recommended. therefore, that specific action with regard to the patent laws be withheld pending the submission of the report devoted exclusively to that subject.

International Exchange of Scientific Information

International exchange of scientific information is of growing importance. Increasing specialization of science will make it more important than ever that scientists in this country keep continually abreast of developments abroad. In addition, a flow of scientific information constitutes one facet of general international accord which should be cultivated.

The Government can accomplish significant results in several ways: by aiding in the arrangement of international science congresses, in the official accrediting of American scientists to such gatherings, in the official reception of foreign scientists of standing in this country, in making possible a rapid flow of technical information, including translation service, and possibly in the provision of international fellowships. Private foundations and other groups partially fulfill some of these functions at present, but their scope is incomplete and inadequate.

The Government should take an active role in promoting the international flow of scientific information.

The Special Need for Federal Support

We can no longer count on ravaged Europe as a source of fundamental knowledge. In the past we have devoted much of our best efforts to the application of such knowledge which has been discovered abroad. In the future we must pay increased attention to discovering this knowledge for ourselves particularly since the scientific applications of the future will be more than ever dependent upon such basic knowledge.

New impetus must be given to research in our country. Such new impetus can come promptly only from the Government. Expenditures for research in the colleges, universities, and research institutes will otherwise not be able to meet the additional demands of increased public need for research.

Further, we cannot expect industry adequately to fill the gap. Industry will fully rise to the challenge of applying new knowledge to new products. The commercial incentive can be relied upon for that. But basic research is essentially noncommercial in nature. It will not receive the attention it requires if left to industry.

For many years the Government has wisely supported research in the agricultural colleges and the benefits have been great. The time has come when such support should be extended to other fields.

In providing Government support, however, we must endeavor to preserve as far as possible the private support of research both in industry and in the colleges, universities, and research institutes. These private sources should continue to carry their share of the financial burden.

The Cost of a Program

It is estimated that an adequate program for Federal support of basic research in the colleges, universities, and research institutes and for financing important applied research in the public interest, will cost about 10 million dollars at the outset and may rise to about 50 million dollars annually when fully underway at the end of perhaps 5 years.

Part Six

THE MEANS TO THE END

New Responsibilities for Government

One lesson is clear from the reports of the several committees attached as appendices. The Federal Government should accept new responsibilities for promoting the creation of new scientific knowledge and the development of scientific talent in our youth.

The extent and nature of these new responsibilities are set forth in detail in the reports of the committees whose recommendations in this regard are fully endorsed.

In discharging these responsibilities Federal funds should be made available. We have given much thought to the question of how plans for the use of Federal funds may be arranged so that such funds will not drive out of the picture funds from local governments, foundations, and private donors. We believe that our proposals will minimize that effect, but we do not think that it can be completely avoided. We submit, however, that the Nation's need for more and better scientific research is such that the risk must be accepted.

It is also clear that the effective discharge of these responsibilities will require the full attention of some over-all agency devoted to that purpose. There should be a focal point within the Government for a concerted program of assisting scientific research conducted outside of Government. Such an agency should furnish the funds needed to support basic research in the colleges and universities, should coordinate where possible research programs on matters of utmost importance to the national welfare, should formulate a national policy for the Government toward science, should sponsor the interchange of scientific information among scientists and laboratories both in this country and abroad, and should ensure that the incentives to research in industry and the universities are maintained. All of the committees advising on these matters agree on the necessity for such an agency.

The Mechanism

There are within Government departments many groups whose interests are primarily those of scientific research. Notable examples are found within the Departments of Agriculture, Commerce, Interior, and the Federal Security Agency. These groups are concerned with science as collateral and peripheral to the major problems of those Departments. These groups should remain where they are, and continue to perform their present functions, including the support of agricultural research by grants to the land grant colleges and experimental stations. Since their largest contribution lies in applying fundamental knowledge to the special problems of the Departments within which they are established.

By the same token these groups cannot be made the repository of the new and large responsibilities in science which belong to the Government and which the Government should accept. The recommendations in this report which relate to research within the Government, to the release of scientific information, to clarification of the tax laws, and to the recovery and development of our scientific talent now in uniform can be implemented by action within the existing structure of the Government.

But nowhere in the governmental structure receiving its funds from Congress is there an agency adapted to supplementing the support of basic research in the universities, both in medicine and the natural sciences; adapted to supporting research on new weapons for both Services; or adapted to administering a program of science scholarships and fellowships.

A new agency should be established, therefore, by the Congress for the purpose. Such an agency, moreover, should be an independent agency devoted to the support of scientific research and advanced scientific education alone. Industry learned many years ago that basic research cannot often be fruitfully conducted as an adjunct to or a subdivision of an operating agency or department. Operating agencies have immediate operating goals and are under constant pressure to produce in a tangible way, for that is the test of their value. None of these conditions is favorable to basic research. Research is the exploration of the unknown and is necessarily speculative. It is inhibited by conventional approaches, traditions, and standards. It cannot be satisfactorily conducted in an atmosphere where it is gauged and tested by operating or production standards. Basic scientific research should not, therefore, be placed under an operating agency whose paramount concern is anything other than research. Research will always suffer when put in competition with operations. The decision that there should be a new and independent agency was reached by each of the committees advising in these matters.

I am convinced that these new functions should be centered in one agency. Science is fundamentally a unitary thing. The number of independent agencies should be kept to a minimum. Much medical progress, for example, will come from fundamental advances in chemistry. Separation of the sciences in tight compartments, as would occur if more than one agency were involved, would retard and not advance scientific knowledge as a whole.

Five Fundamentals

There are certain basic principles which must underlie the program of Government support for scientific research and education if such support is to be effective and if it is to avoid impairing the very things we seek to foster. These principles are as follows:

(1) Whatever the extent of support may be, there must be stability of funds over a period of years so that long-range programs may be undertaken.

(2) The agency to administer such funds should be composed of citizens selected only on the basis of their interest in and capacity to promote the work of the agency. They should be persons of broad interest in and understanding of the peculiarities of scientific research and education.
(3) The agency should promote research through contracts or grants to organizations outside the Federal Government. It should not operate any laboratories of its own.
(4) Support of basic research in the public and private colleges, universities, and research institutes must leave the internal control of policy, personnel, and the method and scope of the research to the institutions themselves. This is of the utmost importance.
(5) While assuring complete independence and freedom for the nature, scope, and methodology of research carried on in the institutions receiving public funds, and while retaining discretion in the allocation of funds among such institutions, the Foundation proposed herein must be responsible to the President and the Congress. Only through such responsibility can we maintain the proper relationship between science and other aspects of a democratic system. The usual controls of audits, reports, budgeting, and the like, should, of course, apply to the administrative and fiscal operations of the Foundation, subject, however, to such adjustments in procedure as are necessary to meet the special requirements of research.

Basic research is a long-term process—it ceases to be basic if immediate results are expected on short-term support. Methods should therefore be found which will permit the agency to make commitments of funds from current appropriations for programs of five years duration or longer. Continuity and stability of the program and its support may be expected (*a*) from the growing realization by the Congress of the benefits to the public from scientific research, and (*b*) from the conviction which will grow among those who conduct research under the auspices of the agency that good quality work will be followed by continuing support.

Military Research

As stated earlier in this report, military preparedness requires a permanent, independent, civilian-controlled organization, having close liaison with the Army and the Navy, but with funds direct from Congress and the clear power to initiate military research which will supplement and strengthen that directly under the control of the Army and Navy. As a temporary measure, the National Academy of Sciences has established the Research Board for National Security at the request of the Secretary of War and the Secretary of the Navy. This is highly desirable in order that there may be no interruption in the relations between scientists and military men after the emergency wartime Office of Scientific Research and Development goes out of existence. The Congress is now considering legislation to provide funds for this Board by direct appropriation.

I believe that, as a permanent measure, it would be appropriate to add to the other functions recommended in this report the responsibilities for civilian initiated and civilian-controlled military research. The function of such a civilian group would be primarily to conduct long-range scientific research on military problems—leaving to the Services research on the improvement of existing weapons.

Some research on military problems should be conducted, in time of peace as well as in war, by civilians independently of the military establishment. It is the primary responsibility of the Army and Navy to train the men, make available the weapons, and employ the strategy that will bring victory in combat. The Armed Services cannot be expected to be experts in all of the complicated fields which make it possible for a great nation to fight successfully in total war. There are certain kinds of research—such as research on the improvement of existing weapons—which can best be done within the military establishment. However, the job of long-range research involving application of the newest scientific discoveries to military needs should be the responsibility of those civilian scientists in the universities and in industry who are best trained to discharge it thoroughly and successfully. It is essential that both kinds of research go forward and that there be the closest liaison between the two groups.

Placing the civilian military research function in the proposed agency would bring it into close relationship with a broad program of basic research in both the natural sciences and medicine. A balance between military and other research could thus readily be maintained.

The establishment of the new agency, including a civilian military research group, should not be delayed by the existence of the Research Board for National Security, which is a temporary measure. Nor should the creation of the new agency be delayed by uncertainties in regard to the postwar organization of our military departments themselves. Clearly, the new agency, including a civilian military research group within it, can remain sufficiently flexible to adapt its operations to whatever may be the final organization of the military departments.

National Research Foundation

It is my judgment that the national interest in scientific research and scientific education can best be promoted by the creation of a National Research Foundation.

1. *Purposes*

The National Research Foundation should develop and promote a national policy for scientific research and scientific education, should support basic research in nonprofit organizations, should develop scientific talent in American youth by means of scholarships and fellowships, and should by contract and otherwise support long-range research on military matters.

Lewis Thomas

1913-1993

The Lives of a Cell

1974

A Princeton educated, Harvard-trained physician, Lewis Thomas was a key player in the development of modern clinical immunology, and he became a recognized master of interdisciplinary collaboration. During his illustrious medical career, he served as an administrator and researcher at many medical colleges including the University of Minnesota, Johns Hopkins, Tulane, the NYU School of Medicine, the Yale Medical School (where he also served as Dean), and later, president of the Sloan-Kettering Institute. In scientific and medical circles, he was considered the father of modern immunology and experimental pathology.

During his tenure at Yale, Thomas began to compose a monthly column for the *New England Journal of Medicine* entitled "Notes of a Biology Watcher." His free-form prose mixed a diverse array of topics, making connections among such themes as man's place in the universe, the nature of the cell membrane, and the evolution of language. He went on to write seven books, at first based on the columns from "Notes of a Biology Watcher," and later delving into broader topics, such as essays titled *The Youngest Science* (1983), *Late Night Thoughts on Listening to Mahler's Ninth Symphony* (1983), *Et Cetera, Et Cetera* (1990), a foray into etymology, and *The Fragile Species* (1992). His writings won many awards, two of which now bear his name, the Lewis Thomas Award for Communications from the American College of Physicians, and the Lewis Thomas Prize from Rockefeller University.

In 1974, his earliest columns became the collected works called *The Lives of a Cell.* The reading below includes three of these columns, one of which what is considered to be his best known column bearing the same title as the book. Also included are two essays that address human society and the nature of information.

1. Consider one of the three columns in the reading. Make connections between basic biology and your own personal experience. Elaborate on why you think your experiences connect to those items described by Thomas.

SOURCE:

Woodlief, Ann. (2003). *The Dictionary of Literary Biography.* Volume 275: Twentieth-Century American Nature Writers: Prose. Retrieved July 17, 2007, from http://www.vcu.edu/engweb/LewisThomas.htm

SELECTION FROM:

Thomas, Lewis. (1974). *The Lives of a Cell.* New York: The Viking Press. 3-5, 11-15, 91-95.

The Lives of a Cell

We are told that the trouble with Modern Man is that he has been trying to detach himself from nature. He sits in the topmost tiers of polymer, glass, and steel, dangling his pulsing legs, surveying at a distance the writhing life of the planet. In this scenario, Man comes on as a stupendous lethal force, and the earth is pictured as something delicate, like rising bubbles at the surface of a country pond, or flights of fragile birds.

But it is illusion to think that there is anything fragile about the life of the earth; surely this is the toughest membrane imaginable in the universe, opaque to probability, impermeable to death. We are the delicate part, transient and vulnerable as cilia. Nor is it a new thing for man to invent an existence that he imagines to be above the rest of life; this has been his most consistent intellectual exertion down the millennia. As illusion, it has never worked out to his satisfaction in the past, any more than it does today. Man is embedded in nature.

The biologic science of recent years has been making this a more urgent fact of life. The new, hard problem will be to cope with the dawning, intensifying realization of just how interlocked we are. The old, clung-to notions most of us have held about our special lordship are being deeply undermined.

Item. A good case can be made for our nonexistence as entities. We are not made up, as we had always supposed, of successively enriched packets of our own parts. We are shared, rented, occupied. At the interior of our cells, driving them, providing the oxidative energy that sends us out for the improvement of each shining day, are the mitochondria, and in a strict sense they are not ours. They turn out to be little separate creatures, the colonial posterity of migrant prokaryocytes, probably primitive bacteria that swam into, ancestral precursors of our eukaryotic cells and stayed there. Ever since, they have maintained themselves and their ways, replicating in their own fashion, privately, with their own DNA and RNA quite different from ours. They are as much symbionts as the rhizobial bacteria in the roots of beans. Without them, we would not move muscle, drum a finger, think a thought.

Mitochondria are stable and responsible lodgers, and I choose to trust them. But what of the other little animals, similarly established in my cells, sorting and balancing me, clustering me together? My centrioles, basal bodies, and probably a good many other more obscure tiny beings at work inside my cells, each with its own special genome are as foreign, and as essential, as aphids in anthills. My cells are no longer the pure line entities I was raised with; they are ecosystems more complex than Jamaica Bay.

I like to think that they work in my interest, that each breath they draw for me, but perhaps it is they who walk through the local park in the early morning, sensing my senses, listening to my music, thinking my thoughts.

I am consoled, somewhat, by the thought that the green plants are in the same fix. They could not be plants, or green, without their chloroplasts, which run the photosynthetic enterprise and generate oxygen for the rest of us. As it turns out, chloroplasts are also separate creatures with their own genomes, speaking their own language.

We carry stores of DNA in our nuclei that may have come in, at one time or another, from the fusion of ancestral cells and the linking of ancestral organisms in symbiosis. Our genomes are catalogues of instructions from all kinds of sources in nature, filed for all kinds of contingencies. As for me, I am grateful for differentiation and speciation, but I cannot feel as separate an entity as I did a few years ago, before I was told these things, nor, I should think, can anyone else.

Item. The uniformity of the earth's life, more astonishing than its diversity, is accountable by the high probability that we derived, originally, from some single cell, fertilized in a bolt of lightening as the earth cooled. It is from the progeny of this parent cell that we take our looks; we still share genes around, and the resemblance of the enzymes of grasses to those of whales is a family resemblance.

The viruses, instead of being single-minded agents of disease and death, now begin to look more like mobile genes. Evolution is still an infinitely long and tedious biologic game, with only the winners staying at the table, but the rules are beginning to look more flexible. We live in a dancing matrix of viruses; they dart, rather like bees, from organism to organism, from plant to insect to mammal to me and back again, and into the sea, tugging along pieces of this genome, strings of genes from that, transplanting grafts of DNA, passing around heredity as though at a great party. They may be a mechanism for keeping new, mutant kinds of DNA in the widest circulation among us. If this is true, the odd virus disease, on which we must focus so much of our attention in medicine, may be looked on as an accident, something dropped.

Item. I have been trying to think of the earth as a kind of organism, but it is no go. I cannot think of it this way. It is too big, too complex, with too many working parts lacking visible connections. The other night, driving through a hilly, wooded part of southern New England, I wondered about this. If not like an organism, what is it like, what is it most like? Then, satisfactorily for that moment, it came to me: it is most like a single cell.

On Societies as Organisms

Viewed from a suitable height, the aggregating clusters of medical scientists in the bright sunlight of the boardwalk at Atlantic City, swarmed there from everywhere for the annual meetings, have the look of assemblages of social insects. There is the same vibrating, ionic movement interrupted by the darting back and forth of jerky individuals to touch antennae and exchange small hits of information; periodically, the mass casts out, like a trout line, a long single file unerringly toward Childs's. If the boards were not fastened down, it would not be a surprise to see them put together a nest of sorts.

It is permissible to say this sort of thing about humans. They do resemble, in their most compulsively social behavior, ants at a distance. It is, however, quite bad form in biological circles to put it the other way round, to imply that the operation of insect societies has any relation at all to human affairs. The writers of books on insect behavior generally take pains, in their prefaces, to caution that insects are like creatures from another planet, that their behavior is absolutely foreign, totally inhuman, unearthly, almost unbiological. They are more like perfectly tooled but crazy little machines, and we violate science when we try to read human meanings in their arrangement.

It is hard for a bystander not to do so. Ants are so much like human beings as to be an embarrassment. They farm fungi, raise aphids as livestock, launch armies into wars, use chemical sprays to alarm and confuse enemies, capture slaves. The families of weaver ants engage in child labor, holding their larvae like shuttles to spin out the thread that sews the leaves together for their fungus gardens. They exchange information ceaselessly. They do everything but watch television.

What makes us most uncomfortable is that they, and the bees and termites and social wasps, seem to live two kinds of lives: they are individuals, going about the day's business without much evidence of thought for tomorrow, and they are at the same time component parts, cellular elements, in the huge, writhing, ruminating organism of the Hill, the nest, the hive. It is because of this aspect, I think, that we most wish for them to be something foreign. We do not like the notion that there can be collective societies with the capacity to behave like organisms. If such things exist, they can have nothing to do with us.

Still, there it is. A solitary ant, afield, cannot be considered to have much of anything on his mind; indeed, with only a few neurons strung together by fibers, he can't be imagined to have a mind at all, much less a thought. He is more like a ganglion on legs. Four ants together, or ten, encircling a dead moth on a path, begin to look more like an idea. They fumble and shove, gradually moving the food toward the Hill, but as though by blind chance. It is only when you watch the dense mass of thousands of ants, crowded together around the Hill, blackening the ground, that you begin to see the whole beast, and now you observe it thinking, planning, calculating. It is an intelligence, a kind of live computer, with crawling bits for its wits.

At a stage in the construction, twigs of a certain size are needed, and all the members forage obsessively for twigs of just this size. Later, when outer walls are to be finished, thatched, the size must change, and as though given new orders by telephone, all the workers shift the search to the new twigs. If you disturb the arrangement of a part of the Hill, hundreds of ants will set it vibrating, shifting, until it is put right again. Distant sources of food are somehow sensed, and long lines, like tentacles, reach out over the ground, up over walls, behind boulders, to fetch it in.

Termites are even more extraordinary in the way they seem to accumulate intelligence as they gather together. Two or three termites in a chamber will begin to pick up pellets and move them from place to place, but nothing comes of it; nothing is built. As more join in, they seem to reach a critical mass, a quorum, and the thinking begins. They place pellets atop pellets, then throw up columns and beautiful, curving, symmetrical arches, and the crystalline architecture of vaulted chambers is created. It is not known how they communicate with each other, how the chains of termites building one column know when to turn toward the crew on the adjacent column, or how, when the time comes, they manage the flawless joining of the arches. The stimuli that set them off at the outset, building collectively instead of shifting things about, may be pheromones released when they reach committee size. They react as if alarmed. They become agitated, excited, and then they begin working, like artists.

Bees live lives of organisms, tissues, cells, organelles, all at the same time. The single bee, out of the hive retrieving sugar (instructed by the dancer: "south-southeast for seven hundred meters, clover—mind you make corrections for the sun drift") is still as much a part of the hive as if attached by a filament. Building the hive, the workers have the look of embryonic cells organizing a developing tissue; from a distance they are like the viruses inside a cell, running off row after row of symmetrical polygons as though laying down crystals. When the time for swarming comes, and the old queen prepares to leave with her part of the population, it is as though the hive were involved in mitosis. There is an agitated moving of bees back and forth, like granules in cell sap. They distribute themselves in almost precisely equal parts, half to the departing queen, half to the new one. Thus, like an egg, the great, hairy, black and golden creature splits in two, each with an equal share of the family genome.

The phenomenon of separate animals joining up to form an organism is not unique in insects. Slime-mold cells do it all the time, of course, in each life cycle. At first they are single amebocytes swimming around, eating bacteria, aloof from each other, untouching, voting straight Republican. Then, a bell sounds, and acrasin is released by special cells toward which the others converge in stellate ranks, touch, fuse together, and construct the slug, solid as a trout. A splendid stalk is raised, with a fruiting body on top, and out of this comes the next generation of amebocytes, ready to swim across the same moist ground, solitary and ambitious.

Herring and other fish in schools are at times so closely integrated, their actions so coordinated, that they seem to be functionally a great multi-fish organism. Flocking birds, especially the seabirds nesting on the slopes of offshore islands in Newfoundland, are similarly attached, connected, synchronized.

Although we are by all odds the most social of all social animals—more interdependent, more attached to each other, more inseparable in our behavior than bees—we do not often feel our conjoined intelligence. Perhaps, however, we are linked in circuits for the storage, processing, and retrieval of information, since this appears to be the most basic and universal of all human enterprises. It may be our biological function to build a certain kind of Hill. We have access to all the information of the biosphere, arriving as elementary units in the stream of solar photons. When we have learned how these are rearranged against randomness, to make, say, springtails, quantum mechanics, and the late quartets, we may have a clearer notion how to proceed. The circuitry seems to be there, even if the current is not always on.

The system of communications used in science should provide a neat, workable model for studying mechanisms of information-building in human society. Ziman, in a recent Nature essay, points out, "the invention of a mechanism for the systematic publication of fragments of scientific work may well have been the key event in the history of modern science . . . " He continues:

> A regular journal carries one research worker to another the various . . . observations which are of common interest . . . A typical scientific paper has never pretended to be more than another little piece in a larger jigsaw—not significant in itself but as an element in a grander scheme. *This technique, of soliciting many modest contributions to the store of human knowledge, has been the secret of Western science since the seventeenth century, for it achieves a corporate, collective power that is far greater than any one individual can exert* [italics mine].

With some alternation of terms, some toning down, the passage could describe the building of a termite nest.

It is fascinating that the word "explore" does not apply to the searching aspect of the activity, but has its origins in the sounds we make while engaged in it. We like to think of exploring in science as a lonely, meditative business, and so it is in the first stages, but always, sooner or later, before the enterprise reaches completion, as we explore, we call to each other, communicate, publish, send letters to the editor, present papers, cry out on finding.

Information

According to the linguistic school currently on top, human beings are all born with a genetic endowment for recognizing and formulating language. This must mean that we possess genes for all kinds of information, with strands of special, peculiarly human DNA for the discernment of meaning in syntax. We must imagine the morphogenesis of deep structures, built into our minds, for coding out, like proteins, the parts of speech. Correct grammar (correct in the logical, not fashionable, sense) is as much a biologic characteristic of our species as feathers on birds.

If this is true, it would mean that the human mind is preset, in some primary sense, to generate more than just the parts of speech. Since everything else that we recognize as human behavior derives from the central mechanism of language, the same sets of genes are at least indirectly responsible for governing such astonishing behavior as in the concert hall, where hundreds of people crowd together, silent, head-tilted, meditating, listening to music as though receiving instructions, or in a gallery, moving along slowly, peering, never looking at each other, concentrating as though reading directions.

This view of things is compatible with the very old notion that a framework for meaning is somehow built into our minds at birth. We start our lives with templates, and attach to them, as we go along, various things that fit. There are neural centers for generating, spontaneously, numberless hypotheses about the facts of life. We store up information the way cells store energy. When we are lucky enough to find a direct match between a receptor and a fact, there is a deep explosion in the mind; the idea suddenly enlarges, rounds up, bursts with new energy, and begins to replicate. At times there are chains of reverberating explosions, shaking everything: the imagination, as we say, is staggered.

This system seems to be restricted to human beings since we are the only beings with language, although chimpanzees may have the capability of manipulating symbols with a certain syntax. The great difference between us and the other animals may be the qualitative difference made by speech. We live by making transformations of energy into words, storing it up, and releasing it uncontrolled explosions.

Speechless animals cannot do this sort of thing, and they are limited to single stage transactions. They wander, as we do, searching for facts to fit their sparser stock hypotheses, but when the receptor meets its match, there is only a single thud. Without language, the energy that is encoiled, springlike, inside information can only by used once. The solitary wasp, Sphex nearing her time of eggs, travels aloft with a single theory about caterpillars. She is, in fact a winged receptor for caterpillars. Finding one to match the hypothesis, she swoops, pins it, paralyzes it, carries it off, and descends to deposit it precisely in front of the door of the round burrow (which, obsessed by a different version of the same theory, she had prepared beforehand). She drops the beast, enters the burrow, inspects the interior for last-minute irregularities, then comes out to pull it in for the egg-laying. It has the orderly, stepwise look of a well thought-out business. But if, while she is inside inspecting, you move the caterpillar a short distance, she has a less sensible second thought about the matter. She emerges, searches for a moment, finds it, drags it back to the original spot, drops it again, and runs inside to check the burrow again. If you move the caterpillar again, she will repeat the program, and you can keep her totally preoccupied for as long as you have the patience and the heart for it. It is a compulsive, essentially neurotic kind of behavior, as mindless as an Ionesco character, but the wasp cannot imagine any other way of doing the thing.

Lymphocytes, like wasps, are genetically programmed for exploration, but each of them seems to be permitted a different, solitary idea. They roam through the tissues, sensing and monitoring. Since there are so many of them, they can make collective guesses at almost anything antigenic on the surface of the earth, but they must do their work one notion at a time. They carry specific information in their surface receptors, presented in the form of a question: is there, anywhere out there, my particular molecular configuration? It seems to be in the nature of biologic information that it not only stores itself up as energy but also instigates a search for more. It is an insatiable mechanism.

Lymphocytes are apparently informed about everything foreign around them, and some of them come equipped for fitting with polymers that do not exist until organic chemists synthesize them in their laboratories. The cells can do more than predict reality; they are evidently programmed with wild guesses as well.

Not all animals have lymphocytes with the same range of information, as you might expect. As with language, the system is governed by genes, and there are genetic differences between species and between inbred animals of the same species. There are polymers that will fit the receptors of one line of guinea pigs or mice but not others; there are responders and nonresponders.

When the connection is made, and a particular lymphocyte with a particular receptor is brought into the presence of the particular antigen, one of the greatest small spectacles in nature occurs. The cell enlarges, begins making new DNA at a great rate, and turns into what is termed, appropriately, a blast. It begins dividing, replicating itself into a new colony of identical cells, all labeled with the same receptor, primed with the same questions. The new cluster is a memory, nothing less.

For this kind of mechanism to be useful, the cells are required to stick precisely to the point. Any ambiguity, any tendency to wander from the matter at hand, will introduce grave hazards for the cells, and even more for the host in which they live. Minor inaccuracies may cause reactions in which neighboring cells are recognized as foreign, and done in. There is a theory that the process of aging may be due to the cumulative effect of imprecision, a gradual degrading of information. It is not a system that allows for deviating.

Perhaps it is in this respect that language differs most sharply from other biologic systems for communication. Ambiguity seems to be an essential, indispensable element for the transfer of information from one place to another by words, where matters of real importance are concerned. It is often necessary, for meaning to come through, that there be an almost vague sense of strangeness and askewness. Speechless animals and cells cannot do this. The specifically locked-on antigen at the surface of a lymphocyte does not send the cell off in search of something totally different; when a bee is tracking sugar by polarized light, observing the sun as though consulting his watch, he does not veer away to discover an unimaginable marvel of a flower. Only the human mind is designed to work in this way, programmed to drift away in the presence of locked-on information, straying from each point in a hunt for a better, different point.

If it were not for the capacity for ambiguity, for the sensing of strangeness, that words in all languages provide, we would have no way of recognizing the layers of counterpoint in meaning, and we might be spending all our time sitting on stone fences, staring into the sun. To be sure, we would always have had some everyday use to make of the alphabet, and we might have reached the same capacity for small talk, but it is unlikely that we would have been able to evolve words to Bach. The great thing about human language is that it prevents us from sticking to the matter at hand.

Paul Feyerabend

1924-1994

Science in a Free Society

1978

Paul Feyerabend was born in Vienna in 1924,spending his earliest years mostly confined to his parents' three-room apartment. Sickly and quite isolated from other children, when enrolled in school at the age of five, he was quite overwhelmed. Once he learned to read, he discovered books, and so began his interests in science and philosophy.

He volunteered for the German army during WW II, advancing to the rank of lieutenant but later confessed he poorly understood the situation around him. In 1945, his military service ended when he was shot in the hand and belly during a retreat from the Russian front. This wound also damaged his spinal nerves.

He began his academic career on a fellowship to study singing and stage management, then returning to Vienna to study history and sociology, before moving to physics. It was at this time that he encountered notable philosophers including Karl Popper, Walter Hollitscher, Ludwig Wittgenstein, and Viktor Kraft. In 1949, he became the leader of the "Kraft Circle" a student philosophy club built around the ideas of his dissertation supervisor, Viktor Kraft. He went on to complete a doctorate in philosophy under Popper at the London School of Economics. He returned to Vienna where he began to publish the earliest in a long career of works on the philosophy of science. In 1958, he joined the faculty of the University of California, Berkeley where he remained until resigning in 1990. He died of an inoperable brain tumor at the Genolier Clinic of Switzerland in February of 1994.

Philosophically, Feyerabend began as a logical positivist. This school of thought greatly revered a scientific and empirical approach, which meshed with Feyerabend's background in physics and fit well in the "Kraft Circle." As his philosophical approach matured, first under Popper and later independently, he moved away from the positivist view and towards a more anarchical view of science. His views changed from an empirical approach to a more theoretical approach to scientific methods and philosophy, culminating in publication of *Against Method* in 1978.

The following selection was also published in 1978, and in it Feyerabend focuses on the modern use and function of science in society.[1] He compares the position of science in modern society to that of religion in the sixteenth through eighteenth centuries, and raises the issue of relativism in the critique of science.

1. What other ways of knowing are employed by humankind? Why is science different from other ways of knowing?

Sources:

Okasha, Samir. (2002). *Philosophy of Science. A Very Short Introduction.* Oxford: Oxford University Press.

Preston, John. (1997). Paul Feyerabend. *Stanford Encyclopedia of Philosophy.* Retrieved
July 25, 2007 from, http://plato.stanford.edu/entries/feyerabend/

Selection from:

Feyerabend, Paul. (1978). *Science in a Free Society.* London: NLB. 73-82. Title also listed as Paul Feyerabend, Against Method—alternate view and belief that science offers just one explanation of phenomenon in our world

---

1 Permission to reprint by Grazia Borrini-Feyerabend. Note from Ms. Borrini-Feyerabend that Paul Feyerbend did not consent to have Science in a Free Society reprinted, and his thinking about relativity evolved considerably in **Farewell to Reason** (Verso, numerous editions) and most of all in **Conquest of Abundance** (Chicago University Press, 1999).

I. Two Questions

There are two questions that arise in the course of any discussion of science. They are:

(A) *What is science?*—how does it proceed, what are its results, how do its standards, procedures, results differ from the standards, procedures, results of other fields?
(B) *What's so great about science?*—what makes science preferable to other forms of existence, using different standards and getting different results as a consequence? What makes modern science preferable to the science of the Aristotelians, or to the cosmology of the Hopi?

Note that in trying to answer question (B) we are not permitted to judge the alternatives to science by scientific standards. When trying to answer question (B) we *examine* such standards, so we cannot make them the basis of our judgements.

Question A has not one answer, but many. Every school in the philosophy of science gives a different account of what science is and how it works. In addition there are the accounts given by scientists, politicians and by so-called spokesmen of the general public. We are not far from the truth when saying that the nature of science is still shrouded in darkness. Still, the matter is discussed and there is a chance that some modest knowledge about science will some day arise.

There exists hardly anyone who asks question B. The excellence of science is *assumed*, it is not *argued for*. Here scientists and philosophers of science act like the defenders of the One and Only Roman Church acted before them: Church doctrine is true, everything else is Pagan nonsense. Indeed, certain methods of discussion and insinuation that were once treasures of theological rhetoric have now found a new home in science.

This phenomenon, though remarkable and somewhat depressing, would hardly bother a sensible person if it were restricted to a small number of the faithful: in a free society there is room for many strange beliefs, doctrines, institutions. But the assumption of the inherent superiority of science has moved beyond science and has become an article of faith for almost everyone. Moreover, science is no longer a particular institution; it is now part of the basic fabric of democracy just as the Church was once part of the basic fabric of society. Of course, Church and State are now carefully separated. State and Science, however, work closely together.

Immense sums are spent on the improvement of scientific ideas. Bastard subjects such as the philosophy of science which shares with science the name but hardly anything else profit from the boom of the sciences. Human relations are subjected to scientific treatment as is shown by education programmes, proposals for prison reform, army training and so on. The power of the medical profession over every stage of our lives already exceeds the power once wielded by the Church. Almost all scientific subjects are compulsory subjects in our schools. While the parents of a six-year-old can decide to have him instructed in the rudiments of Protestantism, or in the rudiments of the Jewish faith, or to omit religious instruction altogether, they do not have similar freedom in the case of the sciences. Physics, astronomy, history *must* be learned; they cannot be replaced by magic, astrology, or by a study of legends.

Nor is one content with a merely historical presentation of physical (astronomical, biological, sociological etc.) facts and principles. One does not say: *some people believe* that the earth moves around the sun while others regard the earth as a hollow sphere that contains the sun, the planets, the fixed stars. One says: the earth *moves* round the sun—everything else is nonsense.

Finally, the manner in which we accept or reject scientific ideas is radically different from democratic decision procedures. We accept scientific laws and facts, we teach them in our schools, we make them the basis of important political decisions, but without having examined them, and without having subjected them to a vote. *Scientists* do not subject them to a vote, or at least this is what they tell us, and laymen certainly do not subject them to a vote. Concrete proposals are occasionally discussed, and a vote is suggested (nuclear reactor initiatives). But the procedure is not extended to general theories and scientific facts. Modern society is 'Copernican' not because Copernicus was put up for vote, discussed in a democratic way, and voted in with a simple majority; it is 'Copernican' because the *scientists* are Copernicans and because one accepts their cosmology as uncritically as one once accepted the cosmology of bishops and of cardinals.

Even bold and revolutionary thinkers bow to the judgement of science. Kropotkin wants to break up all existing institutions, but he does not touch science. Ibsen goes very far in his critique of bourgeois society, but he retains science as a measure of truth. Lévi Strauss has made us realize that Western thought is not the lonely peak of human achievement it was once thought to be, but he and his followers exclude science from their relativization of ideologies.[2] Marx and Engels were convinced that science would aid the workers in their quest for mental and social liberation.

Such an attitude made perfect sense in the 17th, 18th, even 19th centuries when science was one of many competing ideologies, when the state had not yet declared in its favour and when its determined pursuit was more than balanced by alternative views and alternative institutions. In those years science was a liberating force, not because it had found the truth, or the right method (though this was assumed to be *the* reason by the defenders of science), but because it restricted the influence of other ideologies and thus gave the individual room for thought. Nor was it necessary in those years to press a consideration of question B. The opponents of science who still were very much alive tried to show that science was on the wrong track, they belittled its importance and the scientists had to reply to the challenge. The methods and achievements of science were subjected to a critical debate. In this situation it made perfect sense to commit oneself to the cause of science. The very circumstances in which the commitment took place turned it into a liberating force.

It does not follow that the commitment has a liberating effect today. There is nothing in science or in any other ideology that makes them inherently liberating. Ideologies can deteriorate and become dogmatic religions (example: Marxism). They start deteriorating when they become successful, they turn into dogmas the moment the opposition is crushed: their triumph is their downfall. The development of science in the 19th and 20th centuries and especially after the Second World War is a good example. The very same enterprise that once gave man the ideas and the

---

2 Lévi Strauss (*The Savage Mind*, Chicago, 1966, pp. 16ff.) denies that myth, being 'the product of man's "mythmaking faculty" turn[s] its back on reality'. He sees in it an approach to nature that complements science and is characterized by a 'universe of instruments [that is] closed' while the scientist will try new procedures to get results. There can never be a conflict between the results of science and myth and so the question of their relative merit can never arise. Things look different to some Marxist critics. Thus M. Godelier ('Myth et Histoire', *Annales* 1971) lets myth transform the 'numerous objective data about nature into an "imaginative" explanation of reality' where 'objective data' are the data of science. Science, once more, has the upper hand.

strength to free himself from the fears and the prejudices of a tyrannical religion now turns him into a slave of its interests. And let us not be deceived by the libertarian rhetoric and by the great show of tolerance that some propagandists of science are putting on for our benefit. Let us ask whether they would be prepared to give, say the views of the Hopi the same role in basic education which science has today, let us ask a member of the AMA whether he would permit faithhealers into state hospitals and we shall soon see how narrow the limits of this tolerance really are. And, mind you, these limits are not the results of research; they are imposed quite arbitrarily as we shall see later on.

2. The Prevalence of Science a Threat to Democracy

This symbiosis of the state and of an unexamined science leads to an interesting problem for intellectuals and especially for liberals.

Liberal intellectuals are among the chief defenders of democracy and freedom. Loudly and persistently they proclaim and defend freedom of thought, speech, religion and, occasionally, some quite inane forms of political action.

Liberal intellectuals are also 'rationalists'. And they regard rationalism (which for them coincides with science) not just as one view among many, but as a basis for society. The freedom they defend is therefore granted under conditions that are no longer subjected to it. It is granted only to those who have already accepted part of the rationalist (i.e. scientific) ideology.[3]

For a long time this dogmatic element of liberalism was hardly noticed, let alone commented upon. There are various reasons for the oversight. When Blacks, Indians and other suppressed races first emerged into the broad daylight of civic life their leaders and their supporters among Whites demanded equality. But equality, 'racial' equality included, then did not mean *equality of traditions*; it meant *equality of access to one particular tradition*—the tradition of the White Man. The Whites who supported the demand opened the Promised Land—but it was a Promised Land built after their own specifications and furnished with their own favourite playthings.

The situation soon changed. An increasing number of individuals and groups became critical of the gifts offered.[4] They either revived their

---

3 See n. 14, p. 29.

4 White middle class Christians (and liberals, rationalists, even Marxists) felt great satisfaction when they finally offered Indians some of the marvellous opportunities of the great society they think they inhabit and they were

own traditions or adopted traditions different both from rationalism and from the traditions of their forefathers. At this stage intellectuals started developing 'interpretations'. After all, they had studied non-Western tribes and cultures for quite some time. Many descendants of non-Western societies owe whatever knowledge they have of their ancestors to the work of white missionaries, adventurers, anthropologists, some of them with a liberal turn of mind.[5] When later anthropologists collected and systematized this knowledge they transformed it in an interesting way. The [*sic*] emphasized the psychological meaning, the social functions, the existential temper of a culture, they disregarded its ontological implications. According to them oracles, rain dances, the treatment of mind and body *express* the needs of the members of a society, they *function* as a social glue, they *reveal* basic structures of thought, they may even lead to an increased awareness of the relations between man and man and man and nature but without an accompanying *knowledge* of distant events, rain, mind, body. Such interpretations were hardly ever the result of critical thought—most of the time they were simply a consequence of popular antimetaphysical tendencies combined with a firm belief in the excellence first, of Christianity and then of science. This is how intellectuals, Marxists included aided by the forces of a society that is democratic in words only almost succeeded in having it both ways: they could pose as understanding friends of non-Western cultures without endangering the supremacy of their own religion: science.

The situation changed again. There are now individuals, some very gifted and imaginative scientists among them who are interested in a genuine revival not just of the externals of non-scientific forms of life but of the world views and practices (navigation, medicine, theory of life and matter) that were once connected with them. There are societies such

---

displeased and offended when the reaction was disappointment, not abject gratitude. But why should an Indian who never even dreamt of imposing his culture on a white man now be grateful for having white culture imposed on him? Why should he be grateful to the white man who, having stolen his material possessions, his land, his living space now proceeds to steal his mind as well?

5 Christian missionaries occasionally had a better grasp of the inherent rationality of 'barbaric' forms of life than their scientific successors and they were also greater humanitarians. As an example the reader should consult the work of Las Casas as described in Lewis Hanke *All Mankind is One*, Northern Illinois Press 1974.

as mainland China where traditional procedures have been combined with scientific views leading to a better understanding of nature and a better treatment of individual and social dysfunction. And with this the hidden dogmatism of our modern friends of freedom becomes revealed: democratic principles as they are practised today are incompatible with the undisturbed existence, development, growth of special cultures. A rational-liberal (-Marxist) society cannot contain a Black culture in the full sense of the word. It cannot contain a Jewish culture in the full sense of the word. It cannot contain a mediaeval culture in the full sense of the word. It can contain these cultures only as secondary grafts on a basic structure that is an unholy alliance of science, rationalism (and capitalism).[6]

But—so the impatient believer in rationalism and science is liable to exclaim—is this procedure not justified? Is there not a tremendous difference between science on the one side, religion, magic, myth on the other? Is this difference not so large and so obvious that it is unnecessary to point it out and silly to deny it? Does the difference not consist in the fact that magic, religion, mythical world views try to get in touch with reality while science has succeeded in this business and so supersedes its ancestors? Is it therefore not only justified but also required to remove an ontologically potent religion, a myth that claims to describe the world, a system of magic that poses as an alternative to science from the centre of society and to replace them by science? These are some of the questions which the 'educated' liberal (and the 'educated' Marxist) will use to object to any form of freedom that interferes with the central position of science and (liberal or Marxist) rationalism.

---

6 Professor Agassi, see Part Three, Chapter One, has read this passage as suggesting that Jews *should* return to the traditions of their forefathers, that American Indians should resume their old ways, rain dances included, and he has commented on the 'reactionary' character of such suggestions. Reactionary? This assumes that the step into science and technology was not a mistake—which is the question at issue. It also assumes, for example, that rain dances don't work—but who has examined that matter? Besides, I do not make the suggestion Agassi ascribes to me. I don't say that American Indians (for example) *should resume* their old ways, I say that those who want to resume them should be able to do so first, because in a democracy everyone should be able to live as he sees fit and second, because no ideology and no way of life is so perfect that it cannot learn from a comparison with alternatives.

Three assumptions are contained in these rhetorical questions.

Assumption A: scientific rationalism is preferable to alternative traditions.
Assumption B: it cannot be improved by a comparison and/or combination with alternative traditions.
Assumption C: it must be accepted, made a basis of society and education because of its advantages.

In what follows I shall try to show that neither assumption A nor assumption B agrees with the facts where 'facts' are defined in accordance with the type of rationalism implicit in A and B: *rationalists and scientists cannot rationally (scientifically) argue for the unique position of their favourite ideology.*

However, assume they can—does it follow that their ideology must now be imposed on everyone (question C)? Is it not rather the case that traditions that give substance to the lives of people must be given equal rights and equal access to key positions in society no matter what other traditions think about them? Must we not demand that ideas and procedures that give substance to the live1s of people be made full members of a free society *no matter what other traditions think about them*?

There are many people who regard such questions as an invitation to *relativism*. Reformulating them in their own favourite terms they ask us whether we would want to give falsehood the same rights as truth, or whether we would want dreams to be treated as seriously as accounts of reality. From the very beginning of Western Civilization insinuations such as these were used to defend one view, one procedure, one way of thinking and acting to the exclusion of everything else.[7] So, let us take the bull by its horns and let us take a closer look at this frightful monster: relativism.

---

7 In Plutarch's *Life of Solon* we find the following story: 'When the company of Thespis began to exhibit tragedy, and its novelty was attracting the populace but had not yet gone as far as public competition, Solon being fond of listening and learning and being rather given in his old age to leisure and amusements, and indeed to drinking parties and music, went to see Thespis act in his own play, as was the practice of ancient times. Solon approached him after the performance and asked him if he was not ashamed to tell so many lies to so many people. When Thespis said there was nothing dreadful in representing such works and actions in fun, Solon struck the ground

3. The Spectre of Relativism

With the discussion of relativism we enter territory full of treacherous paths, traps, footangles, territory where appeals to emotion count as arguments and where arguments are of a touching simplemindedness. Relativism is often attacked not because one has found a fault, but because one is afraid of it. Intellectuals are afraid of it because relativism threatens their role in society just as the enlightenment once threatened the existence of priests and theologians. And the general public which is educated, exploited and tyrannized by intellectuals has learned long ago to identify relativism with cultural (social) decay. This is how relativism was attacked in Germany's Third Reich, this is how it is attacked again today by Fascists, Marxists, Critical Rationalists. Even the most tolerant people dare not say that they reject an idea or a way of life because they don't like it—which would put the blame on them entirely—they have to add that there are *objective* reasons for their action—which puts at least part of the blame on the thing rejected and on those enamoured by it. What is it about relativism that seems to put the fear of god into everyone?

It is the realization that one's own most cherished point of view may turn out to be just one of many ways of arranging life, important for those brought up in the corresponding tradition, utterly uninteresting and perhaps even a hindrance to others. Only few people are content with being able to think and live in a way pleasing to themselves and would not dream of making their tradition an obligation for everyone. For the great majority—and that includes Christians, rationalists, liberals and a good many Marxists—there exists only one truth and it must prevail. Tolerance does not mean acceptance of falsehood side by side with truth, it means human treatment of those unfortunately caught in falsehood[8]. Relativism would put an end to this comfortable exercise in superiority—therefore the aversion.

---

violently with his walking stick: "If we applaud these things in fun" he said "we shall soon find ourselves honouring them in earnest". Thus began the 'long standing quarrel between poetry and philosophy' (Plato *Republic* 607b6f.), i.e. between those seeing everything in terms of truth and falsehood, and other traditions.

[8] Cf. Henry Kamen, *The Rise of Toleration*, New York 1967.

Fear of moral and political chaos increases the aversion by adding practical disadvantages to the intellectual drawbacks. Relativists, it is said, have no reason to respect the laws of the society to which they belong, they have no reason to keep promises, honour business contracts, respect the lives of others, they are like beasts following the whim of the moment and like beasts they constitute a danger to civilized life.

It is interesting to see how closely this account mirrors the complaints of Christians who witnessed the gradual removal of *religion* from the centre of society. The fears, insinuations and predictions were then exactly the same—but they did not come true. Replacing religion by rationalism and science did not create paradise—far from it—but it did not create chaos either.

It did not create chaos, it is pointed out, because rationalism is itself an orderly philosophy. One order was replaced by another order. But relativism wants to remove *all* ideological ingredients (except those that are convenient, for the time being). Is it possible to have such a society? Can it work? How will it work? These are the questions we have to answer.

Starting with the intellectual (or semantic) difficulties viz. the insinuation that relativism means giving the same rights to truth and falsehood (reason and insanity, virtue and viciousness and so on) we need only remind the reader of theses i. and ii. of Section 2, Part One and the associated explanations. We saw then that classifying traditions as true or false (. . . etc . . . .) means projecting the point of view of other traditions upon them. Traditions are neither good nor bad—they just are. They obtain desirable or undesirable properties only for an agent who participates in another tradition and projects the values of this tradition upon the world. The projections *appear 'objective'* i.e. tradition-independent and the statements expressing its judgements *sound 'objective'* because the subject and the tradition he represents nowhere occur in them. They *are 'subjective'* because this non-occurrence is due to an oversight. The oversight is revealed when the agent adopts another tradition: his value-judgements change. Trying to account for the change the agent has to revise the content of all his value statements just as physicists had to revise the content of even the simplest statement about length when it was discovered that length depends on the reference system. Those who don't carry out the revision cannot pride themselves on forming a special school of especially astute philosophers who have withstood the onslaught of moral relativism just as those who still cling to absolute lengths cannot pride themselves on forming a special school of especially astute physicists who have withstood the onslaught of relativity. They are just pigheaded, or badly informed, or both. So much about seeing relativism in terms of equal rights for falsehood, irrationality, viciousness and so on.

That the appeal to truth and rationality is rhetorical and without objective content becomes clear from the inarticulateness of its defence. In Section I we have seen that the question 'What is so great about science?' is hardly ever asked and has no satisfactory answer. The same is true of other basic concepts.[9] Philosophers inquire into the nature of truth, or the nature of knowledge, but they hardly ever ask why truth should be pursued (the question arises only at the boundary line of traditions—for example, it arose at the boundary line of science and Christianity). The very same notions of Truth, Rationality, Reality that are supposed to eliminate relativism are surrounded by a vast area of ignorance (which corresponds to the arguer's ignorance of the tradition that provides the material for his rhetorical displays).

There is therefore hardly any difference between the members of a 'primitive' tribe who defend their laws because they are the laws of their gods, or of their ancestors and who spread these laws in the name of the tribe and a rationalist who appeals to 'objective' standards, except that the former know what they are doing while the latter does not.[10]

---

9 Can I use 'truth' when criticizing its uncritical use? Of course I can, just as one can use German to explain the disadvantages of German and the advantages of Latin to a German audience.

10 The rules of a rational science, liberal intellectuals say, do not involve special interests. They are 'objective' in the sense that they emphasize truth, reason etc. all of which are independent of the beliefs and wishes of special interest groups. Distinguishing between the *validity* of a demand, a rule, a suggestion and the fact that the demand, rule, suggestion is *accepted* critical rationalists seem to turn knowledge and morals from tribal ideologies into the representation of tribe-independent circumstances. But tribal ideologies do not cease to be tribal ideologies on account of not being openly characterized as such. The demands which rationalists defend and the notions they use *speak* 'objectively' and not in the name of Sir Karl Popper or Professor Gerard Radnitzky because *they have been made to speak that way* and not because the interests of Sir Karl or of Professor Radnitzky are no longer taken into account; and they have been made to speak that way to secure them a wider audience, to keep up the pretence of libertarianism and because rationalists have little sense for what one might call the

This concludes the intellectual, or 'semantic' part of the debate about relativism.

'existential' qualities of life. Their 'objectivity' is in no way different from the 'objectivity' of a colonial official who, having read a book or two now ceases to address the natives in the name of the King and addresses them in the name of Reason instead or from the 'objectivity' of a drill sergeant who instead of shouting 'now, you dogs, listen to me—this is what I want you to do and God have mercy on you if you don't do exactly what I tell you!' purrs 'Well, I think what we ought to do is . . . ". Obedience to the commands and the ideology of the speaker is demanded in either case. The situation becomes even clearer when we examine how rationalists argue. They posit a 'truth' and 'objective' methods for finding it. If the necessary concepts and methods are known to all the parties in the debate, then nothing further needs to be said. The debate can start right away. If one party does not know the methods, or uses methods of its own then it must be *educated* which means *it is not taken seriously* unless its procedure coincides with the procedure of the rationalist. Arguments are tribe-centred and the rationalist is the master.

SECTION II

TECHNOLOGY—GOING FORWARD

Just take a pebble and cast it to the sea,
Then watch the ripples that unfold into me,
My face spill so gently into your eyes,
Disturbing the waters of our lives.

Greg Lake "Take A Pebble"
from Emerson, Lake, and Palmer, 1970

The advent and application of technology has consistently led to the alteration of human society. Whether this technology has led to the purification of iron ore, the construction of the cotton gin, or the advent of genetic engineering, these technologies changed the society into which they were brought forth. In the twenty-first century human society finds itself positioned with a wealth of technical knowledge including the safe, clean, effective application of nuclear energy and genetic engineering, or the ability to manipulate DNA as the basic library of life's features. The questions or difficulties that remain are how to we apply these and other technologies to affect humankind as a species, and our planet as a whole. These technologies are the pebbles, and it is their ripples that must be carefully considered.

Craig Barrett, the former CEO of Intel and a co-author of the *Gathering Storm,* a report on the state of scientific enterprise in the United States, was recently quoted in the "News This Week" section of *Science* saying, "There will be winners and losers, and the losers are the ones who insist on looking backwards." [1] Looking forwards does not necessarily mean the development of new technologies. Those new technologies will take time to be developed and applied. Rather the use of existing technologies applied in new and creative ways will serve to deal with

---

1 Mervis, Jeffrey. *Going From RAGS to Riches Is Proving to Be Very Difficult.* Science 9 May 320. pg. 728-729. 2008.

problems relevant to the twenty-first century, issues such as energy, abuse of the biosphere, and population.

These ideas and issues were embodied within the acceptance speech of Al Gore for the Nobel Peace Prize in 2007.

> We, the human species, are confronting a planetary emergency—a threat to the survival of our civilization that is gathering ominous and destructive potential even as we gather here. But there is hopeful news as well: we have the ability to solve this crisis and avoid the worst—though not all—of its consequences, if we act boldly, decisively and quickly.[2]

Viewing the statements of Barrett and Gore one might be inclined to pessimism. Has humankind gone too far? Have we destroyed the only home we have for our foreseeable future? Has our use of the technological advancements we currently have produced a set of inevitable consequences which can only result in the downfall of *Homo sapiens*?

Probably not. History shows that we as a species have been resourceful. Often it is our resourceful use of technology, such as the proliferation of hydroelectric power in the western United States in the 1930's that allowed for a rapid build up in materials in the war effort against the Axis powers. Without this, our efforts would have been significantly hindered, and our view of the world today may have been colored in a very different light. At the end of that same period, the Manhattan Project brought together a significant cadre of scientists to apply the understanding of atomic physics to the war effort. These uses of technology shaped events and spread forward through time. Our use of the atomic weapons developed by these scientists also changed the shape of the world.

These are but two examples of the double-edged sword of technology. The tools of technology can benefit humankind, or be used to its detriment. Atomic technology ended the conflict in the Pacific theatre, but the ongoing threat of use and the proliferation of atomic weapons produced the Cold War. The continuing potential threat today (whether it be real or imagined) of nuclear weapons in the hands of unscrupulous persons continues to shape decision making around the globe. We must look forward, as Barrett says, and develop this technology to the benefit of humankind.

---

2 Gore, Al. Accessed June 19, 2008.http://nobelprize.org/nobel_prizes/peace/laureates/2007/gore-lecture.html

Thus each piece of technology is like a pebble. The societal ripples continue to spread and interact. It is up to all the members of human society to participate in making informed decisions about the value of these technologies and whether these ripples will amplify one another to the benefit of humankind, or whether they will cancel each other and lead to a continuation of technological applications without true consideration of effects these technologies might have on humankind and the planet which we all inhabit.

James D. Watson

1928-

Francis Crick

1916-2004

A Structure for Deoxyribonucleic Acid

1953

James Watson and Francis Crick can arguably be said to be the most famous duo in the history of the life sciences. Working on the tidbits of evidence provided by early molecular scientists, such as Oswald Avery, Fredrick Griffith, and Erwin Chargaff, they became convinced that understanding the structure of deoxyribonucleic acid would provide insight into the molecular workings of the gene. Until their discovery, an understanding of the molecular structure of the gene had remained vague and was commonly thought to be based on proteins rather than nucleic acids.

Watson was a biologist whose training was in the area of phage genetics, the study of bacteriophages or viruses that affect bacteria. However, he was inspired to seek out the molecular nature of the gene after reading a text by physicist Erwin Schrodinger, called *What is Life?* Crick was then a theoretician who was completing his doctorate in physical chemistry at the Cavendish laboratory at Cambridge. Watson and Crick formed an immediate friendship and defied the orders by superiors to cease and desist from working on the structure of DNA because this work was considered the focus for Maurice Wilkins and Rosalind Franklin at King's College. They were told to concentrate on their assigned studies. Needless to say, they did not follow these directives, and in the autumn of 1952, after Watson had been shown the recent X-ray diffraction pictures by Rosalind Franklin, he and Crick became convinced that DNA had a helical structure. All that remained was to put the pieces together.

From Avery's work, they already knew that DNA was the true hereditary material, and Chargaff had demonstrated that the four component chemical parts of the molecule, Thymine (T), Adenine (A), Guanine (G) and Cytosine (C), existed in quantitatively equal ratios (A=T, G=C). Using cardboard models, later followed by metal and wire structures, and general rules of chemistry, they puzzled out the molecular nature of the structure of DNA that the four component chemicals, called bases, could be arranged in commonly repeated pairs, and that these pairs in long arrangements, form a double helical structure, as shown by the x-ray diffraction evidence of Rosalind Franklin.

In 1962 Watson, Crick, and Wilkins received the Nobel Prize for Physiology or Medicine. Sadly, by this time Rosalind Franklin had died from cancer, most likely developed from long term exposure to x-ray radiation. What follows is their complete paper, perhaps one of the most succinct, elegant, and important pieces of scientific literature ever published.

1. Why do Watson and Crick mention the already proposed structure of Pauling and Corey?
2. How did the understanding of the structure of DNA revolutionize the science of biology?

SOURCE:

Watson, J. D. (1980). *The Double Helix.* Norton Critical Edition. Gunther S. Stent. (Ed.). New York: W.W. Norton.

SELECTION FROM:

J.D. Watson and F.H.C. Crick. (1953). *The Molecular Structure of Nucleic Acids. Nature* Vol. 171 No. 4356 737-738.

April 25, 1953

MOLECULAR STRUCTURE OF NUCLEIC ACIDS

A Structure for Deoxyribose Nucleic Acid[1]

WE wish to suggest a structure for the salt of deoxyribose nucleic acid (D.N.A.). This structure has novel features which are of considerable biological interest.

A structure for nucleic acid has already been proposed by Pauling and Corey[2]. They kindly made their manuscript available to us in advance of publication. Their model consists of three intertwined chains, with the phosphates near the fibre axis, and the bases on the outside. In our opinion, this structure is unsatisfactory for two reasons: (1) We believe that the material which gives the X-ray diagrams is the salt, not the free acid. Without the acidic hydrogen atoms it is not clear what forces would hold the structure together, especially as the negatively charged phosphates near the axis will repel each other. (2) Some of the van der Waals distances appear to be too small.

Another three-chain structure has also been suggested by Fraser (in the press). In his model the phosphates, are on the outside and the bases on the inside, linked together by hydrogen bonds. This structure as described is rather ill-defined, and for this reason we shall not comment on it.

We wish to put forward a radically different structure for the salt of deoxyribose nucleic acid. This structure has two helical chains each coiled round the same axis (see diagram). We have made the usual chemical assumptions, namely, that each chain consists of phosphate diester groups joining β-D-deoryribofuranose residues with linkages. The two chains (but not their bases) are related by a dyad perpendicular to the fibre axis. Both chains follow right-handed helices, but owing to the dyad the sequences of the atoms in the two chains run in opposite directions. Each chain loosely

---

1 permission from Macmillan Publishers Ltd: *Nature* Vol. 171 No. 4356 737-738.

2 Pauling, L., and Corey, R. B., *Nature*, 171, 346 (1953); *Proc. U.S. Nat. Acad. Sci.*, 39, 84. (1953).

resembles Furberg's[3] model No. 1; that is, the bases are on the inside of the helix and the phosphates on the outside. The configuration of the sugar and the atoms near it is close to Furberg's 'standard configuration', the sugar being roughly perpendicular to the attached base. There is a residue WI each chain every 3·4 A. in the z-direction. We have assumed an angle of 36° between adjacent residues in the same chain, so that the structure repeats after 10 residues on each chain, that is, after 34 A. The distance of a phosphorus atom from the fibre axis is 10 A. As the phosphates are on the outside, cations have easy access to them.

The structure is an open one, and its water content is rather high. At lower water contents we would expect the bases to tilt so that the structure could become more compact.

The novel feature of the structure is the manner in which the two chains are held together by the purine and pyrimidine bases. The plane of the bases are perpendicular to the fibre axis. They are joined together in pairs, a single base from one chain being hydrogen-bonded to a single base from the other chain, so that the two lie side by side with identical z-co-ordinates. One of the pair must be a purine and the other a pyrimidine for bonding—to occur. The hydrogen bonds are made as follows : purine position 1 to pyrimidine position 1; purine position 6 to pyrimidine position 6.

If it is assumed that the bases only occur in the structure in the most plausible tautomeric forms (that is, with the keto rather than the enol configurations) it is found that only specific pairs of bases can bond together. These pairs are: adenine (purine) with thymine (pyrimidine), and guanine (purine) with cytosine (pyrimidine).

In other words, if an adenine forms one member of a pair, on either chain, then on these assumptions the other member must be thymine; similarly for guanine and cytosine. The sequence of bases on a single chain does not appear to be restricted in any way. However, if only specific pairs of bases can be formed, it follows that if the sequence of bases on one chain is given, then the sequence on the other chain is automatically determined.

It has been found experimentally[4],[5] that the ratio of the amounts of adenine to thymine, and the ratio of guanine to cytosine, are always very close to unity for deoxyribose nucleic acid.

---

3 Furberg, S., *Ada. Chem. Scand.*, 6, 634 (1952).

4 Chargaff, E., for references see Zamenhof, S., Brawerman, G., and Chargaff, E., *Biochim. et Biophys. Ada*, 9, 402 (1952).

5 Wyatt. G. R., *J. Gen. Physiol.;* 36, 201 (1952).

It is probably impossible to build this structure with a ribose sugar in place of the deoxyribose, as the extra oxygen atom would make too close a van der Waals contact.

The previously published X-ray data[6],[7] on deoxyribose nucleic acid are insufficient for a rigorous test of our structure. So far as we can tell, lit is roughly compatible with the experimental data, but it must be regarded as unproved until it has been checked against more exact results. Some of these are given in the following communications. We were not aware of the details of the results presented there when we devised our structure, which rests mainly though not entirely on published experimental data and stereochemical arguments.

It has not escaped our notice that the specific pairing we have postulated immediately suggests a possible copying mechanism for the genetic material.

Full details of the structure, including the conditions assumed in building it, together with a set of co-ordinates for the atoms, will be published elsewhere.

We are much indebted to Dr. Jerry Donohue for constant advice and criticism, especially on interatomic distances. We have also been stimulated by a knowledge of the general nature of the unpublished experimental results and ideas of Dr. M. H. F. Wilkins, Dr. R. E. Franklin and their co-workers at King's College, London. One of us (J. D. W.) has been aided by a fellowship from the National Foundation for Infantile Paralysis.

J. D. WATSON
F. H. C. CRICK

Medical Research Council Unit for the Study of the Molecular Structure of Biological Systems, Cavendish Laboratory, Cambridge. April 2.

---

6 Astbury, W. T., *Symp.* Soc. Exp. Biol. 1, Nucleic Acid, 66 (Camb. Univ. Press, 1947).

7 Wilkins, M H. F., and Randall, J. T., *Biochim. et Biophy. Ada,* 10, 192 (1953).

Aldous Huxley

1894-1963

Brave New World

1946

Aldous Leonard Huxley was born into an English family of distinguished heritage, the grandson of the renowned biologist Thomas Henry Huxley. T.H. Huxley was known as Darwin's Bulldog for his vociferous defense of *The Origin of the Species* and the theory of natural selection. On his maternal side, his aunt was Mrs. Humphrey Ward a novelist, who was the niece of the poet Matthew Arnold, and the granddaughter of Thomas Arnold a noted educator who became a character in Tom Brown's Schooldays. Huxley's heritage most certainly affected his future work, growing up with a separateness that made him unique for his unusual combination of intelligence, sense of superiority, and moral obligation. At 14, Huxley's mother passed away from cancer and this affected him deeply. An eye illness at age 16 nearly left him blind, but he recovered enough to attend Oxford, but not enough to join the military for World War I or to pursue the scientific work of which he dreamed.

His first publication was a collection of poems. During the next several decades he traveled widely through Europe, Asia, and America gaining a sense of the differences amongst the various cultures he experienced. It was during this period that he began to write, including a number of his most recognized works, such as *Crome Yellow*, *Antic Hay*, and *Point Counter Point*. *Brave New World* was written in 1931, prior to the rise of Hitler's Nazi Germany and has been described as one of the most bewitching and insidious works of literature ever written. In his

1946 Foreword to *Brave New World*, Huxley describes the novel's theme not as the advancement of science as such but rather as the advancement of science as it affects human individuals. [xi]

1. Is science the only means by which humankind can change its direction? Explain your reasoning.
2. Where in current human society do you see social gradations like the alphas, betas etc. on down? Is this the expected product of a science-based society? Explain.
3. How does the speculative technology that Huxley describes in 1931 relate to actual technology today? Could modern science create the society that Huxley envisioned? Would it be the same or different? Explain?

Sources:

Pearce, David. (2007). *Brave New World? A Defense of Paradise-Engineering.* Retrieved August 9, 2007, from http://www.huxley.net/

Aldous Huxley: The Author and His Times. Retrieved August 9, 2007, from http://somaweb.org/w/huxbio.html.

Selection from:

Huxley, A. (1946). *Brave New World.* New York: Harper & Row, Publishers. 1-19, 260-275.

CHAPTER ONE

A squat grey building of only thirty-four stories. Over the main entrance the words, CENTRAL LONDON HATCHERY AND CONDITIONING CENTRE, and, in a shield, the World State's motto, COMMUNITY, IDENTITY, STABILITY.

The enormous room on the ground floor faced towards the north. Cold for all the summer beyond the panes, for all the tropical heat of the room itself, a harsh thin light glared through the windows, hungrily seeking some draped lay figure, some pallid shape of academic goose-flesh, but finding only the glass and nickel and bleakly shining porcelain of a laboratory. Wintriness responded to wintriness. The overalls of the workers were white, their hands gloved with a pale corpse-coloured rubber. The light was frozen, dead, a ghost. Only from the yellow barrels of the microscopes did it borrow a certain rich and living substance, lying along the polished tubes like butter, streak after luscious streak in long recession down the work tables.

"And this," said the Director opening the door, "is the Fertilizing Room."

Bent over their instruments, three hundred Fertilizers were plunged, as the Director of Hatcheries and Conditioning entered the room, in the scarcely breathing silence, the absent-minded, soliloquizing hum or whistle, of absorbed concentration. A troop of newly arrived students, very young, pink and callow, followed nervously, rather abjectly, at the Director's heels. Each of them carried a notebook, in which, whenever the great man spoke, he desperately scribbled. Straight from the horse's mouth. It was a rare privilege. The D.H.C. for Central London always made a point of personally conducting his new students round the various departments.

"Just to give you a general idea," he would explain to them. For of course some sort of general idea they must have, if they were to do their work intelligently—though as little of one, if they were to be good and happy members of society, as possible. For particulars, as every one knows, make for virtue and happiness; generalities are intellectually necessary evils. Not philosophers but fret-sawyers and stamp collectors compose the backbone of society.

"To-morrow," he would add, smiling at them with a slightly menacing geniality, "you'll be settling down to serious work. You won't have time for generalities. Meanwhile . . . "

Meanwhile, it was a privilege. Straight from the horse's mouth into the notebook. The boys scribbled like mad.

Tall and rather thin but upright, the Director advanced into the room. He had a long chin and big, rather prominent teeth, just covered, when he was not talking, by his full, floridly curved lips. Old, young? Thirty? Fifty? Fifty-five? It was hard to say. And anyhow the question didn't arise; in this year of stability, A.F. 632, it didn't occur to you to ask it.

"I shall begin at the beginning," said the D.H.C. and the more zealous students recorded his intention in their notebooks: *Begin at the beginning.* "These," he waved his hand, "are the incubators." And opening an insulated door he showed them racks upon racks of numbered test-tubes. "The week's supply of ova. Kept," he explained, "at blood heat; whereas the male gametes," and here he opened another door, "they have to be kept at thirty-five instead of thirty-seven. Full blood heat sterilizes." Rams wrapped in theremogene beget no lambs.

Still leaning against the incubators he gave them, while the pencils scurried illegibly across the pages, a brief description of the modern fertilizing process; spoke first, of course, of its surgical introduction—"the operation undergone voluntarily for the good of Society, not to mention the fact that it carries a bonus amounting to six months' salary"; continued with some account of the technique for preserving the excised ovary alive and actively developing; passed on to a consideration of optimum temperature, salinity, viscosity; referred to the liquor in which the detached and ripened eggs were kept; and, leading his charges to the work tables, actually showed them how this liquor was drawn off from the test-tubes; how it was let out drop by drop onto the specially warmed slides of the microscopes; how the eggs which it contained were inspected for abnormalities, counted and transferred to a porous receptacle; how (and he now took them to watch the operation) this receptacle was immersed in a warm bouillon containing free-swimming spermatozoa—at a minimum concentration of one hundred thousand per cubic centimetre, he insisted; and how, after ten minutes, the container was lifted out of the liquor and its contents re-examined; how, if any of the eggs remained unfertilized, it was again immersed, and, if necessary, yet again; how the fertilized ova went back to the incubators; where the Alphas and Betas remained until definitely bottled; while the Gammas, Deltas and Epsilons were brought out again, after only thirty-six hours, to undergo Bokanovsky's Process.

"Bokanovsky's Process," repeated the Director, and the students underlined the words in their little notebooks.

One egg, one embryo, one-adult—normality. But a bokanovskified egg will bud, will proliferate, will divide. From eight to ninety-six buds, and every bud will grow into a perfectly formed embryo, and every embryo into a full-sized adult. Making ninety-six human beings grow where only one grew before. Progress.

"Essentially," the D.H.C. concluded, "bokanovskification consists of a series of arrests of development. We check the normal growth and, paradoxically enough, the egg responds by budding."

Responds by budding. The pencils were busy.

He pointed. On a very slowly moving band a rack-full of test-tubes was entering a large metal box, another rack-full was emerging. Machinery faintly purred. It took eight minutes for the tubes to go through, he told them. Eight minutes of hard X-rays being about as much as an egg can stand. A few died; of the rest, the least susceptible divided into two; most put out four buds; some eight; all were returned to the incubators, where the buds began to develop; then, after two days, were suddenly chilled, chilled and checked. Two, four, eight, the buds in their turn budded; and having budded were dosed almost to death with alcohol; consequently burgeoned again and having budded—bud out of bud out of bud—were thereafter—further arrest being generally fatal—left to develop in peace. By which time the original egg was in a fair way to becoming anything from eight to ninety-six embryos—a prodigious improvement, you will agree, on nature. Identical twins—but not in piddling twos and threes as in the old viviparous days, when an egg would sometimes accidentally divide; actually by dozens, by scores at a time.

"Scores," the Director repeated and flung out his arms, as though he were distributing largesse. "Scores."

But one of the students was fool enough to ask where the advantage lay.

"My good boy!" The Director wheeled sharply round on him. "Can't you see? Can't you *see?*" He raised a hand; his expression was solemn. "Bokanovsky's Process is one of the major instruments of social stability!"

Major instruments of social stability.

Standard men and women; in uniform batches. The whole of a small factory staffed with the products of a single bokanovskified egg.

"Ninety-six identical twins working ninety-six identical machines!" The voice was almost tremulous with enthusiasm. "You really know where you are. For the first time in history." He quoted the planetary motto. "Community, Identity, Stability." Grand words. "If we could bokanovskify indefinitely the whole problem would be solved."

Solved by standard Gammas, unvarying Deltas, uniform Epsilons. Millions of identical twins. The principle of mass production at last applied to biology.

"But, alas," the Director shook his head, "we *can't* bokanovskify indefinitely."

Ninety-six seemed to be the limit; seventy-two a good average. From the same ovary and with gametes of the same male to manufacture as many batches of identical twins as possible—that was the best (sadly a second best) that they could do. And even that was difficult.

"For in nature it takes thirty years for two hundred eggs to reach maturity. But our business is to stabilize the population at this moment, here and now. Dribbling out twins over a quarter of a century—what would be the use of that?"

Obviously, no use at all. But Podsnap's Technique had immensely accelerated the process of ripening. They could make sure of at least a hundred and fifty mature eggs within two years. Fertilze and bokanovskify—in other words, multiply by seventy-two—and you get an average of nearly eleven thousand brothers and sisters in a hundred and fifty batches of identical twins, all within two years of the same age.

"And in exceptional cases we can make one ovary yield us over fifteen thousand adult individuals."

Beckoning to a fair-haired, ruddy young man who happened to be passing at the moment, "Mr. Foster," he called. The ruddy young man approached. "Can you tell us the record for a single ovary, Mr. Foster?"

"Sixteen thousand and twelve in this Centre," Mr. Foster replied without hesitation. He spoke very quickly, had a vivacious blue eye, and took an evident pleasure in quoting figures. "Sixteen thousand and twelve; in one hundred and eighty-nine batches of identicals. But of course they've done much better," he rattled on, "in some of the tropical Centres. Singapore has often produced over sixteen thousand five hundred; and Mombasa has actually touched the seventeen thousand mark. But then they have unfair advantages. You should see the way a negro ovary responds to pituitary! It's quite astonishing, when you're used to working with European material. Still," he added, with a laugh (but the light of combat was in his eyes and the lift of his chin was challenging), "still, we mean to beat them if we can. I'm working on a wonderful Delta-Minus ovary at this moment. Only just eighteen months old. Over twelve thousand seven hundred children already, either decanted or in embryo. And still going strong. We'll beat them yet."

"That's the spirit I like!" cried the Director, and clapped Mr. Foster on the shoulder. "Come along with us and give these boys the benefit of your expert knowledge."

Mr. Foster smiled modestly. "With pleasure." They went.

In the Bottling Room all was harmonious bustle and ordered activity. Flaps of fresh sow's peritoneum ready cut to the proper size came shooting up in little lifts from the Organ Store in the sub-basement. Whizz and then, click! the lift-hatches flew open; the bottle-liner had only to reach out a hand, take the flap, insert, smooth-down, and before the lined bottle had had time to travel out of reach along the endless band, whizz, click! another flap of peritoneum had shot up from the depths, ready to be slipped into yet another bottle, the next of that slow interminable procession on the band.

Next to the Liners stood the Matriculators. The procession advanced; one by one the eggs were transferred from their test-tubes to the larger containers; deftly the peritoneal lining was slit, the morula dropped into place, the saline solution poured in . . . and already the bottle had passed, and it was the turn of the labellers. Heredity, date of fertilization, membership of Bokanovsky Group—details were transferred from test-tube to bottle. No longer anonymous, but named, identified, the procession marched slowly on; on through an opening in the wall, slowly on into the Social Predestination Room.

"Eighty-eight cubic metres of card-index," said Mr. Foster with relish as they entered.

"Containing *all* the relevant information," added the Director.

"Brought up to date every morning."

"And co-ordinated every afternoon."

"On the basis of which they make their calculations."

"So many individuals, of such and such quality," said Mr. Foster.

"Distributed in such and such quantities."

"The optimum Decanting Rate at any given moment."

"Unforeseen wastages promptly made good."

"Promptly," repeated Mr. Foster. "If you knew the amount of overtime I had to put in after the last Japanese earthquake!" He laughed good-humouredly and shook his head.

"The Predestinators send in their figures to the Fertilizers."

"Who give them the embryos they ask for."

"And the bottles come in here to be predestinated in detail."

"After which they are sent down to the Embryo Store."

"Where we now proceed ourselves."

And opening a door Mr. Foster led the way down a staircase into the basement.

The temperature was still tropical. They descended into a thickening twilight. Two doors and a passage with a double turn insured the cellar against any possible infiltration of the day.

"Embryos are like photograph film," said Mr. Foster waggishly, as he pushed open the second door. "They can only stand red light."

And in effect the sultry darkness into which the students now followed him was visible and crimson, like the darkness of closed eyes on a summer's afternoon. The bulging flanks of row on receding row and tier above tier of bottles glinted with innumerable rubies, and among the rubies moved the dim red spectres of men and women with purple eyes and all the symptoms of lupus. The hum and rattle of machinery faintly stirred the air.

"Give them a few figures, Mr. Foster," said the Director, who was tired of talking.

Mr. Foster was only too happy to give them a few figures.

Two hundred and twenty metres long, two hundred wide, ten high. He pointed upwards. Like chickens drinking, the students lifted their eyes towards the distant ceiling.

Three tiers of racks: ground floor level, first gallery, second gallery.

The spidery steel-work of gallery above gallery faded away in all directions into the dark. Near them three red ghosts were busily unloading demijohns from a moving staircase.

The escalator from the Social Predestination Room.

Each bottle could be placed on one of fifteen racks, each rack, though you couldn't see it, was a conveyor travelling at the rate of thirty-three and a third centimetres an hour. Two hundred and sixty-seven days at eight metres a day. Two thousand one hundred and thirty-six metres in all. One circuit of the cellar at ground level, one on the first gallery, half on the second, and on the two hundred and sixty-seventh morning, daylight in the Decanting Room. Independent existence—so called.

"But in the interval," Mr. Foster concluded, "we've managed to do a lot to them. Oh, a very great deal." His laugh was knowing and triumphant.

"That's the spirit I like," said the Director once more. "Let's walk round. You tell them everything, Mr. Foster."

Mr. Foster duly told them.

Told them of the growing embryo on its bed of peritoneum. Made them taste the rich blood surrogate on which it fed. Explained why it had to be stimulated with placentin and thyroxin. Told them of the *corpus luteum* extract. Showed them the jets through which at every twelfth metre from zero to 2040 it was automatically injected. Spoke of those gradually increasing doses of pituitary administered during the final ninety-six metres of their course. Described the artificial maternal circulation installed on every bottle at Metre 112; showed them the reservoir of blood-surrogate, the centrifugal pump that kept the liquid moving over the placenta and drove it through the synthetic lung and waste-product filter. Referred to the embryo's troublesome tendency to anæmia, to the massive doses of hog's stomach extract and foetal foal's liver with which, in consequence, it had to be supplied.

Showed them the simple mechanism by means of which, during the last two metres out of every eight, all the embryos were simultaneously shaken into familiarity with movement. Hinted at the gravity of the so-called "trauma of decanting," and enumerated the precautions taken to minimize, by a suitable training of the bottled embryo, that dangerous shock. Told them of the tests for sex carried out in the neighbourhood of metre 200. Explained the system of labelling—a T for the males, a circle for the females and for those who were destined to become freemartins a question mark, black on a white ground.

"For of course," said Mr. Foster, "in the vast majority of cases, fertility is merely a nuisance. One fertile ovary in twelve hundred—that would really be quite sufficient for our purposes. But we want to have a good choice. And of course one must always leave an enormous margin of safety. So we allow as many as thirty per cent of the female embryos to develop normally. The others get a dose of male sex-hormone every twenty-four metres for the rest of the course. Result: they're decanted as freemartins—structurally quite normal (except," he had to admit, "that they *do* have just the slightest tendency to grow beards), but sterile. Guaranteed sterile. Which brings us at last," continued Mr. Foster, "out of the realm of mere slavish imitation of nature into the much more interesting world of human invention."

He rubbed his hands. For of course, they didn't content themselves with merely hatching out embryos: any cow could do that.

"We also predestine and condition. We decant our babies as socialized human beings, as Alphas or Epsilons, as future sewage workers or future . . . " He was going to say "future World controllers," but correcting himself, said "future Directors of Hatcheries," instead.

The D.H.C. acknowledged the compliment with a smile.

They were passing Metre 320 on rack II. A young Beta-Minus mechanic was busy with screwdriver and spanner on the blood-surrogate pump of a passing bottle. The hum of the electric motor deepened by fractions of a tone as he turned the nuts. Down, down . . . A final twist, a glance at the revolution counter, and he was done. He moved two paces down the line and began the same process on the next pump.

"Reducing the number of revolutions per minute," Mr. Foster explained. "The surrogate goes round slower; therefore passes through the lung at longer intervals; therefore gives the embryo less oxygen. Nothing like oxygen-shortage for keeping an embryo below par." Again he rubbed his hands.

"But why do you want to keep the embryo below par?" asked an ingenuous student.

"Ass!" said the Director, breaking a long silence. "Hasn't it occurred to you that an Epsilon embryo must have an Epsilon environment as well as an Epsilon heredity?"

It evidently hadn't occurred to him. He was covered with confusion.

"The lower the caste," said Mr. Foster, "the shorter the oxygen." The first organ affected was the brain. After that the skeleton. At seventy percent of normal oxygen you got dwarfs. At less than seventy eyeless monsters.

"Who are no use at all," concluded Mr. Foster.

Whereas (his voice became confidential and eager), if they could discover a technique for shortening the period of maturation what a triumph, what a benefaction to Society!

"Consider the horse."

They considered it.

Mature at six; the elephant at ten. While at thirteen a man is not yet sexually mature; and is only full-grown at twenty. Hence, of course, that fruit of delayed development, the human intelligence.

"But in Epsilons," said Mr. Foster very justly, "we don't need human intelligence."

Didn't need and didn't get it. But though the Epsilon mind was mature at ten, the Epsilon body was not fit to work till eighteen. Long years of superfluous and wasted immaturity. If the physical development could be speeded up till it was as quick, say, as a cow's, what an enormous saving to the Community!

"Enormous!" murmured the students. Mr. Foster's enthusiasm was infectious.

He became rather technical; spoke of the abnormal endocrine co-ordination which made men grow so slowly; postulated a germinal mutation to account for it. Could the effects of this germinal mutation be undone? Could the individual Epsilon embryo be made a revert, by a suitable technique, to the normality of dogs and cows? That was the problem. And it was all but solved.

Pilkington, at Mombasa, had produced individuals who were sexually mature at four and full-grown at six and a half. A scientific triumph. But socially useless. Six-year-old-men and women were too stupid to do even Epsilon work. And the process was an all-or-nothing one; either you failed to modify at all, or else you modified the whole way. They were still trying to find the ideal compromise between adults of twenty and adults of six. So far without success. Mr. Foster sighed and shook his head.

Their wanderings through the crimson twilight had brought them to the neighbourhood of Metre 170 on Rack 9. From this point onwards Rack 9 was enclosed and the bottles performed the remainder of their journey in a kind of tunnel, interrupted here and there by openings two or three metres wide.

"Heat conditioning," said Mr. Foster.

Hot tunnels alternated with cool tunnels. Coolness was wedded to discomfort in the form of hard X-rays. By the time they were decanted, the embryos had a horror of cold. They were predestined to emigrate to the tropics, to be miners and acetate silk spinners and steel workers. Later on their minds would be made to endorse the judgment of their bodies. "We condition them to thrive on heat," concluded Mr. Foster. "Our colleagues upstairs will teach them to love it."

"And that," put in the Director sententiously, "that is the secret of happiness and virtue—liking what you've *got* to do. All conditioning aims at that: making people like their unescapable social destiny."

In a gap between two tunnels, a nurse was delicately probing with a long fine syringe into the gelatinous contents of a passing bottle. The students and their guides stood watching her for a few moments in silence.

"Well, Lenina," said Mr. Foster, when at last she withdrew the syringe and straightened herself up.

The girl turned with a start. One could see that, for all the lupus and the purple eyes, she was uncommonly pretty.

"Henry!" Her smile flashed redly at him—a row of coral teeth.

"Charming, charming," murmured the Director and, giving her two or three little pats, received in exchange a rather deferential smile for himself.

"What are you giving them?" asked Mr. Foster, making his tone very professional.

"Oh, the usual typhoid and sleeping sickness."

"Tropical workers start being inoculated at Metre 150," Mr. Foster explained to the students. "The embryos still have gills. We immunize the fish against the future man's diseases." Then, turning back to Lenina, "Ten to five on the roof this afternoon," he said, "as usual."

"Charming," said the Director once more, and, with a final pat, moved away after the others.

On Rack 10 rows of next generation's chemical workers were being trained in the toleration of lead, caustic soda, tar, chlorine. The first of a batch of two hundred and fifty embryonic rocket-plane engineers was just passing the eleven hundred metre mark on Rack 3. A special mechanism kept their containers in constant rotation. "To improve their sense of balance," Mr. Foster explained. "Doing repairs on the outside of a rocket in mid-air is a ticklish job. We slacken off the circulation when they're right way up, so that they're half starved, and double the flow of surrogate when they're upside down. They learn to associate topsy-turvydom with well-being; in fact, they're only truly happy when they're standing on their heads."

"And now," Mr. Foster went on, "I'd like to show you some very interesting conditioning for Alpha Plus Intellectuals. We have a big batch of them on Rack 5. First Gallery level," he called to two boys who had started to go down to the ground floor.

"They're round about Metre 900," he explained. "You can't really do any useful intellectual conditioning till the foetuses have lost their tails. Follow me."

But the Director had looked at his watch. "Ten to three," he said. "No time for the intellectual embryos, I'm afraid. We must go up to the Nurseries before the children have finished their afternoon sleep."

Mr. Foster was disappointed. "At least one glance at the Decanting Room," he pleaded.

"Very well then." The Director smiled indulgently. "Just one glance."

CHAPTER SIXTEEN

THE room into which the three were ushered was the Controller's study.

"His fordship will be down in a moment." The Gamma butler left them to themselves.

Helmholtz laughed aloud.

"It's more like a caffeine-solution party than a trial," he said, and let himself fall into the most luxurious of the pneumatic arm-chairs. "Cheer up, Bernard," he added, catching sight of his friend's green unhappy face. But Bernard would not be cheered; without answering, without even looking at Helmholtz, he went and sat down on the most uncomfortable chair in the room, carefully chosen in the obscure hope of somehow deprecating the wrath of the higher powers.

The Savage meanwhile wandered restlessly round the room, peering with a vague superficial inquisitiveness at the books in the shelves, at the sound-track rolls and the reading machine bobbins in their numbered pigeon-holes. On the table under the window lay a massive volume bound in limp black leather-surrogate, and stamped with large golden T's. He picked it up and opened it. MY LIFE AND WORK, BY OUR FORD. The book had been published at Detroit by the Society for the Propagation of Fordian Knowledge. Idly he turned the pages, read a sentence here, a paragraph there, and had just come to the conclusion that the book didn't interest him, when the door opened, and the Resident World Controller for Western Europe walked briskly into the room.

Mustapha Mond shook hands with all three of them; but it was to the Savage that he addressed himself. "So you don't much like civilization, Mr. Savage," he said.

The Savage looked at him. He had been prepared to lie, to bluster, to remain sullenly unresponsive; but, reassured by the good-humoured intelligence of the Controller's face, he decided to tell the truth, straightforwardly. "No." He shook his head.

Bernard started and looked horrified. What would the Controller think? To be labeled as the friend of a man who said that he didn't like civilization—said it openly and, of all people, to the Controller—it was terrible. "But, John," he began. A look from Mustapha Mond reduced him to an abject silence.

"Of course," the Savage went on to admit, "there are some very nice things. All that music in the air, for instance . . . "

"Sometimes a thousand twangling instruments will hum about my ears and sometimes voices."

The Savage's face lit up with a sudden pleasure. "Have you read it too?" he asked. "I thought nobody knew about that book here, in England."

"Almost nobody. I'm one of the very few. It's prohibited, you see. But as I make the laws here, I can also break them. With impunity, Mr. Marx," he added, turning to Bernard. "Which I'm afraid you *can't* do."

Bernard sank into a yet more hopeless misery.

"But why is it prohibited?" asked the Savage. In the excitement of meeting a man who had read Shakespeare he had momentarily forgotten everything else.

The Controller shrugged his shoulders. "Because it's old; that's the chief reason. We haven't any use for old things here."

"Even when they're beautiful?"

"Particularly when they're beautiful. Beauty's attractive, and we don't want people to be attracted by old things. We want them to like the new ones."

"But the new ones are so stupid and horrible. Those plays, where there's nothing but helicopters flying about and you *feel* the people kissing." He made a grimace. "Goats and monkeys!" Only in Othello's words could he find an adequate vehicle for his contempt and hatred.

"Nice tame animals, anyhow," the Controller murmured parenthetically.

"Why don't you let them see *Othello* instead?"

"I've told you; it's old. Besides, they couldn't understand it."

Yes, that was true. He remembered how Helmholtz had laughed at *Romeo and Juliet*. "Well then," he said, after a pause, "something new that's like *Othello*, and that they could understand."

"That's what we've all been wanting to write," said Helmholtz, breaking a long silence.

"And it's what you never will write," said the Controller. "Because, if it were really like *Othello* nobody could understand it, however new it might be. And if it were new, it couldn't possibly be like *Othello.*"

"Why not?"

"Yes, why not?" Helmholtz repeated. He too was forgetting the unpleasant realities of the situation. Green with anxiety and apprehension, only Bernard remembered them; the others ignored him. "Why not?"

"Because our world is not the same as Othello's world. You can't make flivvers without steel—and you can't make tragedies without social instability. The world's stable now. People are happy; they get what they want, and they never want what they can't get. They're well off; they're safe; they're never ill, they're not afraid of death; they're blissfully ignorant of passion and old age; they're plagued with no mothers or fathers; they've got no wives, or children or lovers to feel strongly about; they're so conditioned that they practically can't help behaving as they ought to behave. And if anything should go wrong, there's *soma*. Which you go and chuck out of the window in the name of liberty, Mr. Savage. *Liberty!*" He laughed. "Expecting Deltas to know what liberty is! And now expecting them to understand *Othello!* My good boy!"

The Savage was silent for a little. "All the same," he insisted obstinately, "*Othello*'s good, *Othello*'s better than those feelies."

"Of course it is," The Controller agreed. "But that's the price we have to pay for stability. You've got to choose between happiness and what people used to call high art. We've sacrificed the high art. We have the feelies and the scent organ instead."

"But they don't mean anything."

"They mean themselves; they mean a lot of agreeable sensations to the audience."

"But they're . . . they're told by an idiot."

The Controller laughed. "You're not being very polite to your friend, Mr. Watson. One of our most distinguished Emotional Engineers . . . "

"But he's right," said Helmholtz gloomily. "Because it *is* idiotic. Writing when there's nothing to say . . . "

"Precisely. But that requires the most enormous ingenuity. You're making flivvers out of the absolute minimum of steel—works of art out of practically nothing but pure sensation."

The Savage shook his head. "It all seems to me quite horrible."

"Of course it does. Actual happiness always looks pretty squalid in comparison with the over-compensations for misery. And, of course, stability isn't nearly so spectacular as instability. And being contented has none of the glamour of a good fight against misfortune, none of the picturesqueness of a struggle with temptation, or a fatal overthrow by passion or doubt. Happiness is never grand."

"I suppose not," said the Savage after a silence. "But need it be quite so bad as those twins?" He passed his hand over his eyes as though he were trying to wipe away the remembered image of those long rows of identical midgets at the assembling tables, those queued-up twin-herds at the entrance to the Brentford monorail station, those human maggots swarming round Linda's bed of death, the endlessly repeated face of his assailants. He looked at his bandaged left hand and shuddered. "Horrible!"

"But how useful! I see you don't like our Bokanovsky Groups; but, I assure you, they're the foundation on which every thing else is built. They're the gyroscope that stabilizes the rocket plane of state on its unswerving course." The deep voice thrillingly vibrated; the gesticulating hand implied all space and the onrush of the irresistible machine. Mustapha Mond's oratory was almost up to synthetic standards.

"I was wondering," said the Savage, "why you had them at all—seeing that you can get whatever you want out of those bottles. Why don't you make everybody an Alpha Double Plus while you're about it?"

Mustapha Mond laughed. "Because we have no wish to have our throats cut," he answered. "We believe in happiness and stability. A society of Alphas couldn't fail to be unstable and miserable. Imagine a factory staffed by Alphas—that is to say by separate and unrelated individuals of good heredity and conditioned so as to be capable (within limits) of making a free choice and assuming responsibilities. Imagine it!" he repeated.

The Savage tried to imagine it, not very successfully.

"It's an absurdity. An Alpha-decanted, Alpha-conditioned man would go mad if he had to do Epsilon Semi-Moron work—go mad, or start smashing things up. Alphas can be completely socialized—but only on condition that you make them do Alpha work. Only an Epsilon can be expected to make Epsilon sacrifices, for the good reason that for him they aren't sacrifices; they're the line of least resistance. His conditioning has laid down rails along which he's got to run. He can't help himself; he's foredoomed. Even after decanting, he's still inside a bottle—an invisible bottle of infantile and embryonic fixations. Each one of us, of course," the Controller meditatively continued, "goes through life inside a bottle. But if we happen to be Alphas, our bottles are, relatively speaking, enormous. We should suffer acutely if we were confined in a narrower space. You cannot pour upper-caste champagne-surrogate into lower-caste bottles. It's obvious theoretically. But it has also been proved in actual practice. The result of the Cyprus experiment was convincing."

"What was that?" asked the Savage.

Mustapha Mond smiled. "Well, you can call it an experiment in rebottling if you like. It began in A.F. 473. The Controllers had the island of Cyprus cleared of all its existing inhabitants and re-colonized with a specially prepared batch of twenty-two thousand Alphas. All agricultural and industrial equipment was handed over to them and they were left to manage their own affairs. The result exactly fulfilled all the theoretical predictions. The land wasn't properly worked; there were strikes in all the factories; the laws were set at naught, orders disobeyed; all the people detailed for a spell of low-grade work were perpetually intriguing for high-grade jobs, and all the people with high-grade jobs were counter-intriguing at all costs to stay where they were. Within six years they were having a first-class civil war. When nineteen out of the twenty-two thousand had been killed, the survivors unanimously petitioned the World Controllers to resume the government of the island. Which they did. And that was the end of the only society of Alphas that the world has ever seen."

The Savage sighed, profoundly.

"The optimum population," said Mustapha Mond, "is modelled on the iceberg—eight-ninths below the water line, one-ninth above."

"And they're happy below the water line?"

"Happier than above it. Happier than your friend here, for example." He pointed.

"In spite of that awful work?"

"Awful? *They* don't find it so. On the contrary, they like it. It's light, it's childishly simple. No strain on the mind or the muscles. Seven and a half hours of mild, unexhausting labour, and then the *soma* ration and games and unrestricted copulation and the feelies. What more can they ask for? True," he added, "they might ask for shorter hours. And of course we could give them shorter hours. Technically it would be perfectly simple to reduce all lower-caste working hours to three or four a day. But would they be any the happier for that? No, they wouldn't. The experiment was tried, more than a century and a half ago. The whole of Ireland was put on to the four-hour day. What was the result? Unrest and a large increase in the consumption of *soma*; that was all. Those three and a half hours of extra leisure were so far from being a source of happiness, that people felt constrained to take a holiday from them.

The Inventions Office is stuffed with plans for labour-saving processes. Thousands of them." Mustapha Mond made a lavish gesture. "And why don't we put them into execution? For the sake of the labourers; it would be sheer cruelty to afflict them with excessive leisure. It's the same with agriculture. We could synthesize every morsel of food, if we wanted to. But we don't. We prefer to keep a third of the population on the land. For their own sakes—because it takes *longer* to get food out of the land than out of a factory. Besides, we have our stability to think of. We don't want to change. Every change is a menace to stability. That's another reason why we're so chary of applying new inventions. Every discovery in pure science is potentially subversive; even science must sometimes be treated as a possible enemy. Yes, even science."

Science? The Savage frowned. He knew the word. But what it exactly signified he could not say. Shakespeare and the old men of the pueblo had never mentioned science, and from Linda he had only gathered the vaguest hints: science was something you made helicopters with, something that caused you to laugh at the Corn Dances, something that prevented you from being wrinkled and losing your teeth. He made a desperate effort to take the Controller's meaning.

"Yes," Mustapha Mond was saying, "that's another item in the cost of stability. It isn't only art that's incompatible with happiness; it's also science. Science is dangerous; we have to keep it most carefully chained and muzzled."

"What?" said Helmholtz, in astonishment. "But we're always saying that science is everything. It's a hyponoædic platitude."

"Three times a week between thirteen and seventeen," put in Bernard.

"And all the science propaganda we do at the College . . . "

"Yes; but what sort of science?" asked Mustapha Mond sarcastically. "You've had no scientific training, so you can't judge. I was a pretty good physicist in my time. Too good—good enough to realize that all our science is just a cookery book, with an orthodox theory of cooking that nobody's allowed to question, and a list of recipes that mustn't be added to except by special permission from the head cook. I'm the head cook now. But I was an inquisitive young scullion once. I started doing a bit of cooking on my own. Unorthodox cooking, illicit cooking. A bit of real science, in fact." He was silent.

"What happened?" asked Helmholtz Watson.

The Controller sighed. "Very nearly what's going to happen to you young men. I was on the point of being sent to an island."

The words galvanized Bernard into a violent and unseemly activity. "Send *me* to an island?" He jumped up, ran across the room, and stood gesticulating in front of the Controller. "You can't send *me*. I haven't done anything. It was the others. I swear it was the others." He pointed accusingly to Helmholtz and the Savage. "Oh, please don't send me to Iceland. I promise I'll do what I ought to do. Give me another chance. Please give me another chance." The tears began to flow. "I tell you, it's their fault," he sobbed. "And not to Iceland. Oh please, your fordship, please . . . " And in a paroxysm of abjection he threw himself on his knees before the Controller. Mustapha Mond tried to make him get up; but Bernard persisted in his grovelling; the stream of words poured out inexhaustibly. In the end the Controller had to ring for his fourth secretary.

"Bring three men," he ordered, "and take Mr. Marx into a bedroom. Give him a good *soma* vaporization and then put him to bed and leave him."

The fourth secretary went out and returned with three green-uniformed twin footmen. Still shouting and sobbing, Bernard was carried out.

"One would think he was going to have his throat cut," said the Controller, as the door closed. "Whereas, if he had the smallest sense, he'd understand that his punishment is really a reward. He's being sent to an island. That's to say, he's being sent to a place where he'll meet the most interesting set of men and women to be found anywhere in the world. All the people who, for one reason or another, have got too self-consciously individual to fit into community-life. All the people who aren't satisfied with orthodoxy, who've got independent ideas of their own. Every one, in a word, who's any one. I almost envy you, Mr. Watson."

Helmholtz laughed. "Then why aren't you on an island yourself?"

"Because, finally, I preferred this," the Controller answered. "I was given the choice: to be sent to an island, where I could have got on with my pure science, or to be taken on to the Controllers' Council with the prospect of succeeding in due course to an actual Controllership. I chose this and let the science go." After a little silence, "Sometimes," he added, "I rather regret the science. Happiness is a hard master—particularly other people's happiness. A much harder master, if one isn't conditioned to accept it unquestioningly, than truth." He sighed, fell silent again, then continued in a brisker tone, "Well, duty's duty. One can't consult one's own preferences. I'm interested in truth, I like science. But truth's a menace, science is a public danger. As dangerous as it's been beneficent. It has given us the stablest equilibrium in history. China's was hopelessly insecure by comparison; even the primitive matriarchies weren't steadier than we are. Thanks, I repeat, to science. But we can't allow science to undo its own good work. That's why we so carefully limit the scope of its researches—that's why I almost got sent to an island. We don't allow it to deal with any but the most immediate problems of the moment. All other enquiries are most sedulously discouraged. It's curious," he went on after a little pause, "to read what people in the time of Our Ford used to write about scientific progress. They seemed to have imagined that it could be allowed to go on indefinitely, regardless of everything else. Knowledge was the highest good, truth the supreme value; all the rest was secondary and subordinate. True, ideas were beginning to change even then. Our Ford himself did a great deal to shift the emphasis from truth and beauty to comfort and happiness. Mass production demanded the shift. Universal happiness keeps the wheels steadily turning; truth and beauty can't. And, of course, whenever the masses seized political power, then it was happiness rather than truth and beauty that mattered. Still, in spite of everything, unrestricted scientific research was still permitted. People still went on talking about truth and beauty as though they were the sovereign goods. Right up to the time of the Nine Years' War. *That* made them change their tune all right. What's the point of truth or beauty or knowledge when the anthrax bombs are popping all around you? That was when science first began to be controlled—after the Nine Years' War. People were ready to have even their appetites controlled then. Anything for a quiet life. We've gone on controlling ever since. It hasn't been very good for truth, of course. But it's been very good for happiness. One can't have something for nothing. Happiness has got to be paid for. You're paying for it, Mr. Watson—paying because you happen to be too much interested in beauty. I was too much interested in truth; I paid too."

"But *you* didn't go to an island," said the Savage, breaking a long silence.

The Controller smiled. "That's how I paid. By choosing to serve happiness. Other people's—not mine. It's lucky," he added, after a pause, "that there are such a lot of islands in the world. I don't know what we should do without them. Put you all in the lethal chamber, I suppose. By the way, Mr. Watson, would you like a tropical climate? The Marquesas, for example; or Samoa? Or something rather more bracing?"

Helmholtz rose from his pneumatic chair. "I should like a thoroughly bad climate," he answered. "I believe one would write better if the climate were bad. If there were a lot of wind and storms, for example . . . "

The Controller nodded his approbation. "I like your spirit, Mr. Watson. I like it very much indeed. As much as I officially disapprove of it." He smiled. "What about the Falkland Islands?"

"Yes, I think that will do," Helmholtz answered. "And now, if you don't mind, I'll go and see how poor Bernard's getting on."

H. G. Wells

1866-1946

The Time Machine

1924

A man whose imagination and foresight was notable, Herbert George Wells was born to a mother who was an English maid and a father who was a shopkeeper and professional cricket player. Apprenticed to a draper at age 14, he later won a scholarship to the Normal School of Science in London (1883) where he studied biology and Darwinism under Thomas Henry Huxley. He was unable to fulfill the terms of his scholarship and so became a tutor and a part-time student in his uncle's school. During this time he wrote short stories and several were published.

During his lifetime he was a prolific writer of fiction and non-fiction on themes relating to science, technology, the future, politics, liberalism, democracy, and society, among other topics. Many of his fictional works have been adapted to film and other dramatic media, including as *War of the Worlds*, *The Island of Dr. Moreau*, and *The Time Machine*. His futuristic tales were often accurate, including the development of atomic weapons.

The selections included here are from *The Time Machine*, Wells' first real literary success first published in 1895. In the first portion, he addresses issues and themes of the true nature of reality and human perception of reality, by questioning the nature of time. The excerpt from chapter 4 relates an experience of the Time Traveller in the far future of the eighty-third century where Wells speculates on the nature of civilization and its inhabitants.

1. How can you connect Wells' futuristic view of earth with his understanding of Darwinian evolution? Do they mesh or has he taken liberal artistic license with his view of the future? Explain.
2. Technology appears to be a way to solve the many problems of modern society such as overpopulation, food, crime and related issues. Compare your views with those of Wells. Do you agree that technology and the application of science can solve these problems? Why or why not?

SOURCE:

Merriman, C.D. (2007). *H.G. Wells.* Retrieved July 27, 2007 from http://www.online-literature.com/wellshg/

SELECTION FROM:

Wells, H.G. (1924). *The Time Machine.* New York: Charles Scribner's Sons. 3-10, 29-43.

§1

THE Time Traveller (for so it will be convenient to speak of him) was expounding a recondite matter to us. His grey eyes shone and twinkled, and his usually pale face was flushed and animated. The fire burned brightly, and the soft radiance of the incandescent lights in the lilies of silver caught the bubbles that flashed and passed in our glasses. Our chairs, being his patents, embraced and caressed us rather than submitted to being sat upon, and there was that luxurious after-dinner atmosphere when thought runs gracefully free of the trammels of precision. And he put it to us in this way—marking the points with a lean forefinger—as we sat and lazily admired his earnestness over this new paradox (as we thought it) and his fecundity.

"You must follow me carefully. I shall have to controvert one or two ideas that are almost universally accepted. The geometry, for instance, they taught you at school is founded on a misconception."

"Is not that rather a large thing to expect us to begin upon?" said Filby, an argumentative person with red hair.

"I do not mean to ask you to accept anything without reasonable ground for it. You will soon admit as much as I need from you. You know of course that a mathematical line, a line of thickness *nil*, has no real existence. They taught you that? Neither has a mathematical plane. These things are mere abstractions."

"That is all right," said the Psychologist.

"Nor having only length, breadth, and thickness, can a cube have a real existence."

"There I object," said Filby. "Of course a solid body may exist. All real things—"

"So most people think. But wait a moment. Can an *instantaneous* cube exist?"

"Don't follow you," said Filby.

"Can a cube that does not last for any time at all, have a real existence?"

Filby became pensive. "Clearly," the Time Traveller proceeded, 'any real body must have extension in *four* directions: it must have Length, Breadth, Thickness, and—Duration. But through a natural infirmity of the flesh, which I will explain to you in a moment, we incline to overlook this fact. There are really four dimensions, three which we call the three planes of Space, and a fourth, Time. There is, however, a tendency to draw an unreal distinction between the former three dimensions and the latter, because it happens that our consciousness moves intermittently in one direction along the latter from the beginning to the end of our lives."

"That," said a very young man, making spasmodic efforts to relight his cigar over the lamp; "that . . . very clear indeed."

"Now, it is very remarkable that this is so extensively overlooked," continued the Time Traveller, with a slight accession of cheerfulness. "Really this is what is meant by the Fourth Dimension, though some people who talk about the Fourth Dimension do not know they mean it. It is only another way of looking at Time. *There is no difference between Time and any of the three dimensions of Space except that our consciousness moves along it*. But some foolish people have got hold of the wrong side of that idea. You have all heard what they have to say about this Fourth Dimension?"

"*I* have not," said the Provincial Mayor.

"It is simply this. That Space, as our mathematicians have it, is spoken of as having three dimensions, which one may call Length, Breadth, and Thickness, and is always definable by reference to three planes, each at right angles to the others. But some philosophical people have been asking why *three* dimensions particularly—why not another direction at right angles to the other three?—and have even tried to construct a Four-Dimensional geometry. Professor Simon Newcomb was expounding this to the New York Mathematical Society only a month or so ago. You know how on a flat surface, which has only two dimensions, we can represent a figure of a three-dimensional solid, and similarly they think that by models of three dimensions they could represent one of four—if they could master the perspective of the thing. See?"

"I think so," murmured the Provincial Mayor; and, knitting his brows, he lapsed into an introspective state, his lips moving as one who repeats mystic words. "Yes, I think I see it now," he said after some time, brightening in a quite transitory manner.

"Well, I do not mind telling you I have been at work upon this geometry of Four Dimensions for some time. Some of my results are curious. For instance, here is a portrait of a man at eight years old, another at fifteen, another at seventeen, another at twenty-three, and so on. All these are evidently sections, as it were, Three-Dimensional representations of his Four-Dimensional being, which is a fixed and unalterable thing.

"Scientific people," proceeded the Time Traveller, after the pause required for the proper assimilation of this, "know very well that Time is only a kind of Space. Here is a popular scientific diagram, a weather record. This line I trace with my finger shows the movement of the barometer. Yesterday it was so high, yesterday night it fell, then this morning it rose again, and so gently upward to here. Surely the mercury did not trace this line in any of the dimensions of Space generally recognised? But certainly it traced such a line, and that line, therefore, we must conclude was along the Time-Dimension."

"But," said the Medical Man, staring hard at a coal in the fire, "if Time is really only a fourth dimension of Space why is it, and why has it always been, regarded as something different? And why cannot we move about in Time as we move about in the other dimensions of Space?"

The Time Traveller smiled. "Are you so sure we can move freely in Space? Right and left we can go, backward and forward freely enough, and men always have done so. I admit we move freely in two dimensions. But how about up and down? Gravitation limits us there."

"Not exactly," said the Medical Man. "There are balloons."

"But before the balloons, save for spasmodic jumping and the inequalities of the surface, man had no freedom of vertical movement."

"Still they could move a little up and down," said the Medical Man.

"Easier, far easier down than up."

"And you cannot move at all in Time, you cannot get away from the present moment."

"My dear sir, that is just where you are wrong. That is just where the whole world has gone wrong. We are always getting away from the present moment. Our mental existences, which are immaterial and have no dimensions, are passing along the Time-Dimension with a uniform velocity from the cradle to the grave. Just as we should travel *down* if we began our existence fifty miles above the earth's surface."

"But the great difficulty is this," interrupted the Psychologist. "You *can* move about in all directions of Space, but you cannot move about in Time."

"That is the germ of my great discovery. But you are wrong to say that we cannot move about in Time. For instance, if I am recalling an incident very vividly I go back to the instant of its occurrence: I become absent-minded, as you say. I jump back for a moment. Of course we have no means of staying back for any length of Time, any more than a savage or an animal has of staying six feet above the ground. But a civilised man is better off than the savage in this respect. He can go up against gravitation in a balloon, and why should he not hope that ultimately he may be able to stop or accelerate his drift along the Time-Dimension, or even turn about and travel the other way?"

"Oh, *this*," began Filby, "is all—"

"Why not?" said the Time Traveller.

"It's against reason," said Filby.

"What reason?" said the Time Traveller.

"You can show black is white by argument," said Filby, "but you will never convince me."

"Possibly not," said the Time Traveller. "But now you begin to see the object of my investigations into the geometry of the Four Dimensions. Long ago I had a vague inkling of a machine—"

"To travel through Time!" exclaimed the Very Young Man.

"That shall travel indifferently in any direction of Space and Time, as the driver determines."

Filby contented himself with laughter.

"But I have experimental verification," said the Time Traveller.

"It would be remarkably convenient for the historian," the Psychologist suggested. "One might travel back and verify the accepted account of the Battle of Hastings, for instance!"

"Don't you think you would attract attention?" said the Medical Man. "Our ancestors had no great tolerance for anachronisms."

"One might get one's Greek from the very lips of Homer and Plato," the Very Young Man thought.

"In which case they would certainly plough you for the Little-go. The German scholars have improved Greek so much."

"Then there is the future," said the Very Young Man. "Just think! One might invest all one's money, leave it to accumulate at interest, and hurry on ahead!'

"To discover a society," said I, "erected on a strictly communistic basis."

"Of all the wild extravagant theories!" began the Psychologist.

"Yes, so it seemed to me, and so I never talked of it until—"

"Experimental verification!" cried I. "You are going to verify *that*?"

"The experiment!" cried Filby, who was getting brain-weary.

"Let's see your experiment anyhow" said the Psychologist, "though it's all humbug, you know."

The Time Traveller smiled round at us. Then, still smiling faintly, and with his hands deep in his trousers pockets, he walked slowly out of the room, and we heard his slippers shuffling down the long passage to his laboratory.

The Psychologist looked at us. "I wonder what he's got?"

"Some sleight-of-hand trick or other," said the Medical Man, and Filby tried to tell us about a conjuror he had seen at Burslem; but before he had finished his preface the Time Traveller came back, and Filby's anecdote collapsed . . .

§4

"IN another moment we were standing face to face, I and this fragile thing out of futurity. He came straight up to me and laughed into my eyes. The absence from his bearing of any sign of fear struck me at once. Then he turned to the two others who were following him and spoke to them in a strange and very sweet and liquid tongue.

'There were others coming, and presently a little group of perhaps eight or ten of these exquisite creatures were about me. One of them addressed me. It came into my head, oddly enough, that my voice was too harsh and deep for them. So I shook my head, and pointing to my ears, shook it again. He came a step forward, hesitated, and then touched my hand. Then I felt other soft little tentacles upon my back and shoulders. They wanted to make sure I was real. There was nothing in this at all alarming. Indeed, there was something in these pretty little people that inspired confidence—a graceful gentleness, a certain childlike ease. And besides, they looked so frail that I could fancy myself flinging the whole dozen of them about like ninepins. But I made a sudden motion to warn them when I was their little pink hands feeling at the Time Machine. Happily then, when it was not too late, I thought of a danger I had hitherto forgotten, and reaching over the bars of the machine I unscrewed the little levers that would set in motion, and put these in my pocket. Then I turned again to see what I could do in the way of communication.

"And then, looking more nearly into their features, I saw some further peculiarities in their Dresden-china type of prettiness. Their hair, which was uniformly curly, came to a sharp end at the neck and cheek; there was not the faintest suggestion of it on the face, and their ears were singularly minute. The mouths were small, with bright red, rather thin lips, and the little chins ran to a point. The eyes were large and mild; and—this may seem egotism on my part—I fancied even then that there was a certain lack of the interest I might have expected in them.

"As they made no effort to communicate with me, but simply stood round me smiling and speaking in soft cooing notes to each other, I began the conversation. I pointed to the Time Machine and to myself. Then, hesitating for a moment how to express time, I pointed to the sun. At once a quaintly pretty little figure in chequered purple and white followed my gesture, and then astonished me by imitating the sound of thunder.

"For a moment I was staggered, though the import of his gesture was plain enough. The question had come into my mind abruptly: were these creatures fools? You may hardly understand how it took me. You see, I had always anticipated that the people of the year Eight Hundred and Two Thousand odd would be incredibly in front of us in knowledge, art, everything. Then one of them suddenly asked me a question that showed him to be on the intellectual level of one of our five-year-old children—asked me, in fact, if I had come from the sun in a thunderstorm! It let loose the judgment I had suspended upon their clothes, their frail light limbs and fragile features. A flow of disappointment rushed across my mind. For a moment I felt that I had built the Time Machine in vain.

"I nodded, pointed to the sun, and gave them such a vivid rendering of a thunderclap as startled them. They all withdrew a pace or so and bowed. Then came one laughing towards me, carrying a chain of beautiful flowers altogether new to me, and put it about my neck. The idea was received with melodious applause; and presently they were all running to and fro with flowers and laughingly flinging them upon me until I was almost smothered with blossom. You who have never seen the like can scarcely imagine what delicate and wonderful flowers countless years of culture had created. Then some one suggested that their plaything should be exhibited in the nearest building, and so I was led past the sphinx of white marble, which had seemed to watch me all the while with a smile at my astonishment, towards a very grey edifice of fretted stone. As I went with them the memory of my confident anticipations of a profoundly grave and intellectual posterity came, with irresistible merriment, to my mind.

"The building had a huge entry, and was altogether of colossal dimensions. I was naturally most occupied with the growing crowd of little people, and with the big, open portals that yawned before me shadowy and mysterious. My general impression of the world I saw over their heads was of a tangled waste of beautiful bushes and flowers, a long-neglected and yet weedless garden. I saw a number of tall spikes of strange white flowers, measuring a foot perhaps across the spread of the waxen petals. They grew scattered, as if wild, among the variegated shrubs, but, as I say, I did not examine them closely at this time. The Time Machine was left deserted on the turf among the rhododendrons.

"The arch of the doorway was richly carved, but naturally I did not observe the carving very narrowly, though I fancied I saw suggestions of old Phœnician decorations as I passed through, and it struck me that they were very badly broken and weather-worn. Several more brightly-clad people met me in the doorway, and so we entered, I, dressed in dingy nineteenth-century garments, looking grotesque enough, garlanded with flowers, and surrounded by an eddying mass of bright, soft-coloured robes and shining white limbs, in a melodious whirl of laughter and laughing speech.

"The big doorway opened into a proportionately great hall hung with brown. The roof was in shadow, and the windows, partially glazed with coloured glass and partially unglazed, admitted a tempered light. The floor was made up of huge blocks of some very hard white metal, not plates nor slabs, blocks, and it was so much worn, as I judged by the going to and fro of past generations, as to be deeply channelled along the more frequented ways. Transverse to the length were innumerable tables made of slabs of polished stone, raised perhaps a foot from the floor, and upon these were heaps of fruits. Some I recognised as a kind of hypertrophied raspberry and orange, but for the most part they were strange.

"Between the tables was scattered a great number of cushions. Upon these my conductors seated themselves, signing for me to do likewise. With a pretty absence of ceremony they began to eat the fruit with their hands, flinging peel and stalks and so forth, into the round openings in the sides of the tables. I was not loth to follow their example, for I felt thirsty and hungry. As I did so I surveyed the hall at my leisure.

"And perhaps the thing that struck me most was its dilapidated look. The stained-glass windows, which displayed only a geometrical pattern, were broken many places, and the curtains that hung across the lower end were thick with dust. And it caught my eye that the corner of the marble table near me was fractured. Nevertheless, the general effect was extremely rich and picturesque. There were, perhaps, a couple of hundred people dining in the hall, and most of them, seated as near to me as they could come, were watching me with interest, their little eyes shining over the fruit they were eating. All were clad in the same soft, and yet strong, silky material.

"Fruit, by the bye, was all their diet. These people of the remote future were strict vegetarians, and while I was with them, in spite of some carnal cravings, I had to be frugivorous also. Indeed, I found afterwards that horses, cattle, sheep, dogs, had followed the Ichthyosaurus into extinction. But the fruits were very delightful; one, in particular, that seemed to be in season all the time I was there—a floury thing in a three-sided husk—was especially good, and I made it my staple. At first I was puzzled by all these strange fruits, and by the strange flowers I saw, but later I began to perceive their import.

"However, I am telling you of my fruit dinner in the distant future now. So soon as my appetite was a little checked I determined to make a resolute attempt to learn the speech of these new men of mine. Clearly that was the next thing to do. The fruits seemed a convenient thing to begin upon, and holding one of these up I began a series of interrogative sounds and gestures. I had some considerable difficulty in conveying my meaning. At first my efforts met with a stare of surprise or inextinguishable laughter, but presently a fair-haired little creature seemed to grasp my intention and repeated a name. They had to chatter and explain their business at great length to each other, and my first attempts to make their exquisite little sounds of the language caused an immense amount of amusement. However, I felt like a schoolmaster amidst children, and persisted, and presently I had a score of noun substantives at least at my command; and then I got to demonstrative pronouns, and even the verb 'to eat.' But it was slow work, and the little people soon tired and wanted to get away from my interrogations, so I determined, rather of necessity, to let them give their lessons in little doses when they felt inclined. And very little doses I found they were before long, for I never met people more indolent or more easily fatigued.

"A queer thing I soon discovered about my little hosts, and that was their lack of interest. They would come to me with eager cries of astonishment, like children, but, like children, they would soon stop examining me, and wander away after some other toy. The dinner and my conversational beginnings ended, I noted for the first time that almost all those who had surrounded me at first were gone. It is odd, too, how speedily I came to disregard these little people. I went out through the portal into the sunlit world again so soon as my hunger was satisfied. I was continually meeting more of these men of the future, who would follow me a little distance, chatter and laugh about me, and, having smiled and gesticulated in a friendly way, leave me again to my own devices.

"The calm of evening was upon the world as I emerged from the great hall, and the scene was lit by the warm glow of the setting sun. At first things were very confusing. Everything was so entirely different from the world I had known—even the flowers. The big building I had left was situated on the slope of a broad river valley, but the Thames had shifted, perhaps, a mile from its present position. I resolved to mount to the summit of a crest, perhaps a mile and a half away, from which I could get a wider view of this our planet in the year Eight Hundred and Two Thousand Seven Hundred and One, A.D. For that, I should explain, was the date the little dials of my machine recorded.

As I walked I was watchful for every impression that could possibly help to explain the condition of ruinous spendour in which I found the world—for ruinous it was. A little way up the hill, for instance, was a great heap of granite bound together by masses of aluminium, a vast labyrinth of precipitous walls and crumbled heaps, amidst which were thick heaps of very beautiful pagoda-like plants—nettles possibly—but wonderfully tinted with brown about the leaves, and incapable of stinging. It was evidently the derelict remains of some vast structure, to what end built I could not determine. It was here that I was destined, at a later date, to have a very strange experience—the first intimation of a still stranger discovery—but of that I will speak in its proper place.

"Looking round, with a sudden thought, from a terrace on which I rested for a while, I realised that there were no small houses to be seen. Apparently, the single house, and possibly even the household, had vanished. Here and there among the greenery were palace-like buildings, but the house and the cottage, which form such characteristic features of our own English landscape, had disappeared.

"'Communism,' said I to myself.

"And on the heels of that came another thought. I looked at the half-dozen little figures that were following me. Then, in a flash, I perceived that all had the same form of costume, the same soft hairless visage, and the same girlish rotundity of limb. It may seem strange, perhaps, that I had not noticed this before. But everything was so strange. Now, I saw the fact plainly enough. In costume, and in all the differences of texture and bearing that now mark off the sexes from each other, these people of the future were alike. And the children seemed to my eyes to be but the miniatures of their parents. I judged, then, that the children of that time were extremely precocious, physically at least, and I found afterwards abundant verification of my opinion.

"Seeing the ease and security in which these people were living, I felt that this close resemblance of the sexes was after all what one would expect; for the strength of the man and the softness of a woman, the institution of the family, and the differentiation of occupations are mere militant necessities of an age of physical force. Where population is balanced and abundant, much child-bearing becomes an evil rather than a blessing to the State; where violence comes but rarely and offspring are secure, there is less necessity—indeed there is no necessity—of an efficient family, and the specialisation of the sexes with reference to their children's needs disappears. We see some beginnings of this even in our own time, and in this future age it was complete. This, I must remind you, was my speculation at the time. Later, I was to appreciate how far it fell short of the reality.

"While I was musing upon these things, my attention was attracted by a pretty little structure, like a well under a cupola. I thought in a transitory way of the oddness of wells still existing, and then resumed the thread of my speculations. There were no large buildings towards the top of the hill, and as my walking powers were evidently miraculous, I was presently left alone for the first time. With a strange sense of freedom an adventure I pushed on up to the crest.

"There I found a seat of some yellow metal that I did not recognise, corroded in places with a kind of pinkish rust and half smothered in soft moss, the arm rests cast and filed into the resemblance of griffins' heads. I sat down on it, and I surveyed the broad view of our own world under the sunset of that long day. It was as sweet and fair a view as I have ever seen. The sun had already gone below the horizon and the west was flaming gold, touched with some horizontal bars of purple and crimson. Below was the valley of the Thames, in which the river lay like a band of burnished steel. I have already spoken of the great palaces dotted about among the variegated greenery, some in ruins and some still occupied. Here and there rose a white or silvery figure in the waste garden of the earth, here and there came the sharp vertical line of some cupola or obelisk. There were no hedges, no signs of proprietary rights, no evidences of agriculture; the whole earth had become a garden.

"So watching, I began to put my interpretation upon the things I had seen, and as it shaped itself to me that evening, my interpretation was something in this way. (Afterwards I found I had got only a half truth—or only a glimpse of one facet of the truth.)

"It seemed to me that I had happened upon humanity upon the wane. The ruddy sunset set me thinking of the sunset of mankind. For the first time I began to realise an odd consequence of the social effort in which we are at present engaged. And yet, come to think, it is a logical consequence enough. Strength is the outcome of need; security sets a premium on feebleness. The work of ameliorating the conditions of life—the true civilising process that makes life more and more secure—had gone steadily on to a climax. One triumph of a united humanity over Nature had followed another. Things that are now mere dreams had become projects deliberately put in hand and carried forward. And the harvest was what I saw!

"After all, the sanitation and the agriculture of today are still in the rudimentary stage. The science of our time has attacked but a little department of the field of human disease, but, even so, it spreads its operations very steadily and persistently. Our agriculture and horticulture destroy a weed just here and there and cultivate perhaps a score or so of wholesome plants, leaving the greater number to fight out a balance as they can. We improve our favourite plants and animals—and how few they are—gradually by selective breeding; now a new and better peach, now a seedless grape, now a sweeter and larger flower, now a more convenient breed of cattle. We improve them gradually, because our ideals are vague and tentative, and our knowledge is very limited; because Nature, too, is shy and slow in our clumsy hands. Some day all this will be better organised, and still better. That is the drift of the current in spite of the eddies. The whole world will be intelligent, educated, and cooperating; things will move faster and faster towards the subjugation of Nature. In the end, wisely and carefully we shall readjust the balance of animal and vegetable life to suit our human needs.

"This adjustment, I say, must have been done, and done well: done indeed for all time, in the space of Time across which my machine had leaped. The air was free from gnats, the earth from weeds or fungi; everywhere were fruits and sweet and delightful flowers; brilliant butterflies flew hither and thither. The ideal of preventive medicine was attained. Disease had been stamped out. I saw no evidence of any contagious diseases during all my stay. And I shall have to tell you later that even the processes of putrefaction and decay had been profoundly affected by these changes.

"Social triumphs, too, had been effected. I saw mankind housed in splendid shelters, gloriously clothed, and as yet I had found them engaged in no toil. There were no signs of struggle, neither social nor economical struggle. The shop, the advertisement, traffic, all that commerce which constitutes the body of our world, was gone. It was natural on that golden evening that I should jump at the idea of a social paradise. The difficulty of increasing population had been met, I guessed, and population had ceased to increase.

"But with this change in condition comes inevitably adaptations to the change. What, unless biological science is a mass of errors, is the cause of human intelligence and vigour? Hardship and freedom: conditions under which the active, strong, and subtle survive and the weaker go to the wall; conditions that put a premium upon the loyal alliance of capable men, upon self-restraint, patience, and decision. And the institution of the family, and the emotions that arise therein, the fierce jealousy, the tenderness for offspring, parental self-devotion, all found their justification and support in the imminent dangers of the young. *Now*, where are these imminent dangers? There is a sentiment arising, and it will grow, against connubial jealousy, against fierce maternity, against passion of all sorts; unnecessary things now, and things that make us uncomfortable, savage survivals, discords in a refined and pleasant life.

"I thought of the physical slightness of the people, their lack of intelligence, and those big abundant ruins, and it strengthened my belief in a perfect conquest of Nature. For after the battle comes Quiet. Humanity had been strong, energetic, and intelligent, and had used all its abundant vitality to alter the conditions under which it lived. And now came the reaction of the altered conditions.

"Under the new conditions of perfect comfort and security, that restless energy that with us is strength would become weakness. Even in our own time certain tendencies and desires, once necessary to survival, are a constant source of failure. Physical courage and the love of battle, for instance, are no great help—may even be hindrances—to a civilised man. And in a state of physical balance and security, power, intellectual as well as physical, would be out of place. For countless years I judged there had been no danger of war or solitary violence, no danger from wild beasts, no wasting disease to require strength of constitution, no need of toil. For such a life, what we should call the weak are as well equipped as the strong, are indeed no longer weak. Better equipped indeed they are, for the strong would be fretted by an energy for which there was no outlet. No doubt the exquisite beauty of the buildings I saw was the outcome of the last surgings of the now purposeless energy of mankind before it settled down into perfect harmony with the conditions under which it lived—the flourish of that triumph which began the last great peace. This has ever been the fate of energy in security; it takes to art and to eroticism, and then come languor and decay.

"Even this artistic impetus would at last die away—had almost died in the Time I saw. To adorn themselves with flowers, to dance, to sing in the sunlight; so much was left of the artistic spirit, and no more. Even that would fade in the end into a contented inactivity. We are kept keen on the grindstone of pain and necessity, and it seemed to me that here was that hateful grindstone broken at last!

"As I stood there in the gathering dark I thought that in this simple explanation I had mastered the problem of the world—mastered the whole secret of these delicious people. Possibly the checks they had devised for the increase of population had succeeded too well, and their numbers had rather diminished than kept stationary. That would account for the abandoned ruins. Very simple was my explanation, and plausible enough—as most wrong theories are!

Jonathan Swift

1667-1745

Gulliver's Travels

1726/1735

Jonathan Swift wrote prolifically during an era when science was dominated by men like Keppler, Descartes, Galileo, Newton, and Boyle. During his lifetime, Swift was considered a controversial figure, which continues to present day with over 1,900 articles published just since 1965 (Jaffe, 2005). Soon after he was born on November 30, 1667 in Ireland, his mother moved to England while he remained with an uncle in Dublin. He attended grammar school in Kilkenny until 1681 and then enrolled at Trinity College in Dublin at age 14. He received a bachelor's degree in February, 1686. Political violence in Ireland led him to England and the household of William Temple while he earned a master's degree from Oxford. He became first a deacon, then an ordained priest and vicar of the Church of Ireland (Anglican), before eventually being appointed dean of St. Patrick's Cathedral. In 1714, he returned to Ireland again for investiture.

Swift produced a voluminous body of work on many subjects, and was perhaps the most well-known writer of his time. His work has sparked disputes that continue today and that are laden with emotional content and often lacking in evidentiary substance. His writings are often satirical, with a mocking tone that perturbs many in academic fields and leads to the ongoing disputes about his life and work. When not engaged in his religious duties he was usually writing. His life and writings were strongly influenced by two women, neither of whom he married, though the first was rumored to become his wife and the second hoped it would occur. The first, Esther Johnson, was only 8 years old when Swift met her at William Temple's home while he was at Oxford. The second, Hester (Vanessa) Vanhomrigh came into his life while he was in London in 1708 and followed him back to Ireland hoping he would marry her. This never happened and she died in 1723.

Gulliver's Travels is among the best known works of Jonathan Swift. It was first published anonymously in 1726. In this work, Swift strongly criticizes the advance of technology and its application to the modern society of the eighteenth century. In the excerpt that follows Swift takes aim at the Academy and the vast and useless nature of its constructs and composition. See if you can draw parallels between Gulliver's Academy and that of the modern American university. What is valuable about the way a college or university is organized? What about its organization detracts from its mission? How do these elements contribute to or deter science?

SOURCE:

Jaffe, Lee. (2005). *Travels into Several Remote Nations of the World by Lemuel Gulliver or Gulliver's Travels by Jonathan Swift.* Retrieved August 7, 2007, from http://www.jaffebros.com/lee/gulliver/

SELECTION FROM:

Swift, Jonathan. (1933). *Gulliver's Travels.* New York: The Book League of America. 174-188.

PART THREE

A VOYAGE TO LAPUTA, BALNIBARBI, LUGGNAG, GLUBBDUBDRIB, AND JAPAN

CHAPTER FOUR

The sum of his discourse was to this effect. That about forty years ago certain persons went up to Laputa, either upon business or diversion, and after five months continuance, came back with a very little smattering in mathematics, but full of volatile spirits acquired in that airy region. That these persons upon their return began to dislike the management of every thing below, and fell into schemes of putting all arts, sciences, languages, and mechanics upon a new foot. To this end they procured a royal patent for erecting an Academy of Projectors in Lagado; and the humor prevailed so strongly among the people, that there is not a town of any consequence in the kingdom without such an academy. In these colleges the professors contrive new rules and methods of agriculture and building, and new instruments and tools for all trades and manufacture, whereby, as they undertake, one man shall do the work of ten; a palace may be built in a week, of materials so durable as to last forever without repairing. All the fruits of the earth shall come to maturity at whatever season we think fit to choose, and increase a hundred fold more than they do at present, with innumerable other happy proposals. The only inconvenience is, that none of these projects are yet brought to perfection, and in the meantime, the whole country lies miserably waste, the houses in ruins, and the people without food or clothes. By all which, instead of being discouraged, they are fifty times more violently bent upon prosecuting their schemes, driven equally on by hope and despair; that, as for himself, being not of an enterprising spirit, he was content to go on in the old forms, to live in the houses his ancestors had built, and act as they did in every part of life without innovation. That some few other persons of quality and gentry had done the same, but were looked on with an eye of contempt and ill-will, as enemies to art, ignorant, and ill commonwealth's-men, preferring their own ease and sloth before the general improvement of their country.

His Lordship added, that he would not by any further particulars prevent the pleasure I should certainly take in viewing the grand Academy, whither he was resolved I should go. He only desired me to observe a ruined building upon the side of a mountain about three miles distant, of which he gave me this account. That he had a very convenient mill within half a mile of his house, turned by a current from a large river, and sufficient for his own family as well as a great number of his tenants. That about seven years ago a club of those projectors came to him with proposals to destroy this mill, and build another on the side of that mountain, on the long ridge whereof a long canal must be cut for a repository of water, to be conveyed up by pipes and engines to supply the mill, because the wind and air upon a height agitated the water, and thereby made it fitter for motion, and because the water descending down a declivity would turn the mill with half the current of a river whose course is more upon a level. He said, that being then not very well with the court, and pressed by many of his friends, he complied with the proposal; and after employing an hundred men for two years, the work miscarried, the projectors went off, laying the blame entirely upon him; railing at him ever since, and putting others upon the same experiment, with equal assurance of success, as well as equal disappointment.

In a few days we came back to town, and his Excellency, considering the bad character he had in the Academy, would not go with me himself, but recommended me to a friend of his to bear me company thither. My lord was pleased to represent me as a great admirer of projects, and a person of much curiosity and easy belief; which indeed was not without truth, for I had myself been a sort of projector in my younger days.

CHAPTER FIVE

THIS Academy is not an entire single building, but a continuation of several houses on both sides of a street, which growing waste was purchased and applied to that use.

I was received very kindly by the Warden, and went for many days to the Academy. Every room has in it one or more projectors, and I believe I could not be in fewer than five hundred rooms.

The first man I saw was of a meager aspect, with sooty hands and face, his hair and beard long, ragged and singed in several places. His clothes, shirt, and skin were all of the same color. He had been eight years upon a project for extracting sunbeams out of cucumbers, which were to be put into vials hermetically sealed, and let out to warm the air in raw inclement summers. He told me he did not doubt in eight years more, that he should be able to supply the Governor's gardens with sunshine at a reasonable rate; but he complained that his stock was low, and entreated me to give him something as an encouragement to ingenuity, especially since this had been a very dear season for cucumbers. I made him a small present, for my lord had furnished me with money on purpose, because he knew their practice of begging from all who go to see them.

I went into another chamber, but was ready to hasten back, being almost overcome with a horrible stink. My conductor pressed me forward, conjuring me in a whisper to give no offense, which would be highly resented, and therefore I dare not so much as stop my nose. The projector of this cell was the most ancient student of the Academy; his face and beard were of a pale yellow; his hands and clothes daubed over with filth. When I was presented to him, he gave me a very close embrace (a compliment I could well have excused). His employment from his first coming into the Academy, was an operation to reduce human excrement to its original food, by separating the several parts, removing the tincture which it receives from the gall, making the odor exhale, and scumming off the saliva. He had a weekly allowance from the society, of a vessel filled with human ordure, about the size of a Bristol barrel.

I saw another at work to calcine ice into gunpowder, who likewise showed me a treatise he had written concerning the malleability of fire, which he intended to publish.

There was a most ingenious architect who had contrived a new method for building houses, by beginning at the roof, and working downwards to the foundation, which he justified to me by the like practice of those two prudent insects the bee and the spider.

There was a man born blind, who had several apprentices in his own condition: their employment was to mix colors for painters, which their master taught them to distinguish by feeling and smelling. It was indeed my misfortune to find them at that time not very perfect in their lessons, and the professor himself happened to be generally mistaken; this artist is much encouraged and esteemed by the whole fraternity.

In another apartment I was highly pleased with a projector, who had found a device of plowing the ground with hogs, to save the charges of plows, cattle, and labor. The Method is this: in an acre of ground you bury at six inches distance, and eight deep, a quantity of acorns, dates, chestnuts, and other masts or vegetables whereof these animals are fondest; then you drive six hundred or more of them into the field, where in a few days they will root up the whole ground in search of their food, and make it fit for sowing, at the same time manuring it with their dung. It is true, upon experiment they found the charge and trouble very great, and they had little or no crop. However, it is not doubted that this invention may be capable of great improvement.

I went into another room, where the walls and ceiling were all hung round with cobwebs, except a narrow passage for the artist to go in and out. At my entrance he called aloud to me not to disturb his webs. He lamented the fatal mistake the world had been so long in of using silk worms, while we had such plenty of domestic insects, who infinitely excelled the former, because they understood how to weave as well as spin. And he proposed farther, that by employing spiders, the charge of dyeing silks would be wholly saved, whereof I was fully convinced when he showed me a vast number of flies most beautifully colored, wherewith he fed his spiders, assuring us that the webs would take a tincture from them; and as he had them of all hues, he hoped to fit everybody's fancy, as soon as he could find proper food for the flies, of certain gums, oils, and other glutinous matter to give a strength and consistence to the threads.

There was an astronomer who had undertaken to place a sundial upon the great weathercock on the townhouse, by adjusting the annual and diurnal motions of the earth and sun, so as to answer and coincide with all accidental turnings by the wind.

I was complaining of a small fit of the colic; upon which my conductor led me into a room, where a great physician resided, who was famous for curing that disease by contrary operations from the same instrument. He had a large pair of bellows with a long slender muzzle of ivory. This he conveyed eight inches up the anus, and drawing in the wind, he affirmed he could make the guts as lank as a dried bladder. But when the disease was more stubborn and violent, he let in the muzzle while the bellows was full of wind, which he discharged into the body of the patient; then withdrew the instrument to replenish it, clapping his thumb strongly against the orifice of the fundament; and this being repeated three or four times, the adventitious wind would rush out, bringing the noxious along with it (like water put into a pump) and the patient recovers. I saw him try both experiments upon a dog, but could not discern any effect from the former. After the latter, the animal was ready to burst, and made so violent a discharge, as was very offensive to me and my companions. The dog died on the spot, and we left the doctor endeavoring to recover him by the same operation.

I visited many other apartments, but shall not trouble my reader with all the curiosities I observed, being studious of brevity.

I had hitherto seen only one side of the Academy, the other being appropriated to the advancers of speculative learning, of whom I shall say something when I have mentioned one illustrious person more, who is called among them *the universal artist.* He told us he had been thirty years employing his thoughts for the improvement of human life. He had two large rooms full of wonderful curiosities, and fifty men at work. Some were condensing air into a dry tangible substance, by extracting the nitre, and letting the aqueous or fluid particles percolate; others softening marbles for pillows and pin-cushions; others petrifying the hoofs of a living horse to preserve them from foundering. The artist himself was at that time busy upon two great designs; the first, to sow land with chaff, wherein he affirmed the true seminal virtue to be contained, as he demonstrated by several experiments which I was not skillful enough to comprehend. The other was, by a certain composition of gums, minerals, and vegetables outwardly applied, to prevent the growth of wool upon two young lambs; and he hoped in a reasonable time to propagate the breed of naked sheep all over the kingdom.

We crossed a walk to the other part of the Academy, where, as I have already said, the projectors in speculative learning resided. The first professor I saw was in a very large room, with forty pupils about him. After salutation, observing me to look earnestly upon a frame, which took up the greatest part of both the length and breadth of the room, he said perhaps I might wonder to see him employed in a project for improving speculative knowledge by practical and mechanical operations. But the world would soon be sensible of its usefulness, and he flattered himself that a more noble exalted thought never sprang in any other man's head. Everyone knew how laborious the usual method is of attaining to arts and sciences; whereas by his contrivance, the most ignorant person at a reasonable charge, and with a little bodily labor, may write books in philosophy, poetry, politics, law, mathematics, and theology, without the least assistance from genius or study. He then led me to the frame, about the sides whereof all his pupils stood in ranks. It was twenty feet square, placed in the middle of the room. The superficies was composed of several bits of wood, about the bigness of a die, but some larger than others. They were all linked together by slender wires. These bits of wood were covered on every square with paper pasted on them, and on these papers were written all the words of their language in their several moods, tenses, and declensions, but without any order. The professor then desired me to observe, for he was going to set his engine at work. The pupils at his command took each of them hold of an iron handle, whereof there were forty fixed round the edges of the frame, and giving them a sudden turn, the whole disposition of the words was entirely changed. He then commanded thirty-six of the lads to read the several lines softly as they appeared upon the frame; and where they found three or four words together that might make part of a sentence, they dictated to the four remaining boys who were scribes. This work was repeated three or four times, and at every turn the engine was so contrived, that the words shifted into new places, as the square bits of wood moved upside down.

Six hours a day the young students were employed in this labor, and the professor showed me several volumes in large folio already collected, of broken sentences, which he intended to piece together, and out of those rich materials to give the world a complete body of all arts and sciences; which however might be still improved, and much expedited, if the public would raise a fund for making and employing five hundred such frames in Lagado, and oblige the managers to contribute in common their several collections.

He assured me, that this invention had employed all his thoughts from his youth, that he had emptied[1] the whole vocabulary into his frame, and made the strictest computation of the general proportion there is in books between the numbers of particles, nouns, and verbs, and other parts of speech.

I made my humblest acknowledgment to this illustrious person for his great communicativeness, and promised if ever I had the good fortune to return to my native country, that I would do him justice, as the sole inventor of this wonderful machine; the form and contrivance of which I desired leave to delineate upon paper, as in the figure here annexed.[2] I told him, although it were the custom of our learned in Europe to steal inventions from each other, who had thereby at least this advantage, that it became a controversy which was the right owner, yet I would take such caution, that he should have the honor entire without a rival.

We next went to the school of languages, where three professors sat in consultation upon improving that of their own country.

The first project was to shorten discourse by cutting polysyllables into one, and leaving out verbs and participles; because in reality all things imaginable are but nouns.

The other project was a scheme for entirely abolishing all words whatsoever; and this was urged as a great advantage in point of health as well as brevity. For it is plain that every word we speak is in some degree a diminution of our lungs by corrosion, and consequently contributes to the shortening of our lives. An expedient was therefore offered, that since words are only names for *things*, it would be more convenient for all men to carry about them such things as were necessary to express the particular business they are to discourse on. And this invention would certainly have taken place, to the great ease as well as health of the subject, if the women in conjunction with the vulgar and illiterate had not threatened to raise a rebellion, unless they might be allowed the liberty to speak with their tongues, after the manner of their ancestors; such constant irreconcilable enemies to science are the common people. However, many of the most learned and wise adhere to the new scheme of expressing themselves by things, which has only this inconvenience attending it, that if a man's business be very great, and of various kinds,

---

1 Emptied *Faulkner:* employed *1726, 1727.*

2 See Plate V, page 313.

he must be obliged in proportion to carry a greater bundle of things upon his back, unless he can afford one or two strong servants to attend him. I have often beheld two of those sages almost sinking under the weight of their packs, like pedlars among us; who, when they met in the streets would lay down their loads, open their sacks, and hold conversation for an hour together; then put up their implements, help each other to resume their burdens, and take their leave.

But for short conversations a man may carry implements in his pockets and under his arms, enough to supply him, and in his house he cannot be at a loss. Therefore the room where company meet who practise this art, is full of all things ready at hand, requisite to furnish matter for this kind of artificial converse.

Another great advantage proposed by this invention was that it would serve as a universal language to be understood in all civilized nations, whose goods and utensils are generally of the same kind, or nearly resembling, so that their uses might easily be comprehended. And thus ambassadors would be qualified to treat with foreign princes or ministers of state, to whose tongues they were utter strangers.

I was at the mathematical school, where the master taught his pupils after a method scarce imaginable to us in Europe. The proposition and demonstration were fairly written on a thin wafer, with ink composed of a cephalic tincture. This the student was to swallow upon a fasting stomach, and for three days following eat nothing but bread and water. As the wafer digested, the tincture mounted to his brain, bearing the proposition along with it. But the success has not hitherto been answerable, partly by some error in the *quantum* or composition, and partly by the perverseness of lads, to whom this bolus is so nauseous, that they generally steal aside, and discharge it upwards before it can operate; neither have they been yet persuaded to use so long an abstinence as the prescription requires.

Mary Shelley

1797-1851

Frankenstein

1912

Mary Wollenstonecraft Godwin was born in London, the daughter of feminist Mary Wollenstonecraft and the philosophical anarchist William Godwin. Her mother died soon after her birth leaving her to be raised by a distant father and a cruel step-mother. She was well educated at home by a series of tutors, becoming well versed in the literature of the Enlightenment, including the works of Blake, Coleridge, Defoe, among others. At about age 16, she met the romantic poet Percy Bysshe Shelley, and in 1814, they eloped to France spending six weeks touring the country. The elopement caused an estrangement with her father until the couple was formally married.

During a rainy summer evening of 1816 in Geneva, Mary, Lord Byron, and Byron's physician, Polidori were reading French translations of German ghost stories. This evening inspired her to write perhaps the most famous of modern horror tales. She originally planned a ghost story "which would speak to the mysterious fears of our nature and awake thrilling horror—one to make the reader dread to loo1k round, to curdle the blood, and to quicken the beatings of the heart" (Teuber). The full novel was finished within a year and published anonymously in 1818. Many thought her husband was the author of the work, and it received mixed reviews. It has gone on to become the basis for an innumerable number of plays, movies, and commentaries and remains a work of depth and complexity.

1. What is the meaning of this story?
2. Do you feel the use of Frankenstein or Frankenstein's monster in modern convention has become stretched or overused, compared to the original? Why or how?
3. How does the tale of Frankenstein fit with modern scientific practice? Are there parallels, and what specific areas do you see such parallels or overlap?

SOURCES:

Meriman, C.D. (2006). *Mary Wollenstonecraft Shelley.* Retrieved on March 15, 2008 from http://www.online-literature.com/shelley_mary/

Teuber, Andreas. *Mary Wollenstonecraft Shelley.* Retrieved March 15, 2008, from http://people.brandeis.edu/~teuber/shelleybio.html

SELECTION FROM:

Shelley, Mary. (1912). *Frankenstein; or The Modern Prometheus.* New York: E.P Dutton & Co. 27-33, 39-42, 43-50, 51-53, 99-103.

CHAPTER II

WE were brought up together; there was not quite a year difference in our ages. I need not say that we were strangers to any species of disunion or dispute. Harmony was the soul of our companionship, and the diversity and contrast that subsisted in our characters drew us nearer together. Elizabeth was of a calmer and more concentrated disposition; but, with all my ardour, I was capable of a more intense application, and was more deeply smitten with the thirst for knowledge. She busied herself with following the aerial creations of the poets; and in the majestic and wondrous scenes which surrounded our Swiss home—the sublime shapes of the mountains; the changes of the seasons; tempest and calm; the silence of winter, and the life and turbulence of our Alpine summers,—she found ample scope for admiration and delight. While my companion contemplated with a serious and satisfied spirit the magnificent appearances of things, I delighted in investigating their causes. The world was to me a secret which I desired to divine. Curiosity, earnest research to learn the hidden laws of nature, gladness akin to rapture, as they were unfolded to me, are among the earliest sensations I can remember.

On the birth of a second son, my junior by seven years, my parents gave up entirely their wandering life, and fixed themselves in their native country. We possessed a house in Geneva, and a *campagne* on Belrive, the eastern shore of the lake, at the distance of rather more than a league from the city. We resided principally in the latter, and the lives of my parents were passed in considerable seclusion. It was my temper to avoid a crowd, and to attach myself fervently to a few. I was indifferent, therefore, to my schoolfellows in general; but I united myself in the bonds of the closest friendship to one among them. Henry Clerval was the son of a merchant of Geneva. He was a boy of singular talent and fancy. He loved enterprise, hardship, and even danger, for its own sake. He was deeply read in books of chivalry and romance. He composed heroic songs, and began to write many a tale of enchantment and knightly adventure. He tried to make us act plays, and to enter into masquerades, in which the characters were drawn from the heroes of Roncesvalles, of the Round Table of King Arthur, and the chivalrous train who shed their blood to redeem the holy sepulchre from the hands of the infidels.

No human being could have passed a happier childhood than myself. My parents were possessed by the very spirit of kindness and indulgence. We felt that they were not the tyrants to rule our lot according to their caprice, but the agents and creators of all the many delights which we enjoyed. When I mingled with other families, I distinctly discerned how peculiarly fortunate my lot was, and gratitude assisted the development of filial love.

My temper was sometimes violent, and my passions vehement; but by some law in my temperature they were turned, not towards childish pursuits, but to an eager desire to learn, and not to learn all things indiscriminately. I confess that neither the structure of languages, nor the code of governments, nor the politics of various states, possessed attractions for me. It was the secrets of heaven and earth that I desired to learn; and whether it was the outward substance of things, or the inner spirit of nature and the mysterious soul of man that occupied me, still my enquiries were directed to the metaphysical, or, in its highest sense, the physical secrets of the world.

Meanwhile Clerval occupied himself, so to speak, with the moral relations of things. The busy stage of life, the virtues of heroes, and the actions of men, were his theme; and his hope and his dream was to become one among those whose names are recorded in story, as the gallant and adventurous benefactors of our species. The saintly soul of Elizabeth shone like a shrine-dedicated lamp in our peaceful home. Her sympathy was ours; her smile, her soft voice, the sweet glance of her celestial eyes, were ever there to bless and animate us. She was the living spirit of love to soften and attract: I might have become sullen in my study, rough through the ardour of my nature, but that she was there to subdue me to a semblance of her own gentleness. And Clerval—could aught ill entrench on the noble spirit of Clerval?—yet he might not have been so perfectly humane, so thoughtful in his generosity—so full of kindness and tenderness amidst his passion for adventurous exploit, had she not unfolded to him the real loveliness of beneficence, and made the doing good the end and aim of his soaring ambition.

I feel exquisite pleasure in dwelling on the recollections of childhood, before misfortune had tainted my mind, and changed its bright visions of extensive usefulness into gloomy and narrow reflections upon self. Besides, in drawing the picture of my early days, I also record those events which led, by insensible steps, to my after tale of misery: for when I would account to myself for the birth of that passion, which afterwards ruled my destiny, I find it arise, like a mountain river, from ignoble and almost forgotten sources; but, swelling as it proceeded, it became the torrent which, in its course, has swept away all my hopes and joys.

Natural philosophy is the genius that has regulated my fate; I desire, therefore, in this narration, to state those facts which led to my predilection for that science. When I was thirteen years of age, we all went on a party of pleasure to the baths near Thonon; the inclemency of the weather obliged us to remain a day confined to the inn. In this house I chanced to find a volume of the works of Cornelius Agrippa. I opened it with apathy; the theory which he attempts to demonstrate, and the wonderful facts which he relates, soon changed this feeling into enthusiasm. A new light seemed to dawn upon my mind; and, bounding with joy, I communicated my discovery to my father. My father looked carelessly at the title page of my book, and said, 'Ah! Cornelius Agrippa! My dear Victor, do not waste your time upon this; it is sad trash.'

If, instead of this remark, my father had taken the pains to explain to me, that the principles of Agrippa had been entirely exploded, and that a modern system of science had been introduced, which possessed much greater powers than the ancient, because the powers of the latter were chimerical, while those of the former were real and practical; under such circumstances, I should certainly have thrown Agrippa aside, and have contented my imagination, warmed as it was, by returning with greater ardour to my former studies. It is even possible, that the train of my ideas would never have received the fatal impulse that led to my ruin.

But the cursory glance my father had taken of my volume by no means assured me that he was acquainted with its contents; and I continued to read with the greatest avidity.

When I returned home, my first care was to procure the whole works of this author, and afterwards of Paracelsus and Albertus Magnus. I read and studied the wild fancies of these writers with delight; they appeared to me treasures known to few beside myself. I have described myself as always having been embued with a fervent longing to penetrate the secrets of nature. In spite of the intense labour and wonderful discoveries of modern philosophers, I always came from my studies discontented and unsatisfied. Sir Isaac Newton is said to have avowed that he felt like a child picking up shells beside the great and unexplored ocean of truth. Those of his successors in each branch of natural philosophy with whom I was acquainted appeared, even to my boy's apprehensions, as tyros engaged in the same pursuit.

The untaught peasant beheld the elements around him, and was acquainted with their practical uses. The most learned philosopher knew little more. He had partially unveiled the face of Nature, but her immortal lineaments were still a wonder and a mystery. He might dissect, anatomise, and give names; but, not to speak of a final cause, causes in their secondary and tertiary grades were utterly unknown to him. I had gazed upon the fortifications and impediments that seemed to keep human beings from entering the citadel of nature, and rashly and ignorantly I had repined.

But here were books, and here were men who had penetrated deeper and knew more. I took their word for all that they averred, and I became their disciple. It may appear strange that such should arise in the eighteenth century; but while I followed the routine of education in the schools of Geneva, I was, to a great degree, self taught with regard to my favourite studies. My father was not scientific, and I was left to struggle with a child's blindness, added to a student's thirst for knowledge. Under the guidance of my new preceptors, I entered with the greatest diligence into the search of the philosopher's stone and the elixir of life; but the latter soon obtained my undivided attention. Wealth was an inferior object; but what glory would attend the discovery, if I could banish disease from the human frame, and render man invulnerable to any but a violent death!

Nor were these my only visions. The raising of ghosts or devils was a promise liberally accorded by my favourite authors, the fulfilment of which I most eagerly sought; and if my incantations were always unsuccessful, I attributed the failure rather to my own inexperience and mistake than to a want of skill or fidelity in my instructors. And thus for a time I was occupied by exploded systems, mingling, like an unadept, a thousand contradictory theories, and floundering desperately in a very slough of multifarious knowledge, guided by an ardent imagination and childish reasoning, till an accident again changed the current of my ideas.

When I was about fifteen years old we had retired to our house near Belrive, when we witnessed a most violent and terrible thunder-storm. It advanced from behind the mountains of Jura; and the thunder burst at once with frightful loudness from various quarters of the heavens. I remained, while the storm lasted, watching its progress with curiosity and delight. As I stood at the door, on a sudden I beheld a stream of fire issue from an old and beautiful oak, which stood about twenty yards from our house; and so soon as the dazzling light vanished the oak had disappeared, and nothing remained but a blasted stump. When we visited it the next morning, we found the tree shattered in a singular manner. It was not splintered by the shock, but entirely reduced to thin ribands of wood. I never beheld any thing so utterly destroyed.

Before this I was not unacquainted with the more obvious laws of electricity. On this occasion a man of great research in natural philosophy was with us, and, excited by this catastrophe, he entered on the explanation of a theory which he had formed on the subject of electricity and galvanism, which was at once new and astonishing to me. All that he said threw greatly into the shade Cornelius Agrippa, Albertus Magnus, and Paracelsus, the lords of my imagination; but by some fatality the overthrow of these men disinclined me to pursue my accustomed studies. It seemed to me as if nothing would or could ever be known. All that had so long engaged my attention suddenly grew despicable. By one of those caprices of the mind, which we are perhaps most subject to in early youth, I at once gave up my former occupations; set down natural history and all its progeny as a deformed and abortive creation; and entertained the greatest disdain for a would-be science, which could never even step within the threshold of real knowledge. In this mood of mind I betook myself to the mathematics, and the branches of study appertaining to that science, as being built upon secure foundations, and so worthy of my consideration.

Thus strangely are our souls constructed, and by such slight ligaments are we bound to prosperity or ruin. When I look back, it seems to me as if this almost miraculous change of inclination and will was the immediate suggestion of the guardian angel of my life—the last effort made by the spirit of preservation to avert the storm that was even then hanging in the stars, and ready to envelope me. Her victory was announced by an unusual tranquillity and gladness of soul, which followed the relinquishing of my ancient and latterly tormenting studies. It was thus that I was to be taught to associate evil with their prosecution, happiness with their disregard.

It was a strong effort of the spirit of good; but it was ineffectual. Destiny was too potent, and her immutable laws had decreed my utter and terrible destruction.

CHAPTER III

[* * *]

Such were my reflections during the first two or three days of my residence at Ingolstadt, which were chiefly spent in becoming acquainted with the localities, and the principal residents in my new abode. But as the ensuing week commenced, I thought of the information which M. Krempe had given me concerning the lectures. And although I could not consent to go and hear that little conceited fellow deliver sentences out of a pulpit, I recollected what he had said of M. Waldman, whom I had never seen, as he had hitherto been out of town.

Partly from curiosity, and partly from idleness, I went into the lecturing room, which M. Waldman entered shortly after. This professor was very unlike his colleague. He appeared about fifty years of age, but with an aspect expressive of the greatest benevolence; a few grey hairs covered his temples, but those at the back of his head were nearly black. His person was short, but remarkably erect; and his voice the sweetest I had ever heard. He began his lecture by a recapitulation of the history of chemistry, and the various improvements made by different men of learning, pronouncing with fervour the names of the most distinguished discoverers. He then took a cursory view of the present state of the science, and explained many of its elementary terms. After having made a few preparatory experiments, he concluded with a panegyric upon modern chemistry, the terms of which I shall never forget:—

"The ancient teachers of this science," said he, "promised impossibilities, and performed nothing. The modern masters promise very little; they know that metals cannot be transmuted, and that the elixir of life is a chimera. But these philosophers, whose hands seem only made to dabble in dirt, and their eyes to pore over the microscope or crucible, have indeed performed miracles. They penetrate into the recesses of nature, and show how she works in her hiding places. They ascend into the heavens: they have discovered how the blood circulates, and the nature of the air we breathe. They have acquired new and almost unlimited powers; they can command the thunders of heaven, mimic the earthquake, and even mock the invisible world with its own shadows."

Such were the professor's words—rather let me say such the words of fate, enounced to destroy me. As he went on, I felt as if my soul were grappling with a palpable enemy; one by one the various keys were touched which formed the mechanism of my being: chord after chord was sounded, and soon my mind was filled with one thought, one conception, one purpose. So much has been done, exclaimed the soul of Frankenstein—more, far more, will I achieve: treading in the steps already marked, I will pioneer a new way, explore unknown powers, and unfold to the world the deepest mysteries of creation.

I closed not my eyes that night. My internal being was in a state of insurrection and turmoil; I felt that order would thence arise, but I had no power to produce it. By degrees, after the morning's dawn, sleep came. I awoke, and my yesternight's thoughts were as a dream. There only remained a resolution to return to my ancient studies, and to devote myself to a science for which I believed myself to possess a natural talent. On the same day, I paid M. Waldman a visit. His manners in private were even more mild and attractive than in public; for there was a certain dignity in his mien during his lecture, which in his own house was replaced by the greatest affability and kindness. I gave him pretty nearly the same account of my former pursuits as I had given to his fellow-professor. He heard with attention the little narration concerning my studies, and smiled at the names of Cornelius Agrippa and Paracelsus, but without the contempt that M. Krempe had exhibited. He said, that "these were men to whose indefatigable zeal modern philosophers were indebted for most of the foundations of their knowledge. They had left to us, as an easier task, to give new names, and arrange in connected classifications, the facts which they in a great degree had been the instruments of bringing to light. The labours of men of genius, however erroneously directed, scarcely ever fail in ultimately turning to the solid advantage of mankind." I listened to his statement, which was delivered without any presumption or affectation; and then added, that his lecture had removed my prejudices against modern chemists; I expressed myself in measured terms, with the modesty and deference due from a youth to his instructor, without letting escape (inexperience in life would have made me ashamed) any of the enthusiasm which stimulated my intended labours. I requested his advice concerning the books I ought to procure.

'I am happy,' said M. Waldman, 'to have gained a disciple; and if your application equals your ability, I have no doubt of your success. Chemistry is that branch of natural philosophy in which the greatest improvements have been and may be made: it is on that account that I have made it my peculiar study; but at the same time I have not neglected the other branches of science. A man would make but a very sorry chemist if he attended to that department of human knowledge alone. If your wish is to become really a man of science, and not merely a petty experimentalist, I should advise you to apply to every branch of natural philosophy, including mathematics."

He then took me into his laboratory, and explained to me the uses of his various machines; instructing me as to what I ought to procure, and promising me the use of his own when I should have advanced far enough in the science not to derange their mechanism. He also gave me the list of books which I had requested; and I took my leave.

Thus ended a day memorable to me: it decided my future destiny.

CHAPTER IV

FROM this day natural philosophy, and particularly chemistry, in the most comprehensive sense of the term, became nearly my sole occupation. I read with ardour those works, so full of genius and discrimination, which modern enquirers have written on these subjects. I attended the lectures, and cultivated the acquaintance, of the men of science of the university; and I found even in M. Krempe a great deal of sound sense and real information, combined, it is true, with a repulsive physiognomy and manners, but not on that account the less valuable. In M. Waldman I found a true friend. His gentleness was never tinged by dogmatism; and his instructions were given with an air of frankness and good nature, that banished every idea of pedantry. In a thousand ways he smoothed for me the path of knowledge, and made the most abstruse inquiries clear and facile to my apprehension. My application was at first fluctuating and uncertain; it gained strength as I proceeded, and soon became so ardent and eager, that the stars often disappeared in the light of morning whilst I was yet engaged in my laboratory.

As I applied so closely, it may be easily conceived that my progress was rapid. My ardour was indeed the astonishment of the students, and my proficiency that of the masters. Professor Krempe often asked me, with a sly smile, how Cornelius Agrippa went on? whilst M. Waldman expressed the most heartfelt exultation in my progress. Two years passed in this manner, during which I paid no visit to Geneva, but was engaged, heart and soul, in the pursuit of some discoveries, which I hoped to make. None but those who have experienced them can conceive of the enticements of science. In other studies you go as far as others have gone before you, and there is nothing more to know; but in a scientific pursuit there is continual food for discovery and wonder. A mind of moderate capacity, which closely pursues one study, must infallibly arrive at great proficiency in that study; and I, who continually sought the attainment of one object of pursuit, and was solely wrapt up in this, improved so rapidly, that, at the end of two years, I made some discoveries in the improvement of some chemical instruments, which procured me great esteem and admiration at the university. When I had arrived at his point, and had become as well acquainted with the theory and practice of natural philosophy as depended on the lessons of any of the professors at Ingolstadt, my residence there being no longer conducive to my improvement, I thought of returning to my friends and my native town, when an incident happened that protracted my stay.

One of the phenomena which had peculiarly attracted my attention was the structure of the human frame, and, indeed, any animal endued with life. Whence, I often asked myself, did the principle of life proceed? It was a bold question, and one which has ever been considered as a mystery; yet with how many things are we upon the brink of becoming acquainted, if cowardice or carelessness did not restrain our enquiries. I revolved these circumstances in my mind, and determined thenceforth to apply myself more particularly to those branches of natural philosophy which relate to physiology. Unless I had been animated by an almost supernatural enthusiasm, my application to this study would have been irksome, and almost intolerable. To examine the causes of life, we must first have recourse to death. I became acquainted with the science of anatomy: but this was not sufficient; I must also observe the natural decay and corruption of the human body. In my education my father had taken the greatest precautions that my mind should be impressed with no supernatural horrors. I do not ever remember to have trembled at a tale of superstition, or to have feared the apparition of a spirit. Darkness had no effect upon my fancy; and a churchyard was to me merely the receptacle of bodies deprived of life, which, from being the seat of beauty and strength, had become food for the worm. Now I was led to examine the cause and progress of this decay, and forced to spend days and nights in vaults and charnel-houses. My attention was fixed upon every object the most insupportable to the delicacy of the human feelings. I saw how the fine form of man was degraded and wasted; I beheld the corruption of death succeed to the blooming cheek of life; I saw how the worm inherited the wonders of the eye and brain. I paused, examining and analysing all the minutiæ of causation, as exemplified in the change from life to death, and death to life, until from the midst of this darkness a sudden light broke in upon me—a light so brilliant and wondrous, yet so simple, that while I became dizzy with the immensity of the prospect which it illustrated, I was surprised, that among so many men of genius who had directed their enquiries towards the same science, that I alone should be reserved to discover so astonishing a secret.

Remember, I am not recording the vision of a madman. The sun does not more certainly shine in the heavens, than that which I now affirm is true. Some miracle might have produced it, yet the stages of the discovery were distinct and probable. After days and nights of incredible labour and fatigue, I succeeded in discovering the cause of generation and life; nay, more, I became myself capable of bestowing animation upon lifeless matter.

The astonishment which I had at first experienced on this discovery soon gave place to delight and rapture. After so much time spent in painful labour, to arrive at once at the summit of my desires, was the most gratifying consummation of my toils. But this discovery was so great and overwhelming, that all the steps by which I had been progressively led to it were obliterated, and I beheld only the result. What had been the study and desire of the wisest men since the creation of the world was now within my grasp. Not that, like a magic scene, it all opened upon me at once: the information I had obtained was of a nature rather to direct my endeavours so soon as I should point them towards the object of my search, than to exhibit that object already accomplished. I was like the Arabian who had been buried with the dead, and found a passage to life, aided only by one glimmering, and seemingly ineffectual, light.

I see by your eagerness, and the wonder and hope which your eyes express, my friend, that you expect to be informed of the secret with which I am acquainted; that cannot be: listen patiently until the end of my story, and you will easily perceive why I am reserved upon that subject. I will not lead you on, unguarded and ardent as I then was, to your destruction and infallible misery. Learn from me, if not by my precepts, at least by my example, how dangerous is the acquirement of knowledge, and how much happier that man is who believes his native town to be the world, than he who aspires to become greater than his nature will allow.

When I found so astonishing a power placed within my hands, I hesitated a long time concerning the manner in which I should employ it. Although I possessed the capacity of bestowing animation, yet to prepare a frame for the reception of it, with all its intricacies of fibres, muscles, and veins, still remained a work of inconceivable difficulty and labour. I doubted at first whether I should attempt the creation of a being like myself, or one of simpler organisation; but my imagination was too much exalted by my first success to permit me to doubt of my ability to give life to an animal as complex and wonderful as man. The materials at present within my command hardly appeared adequate to so arduous an undertaking; but I doubted not that I should ultimately succeed. I prepared myself for a multitude of reverses; my operations might be incessantly baffled, and at last my work be imperfect: yet, when I considered the improvement which every day takes place in science and mechanics, I was encouraged to hope my present attempts would at least lay the foundations of future success. Nor could I consider the magnitude and complexity of my plan as any argument of its impracticability. It was with these feelings that I began the creation of a human being. As the minuteness of the parts formed a great hindrance to my speed, I resolved, contrary to my first intention, to make the being of a gigantic stature; that is to say, about eight feet in height, and proportionably large. After having formed this determination, and having spent some months in successfully collecting and arranging my materials, I began.

No one can conceive the variety of feelings which bore me onwards, like a hurricane, in the first enthusiasm of success. Life and death appeared to me ideal bounds, which I should first break through, and pour a torrent of light into our dark world. A new species would bless me as its creator and source; many happy and excellent natures would owe their being to me. No father could claim the gratitude of his child so completely as I should deserve theirs. Pursuing these reflections, I thought, that if I could bestow animation upon lifeless matter, I might in process of time (although I now found it impossible) renew life where death had apparently devoted the body to corruption.

These thoughts supported my spirits, while I pursued my undertaking with unremitting ardour. My cheek had grown pale with study, and my person had become emaciated with confinement. Sometimes, on the very brink of certainty, I failed; yet still I clung to the hope which the next day or the next hour might realise. One secret which I alone possessed was the hope to which I had dedicated myself; and the moon gazed on my midnight labours, while, with unrelaxed and breathless eagerness, I pursued nature to her hiding-places. Who shall conceive the horrors of my secret toil, as I dabbled among the unhallowed damps of the grave, or tortured the living animal to animate the lifeless clay? My limbs now tremble, and my eyes swim with the remembrance; but then a resistless, and almost frantic, impulse, urged me forward; I seemed to have lost all soul or sensation but for this one pursuit. It was indeed but a passing trance, that only made me feel with renewed acuteness so soon as, the unnatural stimulus ceasing to operate, I had returned to my old habits. I collected bones from charnel-houses; and disturbed, with profane fingers, the tremendous secrets of the human frame. In a solitary chamber, or rather cell, at the top of the house, and separated from all the other apartments by a gallery and staircase, I kept my workshop of filthy creation: my eye-balls were starting from their sockets in attending to the details of my employment. The dissecting room and the slaughter-house furnished many of my materials; and often did my human nature turn with loathing from my occupation, whilst, still urged on by an eagerness which perpetually increased, I brought my work near to a conclusion.

The summer months passed while I was thus engaged, heart and soul, in one pursuit. It was a most beautiful season; never did the fields bestow a more plentiful harvest, or the vines yield a more luxuriant vintage: but my eyes were insensible to the charms of nature. And the same feelings which made me neglect the scenes around me caused me also to forget those friends who were so many miles absent, and whom I had not seen for so long a time. I knew my silence disquieted them; and I well remembered the words of my father: 'I know that while you are pleased with yourself, you will think of us with affection, and we shall hear regularly from you. You must pardon me if I regard any interruption in your correspondence as a proof that your other duties are equally neglected.'

I knew well, therefore, what would be my father's feelings; but I could not tear my thoughts from my employment, loathsome in itself, but which had taken an irresistible hold of my imagination. I wished, as it were, to procrastinate all that related to my feelings of affection until the great object, which swallowed up every habit of my nature, should be completed.

I then thought that my father would be unjust if he ascribed my neglect to vice, or faultiness on my part; but I am now convinced that he was justified in conceiving that I should not be altogether free from blame. A human being in perfection ought always to preserve a calm and peaceful mind, and never to allow passion or a transitory desire to disturb his tranquillity. I do not think that the pursuit of knowledge is an exception to this rule. If the study to which you apply yourself has a tendency to weaken your affections, and to destroy your taste for those simple pleasures in which no alloy can possibly mix, then that study is certainly unlawful, that is to say, not befitting the human mind. If this rule were always observed; if no man allowed any pursuit whatsoever to interfere with the tranquillity of his domestic affections, Greece had not been enslaved; Cæsar would have spared his country; America would have been discovered more gradually; and the empires of Mexico and Peru had not been destroyed.

But I forget that I am moralising in the most interesting part of my tale; and your looks remind me to proceed.

My father made no reproach in his letters, and only took notice of my silence by enquiring into my occupations more particularly than before. Winter, spring, and summer passed away during my labours; but I did not watch the blossom or the expanding leaves—sights which before always yielded me supreme delight—so deeply was I engrossed in my occupation. The leaves of that year had withered before my work drew near to a close; and now every day showed me more plainly how well I had succeeded. But my enthusiasm was checked by my anxiety, and I appeared rather like one doomed by slavery to toil in the mines, or any other unwholesome trade, than an artist occupied by his favourite employment. Every night I was oppressed by a slow fever, and I became nervous to a most painful degree; the fall of a leaf startled me, and I shunned my fellow-creatures as if I had been guilty of a crime. Sometimes I grew alarmed at the wreck I perceived that I had become; the energy of my purpose alone sustained me: my labours would soon end, and I believed that exercise and amusement would then drive away incipient disease; and I promised myself both of these when my creation should be complete.

CHAPTER V

IT was on a dreary night of November, that I beheld the accomplishment of my toils. With an anxiety that almost amounted to agony, I collected the instruments of life around me, that I might infuse a spark of being into the lifeless thing that lay at my feet. It was already one in the morning; the rain pattered dismally against the panes, and my candle was nearly burnt out, when, by the glimmer of the half-extinguished light, I saw the dull yellow eye of the creature open; it breathed hard, and a convulsive motion agitated its limbs.

How can I describe my emotions at this catastrophe, or how delineate the wretch whom with such infinite pains and care I had endeavoured to form? His limbs were in proportion, and I had selected his features as beautiful. Beautiful!—Great God! His yellow skin scarcely covered the work of muscles and arteries beneath; his hair was of a lustrous black, and flowing; his teeth of a pearly whiteness; but these luxuriances only formed a more horrid contrast with his watery eyes, that seemed almost of the same colour as the dun white sockets in which they were set, his shrivelled complexion and straight black lips.

The different accidents of life are not so changeable as the feelings of human nature. I had worked hard for nearly two years, for the sole purpose of infusing life into an inanimate body. For this I had deprived myself of rest and health. I had desired it with an ardour that far exceeded moderation; but now that I had finished the beauty of the dream vanished and breathless horror and disgust filled my heart. Unable to endure the aspect of the being I had created, I rushed out of the room, and continued a long time traversing my bedchamber, unable to compose my mind to sleep. At length lassitude succeeded to the tumult I had before endured, and I threw myself on the bed in my clothes, endeavouring to seek a few moments of forgetfulness. But it was in vain: I slept, indeed, but I was disturbed by the wildest dreams. I thought I saw Elizabeth, in the bloom of health, walking in the streets of Ingolstadt. Delighted and surprised, I embraced her; but as I imprinted the first kiss on her lips, they became livid with the hue of death; her features appeared to change, and I thought that I held the corpse of my dead mother in my arms; a shroud enveloped her form, and I saw the grave-worms crawling in the folds of the flannel. I started from my sleep with horror; a cold dew covered my forehead, my teeth chattered, and every limb became convulsed: when, by the dim and yellow light of the moon, as it forced its way through the window shutters, I beheld the wretch—the miserable monster whom I had created. He held up the curtain of the bed; and his eyes, if eyes they may be called, were fixed on me. His jaws opened, and he muttered some inarticulate sounds, while a grin wrinkled his cheeks. He might have spoken, but I did not hear; one hand was stretched out, seemingly to detain me, but I escaped, and rushed down stairs. I took refuge in the courtyard belonging to the house which I inhabited; where I remained during the rest of the night, walking up and down in the greatest agitation, listening attentively, catching and fearing each sound as if it were to announce the approach of the demoniacal corpse to which I had so miserably given life.

Oh! no mortal could support the horror of that countenance. A mummy again endued with animation could not be so hideous as that wretch. I had gazed on him while unfinished; he was ugly then; but when those muscles and joints were rendered capable of motion, it became a thing such as even Dante could not have conceived.

I passed the night wretchedly. Sometimes my pulse beat so quickly and hardly, that I felt the palpitation of every artery; at others, I nearly sank to the ground through languor and extreme weakness. Mingled with this horror, I felt the bitterness of disappointment; dreams that had been my food and pleasant rest for so long a space were now become a hell to me; and the change was so rapid, the overthrow so complete!

Morning, dismal and wet, at length dawned, and discovered to my sleepless and aching eyes the church of Ingolstadt, its white steeple and clock, which indicated the sixth hour. The porter opened the gates of the court, which had that night been my asylum, and I issued into the streets, pacing them with quick steps, as if I sought to avoid the wretch whom I feared every turning of the street would present to my view. I did not dare return to the apartment which I inhabited, but felt impelled to hurry on, although drenched by the rain which poured from a black and comfortless sky.

I continued walking in this manner for some time, endeavouring, by bodily exercise, to ease the load that weighed upon my mind. I traversed the streets, without any clear conception of where I was, or what I was doing. My heart palpitated in the sickness of fear; and I hurried on with irregular steps, not daring to look about me:—

> "Like one who, on a lonely road,
> Doth walk in fear and dread,
> And, having once turned round, walks on,
> And turns no more his head;
> Because he knows a frightful fiend
> Doth close behind him tread."[1]

---

1 Coleridge's *Ancient Mariner*

CHAPTER X

* * *

It was nearly noon when I arrived at the top of the ascent. For some time I sat upon the rock that overlooks the sea of ice. A mist covered both that and the surrounding mountains. Presently a breeze dissipated the cloud, and I descended upon the glacier. The surface is very uneven, rising like the waves of a troubled sea, descending low, and interspersed by rifts that sink deep. The field of ice is almost a league in width, but I spent nearly two hours in crossing it. The opposite mountain is a bare perpendicular rock. From the side where I now stood Montanvert was exactly opposite, at the distance of a league; and above it rose Mont Blanc, in awful majesty. I remained in a recess of the rock, gazing on this wonderful and stupendous scene. The sea, or rather the vast river of ice, wound among its dependent mountains, whose aerial summits hung over its recesses. Their icy and glittering peaks shone in the sunlight over the clouds. My heart, which was before sorrowful, now swelled with something like joy; I exclaimed—"Wandering spirits, if indeed ye wander, and do not rest in your narrow beds, allow me this faint happiness, or take me, as your companion, away from the joys of life."

As I said this, I suddenly beheld the figure of a man, at some distance, advancing towards me with superhuman speed. He bounded over the crevices in the ice, among which I had walked with caution; his stature, also, as he approached, seemed to exceed that of man. I was troubled: a mist came over my eyes, and I felt a faintness seize me; but I was quickly restored by the cold gale of the mountains. I perceived, as the shape came nearer (sight tremendous and abhorred!) that it was the wretch whom I had created. I trembled with rage and horror, resolving to wait his approach, and then close with him in mortal combat. He approached; his countenance bespoke bitter anguish, combined with disdain and malignity, while its unearthly ugliness rendered it almost too horrible for human eyes. But I scarcely observed this; rage and hatred had at first deprived me of utterance, and I recovered only to overwhelm him with words expressive of furious detestation and contempt.

"Devil," I exclaimed, "do you dare approach me? and do not you fear the fierce vengeance of my arm wreaked on your miserable head? Begone, vile insect! or rather, stay, that I may trample you to dust! and, oh! that I could, with the extinction of your miserable existence, restore those victims whom you have so diabolically murdered!"

"I expected this reception," said the dæmon. "All men hate the wretched; how, then, must I be hated, who am miserable beyond all living things! Yet you, my creator, detest and spurn me, thy creature, to whom thou art bound by ties only dissoluble by the annihilation of one of us. You purpose to kill me. How dare you sport thus with life? Do your duty towards me, and I will do mine towards you and the rest of mankind. If you will comply with my conditions, I will leave them and you at peace; but if you refuse, I will glut the maw of death, until it be satiated with the blood of your remaining friends."

"Abhorred monster! fiend that thou art! the tortures of hell are too mild a vengeance for thy crimes. Wretched devil! you reproach me with your creation; come on, then that I may extinguish the spark which I so negligently bestowed."

My rage was without bounds; I sprang on him, impelled by all the feelings which can arm one being against the existence of another.

He easily eluded me, and said—

"Be calm! I entreat you to hear me, before you give vent to your hatred on my devoted head. Have I not suffered enough, that you seek to increase my misery? Life, although it may only be an accumulation of anguish, is dear to me, and I will defend it. Remember, thou hast made me more powerful than thyself; my height is superior to thine; my joints more supple. But I will not be tempted to set myself in opposition to thee. I am thy creature, and I will be even mild and docile to my natural lord and king, if thou wilt also perform thy part, the which thou owest me. Oh, Frankenstein, be not equitable to every other, and trample upon me alone, to whom thy justice, and even thy clemency and affection, is most due. Remember, that I am thy creature; I ought to be thy Adam; but I am rather the fallen angel, whom thou drivest from joy for no misdeed. Every where I see bliss, from which I alone am irrevocably excluded. I was benevolent and good; misery made me a fiend. Make me happy, and I shall again be virtuous."

"Begone! I will not hear you. There can be no community between you and me; we are enemies. Begone, or let us try our strength in a fight, in which one must fall."

"How can I move thee? Will no entreaties cause thee to turn a favourable eye upon thy creature, who implores thy goodness and compassion? Believe me, Frankenstein: I was benevolent; my soul glowed with love and humanity: but am I not alone, miserably alone? You, my creator, abhor me; what hope can I gather from your fellow-creatures, who owe me nothing? they spurn and hate me. The desert mountains and dreary glaciers are my refuge. I have wandered here many days; the caves of ice, which I only do not fear, are a dwelling to me, and the only one which man does not grudge. These bleak skies I hail, for they are kinder to me than your fellow-beings. If the multitude of mankind knew of my existence, they would do as you do, and arm themselves for my destruction. Shall I not then hate them who abhor me? I will keep no terms with my enemies. I am miserable, and they shall share my wretchedness. Yet it is in your power to recompense me, and deliver them from an evil which it only remains for you to make so great, that not only you and your family, but thousands of others, shall be swallowed up in the whirlwinds of its rage. Let your compassion be moved, and do not disdain me. Listen to my tale: when you have heard that, abandon or commiserate me, as you shall judge that I deserve. But hear me. The guilty are allowed, by human laws, bloody as they are, to speak in their own defence before they are condemned. Listen to me, Frankenstein. You accuse me of murder; and yet you would, with a satisfied conscience, destroy your own creature. Oh, praise the eternal justice of man! Yet I ask you not to spare me: listen to me; and then, if you can, and if you will, destroy the work of your hands."

"Why do you call to my remembrance," I rejoined, "circumstances, of which I shudder to reflect, that I have been the miserable origin and author? Cursed be the day, abhorred devil, in which you first saw light! Cursed (although I curse myself) be the hands that formed you! You have made me wretched beyond expression. You have left me no power to consider whether I am just to you, or not. Begone! relieve me from the sight of your detested form."

"Thus I relieve thee, my creator," he said, and placed his hated hands before my eyes, which I flung from me with violence; "thus I take from thee a sight which you abhor. Still thou canst listen to me, and grant me thy compassion. By the virtues that I once possessed, I demand this from you. Hear my tale; it is long and strange, and the temperature of this place is not fitting to your fine sensations; come to the hut upon the mountain. The sun is yet high in the heavens; before it descends to hide itself behind yon snowy precipices, and illuminate another world, you will have heard my story, and can decide. On you it rests, whether I quit for ever the neighbourhood of man, and lead a harmless life, or become the scourge of your fellow-creatures, and the author of your own speedy ruin."

As he said this, he led the way across the ice: I followed. My heart was full, and I did not answer him; but, as I proceeded, I weighed the various arguments that he had used, and determined at least to listen to his tale. I was partly urged by curiosity, and compassion confirmed my resolution. I had hitherto supposed him to be the murderer of my brother, and I eagerly sought a confirmation or denial of this opinion. For the first time, also, I felt what the duties of a creator towards his creature were, and that I ought to render him happy before I complained of his wickedness. These motives urged me to comply with his demand. We crossed the ice, therefore, and ascended the opposite rock. The air was cold, and the rain again began to descend: we entered the hut, the fiend with an air of exultation, I with a heavy heart, and depressed spirits. But I consented to listen; and, seating myself by the fire which my odious companion had lighted, he thus began his tale.

Section III

ENVIRONMENT

> That our Creator made the earth for the use of the living and not of the dead; that those who exist not can have no use nor right in it, no authority or power over it; that one generation of men cannot foreclose or burden its use to another, which comes to it in its own right and by the same divine beneficence; that a preceding generation cannot bind a succeeding one by its laws or contracts; these deriving their obligation from the will of the existing majority, and that majority being removed by death, another comes in its place with a will equally free to make its own laws and contracts; these are axioms so self evident that no explanation can make them plainer; for he is not to be reasoned with who says that non-existence can control existence, or that nothing can move something.
>
> *Thomas Jefferson*[1]

It might be perceived that the green revolution is a development of the twenty-first century. This would be false. The history of environmentalism is marked by the writings and actions of many individuals including such noted figures as Thomas Jefferson, John Muir, Theodore Roosevelt, Aldo Leopold, and Rachel Carson. Their work and ideas provide the nascent core of the current green awakening. The selections that follow provide an entry into the ideas of environmentalism.

Aldo Leopold's poetic and thought provoking writing in *A Sand County Almanac* provides an excellent entry piece to environmentalism for those just beginning to explore the place of humankind in the local, national, and global ecology. His tales of personal events and their impact

---

1 Thomas Jefferson (2005). *Light and Liberty Reflections on the Pursuit of Happiness.* Eric S. Peterson (Ed.). New York, The Modern Library

on his thoughts and actions provide salient focal points for personal reflection on choices made as one considers how to live and maintain good stewardship of the natural world.

In counterpoint to the poetic nature of Leopold's writing, Paul Hawken examines the sustainability of economic practices and the impacts of those practices upon the natural world. He challenges us as citizen's of the planet to consider our actions and to take steps to alter our behaviors, addictions Hawken calls them, which are not sustainable for us, for the global environment or for future generations.

As one begins to develop a sense of environmental awareness, we might be drawn to Daniel Quinn's *Ishmael.* His work contemplates the place of humankind within the global ecology. These fictional characters provide a story through which we can examine our own relationship within the global ecology and perhaps rethink how we choose to act, or not act as may be the case.

Marc Reisner elaborates on the historical background of the dominance of water concerns throughout the western United States. In great detail he brings us from the frontier period, where man tried to dominate and control the environment of the west to serve his ends, and provides a cautionary story where missteps, gaps in understanding, and outright malfeasance contributed to poor environmental decision making.

Finally, Thomas Malthus's 1798 essay on population, in which he argues that rapidly growing populations will ultimately outrun their means of subsistence, provides a forum for many discussions/debates on the need for birth control, whether overpopulation really does mean that plants and animals can never achieve their fullest growth potential, or whether as Darwin argues that such growth supports natural selection and the survival of the fittest.

Mother Earth. The Big Blue Marble. Terra Firma. Gaea. Earth. All of these describe our world, the only one we currently know to possess the conditions and qualities that provide for life. The readings that follow are but a first entry into a process of changing our behaviors to conserve what may turn out to be a unique feature of our universe.

Aldo Leopold

1887-1948

A Sand County Almanac

1966

From a modern perspective, Aldo Leopold can be considered a renaissance man. Born in Burlington, Iowa his love of the natural world developed early with his childhood explorations of the Mississippi river bluffs of Iowa. His keen observational skills in the woods, prairies, and river banks along the bluffs set him on the path to developing the foundation of what was to become his "land ethic."

Upon completion of his degree in Forestry from Yale, he took a position with the U.S. Forest Service and was assigned to the Arizona Territories. It was at this time that his foundation for the "land ethic" began to mature as he used his powers of observation to visualize the land as a living unit, a community which requires proper care and support. This idea expands the definition of community to encompass elements such as soil, water, plants, and animals beyond the human community and its economic interests. In 1924, he transferred to the land office in Madison, Wisconsin and began teaching at the University of Wisconsin in 1928.

Often considered the father of wildlife ecology, his *Game Management* (1933) brought together threads drawn from areas such as agriculture, biology, education, and communication, and Leopold became the founding chair of the Department of Game Management at the University of Wisconsin. Leopold's gift for eloquent writing provides the power to his ideas. His writings were inspired by research conducted on a family farm purchased in 1935 near Baraboo, Wisconsin. An old chicken coop called the "Shack" often housed family, and students provided the location for his many ideas expressed in *A Sand County Almanac.*

Leopold died fighting a brush fire on a neighbor's farm in 1948. The draft of *A Sand County Almanac* was edited by his son, Luna, and first published in 1949. Many of the selections had been published in magazines such as *American Forestry*, *Journal of Forestry*, or *Journal of Wildlife Management*. It is a collection that takes the reader through the seasons, as Leopold interweaves his observations of the land with his subtle, yet powerful ideas of what is the land ethic. The excerpts that follow are two of many possible choices.

SOURCES:

"Ecology Hall of Fame: Aldo Leopold" Retrieved April 15, 2008, from http://www.ecotopia.org/ehof/leopold/extracts.html.

Leopold, Aldo. (1970). *A Sand County Almanac with Essays on Conservation from Round River.* Ballantine Books, New York.

"The Aldo Leopold Foundation." Retrieved April 15, 2008, from http://www.naturenet.com/alnc/aldo.html.

SELECTION FROM:

Leopold, Aldo. (1966). *A Sand County Almanac, With Other Essays on Conservation from Round River.* New York: Oxford University Press. 6-18, 44-50.

February

Good Oak

There are two spiritual dangers in not owning a farm. One is the danger of supposing that breakfast comes from the grocery, and the other that heat comes from the furnace.

To avoid the first danger, one should plant a garden, preferably where there is no grocer to confuse the issue.

To avoid the second, he should lay a split of good oak on the andirons, preferably where there is no furnace, and let it warm his shins while a February blizzard tosses the trees outside. If one has cut, split, hauled, and piled his own good oak, and let his mind work the while, he will remember much about where the heat comes from, and with a wealth of detail denied to those who spend the week end in town astride a radiator.

* * *

The particular oak now aglow on my andirons grew on the bank of the old emigrant road where it climbs the sandhill. The stump, which I measured upon felling the tree, has a diameter of 30 inches. It shows 80 growth rings, hence the seedling from which it originated must have laid its first ring of wood in 1865, at the end of the Civil War. But I know from the history of present seedlings that no oak grows above the reach of rabbits without a decade or more of getting girdled each winter, and re-sprouting during the following summer. Indeed, it is all too clear that every surviving oak is the product either of rabbit negligence or of rabbit scarcity. Some day some patient botanist will draw a frequency curve of oak birth-years, and show that the curve humps every ten years, each hump originating from a low in the ten-year rabbit cycle. (A fauna and flora, by this very process of perpetual battle within and among species, achieve collective immortality.)

It is likely, then, that a low in rabbits occurred in the middle 'sixties, when my oak began to lay on annual rings, but that the acorn that produced it fell during the preceding decade, when the covered wagons were still passing over my road into the Great Northwest. It may have been the wash and wear of the emigrant traffic that bared this roadbank, and thus enabled this particular acorn to spread its first leaves to the sun. Only one acorn in a thousand ever grew large enough to fight rabbits; the rest were drowned at birth in the prairie sea.

It is a warming thought that this one wasn't, and thus lived to garner eighty years of June sun. It is this sunlight that is now being released, through the intervention of my axe and saw, to warm my shack and my spirit through eighty gusts of blizzard. And with each gust a wisp of smoke from my chimney bears witness, to whomsoever it may concern, that the sun did not shine in vain.

My dog does not care where heat comes from, but he cares ardently that it come, and soon. Indeed he considers my ability to make it come as something magical, for when I rise in the cold black pre-dawn and kneel shivering by the hearth making a fire, he pushes himself blandly between me and the kindling splits I have laid on the ashes, and I must touch a match to them by poking it between his legs. Such faith, I suppose, is the kind that moves mountains.

It was a bolt of lightning that put an end to wood-making by this particular oak. We were all awakened, one night in July, by the thunderous crash; we realized that the bolt must have hit near by, but, since it had not hit us, we all went back to sheep. Man brings all things to the test of himself, and this is notably true of lightning.

Next morning, as we strolled over the sandhill rejoicing with the cone-flowers and the prairie clovers over their fresh accession of rain, we came upon a great slab of bark freshly torn from the trunk of the roadside oak. The trunk showed a long spiral scar of barkless sapwood, a foot wide and not yet yellowed by the sun. By the next day the leaves had wilted, and we knew that the lightning had bequeathed to us three cords of prospective fuel wood.

We mourned the loss of the old tree, but knew that a dozen of its progeny standing straight and stalwart on the sands had already taken over its job of wood-making.

We let the dead veteran season for a year in the sun it could no longer use, and then on a crisp winter's day we laid a newly filed saw to its bastioned base. Fragrant little chips of history spewed from the saw cut, and accumulated on the snow before each kneeling sawyer. We sensed that these two piles of sawdust were something more than wood: that they were the integrated transect of a century; that our saw was biting its way, stroke by stroke, decade by decade, into the chronology of a lifetime, written in concentric annual rings of good oak.

* * *

It took only a dozen pulls of the saw to transect the few years of our ownership, during which we had learned to love and cherish this farm. Abruptly we began to cut the years of our predecessor the bootlegger, who hated this farm, skinned it of residual fertility, burned its farmhouse, threw it back into the lap of the County (with delinquent taxes to boot), and then disappeared among the landless anonymities of the Great Depression. Yet the oak had laid down good wood for him; his sawdust was as fragrant, as sound, and as pink as our own. An oak is no respecter of persons.

The reign of the bootlegger ended sometime during the dust-bowl drouths of 1936, 1934, 1933, and 1930. Oak smoke from his still and peat from burning marshlands must have clouded the sun in those years, and alphabetical conservation was abroad in the land, but the sawdust shows no change.

Rest! Cries the chief sawyer, and we pause for breath.

* * *

Now our saw bites into the 1920's, the Babbittian decade when everything grew bigger and better in heedlessness and arrogance—until 1929, when stock markets crumpled. If the oak heard them fall, its wood gives no sign. Nor did it heed the Legislature's several protestations of love for trees: a National Forest and a forest-crop law in 1927, a great refuge on the Upper Mississippi bottomlands in 1924, and a new forest policy in 1921. Neither did it notice the demise of the state's last marten in 1925, nor the arrival of its first starling in 1923.

In March 1922, the 'Big Sleet' tore the neighboring elms limb from limb, but there is no sign of damage to our tree. What is a ton of lee, more or less, to a good oak?

Rest! cries the chief sawyer, and we pause for breath.

* * *

Now the saw bites into 1910-20, the decade of the drainage dream, when steam shovels sucked dry the marshes of central Wisconsin to make farms, and made ash-heaps instead. Our marsh escaped, not because of any caution or forbearance among engineers, but because the river floods it each April, and did so with a vengeance—perhaps a defensive vengeance—in the years 1913-16. The oak laid on wood just the same, even in 1915, when the Supreme Court abolished the state forests and Governor Phillip pontificated that 'state forestry is not a good business proposition.' (It did not occur to the Governor that there might be more than one definition of what is good, and even of what is business. It did not occur to him that while the courts were writing one definition of goodness in the law books, fires were writing quite another one on the face of the land. Perhaps, to be a governor, one must be free from doubt on such matters.)

While forestry receded during this decade, game conservation advanced. In 1916 pheasants became successfully established in Waukesha County; in 1915 a federal law prohibited spring shooting; in 1913 a state game farm was started; in 1912 a 'buck law' protected female deer; in 1911 an epidemic of refuges spread over the state. 'Refuge' became a holy word, but the oak took no heed.

Rest! cries the chief sawyer, and we pause for breath.

* * *

Now we cut 1910, when a great university president published a book on conservation, a great sawfly epidemic killed millions of tamaracks, a great drouth burned the pineries, and a great dredge drained Horicon Marsh.

We cut 1909, when smelt were first planted in the Great Lakes, and when a wet summer induced the Legislature to cut the forest-fire appropriations.

We cut 1908, a dry year when the forests burned fiercely, and Wisconsin parted with its last cougar.

We cut 1907, when a wandering lynx, looking in the wrong direction for the promised land, ended his career among the farms of Dane County.

We cut 1906, when the first state forester took office, and fires burned 17,000 acres in these sand counties; we cut 1905 when a great flight of goshawks came out of the North and ate up the local grouse (they no doubt perched in this tree to eat some of mine). We cut 1902-3, a winter of bitter cold; 1901, which brought the most intense drouth of record (rainfall only 17 inches); 1900, a centennial year of hope, of prayer, and the usual annual ring of oak.

Rest! cries the chief sawyer, and we pause for breath.

* * *

Now our saw bites into the 1890's, called gay by those whose eyes turn cityward rather than landward. We cut 1899, when the last passenger pigeon collided with a charge of shot near Babcock, two counties to the north; we cut 1898 when a dry fall, followed by a snowless winter, froze the soil seven feet deep and killed the apple trees; 1897, another drouth year, when another forestry commission came into being; 1896, when 25,000 prairie chickens were shipped to market from the village of Spooner alone; 1895, another year of fires; 1894, another drouth year; and 1893, the year of 'The Bluebird Storm,' when a March blizzard reduced the migrating bluebirds to near-zero. (The first bluebirds always alighted in this oak, but in the middle 'nineties it must have gone without.) We cut 1892, another year of fires; 1891, a low in the grouse cycle; and 1890, the year of the Babcock Milk Tester, which enabled Governor Heil to boast, half a century later, that Wisconsin is America's Dairyland. The motor licenses which now parade that boast were then not foreseen, even by Professor Babcock.

It was likewise in 1890 that the largest pine rafts in history slipped down the Wisconsin River in full view of my oak, to build an empire of red barns for the cows of the prairie states. Thus it is that good pine now stands between the cow and the blizzard, just as good oak stands between the blizzard and me.

Rest! cries the chief sawyer, and we pause for breath.

* * *

Now our saw bites into the 1880's; into 1889, a drouth year in which Arbor Day was first proclaimed; into 1887, when Wisconsin appointed its first game wardens; into 1886, when the College of Agriculture held its first short course for farmers; into 1885, preceded by a winter 'of unprecedented length and severity'; into 1883, when Dean W. H. Henry reported that the spring flowers at Madison bloomed 13 days later than average; into 1882, the year Lake Mendota opened a month late following the historic 'Big Snow' and bitter cold of 1881-2.

It was likewise in 1881 that the Wisconsin Agricultural Society debated the question, 'How do you account for the second growth of black oak timber that has sprung up all over the country in the last thirty years?' My oak was one of these. One debater claimed spontaneous generation, another claimed regurgitation of acorns by southbound pigeons.

Rest! cries the chief sawyer, and we pause for breath.

* * *

Now our saw bites the 1870's, the decade of Wisconsin's carousal in wheat. Monday morning came in 1879, when chinch bugs, grubs, rust, and soil exhaustion finally convinced Wisconsin farmers that they could not compete with the virgin prairies further west in the game of wheating land to death. I suspect that this farm played its share in the game, and that the sand blow just north of my oak had its origin in over-wheating.

This same year of 1879 saw the first planting of carp in Wisconsin, and also the first arrival of quack-grass as a stowaway from Europe. On 27 October 1879, six migrating prairie chicken is perched on the rooftree of the German Methodist Church in Madison, and took a look at the growing city. On 8 November the markets at Madison were reported to be glutted with ducks at 10 cents each.

In 1878 a deer hunter from Sank Rapids remarked prophetically, 'The hunters promise to outnumber the deer.'

On 10 September 1877, two brothers, shooting Muskego Lake, bagged 210 blue-winged teal in one day.

In 1876 came the wettest year of record; the rainfall piled up 50 inches. Prairie chickens declined, perhaps owing to hard rains.

In 1875 four hunters killed 153 prairie chickens at York Prairie, one county to the eastward. In the same year the U.S. Fish Commission planted Atlantic salmon in Devil's

Lake, 10 miles south of my oak.

In 1874 the first factory-made barbed wire was stapled to oak trees; I hope no such artifacts are buried in the oak now under saw!

In 1873 one Chicago firm received and marketed 25,000 prairie chickens. The Chicago trade collectively bought 600,000 at $3.25 per dozen.

In 1872 the last wild Wisconsin turkey was killed, two counties to the southwest.

It is appropriate that the decade ending the pioneer carousal in wheat should likewise have ended the pioneer carousal in pigeon blood. In 1871, within a 50-mile triangle spreading northwestward from my oak, 136 million pigeons are estimated to have nested, and some may have nested in it, for it was then a thrifty sapling 20 feet tall. Pigeon hunters by scores plied their trade with net and gun, club and salt lick, and trainloads of prospective pigeon pie moved southward and eastward toward the cities. It was the last big nesting in Wisconsin, and nearly the last in any state.

This same year 1871 brought other evidence of the march of empire: the Peshtigo Fire, which cleared a couple of counties of trees and soil, and the Chicago Fire, said to have started from the protesting kick of a cow.

In 1870 the meadow mice had already staged their march of empire; they ate up the young orchards of the young state, and then died. They did not eat my oak, whose bark was already too tough and thick for mice.

It was likewise in 1870 that a market gunner boasted in the *American Sportsman* of killing 6000 ducks in one season near Chicago.

Rest! cries the chief sawyer, and we pause for breath.

* * *

Our saw now cuts the 1860's, when thousands died to settle the question: Is the man-man community lightly to be dismembered? They settled it, but they did riot see, nor do we yet see, that the same question applies to the man-land community.

This decade was not without its gropings toward the larger issue. In 1867 Increase A. Lapham induced the State Horticultural Society to offer prizes for forest plantations. In 1866 the last native Wisconsin elk was killed. The saw now severs 1865, the pith-year of our oak. In that year John Muir offered to buy from his brother, who then owned the home farm thirty miles east of my oak, a sanctuary for the wildflowers that had gladdened his youth. His brother declined to part with the land, but he could not suppress the idea: 1865 still stands in Wisconsin history as the birthyear of mercy for things natural, wild, and free.

We have cut the core. Our saw now reverses its orientation in history; we cut backward across the years, and outward toward the far side of the stump. At last there is a tremor in the great trunk; the saw-kerf suddenly widens; the saw is quickly pulled as the sawyers spring backward to safety; all hands cry "Timber!"; my oak leans, groans, and crashes with earth-shaking thunder, to lie prostrate across the emigrant road that gave it birth.

* * *

Now comes the job of making wood. The maul rings on steel wedges as the sections of trunk are up—ended one by one, only to fall apart in fragrant slabs to be corded by the roadside.

There is an allegory for historians in the diverse functions of saw, wedge, and axe.

The saw works only across the years, which it must deal with one by one, in sequence. From each year the raker teeth pull little chips of fact, which accumulate in little piles, called sawdust by woodsmen and archives by historians; both the character of what lies within by the character of the samples thus made visible without. It is not until the transect is completed that the tree falls, and the stump yields a collective view of a century. By its fall the tree attests the unity of the hodge-podge called history.

The wedge, on the other hand, works only in radial splits; such a split yields a collective view of all the years at once, or no view at all, depending on the skill with which the plane of the split is chosen. (If in doubt, let the section season for a year until a crack develops. Many a hastily driven wedge lies rusting in the woods, embedded in unsplittable cross-grain.)

The axe functions only at an angle diagonal to the years, and this only for the peripheral rings of the recent past. Its special function is to lop limbs, for which both saw and wedge are useless.

The three tools are requisite to good oak, and to good history.

* * *

These things I ponder as the kettle sings, and the good oak burns to red coals on white ashes. Those ashes, come spring, I will return to the orchard at tile foot of the sandhill. They will come back to me again, perhaps as red apples, or perhaps as a spirit of enterprise in some fat October squirrel, who, for reason unknown to himself, is bent on planting acorns.

* * *

Prairie Birthday

During every week from April to September there are, on the average, ten wild plants coming into first bloom. In June as many as a dozen species may burst their buds on a single clay. No man can heed all of these anniversaries; no man can ignore all of them. He who steps unseeing on May dandelions may be hauled up short by August ragweed pollen; he who ignores the ruddy haze of April elms may skid his car on the fallen corollas of June catalpas. Tell me of what plant-birthday a man takes notice, and I shall tell you a good deal about his vocation, his hobbies, his hay fever, and the general level of his ecological education.

* * *

Every July I watch eagerly a certain country graveyard that I pass in driving to and from my farm. It is time for a prairie birthday, and in one corner (if this graveyard lives a surviving celebrant of that once important event.

It is an ordinary graveyard, bordered by the usual spruces, and studded with the usual pink granite or white marble headstones, each with the usual Sunday bouquet of red or pink geraniums. It is extraordinary only in being triangular instead of square, and in harboring, within the sharp angle of its fence, a pin-point remnant of the native prairie on which the graveyard was established in the 1840's. Heretofore unreachable by scythe or mower, this yard-square relic of original Wisconsin gives birth, each July, to a man-high stalk of compass plant or cutleaf Silphium spangled with saucer-yellow blooms resembling sunflowers. It is the sole remnant of this plant along this highway and perhaps the sole remnant in the western half of our county. What a thousand acres of Silphiums looked like when they tickled the bellies of the buffalo is a question never again to he answered, and perhaps not even asked.

This year I found the Silphium in first bloom on 24 July, a week later than usual; during the last six years the average date was 15 July.

When I passed the graveyard again on 3 August, the fence had been removed by a road crew, and the Silphium cut. It is easy now to predict the future; for a few years my Silphium will try in vain to rise above the mowing machine, and then it will die. With it will die the prairie epoch.

The Highway Department says that 100,000 cars pass yearly over this route during the three summer months which the Silphium is in bloom. In them most ride at least 100,000 people who have 'taken' what is called history, and perhaps 25,000 who have 'taken' what is called botany. Yet I doubt whether a dozen have seen the Silphium, and of these hardly one will notice its demise. If I were to tell a preacher of the adjoining church that the road crew has been burning history books in his cemetery under the guise of mowing weeds, he would he amazed and uncomprehending. How could a weed be a book?

This is one little episode in the funeral of the native flora, which in turn is one episode in the funeral of the floras of the world. Mechanized man, oblivious of floras, is proud of his progress in cleaning up the landscape on which, willy-nilly, he must live out his days. It might be wise to prohibit at once all teaching of real botany and real history, lest some future citizen suffer qualms about the floristic price of his good life.

* * *

Thus it comes to pass that farm neighborhoods are good in proportion to the poverty of their floras. My own farm was selected for its lack of goodness and its lack of highway; indeed my whole neighborhood lies in a backwash of the River Progress. My road is the original wagon track of the pioneers, innocent of grades or gravel, brushings or bulldozers. My neighbors bring a sigh to the County Agent. Their fencerows go unshaven for years on end. Their marshes are neither dyked nor drained. As between going fishing and going forward, they are prone to prefer fishing. Thus on week ends my floristic standard of living is that of tile backwoods, while on week days I subsist as best I can on the flora of the university farms, the university campus, and the adjoining suburbs. For a decade I have kept, for pastime, a record of the wild plant species in first bloom on these two diverse areas:

Species First Blooming in	Suburb and Campus	Backward Farm
April	14	26
May	29	59
June	43	70
July	25	56
August	9	14
September	0	1
Total visual diet	120	226

It is apparent that the backward farmer's eye is nearly twice as well fed as the eye of the university student or businessman. Of course neither sees his flora as yet, so we are confronted by the two alternatives already mentioned: either insure the combined blindness of the populace, or examine the question whether we cannot have both progress and plants.

The shrinkage in the flora is due to a combination of clean-farming, woodlot grazing, and good roads. Each of these necessary changes of course requires a larger reduction in the acreage available for wild plants, but none of them requires, or benefits by, the erasure of species from whole farms, townships, or counties. There are idle spots on every farm, and every highway is bordered by an idle strip as long as it is; keep cow, plow, and mower out of these idle spots. and the full native flora, plus dozens of interesting stowaways from foreign parts, could be part of the normal environment of every citizen.

The outstanding conservator of the prairie flora, ironically enough, knows little and cares less about such frivolities: it is the railroad with its fenced right-of-way. Many of these railroad fences were erected before the prairie had been plowed. Within these linear reservations, oblivious of cinders, soot, and annual clean-up fires, the prairie flora still splashes its calendar of colors, from pink shooting-star in May to blue aster in October. I have long wished to confront some hard-boiled railway president with the physical evidence of his soft-heartedness. I have not done so because I haven't met one.

The railroads of course use flame-throwers and chemical sprays to clear the track of weeds, but the cost of such necessary clearance is still too high to extend it much beyond the actual rails. Perhaps further improvements are in the offing.

The erasure of a human subspecies is largely painless—to us—if we know little enough about it. A dead Chinaman is of little import to us whose awareness of things Chinese is bounded by an occasional dish of chow mein. We grieve only for what we know. The erasure of Silphium from western Dane County is no cause for grief if one knows it only as a name in a botany book.

Silphium first became a personality to me when I tried to dig one up to move to my farm. It was like digging an oak sapling. After half an hour of hot grimy labor the root was still enlarging, like a great vertical sweet-potato. As far as I know, that Silphium root went clear through to bedrock. I got no Silphium, but I learned by what elaborate underground stratagems it contrives to weather the prairie drouths.

I next planted Silphium seeds, which are large, meaty, and taste like sunflower seeds. They came up promptly, but after five years of waiting the seedlings are still juvenile, and have not yet borne a flower-stalk.

Perhaps it takes a decade for a Silphium to reach flowering age; how old, then, was my pet plant in the cemetary? It may have been older than the oldest tombstone, which is dated 1850. Perhaps it watched the fugitive Black Hawk retreat from the Madison lakes to the Wisconsin River; it stood on the route of that famous march. Certainly it saw the successive funerals of the local pioneers as they retired, one by one, to their repose beneath the bluestem.

I once saw a power shovel, while digging a roadside ditch, sever the 'sweet-potato' root of a Silphium plant. The root sprouted new leaves, and eventually it again produced a flower stalk. This explains why this plant, which never invades new ground, is nevertheless sometimes seen on recently graded roadsides. Once established, it apparently withstands almost any kind of mutilation except continued glazing, mowing, or plowing.

Why does Silphium disappear from grazed areas? I once saw a farmer turn his cows into a virgin prairie meadow previously used only sporadically for mowing wild hay. The cows cropped the Silphium to the ground before any other plant was visibly eaten at all. One can imagine that the buffalo once had the same preference for Silphium, but he brooked no fences to confine his nibblings all summer long to one meadow. In short, the buffalo's pasturing was discontinuous, and therefore tolerable to Silphium.

It is a kind providence that has withheld a sense of history from the thousands of species of plants and animals that have exterminated each other to build the present world. The same kind providence now withholds it from us. Few grieved when the last buffalo left Wisconsin, and few will grieve when the last Silphium follows him to the prairies of the never-never land.

Paul Hawken

1946-

The Ecology of Commerce

1993

A noted author, economist, and environmentalist, at the age of 20 Paul Hawken began his pursuit of a sustainable culture through a change in the relationship between business and environment. As part of this strategy he has written numerous articles and books and appeared on programs, such as *Larry King Live* and the *Today Show*, among others.

His current pursuits include serving as the head of three companies associated with PAX Scientific, whose goals are focused on energy-saving technologies where biomimicry is applied to fluid dynamics. He also heads the Natural Capital Institute out of Sausalito, California. This organization provides an open-source networking platform link interested parties in creating a hub for a global civil society.

Natural capitalism is an idea based upon changing understanding of driving forces within economics. Most current economic views are based on a concept of unlimited resources and limited labor. The idea of natural capital is that natural resources and their supporting ecological systems are limited, while labor is in abundant supply. By applying these ideas businesses will be prepared for the next industrial revolution, while at the same time be involved in the restoration, rather than the exploitation of our environment.

In 1993, Hawken published what is considered a seminal work at the intersection of environmental concerns and business practice. *The Ecology of Commerce* was voted the number one college text on business and the environment in 1998. The chapter below presents our use and abuse of the environment as a societal addiction. By example, Hawken demonstrates the addictive mindset of the industrial revolution and provides the first step for a change in our economic thinking.

1. You are the CEO or a Board member of a corporation. How could you employ the arguments of Hawken to prepare a business plan that takes into account environmental factors?
2. Is addiction a good analogy for corporate behavior? If so, why? If not, can you propose a different analogy that still takes into account past and current corporate practices in dealing with the environment.

SOURCES:

"Natural Capitalism." (nd). Accessed April 17, 2008 from http://www.natcap.org/.
"Biography." (nd). Accessed April 17, 2008 from http://www.paulhawken.com/paulhawken_frameset.html.

SELECTION FROM:

Hawken, Paul. (1993). *The Ecology of Commerce: A Declaration of Sustainability.* New York: HarperBusiness. 123-136.

8

The Jesse Helms Citizenship Center

We have elevated the ideology and mores of corporate life into a belief system before which we pay homage, and we have allowed it to take over the political system. We may spend an hour in church or temple every week, but we spend forty or fifty or sixty hours at the workplace, in a job that demands and receives the greatest devotion we bestow on anyone or anything outside of (and sometimes including) our families. Work or some form of collective labor has always been a defining element of society, but never before has the output of work become the dominant organizing principle of the world's peoples.

Corporations are portrayed in the media as models of efficiency producing a stream of goods and services. But compelling evidence suggests that the behavior of many individuals in the modern corporation is remarkably similar to that of addicts. The parallels between the way addicts organize their lives and the lives business encourages suggest that there are many aspects to addiction we may not have recognized before—and many ways to define it.

At the core, an addiction is a way to keep ourselves from feeling. Thus, anything we do that keeps us from knowing ourselves and fully experiencing the world around us can become an addiction. Work, television, food, money, sex, sports, and other activities can all be addictive when we rely on them to avoid dealing with inner problems or deeper emotions. For every addiction there is a fix, an experience that we repeat over and over again, giving us the illusion that we are alive, while in fact numbing us to the real world and our real self, until it damages or destroys us.

The extension to corporate behavior is clear. We relate become addicted to the deal, the power, the action, the excitement, the conflict, the aggression, the victories, the defeats, addicted even to the chaos and the stress, addicted to the point at which we feel empowered to do anything as long as it is legal (and perhaps not even legal), oblivious to many if not all of the effects of our actions on the environment, on society, or on ourselves. But like any habit, corporate addictiveness leads to chaos. Pursuing productivity and efficiency, American corporations have found anxiety. The demand to perform had become so overwhelming that, according to a recent poll, 20 to 30 percent of middle managers in the largest corporations confess that they have written memos or progress reports to their superiors that were dishonest. According to Michael Josephson, an ethics consultant for large companies, "We are swimming in enough lies to keep the lawyers busy for the next ten years." Kirk Hanson, Professor of Business Management at Stanford, says that managers feel they must be top achievers, or risk being fired. A recent profile in a business magazine of a prototypical "successful executive" described his *modus operandi* as taking no prisoners, having the hands-on quality of Attila the Hun, and as not suffering fools gladly but shooting them on sight. That was all meant as a compliment Jack Welch, the Chairman of General Electric, nicknamed "Neutron Jack" because of his brutal and sudden firings, has eliminated 170,000 jobs during his reign and is considered one of the most admired CEOs in American by his peers. Some top executives have been summarily sent home from GE without warning, their personal effects shipped home by UPS. It should come as no surprise that another business magazine cover story featured a discussion of a "hot new skill" in the executive ranks, the ability to manage cultural, structural, and emotional chaos.

Business is faced with seemingly irreconcilable forces that sunder old assumptions and play havoc with employee morale. As the job base in Fortune 500 companies continues to decline (four million jobs lost in the past twelve years), as health and pension benefits are curtailed, as real wages continue to fall, and with job security becoming a nostalgic relic, workers can hardly be expected to be their most creative and productive. At the same time, decades of insulating prosperity in America have left our corporations slow in responding to global threats and competitors. Fear of the future has never been an effective human motivator, yet today the loss of jobs and benefits is never far from people's concerns, affecting their willingness to take risks, to speak up, to address critical issues of safety or long-term value.

The victims of an organized addictive system are not only those who lose their jobs, but also those who keep them. You cannot pick up a magazine that does not, at one time or another, praise, envy, or profile a woman or man who "has it all," who regularly puts in sixty hour work weeks, sits on several boards, volunteers for charity, heads the local Chamber of Commerce, works out at the health club, sails a boat, raises three children, and may even run for public office. This "successful" person is rapidly approaching burn-out, of course—you cannot "save the world" if you're destroying yourself on the altar of workaholism, wolfing food, gulping coffee, taking "red-eye" flights in the middle of the night, trying to do the work of three people—but she or he nevertheless was consistently portrayed during the 1980s as living a dazzling life. Many of us who feel inadequate about our own lives will redouble our efforts to climb the corporate ladder through a similar life of constant activity.

A friend tells a story about his business, a regional publishing house that began to build. With the expansion came a feeling of exhilaration and excitement. "Growth was just like being at a party," he recounted. "I could hear the buzzing of the conversation, the tinkling of the champagne glasses, the electricity in the air. I was having a good time but when I looked over at the doorway, there was this goofy, awkward guy standing there, not having fun, and feeling like things had passed him by. And I realized it was me. My business was growing, but part of me had been left behind, the me that is shy, quiet, and reflective." I suspect many people who get involved with business have a modest self that resists being adrenalized and overworked by incessant growth. In most cases, we see this subdued side of ourselves as something to overcome, a limit, a reluctant and unassuming personality that needs motivation tapes and seminars to mold it into the obsessive, success-driven, capable person the late-night cable programs assure us is hiding within.

Nothing in the modern workplace, and very little in society at large, encourages us to take our time, or be satisfied with what we have. We're being presented instead with a future where we will have to work harder, but have even less leisure time than sounds like a positive feedback loop, it is. We are speeding up our lives and working harder in a futile attempt to buy the time to slow down and enjoy it.

Our economic insecurity, drifting and corrupt politics, suffocating debt, and environmental degradation cannot help but reflected in the workplace where we spend most of our waking lives. The connections may be more obvious than we are willing to grant. For example, federal debt reduces the supply of capital for investment, and thus diminishes innovation, jobs, and productivity. High deficits were an attempt to re-create with paper the industrial growth of the past, a type of growth that depended on a unique set of circumstances in relation to the environment and resources. In fact, the 1980's could be seen as a financial end run around the simple economic truth that prosperity can only come from adding value. We have reached a point where the value we do add to our economy is now being outweighed by the value we are removing, not only from ourselves in terms of unlivable cities, deadening jobs, deteriorating health, and rising crime. In biological terms, we have become a parasite and are devouring out host.

For a long time in American society, a large number of people thought they were advancing under the guidance and direction of commerce. As long as we could identify the improvements in the quality of our existence with the continuing growth and influence of big business, criticism of and dissatisfaction with the system were generally discounted or ignored. But during the past twenty years our standard of living has not increased, real wages have not risen, and, for the very first time since the Industrial Revolution, our work week is getting longer, not shorter—a literally epochal development, barley remarked upon in the press. Worldwide, workplace stress has increased in the extent that the U.N. has issued a warning report calling it "one of the most serious health issues of the 20th century". Of the seven top-selling drugs in the United States, three are for hypertension, two are for angina and cholesterol respectively, and two treat ulcers—including Zantac, the top-selling drug in the world. It is estimated that in the United States alone stress-related disease such as ulcers, high blood pressure and heart disease cost $200 billion a year in lost workdays, medical claims, and lost compensation.

The question arises as to how long a company can prevail if its employees, consciously or unconsciously, perceive their products, processes, or corporate goals as harmful to humankind. We must consider whether on some deep or primordial level, we sense and embody within ourselves the strains and demands we place upon the environment. What does it mean to work at a company that produces copious amounts of CO_2, thousands of tons of toxins, dangerous and controversial products? A company that has legal staff larger than its personnel department? Where gag orders are commonplace? Where lawsuits abound? And where safety is sometimes compromised? If such a company was full of depraved people, we would easily understand our dilemma and walk. But instead, it is run and operated by decent people who are friends, neighbors, and associates, people who, like ourselves, are not the least bit interested in harming the environment. Virtually no company exists or has been created to intentionally harm society, so we can assume that destructive acts of commerce are generally well intended, or based on knowledge that was available at the time of inception. But our understanding of the environment and humankind's impact upon it has accelerated and exploded in the past decades, and with that has come a great unease.

One source is quite apparent: An economy oblivious to the environment may be equally insensitive to its workers and managers. Employees will be used in wasteful ways, leading to workplace stress, overwork, ill-health or low morale. That the American workforce lives in a persistent state of anxiety further enlarges the power and control exerted over workers' lives by management. This relationship holds true in both successful and less successful companies, and it is made more acute when rank-and-file sees that a handful of executives and managers are lavishly compensated, in some cases with no apparent correlation to the performance of the company as a whole. In sum, many employees sense (after a decade's worth of "total quality" management, employee involvement programs, and workplace enhancement) that they are still caught in a fundamental inequality that they feel powerless to change. It should come as no surprise that every time a corporation offers a generous early-retirement program as a way to cut costs, it is usually oversubscribed.

It would be one problem—a serious one, granted—if our behavior within the corporate belief system hurt only ourselves, but the damage done is greater than that. It is axiomatic that people will do things in concert that they would not dream of doing as individuals. The actions required in warfare are the standard example, but business offers plenty of its own. The infamous Pinto gas tank was not designed to explode. Rather, an elaborate skein of rationalization, denial, and suppression of information was wrapped around the facts when the safety of the Pinto was questioned within the organization, even when the car was still in the design stage. When a disaster like this strikes and the corporate belief system finds itself at risk in the public eye, public relations is called in to deal with the crisis.

Denial will always prevent us from coming to terms with our actions as they affect the natural world but denial is an understandable reaction in the face of the great gulf between commercial reality and ecological reality. The fact is, if you work for a business—or even more so, if you own a business—it is highly inconvenient to fully acknowledge what is happening in the greater environment. That awareness runs counter to what we have been taught, and what we expect and want from our lives. America was founded on the "Go West, young man" principle of exploiting new lands and resources. Since World War II, we have expanded that principle, and now seek to grow more rapidly, drill deeper, speed up the economy, take more and do it faster. Today, we seem to be entering another phase, which is to deny the downside of present natural resource practices while pretending to be environmentally responsible. Our insatiable appetite for resources and the attendant waste caused by their consumption are being masked in meaningless eco-speak.

The message is much the same whatever the context: Don't worry about too much packaging, too much plastic, or too much waste. We are going to solve the problem with recycling and clean-up. You don't need to change your behavior, and we certainly don't need to change ours in any fundamental way. Recognizing that the greatest threat to their reputation and long-term fiscal health rested with children, their future customers, a number of corporations have entered the classroom, providing teaching kits to schools, many of which have been impoverished by tax-cutting programs supported by business. These teaching materials are, above all, cute: *Planet Patrol* by Procter & Gamble, *The Energy Cube* by Exxon, *Recyclasaurus and Recycle* by Dow Chemicals and Plastics, *Understanding the Waste Cycle* by Browning-Ferris Industries, and *Waste: A Hidden Resource* by Keep America Beautiful, a public relations extension of the packaging industry. In the same vein, Champion International put out advertisements entitled: "Save the Wheatfields. Recycle Toast." The ad goes on to say that environmental issues are "becoming clouded by misconception and confused by a myriad on concerns . . . Sure, trees are a vital natural resource, but they are a renewable resource—and one that is protected by sound forest management . . . The critical issue is garbage dumps." The company would like us to believe that ancient forests are comparable to wheatfields: crops you can grow year after year.

While social issues such as homelessness and poverty are rarely touched by corporations or TV programming because they represent no opportunities to create or maintain illusion, the environment is redolent with benign, endearing imagery. Soft-focus shots of deer in virgin forest are used as totemic proof of a paper company's commitment to the future even as they continue to clear-cut and fight congressional renewal of the Endangered Species Act. Native Americans look approvingly over a littered wildflower meadow being cleaned up by children using plastic bags advertised as biodegradable which in fact are not. (Mobil Oil was sued and chastised by attorney generals in several states for this ad). Simpson Paper introduces a line of "recycled" paper with fractional amounts of post-consumer waste under the names of Thoreau, Whitman, and Leopold. British nuclear power companies announce the nuclear energy is green energy since is does not pollute the air.

Within the forest products industry, one of the leaders in imaginative public relations is Louisiana-Pacific, whose chairman, Harry Merlo, was quoted saying, "We need everything that's out there . . . We log to infinity. Because we need it all, now!" but in a *Fortune* Magazine advertisement Merlo was wordsmith to meet the needs of the 1990's: "Respect for the environment is nothing new to me. From the time I was a small boy in a poor family of Italian immigrants, I've understood how precious our God-given resources are, and how important it is never to waste them. The lessons I learned from my mother, Clotilde Merlo—lessons of thrift, common sense, hard work, and strength of purpose—I have not forgotten for a single day."

It was Simpson Paper Co. and Harry Merlo's Louisiana-Pacific that discharged 40 million gallons per day of toxin-containing effluents into the Pacific Ocean near Eureka, California. After documenting over 40,000 violations of the Clear Water Act, surfers who were getting skin rashes and other ailments from the ocean sued both companies and won, forcing payments of fines totaling $5.6 million. The presiding judge wrote that Louisiana-Pacific "essentially exempted themselves from all environmental protection requirements and therefore [felt] free to discharge potentially chronically toxic effluent into the waters of the Pacific Ocean with impunity. The position is disingenuous and flies in the face of the Clean Water Act."

It is easy to become cynical about corporate PR and promotion, especially in the area of ecology, but cynicism may turn us away from the deeper truth, which is that environmental ad campaigns represent the limit and extent to which corporations are presently willing to accept ecological truths. Corporations do not perceive that present methods of production will deprive future generations, that there is a difference between supporting humankind with goods and services indefinitely and providing for them by relying upon environmental degradation as a means to overcome the carrying capacity of natural systems. What corporations do believe is that genuine environmentalism poses an enormous threat to their well-being. If you define well-being as their ability to continue to grow as they have in the past, they are correct.

Before the Industrial Revolution, commerce and culture were powerfully regulated by natural energy flows—mainly, the solar energy captured by food, wood, and wind. Scholars may debate the exact inflection point at which society turned to *stored* energy and, through it, harnessed the power of steam, railroads, and machinery, but once the process of industrialization commenced, the economic life of culture shifted from working with natural forces to working to overcome them. With the wholesale extraction and exploitation of stored solar energy, human beings are no longer living in synchronization with natural cycles and have accepted, however reluctantly, industrialism's shadow—waste, degradation, and dehumanization.

We have created, in essence, an artificial life, and in so doing, have lost some part of our human nature. Corporations extract resources and manufacture them into saleable products, leaving 11.4 billion tons of hazardous waste behind every year. On one level it appears that we are the customer for these goods, but on another level it is we who are being sold, offered up, and delivered to the corporations. It is we who are being extracted, mined, impoverished, and exploited. It is we who are fungible. Common wisdom holds that ecologists worry about nature while economists are concerned about human beings. But economists are in fact taking care of economics, and human beings are abandoned to the marketplace. What is for sale in America is our welfare.

Author Joanna Macy writes of a type of despair that people feel when they experience the gulf between the grotesqueness of the world and the business-as-usual tenor surrounding it. At the level of the family, the gap between what a child feels and knows is right and reasonable, and what mom and/or dad *tells* the child is right, can lead to schizophrenia. A similar dysfunctionality can affect an entire society that knows the state of the world is one way, yet is told over and over again that the world is something else. That disparity finds its most powerful and pervasive form in advertisements.

By the time he or she graduates from high school, an American teenager will have seen 350,000 commercials. Children watch commercials at school thanks to Whittle Communication's Channel One, which beams two minutes of advertising for every ten minutes of video "news" piped into thousands of classrooms. The average adult sees 21,000 commercials per year. Of these, 75 percent are paid for by the 100 largest corporations in America. In fact, corporations spend more money trying to get us to but their products than we spend on all of secondary education in this country. Besides breathing, what do you do more than 3,000 times a day? What you do—or, more specifically, what is done to you—is receive several thousand messages to buy something. Not all of these are TV hard-sells. Many are marketing messages on T-shirts, shopping bags, license plates, or even stenciled on your oranges and lemons. The others are billboards, radio spots, signs, movies, newspaper ads, labels on the outside of clothing, or sponsorships at operas and sporting events. When you arrive home in the evening, one of the first things you do is collect the flyers, junk mail, catalogs, envelopes from non-profit groups containing "personalized" letters, and free samples of shampoo hanging on your doorknob. Then the computer-generated junk phone calls start during dinner.

Few of the 3,000 daily marketing messages you receive are by invitation. The fact that we are free to ignore any one particular ad doesn't diminish the fact that the commercial environment as a whole is coercive. We cannot ignore it for it is where we live. There is no other place. With newspaper readership trailing off, and book reading likewise, TV has become America's intellectual environment. Our minds are being addressed by addictive media serving corporate sponsors whose purpose is to rearrange "reality" so that viewers forget the world around them.

Advertising *is* needed to inform, direct, and educate, but in its present form, it is an invasive expression of commerce. Advertising creates envy and a sense of inadequacy; it is responsible for mediocre TV programming because the lower denominators of taste produce the highest ratings; it deceives young and old alike into purchases that are inappropriate, unnecessary, or wasteful, feeding the frenzy of consumption that is responsible for civilization's overshooting present carrying capacity. It is a type of "disvalue," the *removal* of value from a product by transferring the monies that should go into quality to promotion and hyperbole instead. Mass-market advertising reinforces economic centralization because of the high costs required; it is antidemocratic because it is not designed to allow dissenting voices that challenge the product's value or merits, and serves no social needs. Advertising permeates our souls, and denigrates women, the intellect, and spirituality. It has been called the "paradigmatic science" of the twentieth century.

The restlessness of corporate promotion is matched by the passivity of consumers. Both parties are implicated, but both exonerate themselves gracelessly and easily by pointing a finger at the other. Businesses say that they are responding to market forces and will change when the consumer changes. Consumers feel economically trapped by corporations and see only the narrowest of options afforded in their daily acts; consciously or not, we feel abused, objectified, taken for granted. American consumers may continually astonish even themselves by their base behavior and wants, but they have also tried to express themselves to business in thousands of other ways, from MADD's campaigns against the promotion of beer and liquor to youth and citizens' clearinghouses on toxic waste issues, to local activist groups concerning open space. People are organizing to fight what they feel are the larger forces that infect their lives and values, forces that are almost invariably rooted in economic self-interest. The giant corporations are silent, immobile and unmoved by our stirrings and longings. When they do speak, it is almost always through the disingenuous voice of "corporate communications." Fixing, restructuring, and reorganizing the corporation to serve a restorative economy will not be a solution unless businesses level with their customers. As the therapist wisely counsels: honesty does not harm, dishonesty always does. Today's deteriorating culture, environment, and economy are the fruits of decades of corporate dishonesty, a dishonesty that we have created, sanctioned, and supported.

The potency of industrial systems is overwhelming. No culture in the world has been able to resist the allure, convenience, ease, and wonder of materialism. Industrial corporations have overturned thousands of years of belief and practices, sometimes overnight, replacing cultural traditions that linked human welfare to deities and great natural laws with a managerial system that showed how mankind could intervene with, overturn, and even replace natural law with engineering, mechanics, technology, and systems. The growing power of corporations has not been accompanied by any comprehensive philosophy, any ethical construct, other than the accumulation of wealth as an end in itself. Very few principles guide the commercial conduct of corporations other than those randomly adduced or self-proclaimed. Everyone—mangers, employees, customers—is left in limbo.

The writer Jeremy Rifkin points out how closely our industrialized concept of time is reflected in our social and environmental attitudes. When time becomes commoditized and scarce, and is constantly being accelerated, there follows an underlying separation of humankind from, a *weltanschauung* that says humankind can create its own world apart from the rhythms and pulses of nature. We live in a runaway commercial culture in which humans dominate and control natural processes to ill-conceived ends, where Faustian problems caused by technology and industry are solved by new technology and industry, where, supposedly, growth is limited only by our imaginations. Those who would carry us to a new world of computerization, robotics, bioengineering, and nano-technology see their role as architects of a future that is controllable, and thereby made secure against the random and seemingly unpredictable patterns of nature. They would create molecular machines that would eat pollution and produce ozone. They would fertilize the oceans with iron dust to reduce global warming. They would engineer our animals and plants and tailor then to human requirements: bacon with less cholesterol, tomatoes that have no genes telling then to decay, chickens without feathers or legs.

Business as practiced today is the opposite of the careful footsteps demanded by the placement of the stones in a Japanese garden, stones that make us conscious of each moment on the path, an arrangement that allows us to stop and consider the environment around us rather than merely walking or rushing through. A careful, attentive path corresponds to an ecological sense of time, honoring all biological connections.

Whenever those moments arise in life when we become aware, fully and wholly, of the transiency of our existence, we seek those tasks and roles that give our hearts, minds, and hands the potential to serve truly another human being. While paying off mortgages and raising the kids can often provide all the "meaning" people can handle in their middle years, people are searching for higher values, both in what they do, as expressed in their work, and in how they interact with the world. As the end of the millennium draws near, what this world desperately needs is to have more value added to it. Too much has been taken away and destroyed. Businesses have this opportunity and challenge to create meaningful work for those who cannot find it in what they are presently doing.

When Pacific Gas & Electric, a utility in northern California, announced a new division called the Energy Efficiency Department, they expected only a trickle of internal applicants. The new division had an agenda that was the opposite of the company's as a whole: It was to institute measures that would create energy out of conservation, and initiate programs, rebates, and incentives to generate "negawatts"—energy created through efficiency rather than new power plants. PG&E was overwhelmed with applications. People are hungry for ways in which they can integrate their need to be employed and support their families with work that improves the world in which they live. The department now has 300 employees.

People are either in denial or anxious that the disparity between what we experience in our own country and how most of the world lives is widening. Our prosperity in the North often results in the victimization of cultures and women and children in southern nations. People should be concerned about the difference between a population in the North that eats high on the food chain, and 1.1 billion people worldwide, especially children, who are malnourished or hungry. It is tragic that America's largest export after food is weaponry, often sent to governments with repressive domestic policies, governments whose military superiority is frequently used to wrest resources away from indigenous cultures to pay the debts incurred in the first place by weapons purchases. And slowly but powerfully, people are becoming concerned with the plight of women in all parts of the world, with the structural imposition of their second-class status with respect to families, education, government, business, and public policy.

Literally thousands of native cultures around the world have been destroyed by economic development. Lost with those cultures been languages, art and craft, family structures, land claims, traditional methods of healing and nourishment, rites and oral histories. Despite all the economic growth in the Third World between 1960 and 1980, the gap in real income between the rich and poor nations increased from a factor of 20 to a factor of 46, and that gap continues to increase. Rather than uplifting the less developed nations, industrial economies have caused increased polarization of rich and poor, unleashed ethnic conflict, destroyed lands, urbanized the poor to marginalized conditions, and made the developed nations richer in the process. According to former World Bank President Robert McNamara, "Even if the growth rate of the poor countries doubled, only seven would close the gap with the rich nations in 100 years. Only another nine would reach our level in 1000 years."

This is, in part, the result of the richer nations expanding their carrying capacity by exploiting resources in other countries. And while the United States may be richer, it has suffered some of the same fate as its neighbors internally: the skewing of the economic pie, a loss of traditions, and the destruction of culture. The top 1 percent of the population increased its wealth 150 times faster than the bottom 99 percent during the 1980s. Within the next decade, California will lose thirty-four Native American languages that have existed for over a thousand years. The people who would have spoken and taught these languages to another generation are driving Ford pick-ups, drinking Bud, or have vanished from the earth.

Business *can* provide meaning for workers and customers but not until it understands that the trust it undertakes and the growth it assumes are part of a larger covenant. As long as nature, children, women, and workers are abused by institutions espousing free-market theories, the *real* deficit will continue to grow—the difference between what business has taken and what it has returned, the difference between value added and value subtracted. For most people meaning is derived from just the opposite relationship, one in which one gives more than one takes, where one's life is intricately bound to the promotion of the common good.

If adding value is what business is, or should be, all about, then it follows that you can't contribute values unless you have them. Our personal values, which have become so distant and removed from the juggernauts of commerce, must become increasingly important and, finally, integral to the healthy functioning of our economy. Business offers us rich and important ways to improve the world. Every transaction in the scheme of the things is small, incremental, seemingly inconsequential, but each moment has the potential to create real change.

When Jerry Kohlberg withdrew from the Kohlberg Kravis Roberts partnership, dismayed that KKR had changed from a friend of innovative small companies to a predator, he said that "Around us there is a breakdown of . . . values in business and government . . . It is not just the overweening, overpowering greed that pervades our business life. It is the fact that we are not willing to sacrifice for the ethics and values we profess. For an ethic is not an ethic, and a value not a value, without some sacrifice for it, something given up, something not taken, something not gained. We do it in exchange for a greater good, for something worth more than just money and power and position."

Daniel Quinn

1872-1970

Ishmael

1992

Born in 1935 in Omaha, Nebraska, Daniel Quinn graduated from Creighton Prep in 1953 and subsequently pursued studies at St. Louis University, the University of Vienna, and at Loyola University of Chicago from which he received his bachelor's degree in English, *cum laude* in 1957.

His notoriety comes from his novel, *Ishmael*, which won him the 1991 Turner Tomorrow Fellowship. This fellowship aims to encourage authors to seek "creative and positive solutions to global problems." (Ishmael.org) In his twenty-plus year career in education and publishing he has served as a "Biography and Fine Arts" editor at the *American Peoples Encyclopedia*, served as the managing editor of the Greater Cleveland Mathematics Program, and heads of the mathematics department at the Encyclopedia Britannica Educational Corporation.

His writings lead the reader into an exploration of humanity's place within the world. His novel, *After Dachau,* raises questions of history, personal identity, and cultural assumptions. His unusual style works to change perspective about common global issues and leaves the reader to question assumptions that would be considered conventional wisdom by many.

In *Ishmael*, he uses the relationship of one character teaching another to explore answers to global problems and issues. The story differentiates between "Leaver" cultures and "Taker" cultures, where a "Leaver" culture strives to coexist with its environment, whereas a "Taker" culture dominates and controls the environment.

1. Propose a means by which the population of earth as a whole can be characterized as a "Leaver" culture. Do the same for earth's population as a "Taker" culture.
2. A simple answer to "Taker" society is proposed. Is it an ethical solution to the issue at hand? What other simple solution could be formulated to aid in the solution of the "Taker" problem?

SOURCES:

"Natural Capitalism." Accessed April 17, 2008 from http://www.natcap.org/.

"Biography." Accessed April 17, 2008 from http://www.paulhawken.com/paulhawken_frameset.html.

SELECTION FROM:

Quinn, Daniel. (1992). *Ishmael.* New York: Bantam/Turner. 56-65, 105-112.

3

This story (Ishmael said) takes place half a billion years ago—an inconceivably long time ago, when this planet would be all but unrecognizable to you. Nothing at all stirred on the land, except the wind and the dust. Not a single blade of grass waved in the wind, not a single cricket chirped, not a single bird soared in the sky. All these things were tens of millions of years in the future. Even the seas were eerily still and silent, for the vertebrates too were tens of millions of years away in the future.

But of course there was an anthropologist on hand. What sort of world would it be without an anthropologist? He was, however, a very depressed and disillusioned anthropologist, for he'd been everywhere on the planet looking for someone to interview, and every tape in his knapsack was as blank as the sky. But one day as he was moping along beside the ocean he saw what seemed to be a living creature in the shallows off shore. It was nothing to brag about, just a sort of squishy blob, but it was the only prospect he'd seen in all his journeys, so he waded out to where it was bobbing in the waves.

He greeted the creature politely and was greeted in kind, and soon the two of them were good friends. The anthropologist explained as well as he could that he was a student of life-styles and customs, and begged his new friend for information of this sort, which was readily forthcoming. "And now," he said at last, "I'd like to get on tape in your own words some of the stories you tell among yourselves."

"Stories?" the other asked.

"You know, like your creation myth, if you have one."

"What is a creation myth?" the creature asked.

"Oh, you know," the anthropologist replied, "the fanciful tale you tell your children about the origins of the world."

Well, at this, the creature drew itself up indignantly—at least as well as a squishy blob can do—and replied that his people had no such fanciful tale.

"You have no account of creation then?"

"Certainly we have an account of creation," the other snapped. "But it is definitely not a *myth*."

"Oh, certainly not," the anthropologist said, remembering his training at last. "I'll be terribly grateful if you share it with me."

"Very well," the creature said. "But I want you to understand that, like you, we are a strictly rational people, who accept nothing that is not based on observation, logic, and the scientific method."

"Of course, of course," the anthropologist agreed.

So at last the creature began its story. "The universe," it said, "was born a long, long time ago, perhaps ten or fifteen billion years ago. Our own solar system—this star, this planet and all the others—seem to have come into being some two or three billion years ago. For a long time, nothing whatever lived here. But then, after a billion years or so, life appeared."

"Excuse me," the anthropologist said. "You say that life appeared. Where did that happen, according to your myth—I mean, according to your scientific account."

The creature seemed baffled by the question and turned a pale lavender. "Do you mean in what precise spot?"

"No. I mean, did this happen on the land or in the sea?"

"Land?" the other asked. "What is land?"

"Oh, you know," he said, waving toward the shore, "the expanse of dirt and rocks that begins over there."

The creature turned a deeper shade of lavender and said, "I can't imagine what you're gibbering about. The dirt and rocks over there are simply the lip of the vast bowl that holds the sea."

"Oh yes," the anthropologist said, "I see what you mean. Quite. Go on."

"Very well," the other said. "For many millions of centuries the life of the world was merely microorganisms floating helplessly in a chemical broth. But little by little, more complex forms appeared: single-celled creatures, slimes, algae, polyps, and so on.

"But finally," the creature said, turning quite pink with pride as he came to the climax of his story, "but finally *jellyfish* appeared!"

4

Nothing much came out of me for ninety seconds or so, except maybe waves of baffled fury. Then I said, "That's not fair."

"What do you mean?"

"I don't exactly know what I mean. You've made some sort of point, but I don't know what it is."

"You don't?"

"No, I don't."

"What did the jellyfish mean when it said, 'But finally jellyfish appeared'?"

"It meant . . . that is what it was all leading up to. This is what the whole ten or fifteen billion years of creation were leading up to: jellyfish."

"I agree. And why doesn't your account of creation end with the appearance of jellyfish?"

I suppose I tittered. "Because there was more to come beyond jellyfish."

"That's right. Creation didn't end with jellyfish. Still to come were the vertebrates and the amphibians and the reptiles and the mammals, and of course, finally, man."

"Right."

"And so your account of creation ends, 'And finally man appeared.'"

"Yes."

"Meaning what?"

"Meaning that there was no more to come. Meaning that creation had come to an end."

"This is what it was all leading up to."

"Yes."

"Of course. Everyone in your culture knows this. The pinnacle was reached in man. Man is the climax of the whole cosmic drama of creation."

"Yes."

"When man finally appeared, creation came to an end, because its objective had been reached. There was nothing left to create."

"That seems to be the unspoken assumption."

"It's certainly not always unspoken. The religions of your culture aren't reticent about it. Man is the end product of creation. Man is the creature for whom all the rest was made: this world, this solar system, this galaxy, the universe itself."

"True."

"Everyone in your culture knows that the world wasn't created for jellyfish or salmon or iguanas or gorillas. It was created for man."

"That's right."

Ishmael fixed me with a sardonic eye. "And this is not mythology?"

"Well . . . the facts are facts."

"Certainly. Facts are facts, even when they're embodied in mythology. But what about the rest? Did the entire cosmic process of creation come to an end three million years ago, right here on this little planet, with the appearance of man?"

"No."

"Did even the planetary process of creation come to an end three million years ago with the appearance of man? Did evolution come to a screeching halt just because man had arrived?"

"No, of course not."

"Then why did you tell it that way?"

"I guess I told it that way, because that's the way it's told."

"That's the way it's told among the Takers. It's certainly not the only way it can be told."

"Okay, I see that now. How would you tell it?"

He nodded toward the world outside his window. "Do you see the slightest evidence anywhere in the universe that creation came to an end with the birth of man? Do you see the slightest evidence anywhere out there that man was the climax toward which creation had been straining from the beginning?"

"No. I can't even imagine what such evidence would look like."

"That should be obvious. If the astrophysicists could report that the fundamental creative processes of the universe came to a halt five billion years ago, when our solar system made its appearance, that would offer at least some support for these notions."

"Yes, I see what you mean."

"Or if the biologists and paleontologists could report that speciation came to a halt three million years ago, this too would be suggestive."

"Yes."

"But you know that neither of these things happened in fact. Very far from it. The universe went on as before, the planet went on as before. Man's appearance caused no more stir than the appearance of jellyfish."

"Very true."

Ishmael gestured toward the tape recorder. "So what are we to make of that story you told?"

I bared my teeth in a rueful grin. "It's a myth. Incredibly enough, it's a myth."

5

"I told you yesterday that the story the people of your culture are enacting is about the meaning of the world, about divine intentions in the world, and about human destiny."

"Yes."

"And according to this first part of the story, what is the meaning of the world?"

I thought about that for a moment. "I don't quite see how it explains the meaning of the world."

"Along about the middle of your story, the focus of attention shifted from the universe at large to this one planet. Why?"

"Because this one planet was destined to be the birthplace of man."

"Of course. As you tell it, the birth of man was a central event—indeed the central event—in the history of the cosmos itself. From the birth of man on, the rest of the universe ceases to be of interest, ceases to participate in the unfolding drama. For this, the earth alone is sufficient; it is the birthplace and home of man, and that's its meaning. The Takers regard the world as a sort of human life-support system, as a machine designed to produce and sustain human life."

"Yes, that's so."

"In your telling of the story, you naturally left out any mention of the gods, because you didn't want it to be tainted with mythology. Since its mythological character is now established, you no longer have to worry about that. Supposing there is a divine agency behind creation, what can you tell me about the gods' intentions?"

"Well, basically, what they had in mind when they started out was man. They made the universe so that our galaxy could be in it. They made the galaxy so that our solar system could be in it. They made our solar system so that our planet could be in it. And they made our planet so that we could be in it. The whole thing was made so that man would have a hunk of dirt to stand on."

"And this is generally how it's understood in your culture—at least by those who assume that the universe is an expression of divine intentions."

"Yes."

"Obviously, since the entire universe was made so that man could be made, man must be a creature of enormous importance to the gods. But this part of the story gives no hint of their intentions toward him. They must have some special destiny in mind for him, but that's not revealed here."

"True."

6

"Every story is based on a premise, is the working out of a premise. As a writer, I'm sure you know that."

"Yes."

"You'll recognize this one: *Two children of warring families fall in love.*"

"Right. *Romeo and Juliet.*"

"The story being enacted in the world by the Takers also has a premise, which is embodied in the part of the story you told me today. See if you can figure out what it is."

I closed my eyes and pretended I was working hard, when in fact I knew I didn't stand a chance. "I'm afraid I don't see it."

"The story the Leavers have enacted in the world has an entirely different premise, and it could be impossible for you to discover it at this point. But you should be able to discover the premise of your own story. It's a very simple notion and the most powerful in all of human history. Not necessarily the most beneficial but certainly the most powerful. Your entire history, with all its marvels and catastrophes, is a working out of this premise."

"Truthfully, I can't even imagine what you're getting at."

"Think . . . Look, the world wasn't made for jellyfish, was it?"

"No."

"It wasn't made for frogs or lizards or rabbits."

"No."

"Of course not. The world was made for man."

"That's right."

"Everyone in your culture knows that, don't they? Even atheists who swear there is no god know that the world was made for man."

"Yes, I'd say so."

"All right. That's the premise of your story: *The world was made for man.*"

"I can't quite grasp it. I mean, I can't quite see why it's a premise."

"The people of your culture *made* it a premise—*took* it as a premise. They said: *What if* the world was made for *us*?"

"Okay. Keep going."

"Think of the consequences of taking that as your premise: If the world was made for you, *then what*?"

"Okay, I see what you mean. I think. If the world was made for us, then it *belongs* to us and we can do what we damn well please with it."

"Exactly. That's what's been happening here for the past ten thousand years: You've been doing what you damn well please with the world. And of course you mean to go right on doing what you damn well please with it, because the whole damn thing *belongs to you.*"

"Yes," I said, and thought for a second. "Actually, that's pretty amazing. I mean, you hear this fifty times a day. People talk about *our* environment, *our* seas, *our* solar system. I've even heard people talk about *our wildlife.*"

"And just yesterday you assured me with complete confidence that there was nothing in your culture remotely resembling mythology."

"True. I did." Ishmael continued to stare at me morosely. "I was wrong," I told him. "What more do you want?"

"Astonishment," he said.

I nodded. "I'm astonished, all right. I just don't let it show."

"I should have gotten you when you were seventeen."

I shrugged, meaning that I wished he had.

7

"Yesterday I told you that your story provides you with an explanation of how things came to be this way."

"Right."

"What contribution does this first part of the story make to that explanation?"

"You mean . . . what contribution does it make to explaining how things came to be the way they are right now?"

"That's right."

"Offhand, I don't see how it makes any contribution to it."

"Think. Would things have come to be this way if the world had been made for jellyfish?"

"No, they wouldn't."

"Obviously not. If the world had been made for jellyfish, things would be entirely different."

"That's right. But it wasn't made for jellyfish, it was made for man."

"And this partly explains *how things came to be this way.*"

"Right. It's sort of a sneaky way of blaming everything on the gods. If they'd made the world for jellyfish, then none of this would have happened."

"Exactly," Ishmael said. "You're beginning to get the idea."

8

"Do you have a feeling now for where you might find the other parts of this story—the middle and the end?"

I gave this some thought. "I'd watch Nova, I think."

"Why?"

"I'd say that if Nova was doing the story of creation, the story I told today would be the outline. All I have to do now is figure out how they'd do the rest."

"Then that's your next assignment. Tomorrow I want to hear the middle of the story."

Section Four
5

Ishmael spent the next few minutes staring at a point about twenty inches in front of his nose, and I began to wonder if he'd forgotten I was there. Then he shook his head and came to. For the first time in our acquaintance, he delivered something like a minilecture.

"The gods have played three dirty tricks on the Takers," he began. "In the first place, they didn't put the world where the Takers thought it belonged, in the center of the universe. They really hated hearing this, but they got used to it. Even if man's home was stuck off in the boondocks, they could still believe he was the central figure in the drama of creation.

"The second of the gods' tricks was worse. Since man was the climax of creation, the creature for whom all the rest was made, they should have had the decency to produce him in a manner suited to his dignity and importance—in a separate, special act of creation. Instead they arranged for him to evolve from the common slime, just like ticks and liver flukes. The Takers really hated hearing this, but they're beginning to adjust to it. Even if man evolved from the common slime, it's still his divinely appointed destiny to rule the world and perhaps even the universe itself.

"But the last of the gods' tricks was the worst of all. Though the Takers don't know it yet, the gods did not exempt man from the law that governs the lives of grubs and ticks and shrimps and rabbits and mollusks and deer and lions and jellyfish. They did not exempt him from this law any more than they exempted him from the law of gravity, and this is going to be the bitterest blow of all to the Takers. To the gods' other dirty tricks, they could adjust. To this one, no adjustment is possible."

He sat there for a while, a hillside of fur and flesh, I guess letting this pronouncement sink in. Then he went on. "Every law has effects or it wouldn't be discoverable as a law. The effects of the law we're looking for are very simple. Species that live in compliance with the law live forever—environmental conditions permitting. This will, I hope, be taken as good news for mankind in general, because if mankind lives in compliance with this law, then it too will live forever—or for as long as conditions permit.

"But of course this isn't the law's only effect. Those species that do *not* live in compliance with the law become extinct. In the scale of biological time, they become extinct very rapidly. And this is going to be very bad news for the people of your culture—the worst they've ever heard."

"I hope," I said, "that you don't think any of this is showing me where to look for this law."

Ishmael thought for a moment, then took a branch from the pile at his right, held it up for me to see, then let it fall to the floor. "That's the effect Newton was trying to explain." He waved a hand toward the world outside. "That's the effect *I'm* trying to explain. Looking out there, you see a world full of species that, environmental conditions permitting are going to go on living indefinitely."

"Yes, that's what I assume. But why does it need explaining?"

Ishmael selected another branch from his pile, held it up, and let it fall to the floor. "Why does *that* need explaining?"

"Okay. So you're saying this phenomenon is not the result of *nothing*. It's the effect of a law. A law is in operation."

"Exactly. A law is in operation, and my task is to show you how it operates. At this point, the easiest way to show you how it operates is by analogy with laws you already know—the law of gravity and the laws of aerodynamics."

"Okay."

6

"You know that, as we sit here, we are in no sense defying the law of gravity. Unsupported objects fall toward the center of the earth, and the surfaces on which we're sitting are our supports."

"Right."

"The laws of aerodynamics don't provide us with a way of defying the law of gravity. I'm sure you understand that. They simply provide us with a way of using the air as a support. A man sitting in an airplane is subject to the law of gravity in exactly the way we're subject to it sitting here. Nevertheless the man sitting in the plane obviously enjoys a freedom we lack: the freedom of the air."

"Yes."

"The law we're looking for is like the law of gravity: There is no escaping it, but there is a way of achieving the equivalent of flight—the equivalent of freedom of the air. In other words, it is possible to build a civilization that flies."

I stared at him for a while, then I said, "Okay."

"You remember how the Takers went about trying to achieve powered flight. They didn't begin with an understanding of the laws of aerodynamics. They didn't begin with a theory based on research and carefully planned experimentation. They just built contraptions, pushed them off the sides of cliffs, and hoped for the best."

"True."

"All right. I want to follow one of those early trials in detail. Let's suppose that this trial is being made in one of those wonderful pedal-driven contraptions with flapping wings, based on a mistaken understanding of avian flight."

"Okay."

"As the flight begins, all is well. Our would-be airman has been pushed off the edge of the cliff and is pedaling away, and the wings of his craft are flapping like crazy. He's feeling wonderful, ecstatic. He's experiencing the freedom of the air. What he doesn't realize, however, is that this craft is aerodynamically incapable of flight. It simply isn't in compliance with the laws that make flight possible—but he would laugh if you told him this. He's never heard of such laws, knows nothing about them. He would point at those flapping wings and say, 'see? Just like a bird!' Nevertheless, whatever he thinks, he's not in flight. He's an unsupported object falling toward the center of the earth. He's not in flight, he's in free fall. Are you with me so far?"

"Yes."

"Fortunately—or, rather, unfortunately for our airman—he chose a very high cliff to launch his craft from. His disillusionment is a long way off in time and space. There he is in free fall, feeling wonderful and congratulating himself on his triumph. He's like the man in the joke who jumps out of a ninetieth-floor window on a bet. As he passes the tenth floor, he says to himself, 'Well, so far so good!'

"There he is in free fall, experiencing the exhilaration of what he takes to be flight. From his great height he can see for miles around, and one thing he sees puzzles him: The floor of the valley is dotted with craft just like his—not crashed, simply abandoned. 'Why,' he wonders, 'aren't these craft in the air instead of sitting on the ground? What sort of fools would abandon their aircraft when they could be enjoying the freedom of the air?' Ah well, the behavioral quirks of less talented, earthbound mortals are none of his concern. However, looking down into the valley has brought something else to his attention. He doesn't seem to be maintaining his altitude. In fact, the earth seems to be rising up toward him. Well, he's not very worried about that. After all, his flight has been a complete success up to now, and there's no reason why it shouldn't go on being a success. He just has to pedal a little harder, that's all.

"So far so good. He thinks with amusement of those who predicted that his flight would end in disaster, broken bones, and death. Here he is, he's come all this way, and he hasn't even gotten a bruise, much less a broken bone. But then he looks down again, and what he sees really disturbs him. The law of gravity is catching up to him at the rate of thirty-two feet per second per second—at an accelerating rate. The ground is now rushing up toward him in an alarming way. He's disturbed but far from desperate. 'My craft has brought me *this* far in safety,' he tells himself. 'I just have to keep going.' And so he starts pedaling with all his might. Which of course does him no good at all, because his craft simply isn't in accord with the laws of aerodynamics. Even if he had the power of a thousand men in his legs—ten thousand, a million—that craft is not going to achieve flight. That craft is doomed—and so is he unless he abandons it."

"Right. I see what you're saying, but I don't see the connection with what we're talking about here."

Ishmael nodded. "Here is the connection. Ten thousand years ago, the people of your culture embarked on a similar flight: a civilization flight. Their craft wasn't designed according to any theory at all. Like our imaginary airman, they were totally unaware that there is a law that must be complied with in order to achieve civilization flight. They didn't even wonder about it. They wanted the freedom of the air, and so they pushed off in the first contraption that came to hand: the Taker Thunderbolt.

"At first all was well. In fact, all was terrific. The Takers were pedaling away and the wings of their craft were flapping beautifully. They felt wonderful, exhilarated. They were experiencing the freedom of the air: freedom from restraints that bind and limit the rest of the biological community. And with that freedom came marvels—all the things you mentioned the other day: urbanization, technology, literacy, mathematics, science.

"Their flight could never end, it could only go on becoming more and more exciting. They couldn't know, couldn't even have guessed that, like our hapless airman, they were in the air but not in flight. They were in free fall, because their craft was simply not in compliance with the law that makes flight possible. But their disillusionment is far away in the future, and so they're pedaling away and having a wonderful time. Like our airman, they see strange sights in the course of their fall. They see the remains of craft very like their own—not destroyed, merely abandoned—by the Maya, by the Hohokam, by the Anasazi, by the peoples of the Hopewell cult, to mention only a few of those found here in the New World. 'Why,' they wonder, 'are these craft on the ground instead of in the air? Why would any people prefer to be earthbound when they could have the freedom of the air, as we do?' It's beyond comprehension, an unfathomable mystery.

"Ah well, the vagaries of such foolish people are nothing to the Takers. They're pedaling away and having a wonderful time. They're not going to abandon *their* craft. They're going to enjoy the freedom of the air forever. But alas, a law is catching up to them. They don't know such a law even exists, but this ignorance affords them no protection from its effects. This is a law as unforgiving as the law of gravity, and it's catching up to them in exactly the same way the law of gravity caught up to our airman: *at an accelerating rate.*

"Some gloomy nineteenth-century thinkers, like Robert Wallace and Thomas Robert Malthus, look down. A thousand years before, even five hundred years before, they would probably have noticed nothing. But now what they see alarms them. It's as though the ground is rushing up to meet them—as though they are going to crash. They do some figuring and say, 'If we go on this way, we're going to be in big trouble in the not-too-distant future.' The other Takers shrug their predictions off.

'We've come all this enormous way and haven't even received so much as a scratch. It's true the ground seems to be rising up to meet us, but that just means we'll have to pedal a little harder. Not to worry.' Nevertheless, just as was predicted, famine soon becomes a routine condition of life in many parts of the Taker Thunderbolt—and the Takers have to pedal even harder and more efficiently than before. But oddly enough, the harder and more efficient they pedal, the worse conditions become. Very strange. Peter Farb calls it a paradox: 'Intensification of production to feed an increased population leads to a still greater increase in population.' 'Never mind,' the Takers said. 'We'll just have to put same people pedaling away on a reliable method of birth control. Then the Taker Thunderbolt will fly forever.'

"But such simple answers aren't enough to reassure the people of your culture nowadays. Everyone is looking down, and it's obvious that the ground is rushing up toward you—and rushing up faster every year. Basic ecological and planetary systems are being impacted by the Taker Thunderbolt, and that impact increases in intensity every year. Basic, irreplaceable resources are being devoured every year—and they're being devoured more greedily every year. Pessimists—or it may be that they're realists—look down and say, 'Well, the crash may be twenty years off or maybe as much as fifty years off. Actually it could happen anytime. There's no way to be sure.' But of course there are optimists as well, who say, 'We must have faith in our craft. After all, it has brought us *this* far in safety. What's ahead isn't doom, it's just a little hump that we can clear if we all just pedal a little harder. Then we'll soar into a glorious, endless future, and the Taker Thunderbolt will take us to the stars and we'll conquer the universe itself.' But your craft isn't going to save you. Quite the contrary, it's your craft that's carrying you toward catastrophe. Five billion of you pedaling away—or ten billion or twenty billion—can't make it fly. It's been in free fall from the beginning, and that fall is about to end."

At last I had something of my own to add to this. "The worst dart of it is this," I said, "that the survivors, if there are any, will immediately set about doing it all over again, exactly the same way."

"Yes, I'm afraid you're right. Trial and error isn't a bad way to learn how to build an aircraft, but it can be a disastrous way to learn how to build a civilization."

Mark Reisner

1949-2000

Cadillac Desert

1986

Marc Reisner was born in St. Paul Minnesota and graduated from Earlham College in Indiana. He was a staff writer for the Natural Resources Defense Council from 1972 to 1979. Upon receiving the Alicia Patterson Journalism Fellowship in 1979, he used this to investigate water resources in the American West. This resulted in his book *Cadillac Desert: The American West and Its Disappearing Water*, published in 1986.

A free-lance writer for most of his life, he remained dedicated to the values he espoused within the pages of *Cadillac Desert*. A devout environmentalist, he made his living writing, while supporting his causes and his family. At the age of 51 he died from cancer.(or cancer took his life.)

As result of this book, Reisner rose to prominence as a writer of national acclaim and went on to be nominated for a National Book Critics Circle Award. The selections included here range from historical information on the establishment of water rights west of the Mississippi, to political wranglings, and the environmental impacts of battles for disbursement of water, to the role of the Bureau of Reclamation in administrating legal decisions.

1. How did (and does) the political and social history of the American West dictate use and distribution of water?
2. How do the human population and the natural ecology of the western United States contribute to water use?

3. Much of the American West operates at least in part on hydroelectric power. How does this compare to other energy sources such as coal, nuclear, or solar?

SOURCES:

Marston, Ed. *Farewell, Marc Reisner.* Accessed May 3, 2007 from High Country News. August 14, 2000. http://www.hcn.org/servlets/hcn.Article?article_id=5929.

Reisner, M. (1986). *Cadillac Desert: The American West and Its Disappearing Water.* New York: Viking Penguin Inc.

SELECTION FROM:

Reisner, M. (1986). *Cadillac Desert: The American West and Its Disappearing Water.* New York: Viking Penguin Inc. 25-26, 43-53, 112-124.

Cadillac Desert

John Wesley Powell belonged to a subspecies of American which flourished briefly during the nineteenth century and went extinct with the end of the frontier. It was an estimable company, one that included the likes of Mark Twain, John Muir, Abraham Lincoln, William Dean Howells, and Hamlin Garland. They were genuine Renaissance men, though their circumstances were vastly different from those of Jefferson or Benjamin Franklin. The founding fathers, the most notable among them, were urban gentlemen or gentlemen farmers who grew up in a society that, though it sought to keep Europe and its mannerisms at arm's length, had a fair amount in common with the Old World. They lived in very civilized style, even if they lived at the edge of a frontier. Powell, Howells, Lincoln, and the others were children of the real frontier. Most grew up on subsistence farms hacked out of ancient forests or grafted onto tallgrass prairie; they lacked formal education, breeding, and refinement. Schooled by teachers who knew barely more than they did, chained to the rigors of farm life, they got their education from borrowed books devoured by the embers of a fireplace or surreptitiously smuggled into the fields. What they lacked in worldliness and schooling, however, they more than made up in vitality, originality, and circumambient intelligence. John Wesley Powell may be one of the lesser-known of this group, but he stood alone in the variety of his interests and the indefatigability of his pursuits.

Powell's father was a poor itinerant preacher who transplanted his family westward behind the breaking wave of the frontier. As a boy in the 1840s, Powell moved from Chillicothe, Ohio, to Walworth County, Wisconsin, to Bonus Prairie, Illinois. Nothing was paved, little was fenced; the forests were full of cougars and the streams full of fish. To Powell, the frontier was a rapturous experience. Like John Muir, he got a vagabond's education, rambling cross-country in order to become intimate with forests and fauna, with hydrology and weather. In the summer of 1855, Powell struck out for four months and walked across Wisconsin. Two years later he floated down the Ohio River from Pittsburgh to St. Louis. A few months later, he was gathering fossils in interior Missouri. The next spring he was rowing alone down the Illinois River and up the Mississippi and the Des Moines River to the middle of Iowa, then a wilderness. Between his peregrinations Powell picked up some frantic education—Greek, Latin, botany, a bit of philosophy—at Wheaton, Oberlin, and Illinois College, but he never graduated and he never stayed long. Powell learned on the run.

When the Civil War broke out, Powell enlisted on the Union side, fought bravely, and came out a major, a confidant of Ulysses Grant, and minus an arm, which was removed by a steel ball at the Battle of Shiloh. To Powell, the loss of an arm was merely a nuisance, though the raw nerve endings in his amputated stump kept him in pain for the rest of his life. After the war he tried a stint at teaching, first at Illinois Wesleyan and then at Illinois State, but it didn't satisfy him. He helped found the Illinois Museum of Natural History, and was an obvious candidate for the position of curator, but decided that this, too, was too dull an avenue with too visible an end. Powell, like the mountain men, was compulsively drawn to the frontier. In the United States of the late 1860s, there was but one place where the frontier was still nearly intact . . . .

[* * *]

. . . By 1869, the population of New York City had surpassed one million. The city had built a great water-supply aqueduct to the Croton River and was imagining its future subway system. Chicago, founded thirty years earlier, was already a big sprawling industrial town. The millionaires of San Francisco were building their palatial mansions on Nob Hill. New England was deforested, farms and settlements were spilling onto the prairie. However, on maps of the United States Capitalists, newspaper editors, lonely pioneers, local emperors of Gilpin's ilk—all had a stake in retreating deserts. But they were not the only ones. Abolitionists, for example, did, too. In the 1850s, when Kansas seemed likely to be the next state admitted to the Union, something approaching warfare broke out between those who would have made it a free state and those who would have tolerated slavery. Horace Greeley, an avowed abolitionist with considerable interest in the West, found the climate in Kansas wonderful and the rainfall abundant. In such a state, Greeley said in his influential editorials, a 160-acre homestead could produce an ample living. A plantation, of course, demanded more land—but if Kansas was full of yeoman farmers working 160-acre plots, plantations and slaves were not likely to intrude.

One hundred and sixty acres. If anything unifies the story of the American West—its past and its present, its successes and its dreadful mistakes—it is this mythical allotment of land. Its origins are found in the original Homestead Act of 1862, which settled on such an amount—a quarter-mile square, more often referred to as a quarter section—as the ideal acreage for a Jeffersonian utopia of small farmers. The idea was to carve millions of quarter sections out of the public domain, sell them cheaply to restless Americans and arriving immigrants, and, by letting them try to scratch a living out of them, develop the nation's resources and build up its character.

In the West, the Homestead Act had several later incarnations. The Desert Lands Act, the Timber Culture Act, and the Timber and Stone Act were the principal ones. Neither Congress nor the General Land Office, which was responsible for administering the acts, could ever comprehend that the relative success of the land program east of the Mississippi River had less to do with the perseverance of the settlers or the wisdom of the legislation than with the forgiving nature of the climate. In the East, virtually every acre received enough rainfall, except during years of extraordinary drought, to grow most anything that didn't mind the soil and the temperature. (Unlike much of the West, which suffers through months of habitual drought, the East gets precipitation year-round; in the spring and early summer, when crops need water most, much of the East is exceptionally wet.) Since the growing season, except in the extreme north, was at least five months long, even an ignorant or lazy farmer could raise *some* kind of crop.

In the West, even if you believed that the rainfall was magically increasing, you still had to contend with high altitudes (the western plains, the Snake River Valley, and most of the irrigable lands in the Great Basin would float over the tops of all but the highest Appalachian Mountains) and, as a result, chronic frost danger even in May and September. Then there were the relentless winds, hailstones bigger than oranges, tornadoes, and breathtaking thunderstorms. There were sandy lands that would not retain moisture and poorly drained lands that retained too much; there were alkaline lands that poisoned crops.

The General Land Office bureaucrats sat in Washington pretending that such conditions did not exist. Their job, as they perceived it, was to fill little squares with people. They extended no credit, provided no water, offered no services. And the permutations of the Homestead Act that found their way into the western versions of the law sometimes added to the farmers' burdens. Under the Timber Culture Act, for example, you had to plant one-quarter of your quarter section with trees, a stipulation inserted because it was thought that trees increased the rainfall. In West Texas, where, meteorologically speaking, all that is predictable is the wind, you would have to spend most of your time replanting your fallen-down trees. Under the Desert Lands Act, which applied to land so arid even the government realized that farming was hopeless without irrigation, you had to demonstrate "proof of irrigation" before you could own the land. Unless you owned reasonably flat land immediately adjacent to a relatively constant stream which did not, as most western rivers do for much of their length, flow in a canyon, complying with the Desert Lands Act was almost out of the question. A mutual irrigation effort by the inhabitants of a valley was, perhaps, a possibility. That was what the Mormons had done, but they were a close-knit society linked by a common faith and a history of persecution.

The members of Congress who wrote the legislation, the land office agents who doled out land, and the newspaper editors who celebrated the settlers' heroism had, in a great many cases, never laid eyes on the land or the region that enclosed it. They were unaware that in Utah, Wyoming, and Montana—to pick three of the colder and drier states—there was not a single quarter section on which a farmer could subsist, even with luck, without irrigation, because an unirrigated quarter section was enough land for about five cows. The Indians accepted things as they were; that is why they were mostly nomadic, wandering toward greener grass and fuller herds and flowing water. If whites were going to insist on living there—fixed, settled, mortgaged, fenced—the best they could do with the land was graze it. But in those three states, an economical grazing unit was, say, twenty-five hundred to five thousand acres, depending on the circumstances. To amass that much land you had to cheat—on a magnificent scale. If you didn't, you had to overgraze the land and ruin it, and many millions of acres were damaged or ruined in exactly this way. Many settlers were tasting property ownership for the first time in their lives, and all they had in common was greed.

Speculation. Water monopoly. Land monopoly. Erosion. Corruption. Catastrophe. By 1876, after several trips across the plains and through the Rocky Mountain states, John Wesley Powell was pretty well convinced that those would be the fruits of a western land policy based on wishful thinking, willfulness, and lousy science. And by then everything he predicted was happening, especially land monopoly, water monopoly, graft, and fraud.

Homesteads fronting on streams went like oranges aboard a scurvy-ridden ship. The doctrine of riparian rights, which had been unthinkingly imported from the East, made it possible to monopolize the water in a stream if you owned the land alongside it. But if the stream was anything larger than a creek, only the person who owned land upstream, where it was still small, could manage to build a dam or barrage to guarantee a summer flow; then he could divert all he wanted, leaving his downstream neighbors with a bed of dry rocks. Riparian doctrine alone, therefore, made it possible for a tiny handful of landowners to monopolize the few manageable rivers of the West. When their neighbors saw their predicament and sold out, they could monopolize the best land, too.

As for the Desert Land Act and the Timber and Stone Act, they could not have promoted land monopoly and corruption more efficiently if they had been expressly designed for that purpose. A typical irrigation scene under the Desert Land Act went as follows: A beneficiary hauled a hogshead of water and a witness to his barren land, dumped the water on the land, paid the witness $20, and brought him to the land office, where the witness swore he had seen the land irrigated. Then, with borrowed identification and different names, another land application was filed, and the scene was repeated. If you could pull it off six or seven times, you had yourself a ranch. Foreign sailors arriving in San Francisco were offered a few dollars, a jug of whiskey, and an evening in a whorehouse in exchange for filing a land claim under the Timber and Stone Act. Before shipping out, the sailors abdicated title; there were no restrictions on transfer of ownership. Whole redwood forests were acquired in such a manner.

Then there was the Swamplands Act, or Swamp and Overflow Act—a Desert Lands Act of the bulrushes. If there was federal land that overflowed enough so that you could traverse it at times in a flat-bottomed boat, and you promised to reclaim it (which is to say, dike and drain it), it was yours. Henry Miller, a mythical figure in the history of California land fraud, acquired a large part of his 1,090,000-acre empire under this act. According to legend, he bought himself a boat, hired some witnesses, put the boat and witnesses in a wagon, hitched some horses to it, and hauled the boat and witnesses over county-size tracts near the San Joaquin River where it rains, on the average, about eight or nine inches a year. The land became his. The sanitized version of the story, the one told by Miller's descendants, has him benefiting more from luck than from ruse. During the winter of 1861 and 1862, most of California got three times its normal precipitation, and the usually semiarid Central Valley became a shallow sea the size of Lake Ontario. But the only difference in this version is that Miller didn't need a wagon for his boat; he still had no business acquiring hundreds of thousands of acres of the public domain, yet he managed it with ease.

One of the unforeseen results of the homestead legislation was a high rate of employment among builders of birdhouses. In most instances, you were required to display an "erected domicile" on your land. The Congress, after all, was much too smart to give people land without requiring them to live on it. In a number of instances, the erected domicile was a birdhouse, put there to satisfy a paid witness with a tender conscience. It is quite possible that the greatest opportunity offered by the homestead legislation in the West was the opportunity to earn a little honest graft. By conservative estimates, 95 percent of the final proofs under the Desert Land Act were fraudulent. "Whole townships have been entered under this law in the interest of one person or firm," thundered Binger Hermann, a commissioner of the General Land Office, about the Timber and Stone Act. Not long afterward, Hermann himself was fired for allowing unrestricted fraud.

Mark Twain might have written it off to the human condition, but Powell, who subscribed to a more benevolent view of humanity, wrote it off to the conditions of the desert and the failure to understand them. Americans were making a Procrustean effort to turn half a continent into something they were used to. It was a doomed effort. Even worse, it was unscientific. The document that Powell hoped would bring the country to its senses was called *A Report on the Lands of the Arid Region of the United States, with a More Detailed Account of the Lands of Utah*. Published in 1876, the volume was seven years in preparation—though Powell took time out for a second expedition down the Colorado, in 1871, and for his usual plethora of intermittent pursuits. Powell's *Report* is remarkably brief, a scant two hundred pages in all. Unlike many of his rivals, such as the bombastic Ferdinand V. Hayden, Powell was more interested in being right than in being long. But his portrait of the American West has revolutionary implications even today.

At the beginning, Powell reconfirmed his view, which he had already submitted to an unbelieving Congress, that two-fifths of the United States has a climate that generally cannot support farming without irrigation. On top of that, irrigation could reclaim only a fraction of it. "When all the waters running in the streams found in this region are conducted on the land," Powell said, "there will be but a small portion of the country redeemed, varying in the different territories perhaps from *one to three percent*" (emphasis added). Powell regarded the theory that increased rainfall accompanied human settlement as bunk, but, typically, he disposed of it in a sympathetic and felicitous way: "If it be true that increase of the water supply is due to increase in precipitation, as many have supposed, the fact is not cheering to the agriculturalist of the arid region . . . . Any sudden great change [in climate] is ephemeral, and usually such changes go in cycles, and the opposite or compensating change may reasonably be anticipated . . . . [W]e shall have to expect a speedy return to extreme aridity, in which case a large portion of the agricultural industries of these now growing up would be destroyed."

The whole problem with the Homestead Acts, Powell went on, was that they were blind to reality. In the West, a 160-acre *irrigated* farm was too *large*, while a 160-acre *unirrigated* farm was too *small*. Most western valley soil was fertile, and a good crop was a near certainty once irrigation water was applied; in the milder regions the growing season was very long and two crops were possible, so one could often subsist on eighty irrigated acres or less. That, in fact, was about all the irrigated land one family could be expected to work. Remove the irrigation water, however, and things were drastically different. Then even a whole section was too small a piece of land. Under most circumstances, Powell claimed, no one could make a living through dryland ranching on fewer than 2,560 acres—four full sections. And even with that much land, a settler's prospects would be dicey in times of drought, because the land might lie utterly bare. Therefore, every pasturage farm should ideally have a water right sufficient to irrigate twenty acres or so during emergencies.

Having thrown over the preeminent myths about agriculture in the American West, Powell went on to the truly revolutionary part of his report. Under riparian water law, to give everyone a water right for twenty irrigated acres was impossible if you gave everyone a neat little square of land. Some squares would contain much greater stream footage than others, and their owners would have too much water compared with the others. The property boundaries would therefore have to be gerrymandered to give everyone a sufficient piece of the stream. That was one way you could help avert the monopolization of water. Another way was to insist that people *use* their water rights, not hold on to them in the hope that cities would grow up and one could make a killing someday selling water to them. An unused water right should revert—let us say after five years—to the public trust so someone else could claim it.

Doing all this, Powell reasoned, might help assure that water would be used equitably, but not necessarily efficiently. Ideally, to get through drier months and times of drought, you needed a reservoir in a good location—at a low altitude, and on the main branch of a stream. That way you could get more efficient storage of water—a dam only twice as large, but lower down, might capture five times as much water as a smaller one upstream. Also, you could then irrigate the lower valley lands, which usually have better soil and a longer growing season. In any event, an on-stream storage reservoir was, from the point of view of irrigation, preferable to small shallow ponds filled with diverted streamwater, the typical irrigation reservoirs of his day; the ponds evaporated much greater amounts of water and displaced valuable cropland.

But who, Powell asked, was building on-stream reservoirs? Practically no one. Homesteaders couldn't build them at all, let alone build them right, nor could groups of homesteaders—unless perhaps they were Mormons. Such dams required amounts of capital and commitment that were beyond the limits of aggregations of self-interested mortals. Private companies probably couldn't build good irrigation projects, either, nor even states. Sooner or later, the federal government would have to get into the irrigation business or watch its efforts to settle the West degenerate into failure and chaos. Once it realized that, it would have to undertake a careful survey of the soil characteristics so as not to waste a lot of money irrigating inferior land with drainage problems. And (he implied rather than stated) the government ought to put J. W. Powell in charge; the General Land Office, which would otherwise be responsible, was, as anyone could see, "a gigantic illustration of the evils of badly directed scientific work."

Having gone this far, Powell figured he might as well go the whole route. Fences, for example, bothered him. What was the sense of every rancher enclosing his land with a barbed-wire fence? Fenced lands tended to be unevenly grazed, and fences were obvious hazards to cattle in winter storms. Fencing was also a waste of time and money, especially in a region where rainfall could skid from twenty to six inches in successive years and someone was lucky to survive at all, let alone survive while constantly repairing and replacing fences. Individually fenced lands were a waste of resources, too; it takes a lot more tin, Powell reasoned, to make five eight-ounce cans than to make one forty-ounce can. The sensible thing was for farms to be clustered together and the individually owned lands treated as a commons, an *ejido*, with a single fence around the perimeter.

States bothered Powell, too. Their borders were too often nonsensical. They followed rivers for convenience, then struck out in a straight line, bisecting mountain ranges, cutting watersheds in half. Boxing out landscapes, sneering at natural reality, they were wholly arbitrary and, therefore, stupid. In the West, where the one thing that really mattered was water, states should logically be formed around watersheds. Each major river, from the glacial drip at its headwaters to the delta at its mouth, should be a state or semistate. The great state of Upper Platte River. Will the Senator from the state of Rio Grande yield? To divide the West any other way was to sow the future with rivalries, jealousies, and bitter squabbles whose fruits would contribute solely to the nourishment of lawyers.

While Powell knew that his plan for settling the American West would be considered revolutionary, he saw a precedent. After all, what was the difference between a cooperative irrigation district and a New England barn-raising? One was informal, the other organized and legalized, but otherwise they were the same thing. Communal pasturelands might be a gross affront to America's preoccupation with private property rights, but they were common in Europe. In the East, where inland navigation was as important as irrigation was in the West, you already had a strong federal presence in the Corps of Engineers. If anything was revolutionary, it was trying to graft English common law and the principles and habits of wet-zone agriculture onto a desert landscape. There was not a desert civilization in the world where that had been tried—and most of those civilizations had withered even after following sensible rules.

Powell was advocating cooperation, reason, science, an equitable sharing of the natural wealth, and—implicitly if not explicitly—a return to the Jeffersonian ideal. He wanted the West settled slowly, cautiously, in a manner that would work. If it was done intelligently instead of in a mad, unplanned rush, the settlement of the West could help defuse the dangerous conditions building in the squalid industrial cities of the East. If it was done wrong, the migration west might go right into reverse.

The nation at large, however, was in no mood for any such thing. It was avid for imperial expansion, and the majority of its citizens wanted to get rich. New immigrants were arriving, dozens of boatloads a day, with that motive burning in their brains. To them America was not so much a democratic utopia as a gold mine. If monopolists reigned here, they could accept that; someday *they* would be monopolists, too. Forty years earlier, Alexis de Tocqueville had captured the raw new country's soul: "To clear, to till, and to transform the vast uninhabited continent which is his domain, the American requires the daily support of an energetic passion; that passion can only be the love of wealth; the passion for wealth is therefore not reprobated in America, and, provided it does not go beyond the bounds assigned to it for public security, it is held in honor." In Powell's day, that passion for wealth had if anything grown more intense. A pseudoscientific dogma, Social Darwinism, had been invented to give predatory behavior a good name. Darwin could not be taught in the schools; but a perversion of Darwin could be practiced in real life.

The unpeopled West, naturally, was where a great many immigrants hoped to find their fortunes. They didn't want to hear that the West was dry. Few had ever seen a desert, and the East was so much like Europe that they imagined the West would be, too. A tiny bit semiarid, perhaps, like Italy. But a desert? Never! They didn't want to hear of communal pasturelands—they had left those behind, in Europe, in order that they could become the emperors of Wyoming. They didn't want the federal government parceling out water and otherwise meddling in their affairs; that was another European tradition they had left an ocean away. Agricultural fortunes were being made in California by rampant capitalists like Henry Miller; acreages the size of European principalities were being amassed in Texas, in Montana. If the federal government controlled the water, it could also control the land, and then the United States might become a nation of small farmers after all—which was exactly what most Americans didn't want. For this was the late nineteenth century, when, as Henry Adams wrote, "the majority at last declared itself, once and for all, in favor of the capitalistic system with all its necessary machinery . . . the whole mechanical consolidation of force . . . ruthlessly . . . created monopolies capable of controlling the new energies that America adored."

It was bad enough for Powell that he was pulling against such a social tide. He also had to deal with the likes of William Gilpin, who had traded his soapbox for the governor's mansion in Denver; he had to fight with the provincial newspapers, the railroads, and all the others who were already there and had a proprietary interest in banishing the Great American Desert; he had to deal with western members of Congress who could not abide anyone calling their states arid (although a hundred years later, when the Bureau of Reclamation had become their prime benefactor, members of Congress from these same states would argue at length over whose state was the *more* arid and hostile).

Powell seemed at first to have everything going in his favor. The West was coming hard up against reality, as more hundreds of thousands of settlers ventured each year into the land of little rain. His exploits on the Colorado River had made him a national hero, the most celebrated adventurer since Lewis and Clark. He was on friendly if not intimate terms with a wide cross-section of the nation's elite—everyone from Henry Adams to Othniel C. Marsh, the great paleontologist, to Carl Schurz, the Interior Secretary, to Clarence King, the country's foremost geologist, to numerous strategically placed members of Congress. By 1881, he was head of both the Bureau of Ethnology and the Geologic Survey, two prestigious appointments that made him probably the most powerful, if not the most influential, scientist in America. But none of this prestige and power, none of these connections, was a match for ignorance, nonsense, and the nineteenth century's fulsome, quixotic optimism. When he testified before Congress about his report and his irrigation plan, the reception from the West—the region with which he was passionately involved, the region he wanted to *help*—was icily hostile. In his biography of Powell, Wallace Stegner nicely characterized the frame of mind of the typical western booster-politician when he surveyed Powell's austere, uncompromising monument of facts:

> What, they asked, did he know about the West? What did he know about South Dakota? Had he ever been there? When? Where? For how long? Did he know the average rainfall of the James River Valley? Or the Black Hills? . . . [Did he] really know anything about the irrigable lands in the Three Forks country in Montana? They refused to understand his distinction between arid and subhumid, they clamored to know how their states had got labelled "arid" and thus been closed to settlement . . . . [W]hat about the artesian basin in the Dakotas? What about irrigation from that source? So he gave it to them: artesian wells were and always would

> be a minor source of water as compared to the rivers and the storm-water reservoirs. He had had his men studying artesian wells since 1882 . . . . If all the wells in the Dakotas could be gathered into one county they would not irrigate that county.
>
> Senator Moody [of South Dakota] thereupon remarked that he did not favor putting money into Major Powell's hands when Powell would clearly not spend it as Moody and his constituents wanted it spent. We ask you, he said in effect, your opinion of artesian wells. You think they're unimportant. All right, the hell with you. We'll ask somebody else who will give us the answer we want. Nothing personal.

The result, in the end, was that Powell got some money to conduct his Irrigation Survey for a couple of years—far less than he wanted, and needed—and then found himself frozen permanently out of the appropriations bills. The excuse was that he was moving too slowly, too deliberately; the truth was that he was forming opinions the West couldn't bear to hear. There was inexhaustible land but far too little water, and what little water there was might, in many cases, be too expensive to move. Having said this, held to it, and suffered for it, Powell spent his last years in a kind of ignominy. Unable to participate in the settlement of the West, he retreated into the Bureau of Ethnology, where his efforts, ironically, helped prevent the culture of the West's original inhabitants from being utterly trampled and eradicated by that same settlement. On September 23, 1902, he died at the family compound near Haven, Maine, about as far from the arid West as he could get.

Powell had felt that the western farmers would stand behind him, if not the politicians themselves; there he made one of the major miscalculations of his life. "Apparently he underestimated the capacity of the plains dirt farmer to continue to believe in myths even while his nose was being rubbed in unpleasant fact," Stegner wrote. "The press and a good part of the public in the West was against him more than he knew . . . . The American yeoman might clamor for government assistance in his trouble, but he didn't want any that would make him change his thinking."

What is remarkable, a hundred years later, is how little has changed. The disaster that Powell predicted—a catastrophic return to a cycle of drought—did indeed occur, not once but twice: in the late 1800s and again in the 1930s. When that happened, Powell's ideas—at least his insistence that a federal irrigation program was the only salvation of the arid West—were embraced, tentatively at first, then more passionately, then with a kind of desperate insistence. The result was a half-century rampage of dam-building and irrigation development which, in all probability, went far beyond anything Powell would have liked. But even as the myth of the welcoming, bountiful West was shattered, the myth of the independent yeoman farmer remained intact. With huge dams built for him at public expense, and irrigation canals, and the water sold for a quarter of a cent per ton—a price which guaranteed that little of the public's investment would ever be paid back—the West's yeoman farmer became the embodiment of the welfare state, though he was the last to recognize it. And the same Congress which had once insisted he didn't need federal help was now insisting that such help be continued, at any cost. Released from a need for justification, released from logic itself, the irrigation program Powell had wanted became a monster, redoubling its efforts and increasing its wreckage, both natural and economic, as it lost sight of its goal. Powell's ideal was a future in which the rivers of the American West would help create a limited bounty on that tiny fraction of the land which it made sense to irrigate. It is hard to imagine that the first explorer of the Colorado River would have welcomed a future in which there might be no rivers left at all . . . .

. . . The rapid rise of the federal irrigation movement in the early 1890s was due in part to this succession of overawing catastrophes. But it had just as much to do with the fact that by the late 1880s, private irrigation efforts had come to an inglorious end. The good sites were simply gone. Most of the pioneers who had settled successfully across the hundredth meridian had gone to Washington and California and Oregon, where there was rain, or had chosen homesteads along streams whose water they could easily divert. Such opportunities, however, were quick to disappear. Groundwater wasn't much help either. A windmill could lift enough drinking water for a family and few cattle; but it would require thirty or forty windmills, and reliable wind, to lift enough water to irrigate a quarter section of land—a disheartening prospect to a farmer with no money in a region with no wood.

Even if their land abutted a stream with some surplus water rights, few farmers had the confidence, cooperative spirit, and money to build a dam and lead the stored water to their lands through a long canal. It was one thing to throw a ten-foot-high earthen plug across a freshet in order to create a two-acre stock pond—though even that taxed the resources of most farmers in the West, who had invested all their savings simply to get there from Kentucky or Maine. It was quite another thing to build a dam on a stream large enough to supply a year-round flow, and to dig a canal—by horse and by hand—that was long enough, and deep enough, and wide enough, to irrigate hundreds or thousands of acres of land. The work involved was simply stupefying; clearing a field, by comparison, seemed like the simplest, most effortless job.

The farmers' predicament, on the other hand, was an opportunity for the legions of financial swashbucklers who had gone west in pursuit of quick wealth. In the 1870s and 1880s, hundreds of irrigation companies, formed with eastern capital, set themselves to the task of reclaiming the arid lands. Almost none survived beyond ten years. At the eighth National Irrigation Congress in 1898, a Colorado legislator likened the American West to a graveyard, littered with the "crushed and mangled skeletons of defunct [irrigation] corporations . . . [which] suddenly disappeared at the end of brief careers, leaving only a few defaulted obligations to indicate the route by which they departed."

There was, indeed, a kind of cruel irony in the collapse of the irrigation companies. Most of them operated in the emphatically arid regions—the Central Valley of California, Nevada, Arizona, southeastern Colorado, New Mexico—where agriculture without irrigation is daunting or hopeless, but otherwise the climate is well suited for growing crops. The drought, on the other hand, struck hardest in the region just east of the hundredth meridian, where, in most years, a nonirrigating farmer had been able to make a go of it. Kansas was emptied by the drought and the white winter, Nevada by irrigation companies gone defunct. In the early 1890s, the exodus from Nevada, as a percentage of those who hung on, was unlike anything in the country's history. Even California, in the midst of a big population boom, saw the growth of its *agricultural* population come to a standstill in 1895.

California, the perennial trend-setting state, was the first to attempt to rescue its hapless farmers, but the result, the Wright Act, was another in the long series of doomed efforts to apply eastern solutions to western topography and climate. The act, which took its inspiration from the township governments of New England, established self-governing mini-states, called irrigation districts, whose sole function was to deliver water onto barren land. Like the western homestead laws, it was a good idea that foundered in practice. The districts soon buckled under their responsibilities—issuing bonds that wouldn't sell, building reservoirs that wouldn't fill, allocating water unfairly, distributing it unevenly, then throwing up their hands when anarchy prevailed. Elwood C. Mead, then the state engineer of Wyoming and probably the country's leading authority on irrigation, called the Wright Act "a disgrace to any self-governing people." George Maxwell, a Californian and founder of the National Irrigation Association, said "the extravagance or stupidity or incompetence of local [irrigation] directors" had left little beyond a legacy of "waste and disaster." Though the Wright Act was in most ways a failure, Colorado, thinking it had learned something from California's mistakes, adopted its own version, which added a modest subsidy for private irrigation developers in order to improve their odds of success. By 1894, under Colorado's new program, five substantial storage reservoirs had been built. Three were so poorly designed and situated that they stored no water at all; the fourth was declared unsafe and was never even filled; and the fifth was so far from the land it was supposed to irrigate that most of the meager quantity of water it could deliver disappeared into the ground before it got there.

In that same year—1894—Senator Joseph Carey of Wyoming, thinking he had learned something from California's and Colorado's mistakes, introduced a bill that offered another approach: the federal government would cede up to a million acres of land to any state that promised to irrigate it. But, by some elusive reasoning, the states were forbidden to use land as the collateral they would need to raise the money to build the irrigation works—and land, at the time, was the only thing of value most of them had. Sixteen years later, using a generous estimate, the Carey Act had caused 288,553 acres to come under irrigation throughout the entire seventeen-state West—about as much developed farmland as there was in a couple of counties in Illinois.

As the private and state-fostered experiments with irrigation lay in shambles, many of the western reclamation advocates heaped blame on the East and "Washington" for not doing more to help, just as their descendants, four generations later, would vilify Jimmy Carter, an easterner and southerner, for not "understanding" their "needs" when he tried to eliminate some water projects that would have subsidized a few hundred of them to the tune of hundreds of thousands of dollars apiece. In each case, the West was displaying its peculiarly stubborn brand of hypocrisy and blindness. Midwestern members of Congress were understandably uneager to subsidize competition for their own farmer constituents, but they had little to do with making reclamation fail; the West was up to the task itself. Its faith in private enterprise was nearly as absolute as its earlier faith that settlement would make the climate wetter. John Wesley Powell, a midwesterner, knew that all the private initiative in the world would never make it bloom. Theodore Roosevelt, an easterner, had returned from the West convinced that there were "vast areas of public land which can be made available for . . . settlement," but only, he added, "by building reservoirs and main-line canals impractical for private enterprise." But the West wasn't listening. For the first time in their history, Americans had come up against a problem they could not begin to master with traditional American solutions—private capital, individual initiative, hard work—and yet the region confronting the problem happened to believe most fervently in such solutions. Through the 1890s, western Senators and Congressmen resisted all suggestions that reclamation was a task for government alone—not even for the states, which had failed as badly as the private companies, but for the national government. To believe such a thing was to imply that their constituents did not measure up to the myth that enshrouded them—that of the indomitable individualist. When they finally saw the light, however, their attitude miraculously changed—though the myth didn't—and the American West quietly became the first and most durable example of the modern welfare state.

The passage of the Reclamation Act of 1902 was such a sharp left turn in the course of American politics that historians still gather and argue over why it was passed. To some, it was America's first flirtation with socialism, an outgrowth of the Populist and Progressive movements of the time. To others, it was a disguised reactionary measure, an effort to relieve the mobbed and riotous conditions of the eastern industrial cities—an act to save heartless capitalism from itself. To some, its roots were in Manifest Destiny, whose incantations still held people in their sway; to others, it was a military ploy to protect and populate America's western flank against the ascendant Orient.

What seems beyond question is that the Reclamation Act, or some variation of it, was, by the end of the nineteenth century, inevitable. To resist a federal reclamation program was to block all further migration to the West and to ensure disaster for those who were already there—or for those who were on their way. Even as the victims of the great white winter and the drought of the 1880s and 1890s were evacuating the arid regions, the trains departing Chicago and St. Louis for points west were full. The pull of the West reached deep into the squalid slums of the eastern cities; it reached back to the ravined, rock-strewn farms of New England and down into the boggy, overwet farmlands of the Deep

South. No matter what the government did, short of erecting a wall at the hundredth meridian, the settlement of the West was going to continue. The only way to prevent more cycles of disaster was to build a civilization based on irrigated farming. Fifty years of effort by countless numbers of people had resulted in 3,631,000 acres under irrigation by 1889. There were counties in California that contained more acreage than that, and the figure included much of the easily irrigable land. Not only that, but at least half the land had been irrigated by Mormons. Each additional acre, therefore, would be won at greater pain. Everything had been tried—cheap land, free land, private initiative, local initiative, state subsidy—and everything, with a few notable exceptions, had failed. One alternative remained.

There seemed to be only one politician in the arid West who fathomed his region's predicament well enough to end it. He had emigrated to San Francisco from the East, made a fortune through a busy law practice and the inheritance of his father-in-law's silver mine, moved to Nevada, and in 1888 launched the Truckee Irrigation Project. It was one of the most ambitious reclamation efforts of its day, and it failed—not because it was poorly conceived or executed (hydrologically and economically, it was a good project) but because squabbles among its beneficiaries and the pettiness of the Nevada legislature ruined its hopes. In the process Francis Griffith Newlands lost half a million dollars and whatever faith he had in the ability of private enterprise to mount a successful reclamation program. "Nevada," he said bitterly as his project went bust in 1891, "is a dying state."

Newlands, who succeeded at everything else he tried, gave up on irrigation, ran for Congress, and won. For the remainder of the decade, he kept out of the reclamation battles, if only to give everyone else's solutions an opportunity to fail. All the while, however, he was waiting for his moment. It came on September 14, 1901, when a bullet fired by an anarchist ended the life of President William McKinley. Theodore Roosevelt, the man who succeeded McKinley as President, was, like Francis Newlands, a student and admirer of John Wesley Powell. Infatuated with the West, he had traveled extensively there and been struck by the prescience and accuracy of Powell's observations. Roosevelt was first of all a politician, and had no interest in sharing Powell's ignominious fate; nonetheless, he knew that Powell's solutions were the only ones that would work, and he wanted a federal reclamation effort badly. A military thinker, he was concerned about Japan, bristling with expansionism and dirt-poor in resources, and knew that America was vulnerable on its underpopulated western flank. A bug for efficiency, he felt that the waste of money and effort on doomed irrigation ventures was a scandal. Roosevelt was also a conservationist, in the utilitarian sense, and the failure to conserve—that is, use—the water in western rivers irritated him. "The western half of the United States would sustain a population greater than that of our whole country today if the waters that now run to waste were saved and used for irrigation," he said in a speech in December of 1901. For all his enthusiasm, however, Roosevelt knew that his biggest problem would be not the eastern states in Congress but the myth-bound western bloc, whose region he was trying to help. His second-greatest problem, ironically, would be his chief ally, Francis Newlands.

As soon as Roosevelt was in the White House, Newlands introduced a bill creating a federal program along the lines suggested by Powell. But the bitterness he felt over his huge financial loss was so strong that he described his bill in language almost calculated to infuriate his western colleagues, who were clinging to the myth that the hostile natural forces  of the West could be overcome by individual initiative. In a long speech on the floor of the Congress, Newlands said outright that the legislation he was introducing would "nationalize the works of irrigation"—which was like saying today that one intended to nationalize the automobile industry. Then he launched into a long harangue about the failures of state reclamation programs, blaming them on "the ignorance, the improvidence, and the dishonesty of local legislatures"—even though many of his listeners had recently graduated from such legislatures themselves. He even suggested that *Congress* should have no oversight powers, implying that he distrusted that body as much as he did the thieves, opportunists, and incompetents whom he saw controlling the state legislatures.

Newlands's bill, as expected, ran into immediate opposition. When it came up for a vote in March, it was soundly defeated. Western members then began to support a rival bill, proposed by Senator Francis E. Warren of Wyoming, that contained none of the features Newlands wanted. By February of 1902, Warren's bill was finally passed by the Senate and seemed destined to become law. At that point, however, fate and Theodore Roosevelt intervened. Mrs. Warren became gravely ill, necessitating the Senator's return to Wyoming. In Warren's absence, Roosevelt leaned on Newlands to tone down his language, and before long the Congressman was describing his defeated measure, which he had already reintroduced, as a "conservative" and "safe" bill. Roosevelt still wouldn't risk supporting it, but he came up with a brilliant ploy. Announcing his "sympathy with the spirit" of Warren's bill, he said he would support it with "a few minor changes." The person whom he wanted to make the changes and lead the bill through Congress was Wyoming's young Congressman-at-large, Frank Mondell, the future Republican leader of the House. Mondell had a weakness for flattery and a less than athletic mind, and Roosevelt was a master at exploiting both. Before long, he had persuaded Mondell to incorporate as "minor changes" in Warren's bill almost all of Newlands's language. Roosevelt then softened up his eastern opposition with some implied threats that their river and harbor projects might be in jeopardy if they did not go along—a strategy that has seen long useful service. By the time Warren returned from Wyoming, Newlands's bill, disguised as his own, had cleared both houses. On June 17, 1902, the Reclamation Act became law.

The newly created Reclamation Service exerted a magnetic pull on the best engineering graduates in the country. The prospect of reclaiming a desert seemed infinitely more satisfying than designing a steel mill in Gary, Indiana, or a power dam in Massachusetts, and the graduates headed west in a fog of idealism, ready to take on the most intractable foe of mankind: the desert. But the desert suffers improvement at a steep price, and the early Reclamation program was as much a disaster as its dams were engineering marvels.

The underlying problems were politics and money. Under the terms of the Reclamation Act, projects were to be financed by a Reclamation Fund, which would be filled initially by revenues from sales of federal land in the western states, then paid back gradually through sales of water to farmers. (It should be mentioned right away that the farmers, under the law, were exempted from paying interest on virtually all of their repayment obligations—a subsidy which was substantial to begin with, and which was to become breathtaking in later decades, as interest rates topped 10 percent. In some cases, the interest exemption alone—which is, of course, an indirect burden on the general taxpayer—has amounted to a subsidy of ninety cents on the dollar.) Section 9 of the Reclamation Act implied, if it didn't require, that all money accruing to the Reclamation Fund from sales of land in any given state should be spent in that state as well. Frederick Newell, the Service's first director, was particularly anxious to locate a few projects in each state anyway, because that might dispel some of the antipathy that had attended the Service's creation. By 1924, twenty-seven projects were completed or under construction. Of those, twenty-one had been initiated before the Service was even half a decade old.

The engineers who staffed the Reclamation Service tended to view themselves as a godlike class performing hydrologic miracles for grateful simpletons who were content to sit in the desert and raise fruit. About soil science, agricultural economics, or drainage they sometimes knew less than the farmers whom they regarded with indulgent contempt. As a result, some of the early projects were to become painful embarrassments, and expensive ones. The soil turned out to be demineralized, alkaline, boron-poisoned; drainage was so poor the irrigation water turned fields into saline swamps; markets for the crops didn't exist; expensive projects with heavy repayment obligations were built in regions where only low-value crops could be grown. In the Bureau of Reclamation's quasi-official history, *Water for the West,* Michael Robinson (the son-in-law of a Commissioner of Reclamation) discreetly admits all of this: "Initially, little consideration was given to the hard realities of irrigated agriculture. Neither aid nor direction was given to settlers in carrying out the difficult and costly work of clearing and leveling the land, digging irrigation ditches, building roads and houses, and transporting crops to remote markets . . . ."

Robinson also acknowledges the political pressures that have bedeviled the Reclamation program ever since it was born. The attitude of most western members of Congress was quaintly hypocritical: after resisting this experiment in pseudosocialism, or even voting against it, they decided, after it became law, that they might as well make the best of it. "The government was immediately flooded with requests for project investigations," Robinson writes. "Local chambers of commerce, real estate interests, and congressmen were convinced their areas were ideal for reclamation development. State legislators and officials joined the chorus of promoters seeking Reclamation projects . . . . Legislative requirements and political pressures sometimes precluded careful, exhaustive surveys of proposed projects . . . . Projects were frequently undertaken with only a sketchy understanding of the area's climate, growing season, soil productivity, and market conditions."

Congress's decision, in passing the act, to ignore much of John Wesley Powell's advice made things worse. Powell had proposed that in those inhospitable regions where only livestock could be raised, settlers should be allowed to homestead 2,560 acres of the public domain—but allocated enough water to irrigate only twenty. The Reclamation Act gave everyone up to 160 acres (a man and wife could jointly farm 320 acres), whether they settled in Mediterranean California or in the frigid interior steppes of Wyoming, where the extremes of climate rival those in

Mongolia. You could grow wealthy on 160 acres of lemons in California and starve on 160 acres of irrigated pasture in Wyoming or Montana, but the act was blind to such nuances. And by building so many projects in a rush, the Reclamation Service was repeating its mistakes before it had a chance to learn from them.

All of these problems were compounded by the fact that few settlers had any experience with irrigation farming—nor were they required to. They overwatered and mismanaged their crops; they let their irrigation systems silt up. Many had optimistically filed on more acreage than they had resources to irrigate, and they ended up with repayment obligations on land they were forced to leave fallow. From there, it was a short, swift fall into bankruptcy. Fifty years earlier, the ancestors of the first Reclamation farmers had endured adversity by putting their faith in God and feeding themselves on game. But this was the twentieth century; the game was vanishing, and government was replacing God as the rescuer of last resort. As Michael Robinson wrote, "Western economic and social determinants were changing rapidly. Nineteenth-century irrigation pioneers were better suited to endure hardships than settlers who struggled to survive on Federal Reclamation projects after 1902. In the nineteenth century, wild game was plentiful, livestock could graze on the public domain outside irrigated areas, and the settlers were inured to privation." And so, after a few years of trial and a lot of error, the Reclamation Act began to undergo a long and remarkable series of "reforms."

The first reform was humble—a $20 million loan from the Treasury to the bankrupt Reclamation Fund to keep the program from falling on its face. It was approved in 1910, the same year that Section 9—the ill-advised clause promoting the construction of projects where they couldn't work—was repealed. New projects were also required to have the explicit consent of the President before they were launched. A paper reform, however, is not necessarily a reform in real life. Every Senator still wanted a project in his state; every Congressman wanted one in his district; they didn't care whether they made economic sense or not. The Commissioner of Reclamation and the President were only human. If Congress authorized a bad project and voted funding for it, a President might have good reasons not to veto the bill—especially if it also authorized a lot of things the President *did* want. Congress caught on quickly, and was soon writing "omnibus" authorization bills, in which bad projects were thrown in, willy-nilly, with good ones. (Later, Congress would learn a new trick: attaching sneaky little amendments authorizing particularly wretched projects to legislation dealing with issues such as education and hurricane relief.) As a result, instead of weeding out or discouraging bad projects, the "reforms" began to concentrate on making bad projects work—or, to put it more bluntly, on bailing them out.

The first of these adjustments came in 1914, when the repayment period, which had been set in the act at a rather unrealistic ten years, was extended to twenty. It was quite a liberal adjustment, but failed to produce any measurable results. By 1922, twenty years after the Reclamation program began, only 10 percent of the money loaned from the Reclamation Fund had been repaid. Sixty percent of the irrigators—an astounding number—were defaulting on their repayment obligations, even though they paid no interest on irrigation features.

In 1924, Congress commissioned a Fact Finder's report on the Reclamation program, which recommended an even more drastic adjustment—raising the repayment period from twenty years to forty. No sooner was that done, however, than the most chronic and intractable problem of twentieth-century American agriculture began to appear: huge crop surpluses. Production and prices reached record levels during the First World War; when the war ended, production remained high, but crop prices did not. The value of all crops grown on Reclamation land fell from $152 million in 1919 to $83.6 million in 1922—as morose a statistic as the number of farmers in default. With their profits shriveling, the beleaguered farmers were reluctant to pay for water they were beginning to regard as rightful recompense for attempting to civilize the desert, especially when the Reclamation Service, in most cases, didn't dare shut it off when they refused to pay. So Congress took further steps to bail the Reclamation program out, rerouting royalties from oil drilling and potassium mining to the Reclamation Fund on the theory that the West, while being stripped of its mineral resources, ought to get something in return. But even after all these measures had been adopted a number of projects continued to operate at a hopeless loss.

Nonetheless, the psychic value of the Reclamation farms remained high. The only relief in a pitiless desert landscape, their worth was computed in almost ethereal terms, as if they were art. And their investment value to speculators remained high, too. An acre which in pre-project years was worth $5 or $10—if that—was suddenly worth fifty times as much. At such prices, many farmers found the temptation to sell out irresistible; by 1927, at least a third of the Reclamation farmers had. The buyers were usually wealthy speculators who figured they could absorb some minor losses for a while—especially if they could convince Congress to give them tax breaks—as long as they could make money when agricultural prices went back up. The Salt River Project in Arizona was notable for having been all but taken over by speculators. Elwood Mead, who succeeded Newell and Arthur Powell Davis as Commissioner of Reclamation, called speculation "a vampire which has done much to destroy the desirable social and economic purposes of the Reclamation Act." But the big, distant new owners were often better at paying their water bills than the stone-broke small farmers, so the Reclamation Service, in a number of instances, turned a blind eye toward what was going on. It was a case of lawlessness becoming de facto policy, and it was to become more and more commonplace.

Part of the reason the Reclamation Service (which metamorphosed, fittingly, into the *Bureau* of Reclamation in 1923) seemed so hapless at enforcing its social mandate had to do with the Omnibus Adjustment Act of 1926, one of those well-meaning pieces of legislation that make everything worse. Intended to clamp down on speculation, the act demanded that landowners owning excess amounts of land sign recordable contracts in which they promised to sell such lands within a designated period, at prices reflecting the lands' pre-project worth. But the contracts were to be signed with the local irrigation district acting as wholesaler of the Bureau's water—not with the Bureau itself. It was an ideal opportunity to camouflage acreage violations, since the same people who were in violation of the Reclamation Act often sat on the local irrigation district's board of directors.

A more important and insidious reason, however, had to do with the nature of the Bureau itself. "There was a tendency for some engineers to view public works as ends in themselves," admits Michael Robinson. "Despite official declarations from more sensitive administrators that 'Reclamation is measured not in engineering units but in homes and agricultural values' . . . the Service regarded itself as an 'engineering outfit.'"

That may have been the understatement of the year. To build a great dam on a tempestuous river like the Snake was terrifically exhilarating work; enforcing a hodgepodge of social ideals was hardly that. Stopping a wild river was a straightforward job, subjugable to logic, and the result was concrete, heroic, real: a dam. Enforcing repayment obligations and worrying about speculators and excess landowners was a cumbersome, troublesome, time-consuming nuisance—a nuisance without reward. Was the Bureau to abandon the most spellbinding effort of modern times—transforming the desert into a garden—just because a few big landowners were taking advantage of the program, just because some farmers couldn't pay as much as Congress hoped?

There were to be still more "reforms" tacked onto the Reclamation Act: reforms extending the repayment period to fifty years, setting water prices according to the farmers' "ability to pay," using hydroelectric revenues to subsidize irrigation costs. It wasn't until the 1930s, however, that the Reclamation program went into high gear. In the 1920s and early 1930s, the nation's nexus of political power still lay east of the Mississippi River; the West simply didn't have the votes to authorize a dozen big water projects each year. Western politicians who were to exercise a near-despotic rule over the Bureau's authorizing committees in later years, men like Wayne Aspinall and Bernie Sisk and Carl Hayden, were still working their way up the political ranks. (In 1902, the year the Reclamation program began, Arizona was still ten years away from becoming a state.) Presidents Harding and Coolidge were ideological conservatives from the East who sternly resisted governmental involvement in economic affairs, unless it was an opportunity for their friends to earn a little graft. And even Herbert Hoover, though a Californian and an engineer, was not regarded by the western water lobby and the Bureau as a particularly loyal friend.

All of this was to change more abruptly than the Bureau of Reclamation and its growing dependency could have hoped. The most auspicious event in its entire history was the election to the presidency in 1932 of a free-wheeling, free-spending patrician. The second most auspicious event was the passage, during the four-term Roosevelt-Truman interregnum, of several omnibus river-basin bills that authorized not one, not five, not even ten, but dozens of dams and irrigation projects at a single stroke. Economics mattered little, if at all; if the irrigation ventures slid into an ocean of debt, the huge hydroelectric dams authorized within the same river basin could generate the necessary revenues to bail them out (or so it was thought). It was a breathtakingly audacious solution to an intractable problem, and the results were to be breathtaking as well. Between Franklin Roosevelt and the river-basin approach—which, in an instant, could authorize dams and canals and irrigation projects from headwaters to river mouth, across a thousand miles of terrain—the natural landscape of the American West, the rivers and deserts and wetlands and canyons, was to undergo a man-made transformation the likes of which no desert civilization has ever seen. The first, and perhaps the most fateful, such transformation was wrought in the most arid and hostile quarter of the American West, a huge desert basin transected by one comparatively miniature river: the Colorado.

Thomas R. Malthus

1766-1834

An Essay on the Principle of Population

1798

In his famous essay on population control, Malthus argued that populations of humans and animals grow geometrically while food stuffs increase arithmetically. Noting the population explosion in Great Briton during the nineteenth century, he was concerned that if the population were to increase more rapidly than the means of subsistence, and if no checks were placed upon the increase in population, many would starve or everyone would be poorly fed. His primary concern was that larger numbers of people meant more workers and that wages would suffer as too many laborers would vie for a limited number of positions, that over-population or population unchecked would lead to lowering the quality of subsistence for everyone. While he believed that wars, famines, plagues, and natural disasters could serve as checks on population growth, he did not think these sufficient. He argued for limiting the number of children based on economic circumstances. Although never explaining how he arrived at this conclusion, he wrote prolifically on the subject to the extent that his was considered to be a total pessimist when it came to the plight of future generations.

However, Charles Darwin credited Malthus' argument, that in nature more plants and animals are produced than can survive, as giving him the understanding for his theory of natural selection. Rather than being pessimistic about over-population, Darwin understood that with more offspring, there would be more competition leading to greater variation, and thus a greater chance that some would survive. Darwin was very optimistic about natural selection and its power in evolution.

Malthus was born in 1766, at Dorking, near London, and was one of eight children. His father, Daniel Malthus, tutored him and also hired tutors for young Robert until he enrolled in Cambridge in 1784. Robert was an able student and studied economics and for the ministry in the Church of England. He married late and fathered three children. In 1805, he was appointed professor of Political Economy at the college at Haileybury where he spent the remainder of his career.

Malthus was controversial in his day, as scholars accused him of being too pessimistic and not fully explaining how he arrived at his predictions in the lengthy essay. His call for temperance among married couples and for limiting the number of children born was not only contentious, but he also offended the sensibilities of some readers during his day. His predictions of crop failure and starvation did not occur. He could not have known about the coming industrial revolution with its advances in food production, sanitation, and the growth of technology. Yet, today, there are those, such as the members of the Malthus Society, who argue that his thoughts were prescient and who argue for birth control and less government programs for the poor.

After reading this essay, students should ask themselves

1. Is the world becoming dangerously over-populated?
2. Are we running out of the essential natural resources to sustain the population growth?
3. Can technology address this situation in the future as it has in the past?

SOURCES:

Thomas Malthus. (1995) Assessed on April 20, 2009 from http://www.ucmp.berkeley.edu/history/malthus.html.

Malthus Theory. (2009) Assessed April 20, 2009 from http://www.tiscali.co.uk/reference/encyclopaedia/hutchinson/m0034800.html

Life after People, (2006). Assessed April 20, 2009 from http://www.blupete.com/Literature/Biographies/Philosophy/Malthus.htm#Life.

SELECTION FROM:

Malthus, T. R. (1914). *On the Principles of Population*. New York: J. M. Dent & Sons Limited. 5-11.

Book I

OF THE CHECKS TO POPULATION IN THE LESS CIVILIZED PARTS OF THE WORLD AND IN PAST TIMES

Chapter I

Statement of the Subject—Ratios of the Increase of Population and Food.

In an inquiry concerning the improvement of society, the mode of conducting the subject which naturally presents itself, is,

1. To investigate the causes that have hitherto impeded the progress of mankind towards happiness; and,
2. To examine the probability of the total or partial removal of these causes in future.

To enter fully into this question, and to enumerate all the causes that have hitherto influenced human improvement, would be much beyond the power of an individual. The principal object of the present essay is to examine the effects of one great cause intimately united with the very nature of man; which, though it has been constantly and powerfully operating since the commencement of society, has been little noticed by the writers who have treated this subject. The facts which establish the existence of this cause have, indeed, been repeatedly stated and acknowledged; but its natural and necessary effects have been almost totally overlooked; though probably among these effects may be reckoned a very considerable portion of that vice and misery, and of that unequal distribution of the bounties of nature, which it has been the unceasing object of the enlightened philanthropist in all ages to correct.

The cause to which I allude, is the constant tendency in all animated life to increase beyond the nourishment prepared for it.

It is observed by Dr. Franklin, that there is no bound to the prolific nature of plants or animals, but what is made by their crowding and interfering with each other's means of subsistence. Were the face of the earth, he says, vacant of other plants, it might be gradually sowed and overspread with one kind only, as for instance with fennel: and were it empty of other inhabitants, it might in a few ages be replenished from one nation only, as for instance with Englishmen.[1]

This is incontrovertibly true. Through the animal and vegetable kingdoms Nature has scattered the seeds of life abroad with the most profuse and liberal hand; but has been comparatively sparing in the room and the nourishment necessary to rear them. The germs of existence contained in this earth, if they could freely develop themselves, would fill millions of worlds in the course of a few thousand years. Necessity, that imperious, all-pervading law of nature, restrains them within the prescribed bounds. The race of plants and the race of animals shrink under this great restrictive law; and man cannot by any efforts of reason escape from it.

In plants and irrational animals, the view of the subject is simple. They are all impelled by a powerful instinct to the increase of their species; and this instinct is interrupted by no doubts about providing for their offspring. Wherever therefore there is liberty, the power of increase is exerted; and the superabundant effects are repressed afterwards by want of room and nourishment.

The effects of this check on man are more complicated. Impelled to the increase of his species by an equally powerful instinct, reason interrupts his career, and asks him whether he may not bring beings into the world, for whom he cannot provide the means of support. If he attend to this natural suggestion, the restriction too frequently produces vice. If he hear it not, the human race will be constantly endeavouring to increase beyond the means of subsistence. But as, by that law of our nature which makes food necessary to the life of man, population can never actually increase beyond the lowest nourishment capable of supporting it, a strong check on population, from the difficulty of acquiring food, must be constantly in operation. This difficulty must fall somewhere, and must necessarily be severely felt in some or other of the various forms of misery, or the fear of misery, by a large portion of mankind.

That population has this constant tendency to increase beyond the means of subsistence, and that it is kept to its necessary level by these causes, will sufficiently appear from a review of the different states of society in which man has existed. But, before we proceed to this review, the subject will, perhaps, be seen in a clearer light, if we endeavour to ascertain what would be the natural increase of population, if left to exert itself with perfect freedom; and what might be expected to be the rate

---

1 Franklin's Miscell. p. 9

of increase in the productions of the earth, under the most favourable circumstances of human industry.

It will be allowed that no country has hitherto been known, where the manners were so pure and simple, and the means of subsistence so abundant, that no check whatever has existed to early marriages from the difficulty of providing for a family, and that no waste of the human species has been occasioned by vicious customs, by towns, by unhealthy occupations, or too severe labour. Consequently in no state that we have yet known, has the power of population been left to exert itself with perfect freedom.

Whether the law of marriage be instituted, or not, the dictate of nature and virtue seems to be an early attachment to one woman; and where there were no impediments of any kind in the way of an union to which such an attachment would lead, and no causes of depopulation afterwards, the increase of the human species would be evidently much greater than any increase which has been hitherto known.

In the northern states of America, where the means of subsistence have been more ample, the manners of the people more pure, and the checks to early marriages fewer, than in any of the modern states of Europe, the population has been found to double itself, for above a century and a half successively, in less than twenty-five years.[2] Yet, even during these periods, in some of the towns, the deaths exceeded the births,[3] a circumstance which clearly proves that, in those parts of the country which supplied this deficiency, the increase must have been much more rapid than the general average.

In the back settlements, where the sole employment is agriculture, and vicious customs and unwholesome occupations are little known, the population has been found to double itself in fifteen years.[4] Even this extraordinary rate of increase is probably short of the utmost power of population. Very severe labour is requisite to clear a fresh country; such situations are not in general considered as particularly healthy; and the inhabitants, probably, are occasionally subject to the incursions of the

---

2 It appears, from some recent calculations and estimates, that from the first settlement of America, to the year 1800, the periods of doubling have been but very little above twenty years. See a note on the increase of American population in Book ii. chap. xi.

3 Price's Observ. on Revers. Pay. vol. i. p. 274. 4th edit.

4 Id. p. 282.

Indians, which may destroy some lives, or at any rate diminish the fruits of industry.

According to a table of Euler, calculated on a mortality of 1 in 36, if the births be to the deaths in the proportion of 3 to 1, the period of doubling will be only 12 years and 4-5ths.[5] And this proportion is not only a possible supposition, but has actually occurred for short periods in more countries than one.

Sir William Petty supposes a doubling possible in so short a time as ten years.[6]

But, to be perfectly sure that we are far within the truth, we will take the slowest of these rates of increase, a rate in which all concurring testimonies agree, and which has been repeatedly ascertained to be from procreation only.

It may safely be pronounced, therefore, that population, when unchecked, goes on doubling itself every twenty-five years, or increases in a geometrical ratio.

The rate according to which the productions of the earth may be supposed to increase, it will not be so easy to determine. Of this, however, we may be perfectly certain, that the ratio of their increase in a limited territory must be of a totally different nature from the ratio of the increase of population. A thousand millions are just as easily doubled every twenty-five years by the power of population as a thousand. But the food to support the increase from the greater number will by no means be obtained with the same facility. Man is necessarily confined in room. When acre has been added to acre till all the fertile land is occupied, the yearly increase of food must depend upon the melioration of the land already in possession. This is a fund; which, from the nature of all soils, instead of increasing, must be gradually diminishing. But population, could it be supplied with food, would go on with unexhausted vigour; and the increase of one period would furnish the power of a greater increase the next, and this without any limit.

From the accounts we have of China and Japan, it may be fairly doubted, whether the best-directed efforts of human industry could double the produce of these countries even once in any number of years. There are many parts of the globe; indeed, hitherto uncultivated, and almost unoccupied; but the right of exterminating, or driving into a corner where they must starve, even the inhabitants of these thinly-peopled

---

5 See this table at the end of chap. iv. book ii.

6 Polit. Arith. p. 14

regions, will be questioned in a moral view. The process of improving their minds and directing their industry would necessarily be slow; and during this time, as population would regularly keep pace with the increasing produce, it would rarely happen that a great degree of knowledge and industry would have to operate at once upon rich unappropriated soil. Even where this might take place, as it does sometimes in new colonies, a geometrical ratio increases with such extraordinary rapidity, that the advantage could not last long. If the United States of America continue increasing, which they certainly will do, though not with the same rapidity as formerly, the Indians will be driven further and further back into the country, till the whole race is ultimately exterminated, and the territory is incapable of further extension.

These observations are, in a degree, applicable to all the parts of the earth, where the soil is imperfectly cultivated. To exterminate the inhabitants of the greatest part of Asia and Africa, is a thought that could not be admitted for a moment. To civilise and direct the industry of the various tribes of Tartars and Negroes, would certainly be a work of considerable time, and of variable and uncertain success.

Europe is by no means so fully peopled as it might be. In Europe there is the fairest chance that human industry may receive its best direction. The science of agriculture has been much studied in England and Scotland; and there is still a great portion of uncultivated land in these countries. Let us consider at what rate the produce of this island might be supposed to increase under circumstances the most favourable to improvement.

If it be allowed that by the best possible policy, and great encouragements to agriculture, the average produce of the island could be doubled in the first twenty-five years, it will be allowing, probably, a greater increase than could with reason be expected.

In the next twenty-five years, it is impossible to suppose that the produce could be quadrupled. It would be contrary to all our knowledge of the properties of land. The improvement of the barren parts would be a work of time and labour; and it must be evident to those who have the slightest acquaintance with agricultural subjects, that in proportion as cultivation extended, the additions that could yearly be made to the former average produce must be gradually and regularly diminishing. That we may be the better able to compare the increase of population and food, let us make a supposition, which, without pretending to accuracy, is clearly more favourable to the power of production in the earth, than any experience we have had of its qualities will warrant.

Let us suppose that the yearly additions which might be made to the former average produce, instead of decreasing, which they certainly would do, were to remain the same; and that the produce of this island might be increased every twenty-five years, by a quantity equal to what it at present produces. The most enthusiastic speculator cannot suppose a greater increase than this. In a few centuries it would make every acre of land in the island like a garden.

If this supposition be applied to the whole earth, and if it be allowed that the subsistence for man which the earth affords might be increased every twenty-five years by a quantity equal to what it at present produces, this will be supposing a rate of increase much greater than we can imagine that any possible exertions of mankind could make it.

It may be fairly pronounced, therefore, that, considering the present average state of the earth, the means of subsistence, under circumstances the most favourable to human industry, could not possibly be made to increase faster than in an arithmetical ratio.

The necessary effects of these two different rates of increase, when brought together, will be very striking. Let us call the population of this island eleven millions; and suppose the present produce equal to the easy support of such a number. In the first twenty-five years the population would be twenty-two millions, and the food being also doubled, the means of subsistence would be equal to this increase. In the next twenty-five years, the population would be forty-four millions, and the means of subsistence only equal to the support of thirty-three millions. In the next period the population would be eighty-eight millions, and the means of subsistence just equal to the support of half that number. And, at the conclusion of the first century, the population would be a hundred and seventy-six millions, and the means of subsistence only equal to the support of fifty-five millions, leaving a population of a hundred and twenty-one millions totally unprovided for.

Taking the whole earth, instead of this island, emigration would of course be excluded; and, supposing the present population equal to a thousand millions, the human species would increase as the numbers, 1, 2, 4, 8, 16, 32, 64, 128, 256, and subsistence as 1, 2, 3, 4, 5, 6, 7, 8, 9. In two centuries the population would be to the means of subsistence as 256 to 9; in three centuries as 4096 to 13, and in two thousand years the difference would be almost incalculable.

In this supposition no limits whatever are placed to the produce of the earth. It may increase for ever and be greater than any assignable quantity; yet still the power of population being in every period so much superior, the increase of the human species can only be kept down to the level of the means of subsistence by the constant operation of the strong law of necessity, acting as a check upon the greater power.

Section IV

Society

Throughout the ages society has been shaped by developments in technology. From the Stone Age to the Information Age, new developments have expanded our capacity to feed, clothe, shelter, and protect ourselves. We live longer, communicate with each other instantly, and generally have more freedoms, all because of technological advancements. Modern powerful technological developments, such as the invention of computers and the internet, weapons of mass destruction, genetic engineering and cloning, assure that the future will be very different from yesterday. Our decisions as a society about the uses of what we have invented, and what we are capable of inventing, must become more measured. James Childress argues in *The Art of Technology Assessment* that society must consider its values in light of its advances because true technology assessment "predicts and evaluates for the future and is less interested in the evaluation of technologies already developed." (207) As Bertrand Russell points out in the *Impact of Science on Society*, although the invention of gun powder and the compass ushered in the modern power of the state in the latter half of the fifteenth century and the state has become more powerful ever since, the current level of sophistication in these technologies begs us to exercise restraint and live by the rule of law for the good of civilization.

Perhaps the environment serves as the interface, showcasing the prominence of human decisions about the development and use of technologies of all kinds. In the past, society's concern for the environment has faded in and out of the public consciousness and public dialogue depending on the latest catastrophic event. However, since the beginning of the twenty-first century environmental issues have become more prominent; they will continue to be central to our social dialogue concerning ways to best protect and manage the environment while at the same time giving people the access and freedom to enjoy the quality of life they desire. More global issues such as pollutants in the air, global warming, population growth, and public health will continue to challenge our abilities to find workable solutions to the many issues.

In "Environmental Degradation and the Tyranny of Small Decisions," William Odum points to the wholesale loss of valuable wetlands, not because of a single decision, but as a result of the many smaller decisions made at many different local levels. Insidious smaller decisions to build subdivisions, roads, cut trees, all have led to water and air pollution problems with more global effect. Garrett Hardin, in "The Tragedy of the Commons," argues that the tragedy of communal access to and ownership of property often leads to the demise of that property, that individual self-interests often in conflict with the collective interest. Even personal decisions as to how many children we shall have will lead to over population in many countries, a result from the desire of the individual at the expense of the collective. Eventually, these small decisions will affect the quality of life for all. Finally Schumacher warns that society may be overconfident that it has solved issues of production. But as we produce in the modern industrial age we are rapidly consuming our land, labor and capital on an ever increasing larger scale. He urges us to consider that smaller may in fact be more beautiful—certainly smaller may be less wasteful, and in the long run, our salvation.

Bertrand Russell

1872-1970

The Impact of Science on Society

1951

Bertrand Russell was a British Philosopher and social critic who made significant contributions to logic, mathematics, philosophy, politics, and religion. He was awarded the Order of Merit in 1949, an award that recognizes those who make outstanding contributions in the arts and sciences in England, and he also won the Nobel Prize in Literature in 1950. His writings on a wide range of topics in the humanities and in the sciences, and well as on social justice, made him simultaneously a revered philosopher and controversial figure of his day.

Although from a noble heritage, Bertrand Russell was the third Earl Russell and his grandfather was Prime Minister of England, he was known in many quarters for his opposition to the proliferation of nuclear weapons and his opposition to war. A life-long pacifist, his public protests against war went back to the World War I when he was fined and jailed in England for his public opposition to that war. Graduating from Trinity College, Cambridge in 1890 with first-class honors in mathematics, he remained to complete an advanced degree in the moral sciences in 1894; he was named a fellow soon thereafter but his war protests led to his dismissal from Trinity College in 1916. His life of protests for his social causes led to the revocation of an offer to teach at City College of New York in 1940, and to his dismissal from the Barnes Foundation in Pennsylvania in 1943. He was jailed in the United States for his anti-nuclear war protests in 1961.

Perhaps best known for his collaborative work with Alfred North Whitehead in *Principia Mathematica* (1910, 1912, 1913), as well as his works including *Principles of Mathematics* (1903), *An Essay on the Foundations of Geometry* (1897), and his *Introduction to Mathematical Philosophy* (1919), he is considered to be one of the most important mathematicians and logicians of the twentieth century. With an emphasis on analytical philosophy, he believed in the importance of scientific knowledge and the scientific method in helping to promote human understanding.

In the following excerpt, Russell allows that science helps us to *know* things and to *do* things, but he warns that at the same time, the scientific technique can bring about cruelty and misery, particularly to the laborers. The development and use of weapons gives centralized governments more power, creating a tyranny over the masses. Thus science and technology can provide humankind with great prosperity or great misery.

1. How is science a way of knowing, different from other fields of endeavor?
2. Is there a connection between science and technology? If so explain the connection. If not, why do you think there is no connection?
3. Has the nature of science as a way of knowing changed from the periods Russell describes (antiquity, civil war) to the present? If so, how has science changed?

SOURCES:

www.http://plato.standord.edu/entries/russell/. Accessed November 2, 2006 from Bertrand Russell (Stanford Encyclopedia of Philosophy November 2, 2006.

Bertrand Russell. Nobel Prizes in Literature. Accessed November 2, 2006 from http://nobelprize.org.

SELECTION FROM:

Russell, B., (1951). "Effects of Scientific Technique," *The Impact of Science on a Free Society*. New York: Columbia University Press. 21-43.

Chapter II

General Effects of Scientific Technique

SCIENCE, ever since the time of the Arabs, has had two functions: first, to enable us to *know* things, and, second, to enable us to *do* things. The Greeks, with the exception of Archimedes, were only interested in the first of these. They had much curiosity about the world, but, since civilized people lived comfortably on slave labor, they had no interest in technique. Interest in the practical uses of science came first through superstition and magic. The Arabs wished to discover the philosopher's stone, the elixir of life, and how to transmute base metals into gold. In pursuing investigations having these purposes, they discovered many facts in chemistry, but they did not arrive at any valid and important general laws, and their technique remained elementary.

However, in the late Middle Ages two discoveries were made which had a profound importance: they were gunpowder and the mariner's compass. It is not known who made these discoveries—the only thing certain is that it was *not* Roger Bacon, as English children were taught when I was young.

The main importance of gunpowder, at first, was that it enabled central governments to subdue rebellious barons. Magna Carta would have never been won if John had possessed artillery. But although in this instance we may side with the barons against the king, in general the Middle Ages suffered from anarchy, and what was needed was a way of establishing order and respect for law. At that time, only royal power could achieve this. The barons had depended upon their castles, and the castles could not stand against artillery. That is why the Tudors were more powerful than earlier kings. And the same kind of change occurred at the same time in France and Spain. The modern power of the State began in the late fifteenth century and began as a result of gunpowder. From that day to this, the authority of states has increased, and throughout it has been mainly improvements in weapons of war that has made this increase possible. This development was begun by Henry VII, Louis XI, and Ferdinand and Isabella. It was artillery that enabled them to succeed.

The mariner's compass was equally important. It made possible the age of discovery. The New World was opened to white colonists; the route to the East round Cape of Good Hope made possible the conquest of India and brought about important contacts between Europe and China.

The importance of sea power was enormously increased, and through sea power Western Europe came to dominate the world. It is only in the present century that this domination has come to an end.

Nothing of equal importance occurred in the way of new scientific technique until the age of steam and the Industrial Revolution. The atom bomb has caused many people during the last seven years to think that scientific technique may be carried too far. But there is nothing new in this. The Industrial Revolution caused unspeakable misery both in England and in America. I do not think any student of economic history can doubt that the average of happiness in England in the early nineteenth century was lower than it had been a hundred years earlier; and this was due almost entirely to scientific technique.

Let us consider cotton, which was the most important example of early industrialization. In the Lancashire cotton mills (from which, by the way, Marx and Engels derived their livelihood), children worked from 12 to 16 hours a day; they often began working at the age of six or seven. Children had to be beaten to keep them from falling asleep while at work; in spite of this, many failed to keep awake and rolled into the machinery, by which they were mutilated or killed. Parents had to submit to the infliction of these atrocities upon their children, because they themselves were in a desperate plight. Handicraftsmen had been thrown out of work by the machines; rural laborers were compelled to migrate to the towns by the Enclosure Acts, which used Parliament to make landowners richer by making peasants destitute; trade unions in England were illegal until 1824; the government employed *agents provocateurs* to try to get revolutionary sentiments out of wage-earners, and when they succeeded, the wage earners were denounced and hanged.

Such was the first effect of machinery in England.

Meanwhile the effects in the United States had been equally disastrous. At the time of the War of Independence, and for some years after its close, the Southern States were quite willing to contemplate the abolition of slavery in the near future. Slavery in the Old Northwest was abolished by a unanimous vote in 1787, and Jefferson, not without reason, hoped to see it abolished in the South. But in the year 1793 Whitney invented the cotton gin, which enabled a Negro to clean fifty pounds of fibre a day instead of only one, as formerly. "Labor-saving" devices, so called, in England had caused children to have to work 15 hours a day; "labor-saving" devices in America inflicted upon slaves a life of toil far more severe than what they had to endure before Mr. Whitney's invention. The slave trade having been abolished in 1808, the immense increase in the cultivation of cotton after that date had to be made possible by importing Negroes from the less southerly States in which cotton could not be grown. The Deep South was unhealthy, and the slaves on the cotton plantations were cruelly overworked. The less southern slave states thus became breeding grounds for the profitable Southern graveyards.

The ultimate outcome was the Civil War, which would almost certainly not have occurred if the cotton industry had remained unscientific.

There were also results in other continents. Cotton goods could find a market in India and Africa; this was a stimulus to British imperialism. Africans had to be taught that nudity is wicked; this was done very cheaply by missionaries. In addition to cotton goods, we exported tuberculosis and syphilis, but for these there was no charge.

I have dwelt upon the case of cotton because I want to emphasize that evils due to a new scientific technique are no new thing. The evils I have been speaking of ceased in time, child labor was abolished in England, slavery was abolished in America, imperialism is now at an end in India. The evils that persist in Africa have now nothing to do with cotton.

Steam, which was one of the most important elements in the industrial revolution, had its most distinctive sphere of operation in transport—steamers and railways. The really large-scale effects of steam transportation did not develop fully until after the middle of the nineteenth century, when they led to the opening of the Middle West and the use of its grain to feed the industrial populations of England and New England. This led to a very general increase of prosperity, and had more to do than any other single cause with Victorian optimism. It made possible a very rapid increase in population in every civilized country—except France, where the Code Napoléon had prevented it by decreeing equal division of a man's property among all his children and where a majority were peasant proprietors owning very little land.

This development was not attended with the evils of early industrialism, chiefly, I think, because of the abolition of slavery and the growth of democracy. Irish peasants and Russian serfs, who were not self-governing, continued to suffer. Cotton operatives would have continued to suffer if English landowners had been strong enough to defeat Cobden and Bright.

The next important stage in the development of scientific technique is connected with electricity and oil and the internal-combustion engine.

Long before the use of electricity as a source of power, it was used in the telegraph. This had two important consequences: first, messages could now travel faster than human beings; secondly, in large organizations detailed control from a center became much more possible than it had formerly been.

The fact that messages could travel faster than human beings was useful, above all, to the police. Before the telegraph, a highwayman on a galloping horse could escape to a place where his crime had not yet been heard of, and this made it very much harder to catch him. Unfortunately, however, the men whom the police wish to catch are frequently benefactors of mankind. If the telegraph had existed, Polycrates would have caught Pythagoras, the Athenian government would have caught Anaxagoras, the pope would have caught William of Occam, and Pitt would have caught Tom Paine. A large proportion of the best Germans and Russians have suffered under Hitler and Stalin; many more would have escaped but for the rapid transmission of messages. The increased power of the police therefore, is not wholly a gain.

Increase of central control is an even more important consequence of the telegraph. In ancient empires satraps or proconsuls in distant provinces could rebel, and had time to entrench themselves before the central government knew of their disaffection. When Constantine proclaimed himself Emperor at York and marched on Rome, he was almost under the walls of the city before the Roman authorities knew he was coming. Perhaps if the telegraph had existed in those days, the Western world would not now be Christian. In the War of 1812, the battle of New Orleans was fought after peace had been concluded, but neither army was aware of the fact. Before the telegraph, ambassadors had an independence which they have now completely lost, because they had to be allowed a free hand if swift action was necessary in a crisis.

It was not only in relation to government, but wherever organizations covering large areas were concerned, that the telegraph effected a transformation. Read, for instance, in Hakluyt's *Voyages,* the accounts of attempts to foster trade with Russia that were made by English commercial interests in the time of Elizabeth. All that could be done was to choose an energetic and tactful emissary, give him letters, goods, money, and leave him to make what headway he could. Contact with his employers was possible only at long intervals, and their instructions could never be up to date.

The effect of the telegraph was to increase the power of the central government and diminish the initiative of distant subordinates. This applied not only to the state, but to every geographically extensive organization. We shall find that a great deal of scientific technique has a similar effect. The result is that fewer men have executive power, but those few have more power than such men had formerly.

In all these respects, broadcasting has completed what the telegraph began.

Electricity as a source of power is much more recent than the telegraph, and has not yet had all the effects of which it is capable. As an influence on social organization its most notable feature is the importance of power stations, which inevitably promote centralization. The philosophers of Laputa, as you all will remember, could reduce a rebellious dependency to submission by interposing their floating island between the rebels and the sun. Something very analogous can be done by those who control power stations, as soon as a community has become dependent upon them for lighting and heating and cooking. I lived in America in a farmhouse which depended entirely upon electricity, and sometimes, in a blizzard, the wires would be blown down. We sat shivering in the dark, with only uncooked food. If we had been deliberately cut off for being rebels, we should soon have had to give in.

The importance of oil and the internal-combustion engine in our present technique is obvious to everybody. For technical reasons, it is advantageous if oil companies are very large, since otherwise they cannot afford such things as long pipe lines. The importance of oil companies in the politics of the last thirty years has been very generally recognized. This applies especially to the Middle East and the Dutch East Indies. Oil is a serious source of friction between the West and the U.S.S.R. and tends to generate friendliness towards Communism in some regions that are strategically important to the West.

But what is of most importance in this connection is the development of flying. Airplanes have increased immeasurably the power of governments. No rebellion can hope to succeed unless it is favored by at least a portion of the air force. Not only has air warfare increased the power of governments, but it has increased the disproportion between great and small powers. Only great powers can afford a large air force, and no small power can stand out against a great power which has secured air supremacy.

This brings me to the most recent technical application of physical knowledge—I mean the utilization of atomic energy. It is not yet possible to estimate its peaceful uses. Perhaps it will become a source of power for certain purposes, thus carrying further the concentration at present represented by power stations. Perhaps it will be used as the Soviet Government says it intends to use it—to alter physical geography by abolishing mountains and turning deserts into lakes. But as far as can be judged at present, atomic energy is not likely to be as important in peace as in war.

War has been, throughout history, the chief source of social cohesion; and since science began, it has been the strongest incentive to technical progress. Large groups have a better chance of victory than small ones, and therefore the usual result of war is to make states larger. In any given state of technique there is a limit to size. The Roman Empire was stopped by German forests and African deserts. The British conquests in India were halted by the Himalayas; Napoleon was defeated by the Russian winter. And before the telegraph, large empires tended to break up because they could not be effectively controlled from a center.

Communications have been hitherto the chief factor limiting the size of empires. In antiquity, the Persians and the Romans depended upon roads, but since nothing traveled faster than a horse, empires became unmanageable when the distance from the capital to the frontier was very great. This difficulty was diminished by railways and the telegraph, and is on the point of disappearing with the improvement of the long-range bomber. There would now be no technical difficulty about a single world-wide empire. Since war is likely to become more destructive of human life than it has been in recent centuries, unification under a single government is probably necessary unless we are to acquiesce in either a return to barbarism or the extinction of the human race.

There is, it must be confessed, a psychological difficulty about a single world government. The chief source of social cohesion in the past, I repeat, has been war: the passions that inspire a feeling of unity are hate and fear. These depend upon the existence of an enemy, actual or potential. It seems to follow that a world government could only be kept in being by force, not by the spontaneous loyalty that now inspires a nation at war—unless, of course, the world government were to compel journalists to say that an invasion from Mars was imminent. That would cause perfect terrestrial cohesion.

So far, I have been considering only techniques derived from physics and chemistry. These have, up to the present, been the most important, but biology, physiology, and psychology are likely in the long run to affect human life quite as much as physics and chemistry.

Take first the question of food and population. At present the population of the globe is increasing at the rate of about 20 millions a year. Most of this increase is in Russia and Southeast Asia. The population of Western Europe and the United States is nearly stationary. Meanwhile, the food supply of the world as a whole threatens to diminish, as a result of unwise methods of cultivation and destruction of forests. This is an explosive situation. Left to itself, it must lead to a food shortage and thence to a world war. Technique, however, makes other issues possible.

Vital statistics in the West are dominated by medicine and birth control: the one diminishes the deaths, the other the births. The result is that the average age in the West increases: there is a smaller percentage of young people and a larger percentage of old people. Some people consider that this must have unfortunate results, but, speaking as an old person, I am not sure.

The danger of a world shortage of food may be averted for a time by improvements in the technique of agriculture. But, if population continues to increase at the present rate, such improvements cannot long suffice. There will then be two groups, one poor with an increasing population, the other rich with a stationary population. Such a situation can hardly fail to lead to world war. If there is not to be an endless succession of wars, population will have to become stationary throughout the world, and this will probably have to be done, in many countries, as a result of governmental measures. This will require an extension of scientific technique into very intimate matters.

Biology is likely to affect human life through the study of heredity. Without science, men have changed domestic animals and food plants enormously in advantageous ways. It may be assumed that they will change them much more, and much more quickly, by bringing the science of genetics to bear. Perhaps it may even become possible artificially to induce desirable mutations in genes. (Hitherto the only mutations that can be artificially caused are neutral or harmful.) In any case, it is pretty certain that scientific technique will very soon effect great improvements in the animals and plants that are useful to man.

When such methods of modifying the congenital character of animals and plants have been pursued long enough to make their success obvious, it is probable that there will be a powerful movement for applying scientific methods to human propagation. There would at first be strong religious and emotional obstacles to the adoption of such a policy. But suppose, say, Russia were able to overcome these obstacles and to breed a race stronger, more intelligent, and more resistant to disease than any race of men that has hitherto existed, and suppose the other nations perceived that unless they followed suit they would be defeated in war, then either the other nations would voluntarily forgo their prejudices, or, after defeat, they would be compelled to forgo them.

Any scientific technique, however beastly, is bound to spread if it is useful in war—until such time as men decide that they have had enough of war and will henceforth live in peace. As that day does not seem to be at hand, scientific breeding of human beings must be expected to come about, much as I should regret it.

Physiology and psychology afford fields for scientific technique which still await development. There are two great men here who have laid the foundations and are popularly supposed to be opposites, Pavlov and Freud. I do not myself believe that they are in any essential conflict, but what structure will be built upon their foundations remains still doubtful.

I think the subject which would be of most importance, politically, is mass psychology. Mass psychology is, scientifically speaking, not a very advanced study, and so far its professors have not been in universities: they have been advertisers, politicians, and, above all, dictators. This study is immensely useful to practical men, whether they wish to become rich or to acquire the government. It is, of course, as a science founded upon individual psychology, but hitherto it has employed rule-of-thumb methods which were based upon a kind of intuitive common sense. Its importance has been enormously increased by the growth of modern methods of propaganda. Of these the most influential is what is called "education." Religion plays a part, though a diminishing one; the press, the cinema, and the radio play an increasing part.

What is essential in mass psychology is the art of persuasion. If you compare a speech of Hitler's with a speech of, say, Edmund Burke, you will see what strides have been made in the art since the eighteenth century. What went wrong formerly was that people had read in books that man is a rational animal, and framed their arguments on this hypothesis. We now know that limelight and a brass band do more to persuade than can be done by the most elegant train of syllogisms. It may be hoped that in time anybody will be able to persuade anybody of anything if he can catch the patient young and is provided by the state with money and equipment.

This subject will make great strides when it is taken up by scientists under a scientific dictatorship. Anaxagoras maintained that snow is black, but no one believed him. The social psychologists of the future will have a number of classes of school children on whom they will try different methods of producing an unshakable conviction that snow is black. Various results will soon be arrived at: first, that the influence of home is obstructive; second, that not much can be done unless indoctrination begins before the age of ten; third, that verses set to music and repeatedly intoned are very effective; fourth, that the opinion that snow is white must be held to show a morbid taste for eccentricity. But I anticipate. It is for future scientists to make these maxims precise and discover exactly how much it costs per head to make children believe that snow is black and how much less it would cost to make them believe it is dark gray.

Although this science of mass psychology will be diligently studied, it will be rigidly confined to the governing class. The populace will not be allowed to know how its convictions are generated. When the technique has been perfected, every government that has been in charge of education for a generation will be able to control its subjects securely without the need of armies or policemen. As yet, there is only one country which has succeeded in creating this politician's paradise. And this brings me on to a more explicit consideration. I want now to come more explicitly to the social effects of scientific technique as opposed to the technique itself. They have already been many and important and are likely to be even more noteworthy in the future. Some depend upon the political and economic character of the country concerned; others are inevitable, whatever the character of the government may be. I shall come in my last lecture tomorrow to the connection of this entire subject with values, but for the present, I am not considering values.

The most obvious and inescapable effect of scientific technique is that it makes society more organic, in the sense of increasing the interdependence of its various parts. In the sphere of production, this has two forms. There is, first, the very intimate interconnection of individuals engaged in a common enterprise, for instance a single factory; and, secondly, there is the relation, less intimate but still essential, between one enterprise and another. Each of these becomes more important with every advance in scientific technique.

A peasant in an unindustrialized country may produce almost all his own food by means of very inexpensive tools. These tools, some of his clothes, and a few things such as salt, are all that he needs to buy. His children did not go to school, and when they are ill, they get no medical attention. His relations with the outer world are thus reduced to a minimum. So long as he produces, with the help of his wife and children, a little more food than the family requires, he can enjoy almost complete independence, though at the cost of hardship and poverty. But in a time of famine he goes hungry, and probably most of his children die. His liberty is so dearly bought that few civilized men would change places with him. This was the lot of most of the population of civilized countries till the rise of industrialism.

Although the peasant's lot is in any case a hard one, it is apt to be rendered harder by one or both of two enemies—the moneylender and the landowner. In any history of any period, you will find roughly the following gloomy picture. "At this time the old hardy yeoman stock had fallen upon evil days. Under threat of starvation from bad harvests, many of them had borrowed from urban landowners, who had none of their traditions, their ancient piety, or their patient courage. Those who had taken this fatal step became, almost inevitably, the slaves or serfs of members of the new commercial class. And so the sturdy farmers, who had been the backbone of the nation, were submerged by supple men who had the skill to amass new wealth by dubious methods." You will find, as I say, substantially this account in the history of Attica before Solon, of Latium after the Punic Wars, of England in the early nineteenth century, of Southern California as depicted in Norris's *Octopus,* of India under the British raj, and of the reasons which have led Chinese peasants to support communism. The process, however regrettable, is an inevitable stage in the integration of agriculture into a larger economy. And I may say that, for my part, I believe all this talk about the sturdy yeoman is considering being humbug. There seems to have never been an age when the sturdy yeoman was not falling into decay.

By way of contrast with the primitive peasant, consider the agrarian interests in modern California or Canada or Australia or the Argentine. Everything is produced for export, and the prosperity to be brought by exporting depends upon such distant matters as war in Europe or Marshall aid or the devaluation of the pound. Everything turns on politics—on whether the farm bloc is strong in Washington, whether there is reason to fear that Argentina may make friends with Russia, and so on. There may still be nominally independent farmers, but in fact they are in the power of the vast financial interests that are concerned in manipulating political issues. This interdependence is in no degree lessened—perhaps it is even increased—if the countries concerned are socialist, as, for example, if the Soviet government and the British government make a deal to exchange food for machinery. All this is the effect of scientific technique on agriculture. Malthus, at the beginning of the nineteenth century, wrote: "In the wildness of speculation it has been suggested (of course more in jest than in earnest) that Europe should grow its corn in America, and devote itself solely to manufactures and commerce." It turned out that the speculation was by no means "wild."

So much for agriculture. In industry, the integration brought about by scientific technique is much greater and more intimate.

One of the most obvious results of industrialism is that a much larger percentage of the population lives in towns than was formerly the case. The town dweller is a more social being than the agriculturist and is much more influenced by discussion. In general, he works in a crowd, and his amusements are apt to take him into still larger crowds. The course of nature, the alternations of day and night, summer and winter, wet or shine, make little difference to him; he has no occasion to fear that he will be ruined by frost or drought or sudden rain. What matters to him is his human environment and his place in various organizations.

Take a man who works in a factory, and consider how many organizations affect his life. There is, first of all, the factory itself, and any large organization of which it may be a part. Then there are the man's trade union and his political party. He probably gets house room from a building society or public authority. His children go to school. If he reads a newspaper or goes to a cinema or looks at a football match, these things are provided by powerful organizations. Indirectly, through his employers, he is dependent upon those from whom they buy their raw material and those to whom they sell their finished product. Above all, there is the state, which taxes him and may at any moment order him to go and get killed in war, in return for which it protects him against murder and theft so long as there is peace.

The capitalist is almost equally hemmed in. In nostalgic moments he may talk about *laissez faire,* but in fact he sees no hope of safety except in new organizations to fight existing ones that he dislikes, for he knows that as an isolated unit he would be powerless and as an isolated state his country would be powerless.

The increase of organization has brought into existence new positions of power. Every body has to have executive officials, in whom, at any one moment, its power is concentrated. It is true that officials are usually subject to control, but the control may be slow and distant. From the young lady who sells stamps in a post office all the way up to the president, every official is invested, for the time being, with some part of the power of the state. You can complain of the young lady if her manners are bad, and you can vote against the president at the next election if you disapprove of his policy. But both the young lady and the president can have a very considerable run for their money before (if ever) your discontent has any effect. This increase in the power of officials is a constant source of irritation to everybody else. In most countries they are much less polite than in—some countries. There are countries where the police seem to think you must be a rare exception if you are not a criminal. This tyranny of officials is one of the worst results of increasing organization and one against which it is of the utmost importance to find safeguards if a scientific society is not to be intolerable to all but an insolent minority of Jacks-in-office.

The power of officials is, usually, distinct from that of people who are theoretically in ultimate control. In large corporations, although the directors are nominally elected by the shareholders, they usually manage, by various devices, to be in fact self-perpetuating and to acquire new directors, when necessary, by cooption more or less disguised as election. In British politics, it is a commonplace that most ministers find it impossible to cope with their civil servants, who in effect dictate policy except on party questions that have been prominently before the public. In many countries, the armed forces are apt to get out of hand and defy the civil authorities. Of the police I have already spoken. In countries where the Communists enter coalition governments, they always endeavor to make sure of control of the police. When once this is secured, they can manufacture plots, make arrests, and extort confessions freely. But this means, they pass from being participants in a coalition to being the whole government. The problem of causing the police to obey the law is a very difficult one. I read a book called *Our Lawless Police* by Ernest Jerome Hopkins, which, if correct, would seem to show that the problem of causing the police to obey the law has not been completely solved in your country.

The increased power of officials is an inevitable result of the greater degree of organization that scientific technique brings about. It has the drawback that it is apt to be irresponsible, behind-the-scenes power, like that of emperors' eunuchs and kings' mistresses in former times. To discover ways of controlling it is one of the most important political problems of our time. Liberals protested, successfully, against the power of kings and aristocrats; socialists protested against the power of capitalists. But unless the power of officials can be kept within bounds, socialism will mean little more than the substitution of one set of masters for another: all the former powers of the capitalist will be inherited by the official. In 1942, when I lived in Pennsylvania in the country, I had a part-time gardener, who spent the bulk of his working day making munitions. He told me with triumph that his union had secured the "closed shop." A little while later he told me, without triumph, that the union dues had been raised and that the extra money went wholly to increase the salary of the secretary of the union. Owing to what was practically a war situation between labor and capital, any agitation against the secretary could be represented as treachery. This little story illustrates the helplessness of the public against its own officials, even where there is nominally complete democracy.

One of the drawbacks to the power of officials is that they are apt to be quite remote from the things they control. As to this, I shall speak about English conditions because I don't know so much about your conditions. But speaking of England, what do the men in the Education Office know about education? Only what they dimly remember of their public school and university some twenty or thirty years ago. What does the Ministry of Agriculture know about mangold-wurzels? Only how they are spelt. What does the British Foreign Office know about modern China? After I had returned from China in 1921, I had some dealings with the permanent officials who determined our Far Eastern policy—British Far Eastern policy—and I found their ignorance unsurpassed except by their conceit. America has invented the phrase "yes-men" for those who flatter great executives. In Britain, we are more troubled by "no-men," who make it their business to employ clever ignorance in opposing and sabotaging every scheme suggested by those who have knowledge and imagination and enterprise. I am afraid our "no-men" are a thousand times more harmful than the American "yes-men." If we are to recover prosperity in Britain, we shall have to find ways of emancipating energy and enterprise from the frustrating control of constitutionally timid ignoramuses.

Owing to increase of organization, the question of the limits of individual liberty needs completely different treatment from that of nineteenth-century writers such as Mill. The acts of a single man are as a rule unimportant, but the acts of groups are more important than they used to be. Take, for example, refusal to work. If one man, on his own initiative, chooses to be idle, that may be regarded as his own affair; he loses his wages, and there is an end of the matter. But if there is a strike in a vital industry, the whole community suffers. I am not arguing that the right to strike should be abolished; I am only arguing that, if it is to be preserved, it must be for reasons concerned with this particular matter, and not on general grounds of personal liberty. In a highly organized country, there are many activities which are important to everybody and without which there would be widespread hardship. Matters should be so arranged that large groups seldom think it to their interest to strike. This can be done by arbitration and conciliation or, as under the dictatorship of the proletariat, by starvation and police action. But in one way or another it must be done if an industrial society is to prosper.

War is a more extreme case than strikes, but raises very similar questions of principle. When two men fight a duel, the matter is trivial; but when 200 million people fight 200 million other people, the matter is serious. And with every increase of organization, war becomes more serious. Until the present century, the great majority of the population, even in nations engaged in such contests as the Napoleonic wars, were still occupied with peaceful pursuits and as a rule little disturbed in their ordinary habits of life. Now, almost everybody, women as well as men, are set to some kind of war work. The resulting dislocation makes the peace, when it comes, almost worse than the war. Since the end of the late war, throughout Central Europe enormous numbers, men, women, and children, have died in circumstances of appalling suffering, and many millions of survivors have become homeless wanderers, uprooted, without work, without hope, a burden equally to themselves and to those who feed them. This sort of thing is to be expected when defeat introduces chaos into highly organized communities.

The right to make war, like the right to strike, but in a far higher degree, is very dangerous in a world governed by scientific technique. Neither can be simply abolished, since that would open the road to tyranny. But in each case it must be recognized that groups cannot, in the name of freedom, justly claim the right to inflict great injuries upon others. As regards war, the principle of unrestricted national sovereignty, cherished by liberals in the nineteenth century and by the Kremlin in the present day, must be abandoned. Means must be found of subjecting the relations of nations to the rule of law, so that a single nation will no longer be, as at present, the judge in its own cause. If this is not done, the world will quickly return to barbarism. In that case, scientific technique will disappear along with science, and men will be able to go on being quarrelsome because their quarrels will no longer do much harm. It is, however, just possible that mankind may prefer to survive and prosper rather than to perish in misery, and, if so, national liberty will have to be effectively restrained.

As we have seen, the question of freedom needs a completely fresh examination. There are forms of freedom that are desirable and that are gravely threatened; there are other forms of freedom that are undesirable, but that are very difficult to curb. There are two dangers, both rapidly increasing. Within any given organization, the power of officials, or of what may be called the "government," tends to become excessive, and to subject individuals to various forms of tyranny. On the other hand, conflicts between different organizations become more and more harmful as organizations acquire more power over their members. Tyranny within and conflict without are each other's counterpart. Both spring from the same source: the lust for power. A state which is internally despotic will be externally warlike, in both respects because the men who govern the state desire the greatest attainable extent and intensity of control over the lives of other men. The resultant twofold problem, of preserving liberty internally and diminishing it externally, is one that the world must solve, and solve soon, if scientific societies are to survive.

Let us consider for a moment the social psychology involved in this situation.

Organizations are of two kinds, those which aim at getting something done and those which aim at preventing something from being done. The Post Office is an example of the first kind; a fire brigade is an example of the second kind. Neither of these arouses much controversy, because no one objects to letters being carried, and incendiaries dare not avow a desire to see buildings burnt down. But when what is to be prevented is something done by human beings, not by nature, the matter is otherwise. The armed forces of one's own nation exist—so each nation asserts—to *prevent* aggression by other nations. But the armed forces of other nations exist—or so many people believe—to *promote* aggression. If you say anything against the armed forces of your own country, you are a traitor, wishing to see your fatherland ground under the heel of a brutal conqueror. If, on the other hand, you defend a potential enemy state for thinking armed forces necessary to its safety, you malign your own country, whose unalterable devotion to peace only perverse malice could lead you to question. Please imagine that it is a Russian who is speaking. I heard all this said about Germany by a thoroughly virtuous German lady in 1936, in the course of a panegyric on Hitler, whom she regarded as the sole safeguard of the peace of the world.

The same sort of thing applies, though with slightly less force, to other combatant organizations. My Pennsylvania gardener would not publicly criticize his trade-union secretary for fear of weakening the union in contest with capitalism. It is difficult for a man of ardent political convictions to admit either the shortcomings of politicians of his own party or the merits of those of the opposite party.

And so it comes about that, whenever an organization has a combatant purpose, its members are reluctant to criticize their officials and tend to acquiesce in usurpations and arbitrary exercises of power which, but for the war mentality, they would bitterly resent. It is the war mentality that gives officials and governments their opportunity.

It is therefore only natural that officials and governments are prone to foster war mentality.

The only escape is to have the greatest possible number of disputes settled by legal process and not by a trial of strength. Thus, here again the preservation of internal liberty and external control go hand in hand, and both equally depend upon what is *prima facie* a restraint upon liberty, namely an extension of the domain of law and of the public force necessary for its enforcement.

In what I have been saying so far, I feel that I have not sufficiently emphasized the gains that we derive from scientific technique. It is obvious that the average inhabitant of the United States at the present day is very much richer than the average inhabitant of England in the eighteenth century, and this advance is almost entirely due to scientific technique. The gain in the case of England is not so great, but that is because the British spent so much money on killing Germans. But even in England, there are enormous material advances. In spite of shortages, almost everybody in England has as much to eat as is necessary for health and efficiency. Most people have warmth in winter and adequate light after sunset. The streets, except in time of war, are not pitch dark at night. All children go to school. Everyone can get medical attendance. Life and property are much more secure (in peacetime) than they were in the eighteenth century. A much smaller percentage of the population lives in slums. Travel is vastly easier, and many more amusements are available than in former times. The improvement in health would in itself be sufficient to make this age preferable to those earlier times for which some people feel nostalgia. On the whole, I think this age is an improvement on all its predecessors except for the rich and privileged.

Our advantages are due entirely, or almost entirely, to the fact that a given amount of labor is more productive than it was in pre-scientific days. I used to live on a hilltop surrounded by trees, where I could pick up firewood with the greatest ease. But to secure a given amount of fuel in this way cost more human labor than to have it brought across half England in the form of coal, because the coal was mined and brought scientifically, whereas I could employ only primitive methods in gathering sticks. In old days, one man produced not much more than one man's necessaries; a tiny aristocracy lived in luxury, a small middle class lived in moderate comfort, but the great majority of the population had very little more than was required to keep them alive. It is true that we do not always spend our surplus of labor wisely. We are able to set aside a much larger proportion for war than our ancestors could. But almost all the large-scale disadvantages of our time arise from failure to extend the domain of law to the settlement of disputes which, when left to the arbitrament of force, have become, through our very efficiency, more harmful than in previous centuries. This survival of formerly endurable anarchy must be dealt with if our civilization is to survive. Where liberty is harmful, it is to law that we must look.

William E. Odum

1942-1991

"Environmental Degradation and the Tyranny of Small Decisions"

1982

William E. Odum was an environmental scientist and ecologist with a long family history of intellectual and academic pursuits. His grandfather was the noted sociologist Howard Washington Odum. Eugene P. Odum, his father, often called the father of modern ecology was the first proponent of the concept of the ecosystem. His father and his uncle, Howard Thomas Odum were both ecologists. Following them into ecology, he spent many years teaching in the Department of Environmental Science at the University of Virginia, before succumbing to liver cancer in September 1991.

He specialized in marsh and wetland ecology, with specific focus on the disturbance, succession and change of estuarine ecosystems. Among his more notable achievements in the pursuit of a broad understanding of human disturbance of wetlands and estuarine ecology was an advance in a more precise understanding of trophic level through analysis of actual observations of diet within the trophic system. This insight, in conjunction with Eric J. Heald spurred an advance from linear thinking in trophic level understanding to the creation of the concept of food networks or webs.

In the paper that follows Odum uses Alfred E. Kahn's economic premise on the tyranny of small decisions to illustrate how an individual can affect the global environment (biosphere). The everyday choices we all face to recycle, carpool, or not and engage in other potential environmentally damaging decisions are reflected in the individual choices we make at the local level.

1. What green or environmentally supportive choices do you make on a daily basis? List as many as possible.
2. What actions could you take, keeping Odum's argument in mind, which would improve rather than degrade the environment?
3. Which of your choices or lack thereof might be magnified at a regional, national, or global environmental level? Why?
4. How have current and past governments acted in ways which influence the environmental effect of the tyranny of small decisions?
5. Are there other principles of social science, economics, government, or psychology that might also apply to the theory and practice of environmental conservation and management?
6. What does Odum mean by the heading "Loosing the Chains"?

Source:

Rickards, B. *William E. Odum, 1942-1991. Estuaries* 14(3):343, Sept. 1991.

Selection from:

Odum, W.E. (1982, October). Environmental Degradation and the Tyranny of Small Decisions. *BioScience, 32*(9), 728-729.

"Environmental Degradation and the Tyranny of Small Decisions"

Economist Alfred E. Kahn's premise of "the tyranny of small decisions" is applicable to environmental issues. Examples of so-called "small decision effects" range from loss of prime farmland and acid precipitation to mismanagement of the Florida Everglades. A holistic rather than reductionist perspective is needed to avoid the undesirable, cumulative effects of small decisions. (Accepted for publication 2 March 1982)

Ideally, society's problems are resolved through a system of nested levels of public decisions. At the lowest level, decisions are made by the individual or by small groups of individuals. Higher decision-making levels range from local and state governments to the highest levels of the federal government. Theoretically, the highest levels are composed of experts whose joint decisions provide constraints in the form of "rules" for decisions made at the lower levels.

Unfortunately, important decisions are often reached in an entirely different manner. A series of small, apparently independent decisions are made, often by individuals or small groups of individuals. The end result is that a big decision occurs (post hoc) as an accretion of these small decisions; the central question is never addressed directly at the higher decision-making levels. Usually, this process does not produce an optimal, desired, or preferred solution for society.

This process of post hoc decision-making has been termed "the tyranny of small decisions" by the economist Alfred E. Kahn (1966). As Kahn has pointed out, this is a common problem in market economics. He gives as an example the loss of passenger train service to Ithaca, New York. Even though the majority of the inhabitants of Ithaca would have preferred to retain passenger train service, they "decided" to terminate service through the combined effects of a series of small, independent decisions to travel by automobile, airplane, and bus.

SMALL DECISIONS AND THE ENVIRONMENT

Clearly, "the tyranny of small decisions," or what might be called "small decision effects," applies to much more than market economics. Much of the current confusion and distress surrounding environmental issues can be traced to decisions that were never consciously made, but simply resulted from a series of small decisions. Consider, for example, the loss of coastal wetlands on the east coast of the United States between 1950 and 1970. No one purposely planned to destroy almost 50% of the existing marshland along the coasts of Connecticut and Massachusetts. In fact, if the public had been asked whether coastal wetlands should be preserved or convened to some other use, preservation would probably have been supported. However, through hundreds of little decisions and the conversion of hundreds of small tracts of marshland, a major decision in favor of extensive wetlands conversion was made without ever addressing the issue directly.

Regional problems are highly vulnerable to small decision effects. The ecological integrity of the Florida Everglades has suffered, not from a single adverse decision, but from a multitude of small pin pricks. These include a series of independent choices to add one more drainage canal, one more roadway, one more retirement village, and one more well to provide Miami with drinking water. No one chose to reduce the annual surface flow of water into the Everglades National Park, to intensify the effects droughts, or to encourage unnaturally hot, destructive fires. Yet all of these things have happened, and. at this point, it is not clear how the "decision" to degrade the Everglades can be reversed.

Each threatened and endangered species, with a few exceptions, owes it special status to a series of small decisions. Polar bears, key deer, bald eagles, California condors, Everglades kites, humpback whales, and green turtles have all suffered from the combined effects of single decisions about habitat conversion or over-exploitation. In the case of the green turtle, the removal of nesting beaches one by one through development and human intervention has paralleled the decline of green turtle populations. Furthermore, this decline has been accelerated by a multitude of independent decisions by individual fishermen to harvest one more turtle despite their recognized threatened status.

The insidious quality of small decision effects is probably best exemplified by water and air pollution problems. Few cases of cultural eutrophication of lakes are the result of intentional and rational choice. Instead, lakes gradually become more and more eutrophic through the cumulative effects of small decisions: the addition of increasing numbers of domestic sewage and industrial outfalls along with increasing run-off from more and more housing developments, highways, and agricultural fields. Similarly, the gradual decline in air quality of the Los Angeles basin during the 1940s and 1950s was produced by thousands of small decisions to add one more factory or one more family automobile.

Obviously, Alfred Kahn's observation concerning the net effect of small decisions has great applicability to environmental problems. We could add many more examples to our list, including the decline of prime farmland in the United States, desertification, misuse of groundwater resources, the impact of persistent pesticides, the side-effects of single-species management in fisheries and wildlife management, the threat of tropical forest clearing, and the increasing severity of acid precipitation.

LOOSING THE CHAINS

While it is easy to recognize this basic problem in the environmental decision—making process, it is not so simple to do anything of a corrective nature. One apparent step would be to strengthen and protect the upper levels of environmental decision-makers (Department of the Interior, NOAA, EPA, etc.). Unfortunately, these organizations do not always operate with the greatest efficiency, become entangled in their own bureaucratic red tape, and in the end, leave decisions to the lower levels by default.

Moreover, most of the rewards and pressures within both contemporary political and scientific systems force us toward specific problems and specific solutions, in other words, small decisions. In the political realm, the trend is toward decision-making at lower levels of the system (e.g. the "new federalism" of Ronald Reagan). Although this may be successful for relatively simple problems, such as building schools, this type of approach offers little hope for solving complex problems of environmental management. Unfortunately, it is much easier and politically more feasible for a planner or politician to make a decision on a single tract of land or a single issue rather than attempting policy or land-use plans on a large scale.

This pattern of rewards, pressures, and trends is not unique to politics but also permeates academic science. The majority of scientists are most comfortable concentrating upon pieces of problems rather than an entire system. In medicine the trend since the time of Louis Pasteur has been toward single-effect medicine ("germ theory") with modest emphasis on total body responses ("holistic medicine"). Reinforcing this reductionist tendency in science is the coordination of both grant money and academic tenure with the solution of short-term problems (i.e., small problems).

One key to avoiding the problem of cumulative effects of small environmental decisions lies in a holistic view of the world around us. Scientists, no matter how reductionist their research, should be able to understand and predict how their specialty fits into whole-system processes. In addition, we must have at least a few scientists who study whole **systems** and help us to avoid the consequences of small decisions. Conversely, planners and politicians must have a large-scale perspective encompassing the effects of all their little decisions. Most important of all, environmental science teachers should include in their courses examples of large-scale processes and resulting man-induced problems (e.g., the Florida Everglades, the Colorado River, the Amazon Basin).

Sadly, prospects are not encouraging. Few politicians, planners, or scientists have been trained with, or have developed a truly holistic perspective. Considering all of the pressures and short-term rewards that guide society toward simple solutions, it seems safe to assume that the "tyranny of small decisions" will be an integral part of environmental policy for a long time to come.

REFERENCE CITED

Kahn, Alfred E. (1966).The tyranny of small decisions: market failures, imperfections, and the limits of economics. *Kyklos* 19: 23-47.

Garrett Hardin

1915-2003

"The Tragedy of the Commons"

1968

A trained ecologist and microbiologist, Garrett Hardin's most significant writings overlapped with bioethics, concerns which are highlighted by the following selection from his 1968 essay "The Tragedy of the Commons." Garrett Hardin earned his bachelor of science in zoology from the University of Chicago in 1936, and went on to complete his doctorate in microbiology at Stanford. The majority of his career was spent as a faculty member of the Department of Biological Sciences at the University of California, Santa Barbara (1946-1978) where he was a professor of human ecology.

His numerous writings center on bioethical issues, but rather than simply juxtaposing ethics onto biological issues, he builds his ethical arguments upon a biological foundation. Such arguments include elements of relative quantities, feedback processes, and the impact of time. He was also unabashed in his public stance on a number of issues, including public debates on abortion, immigration, and nuclear power, issues that remain at the forefront of social, political, and environmental public discussion to this day.

After his retirement from the UCSB faculty in 1978, he devoted himself to writing and speaking and his career includes over 350 articles and 27 books. His 1993 volume "Living Within Limits: Ecology, Economics and Population Taboos" won the Award in Science from the honor society, Phi Beta Kappa.

Below is the full text of his 1978 essay, which has been reprinted over 100 times in various anthologies and other works. He delves into issues that only grow in importance as time passes, and his arguments could be used to form the basis for a new social order if the ever-burgeoning human populace would heed his words.

1. What is the commons? What is the problem that Hardin discusses?
2. How do local, regional, and global populations influence other social and planetary issues?
3. Are there social and environmental ethics in the decision to have a family and the size of that family? If so why?

Source:

"About Garrett Hardin" Accessed April 1, 2008 from http://www.garretthardinsociety.org/gh/about_gh.html.

Selection from:

Hardin, G. (1968). "The Tragedy of the Commons." *Science*, 162. 1243-1248.

The Tragedy of the Commons[1]

At the end of a thoughtful article on the future of nuclear war, J.B. Wiesner and H.F. York concluded that: "Both sides in the arms race are . . . confronted by the dilemma of steadily increasing military power and steadily decreasing national security. *It is our considered professional judgment that this dilemma has no technical solution.* If the great powers continue to look for solutions in the area of science and technology only, the result will be to worsen the situation." [1]

I would like to focus your attention not on the subject of the article (national security in a nuclear world) but on the kind of conclusion they reached, namely that there is no technical solution to the problem. An implicit and almost universal assumption of discussions published in professional and semipopular scientific journals is that the problem under discussion has a technical solution. A technical solution may be

---

1 Reprinted with permission from SCIENCE 162:1243-1248 (1968) AAAS.

defined as one that requires a change only in the techniques of the natural sciences, demanding little or nothing in the way of change in human values or ideas of morality.

In our day (though not in earlier times) technical solutions are always welcome. Because of previous failures in prophecy, it takes courage to assert that a desired technical solution is not possible. Wiesner and York exhibited this courage; publishing in a science journal, they insisted that the solution to the problem was not to be found in the natural sciences. They cautiously qualified their statement with the phrase, "It is our considered professional judgment . . . ." Whether they were right or not is not the concern of the present article. Rather, the concern here is with the important concept of a class of human problems which can be called "no technical solution problems," and more specifically, with the identification and discussion of one of these.

It is easy to show that the class is not a null class. Recall the game of tick-tack-toe. Consider the problem, "How can I win the game of tick-tack-toe?" It is well known that I cannot, if I assume (in keeping with the conventions of game theory) that my opponent understands the game perfectly. Put another way, there is no "technical solution" to the problem. I can win only by giving a radical meaning to the word "win." I can hit my opponent over the head; or I can falsify the records. Every way in which I "win" involves, in some sense, an abandonment of the game, as we intuitively understand it. (I can also, of course, openly abandon the game—refuse to play it. This is what most adults do.)

The class of "no technical solution problems" has members. My thesis is that the "population problem," as conventionally conceived, is a member of this class. How it is conventionally conceived needs some comment. It is fair to say that most people who anguish over the population problem are trying to find a way to avoid the evils of overpopulation without relinquishing any of the privileges they now enjoy. They think that farming the seas or developing new strains of wheat will solve the problem—technologically. I try to show here that the solution they seek cannot be found. The population problem cannot be solved in a technical way, any more than can the problem of winning the game of tick-tack-toe.

What Shall We Maximize?

Population, as Malthus said, naturally tends to grow "geometrically," or, as we would now say, exponentially. In a finite world this means that the per-capita share of the world's goods must decrease. Is ours a finite world?

A fair defense can be put forward for the view that the world is infinite or that we do not know that it is not. But, in terms of the practical problems that we must face in the next few generations with the foreseeable technology, it is clear that we will greatly increase human misery if we do not, during the immediate future, assume that the world available to the terrestrial human population is finite. "Space" is no escape. [2]

A finite world can support only a finite population; therefore, population growth must eventually equal zero. (The case of perpetual wide fluctuations above and below zero is a trivial variant that need not be discussed.) When this condition is met, what will be the situation of mankind? Specifically, can Bentham's goal of "the greatest good for the greatest number" be realized?

No—for two reasons, each sufficient by itself. The first is a theoretical one. It is not mathematically possible to maximize for two (or more) variables at the same time. This was clearly stated by von Neumann and Morgenstem, [3] but the principle is implicit in the theory of partial differential equations, dating back at least to D'Alembert (1717-1783).

The second reason springs directly from biological facts. To live, any organism must have a source of energy (for example, food). This energy is utilized for two purposes: mere maintenance and work. For man maintenance of life requires about 1600 kilocalories a day ("maintenance calories"). Anything that he does over and above merely staying alive will be defined as work, and is supported by "work calories" which he takes in. Work calories are used not only for what we call work in common speech; they are also required for all forms of enjoyment, from swimming and automobile racing to playing music and writing poetry. If our goal is to maximize population it is obvious what we must do: We must make the work calories per person approach as close to zero as possible. No gourmet meals, no vacations, no sports, no music, no literature, no art . . . I think that everyone will grant, without argument or proof, that maximizing population does not maximize goods. Bentham's goal is impossible.

In reaching this conclusion I have made the usual assumption that it is the acquisition of energy that is the problem. The appearance of atomic energy has led some to question this assumption. However, given an infinite source of energy, population growth still produces an inescapable problem. The problem of the acquisition of energy is replaced by the problem of its dissipation, as J. H. Fremlin has so wittily shown. [4] The arithmetic signs in the analysis are, as it were, reversed; but Bentham's goal is unobtainable.

The optimum population is, then, less than the maximum. The difficulty of defining the optimum is enormous; so far as I know, no one has seriously tackled this problem. Reaching an acceptable and stable solution will surely require more than one generation of hard analytical work—and much persuasion.

We want the maximum good per person; but what is good? To one person it is wilderness, to another it is ski lodges for thousands. To one it is estuaries to nourish ducks for hunters to shoot; to another it is factory land. Comparing one good with another is, we usually say, impossible because goods are incommensurable. Incommensurables cannot be compared.

Theoretically this may be true; but in real life incommensurables *are* commensurable. Only a criterion of judgment and a system of weighting are needed. In nature the criterion is survival. Is it better for a species to be small and hideable, or large and powerful? Natural selection commensurates the incommensurables. The compromise achieved depends on a natural weighting of the values of the variables.

Man must imitate this process. There is no doubt that in fact he already does, but unconsciously. It is when the hidden decisions are made explicit that the arguments begin. The problem for the years ahead is to work out an acceptable theory of weighting. Synergistic effects, nonlinear variation, and difficulties in discounting the future make the intellectual problem difficult, but not (in principle) insoluble.

Has any cultural group solved this practical problem at the present time, even on an intuitive level? One simple fact proves that none has: there is no prosperous population in the world today that has, and has had for some time, a growth rate of zero. Any people that has intuitively identified its optimum point will soon reach it, after which its growth rate becomes and remains zero.

Of course, a positive growth rate might be taken as evidence that a population is below its optimum. However, by any reasonable standards, the most rapidly growing populations on earth today are (in general) the most miserable. This association (which need not be invariable) casts doubt on the optimistic assumption that the positive growth rate of a population is evidence that it has yet to reach its optimum.

We can make little progress in working toward optimum population size until we explicitly exorcise the spirit of Adam Smith in the field of practical demography. In economic affairs, *The Wealth of Nations* (1776) popularized the "invisible hand," the idea that an individual who "intends only his own gain," is, as it were, "led by an invisible hand to promote . . . the public interest." [5] Adam Smith did not assert that this was invariably true, and perhaps neither did any of his followers. But he contributed to a dominant tendency of thought that has ever since interfered with positive action based on rational analysis, namely, the tendency to assume that decisions reached individually will, in fact, be the best decisions for an entire society. If this assumption is correct it justifies the continuance of our present policy of *laissez faire* in reproduction. If it is correct we can assume that men will control their individual fecundity so as to produce the optimum population. If the assumption is not correct, we need to reexamine our individual freedoms to see which ones are defensible.

Tragedy of Freedom in a Commons

The rebuttal to the invisible hand in population control is to be found in a scenario first sketched in a little-known Pamphlet in 1833 by a mathematical amateur named William Forster Lloyd (1794-1852). [6] We may well call it "the tragedy of the commons," using the word "tragedy" as the philosopher Whitehead used it [7]: "The essence of dramatic tragedy is not unhappiness. It resides in the solemnity of the remorseless working of things." He then goes on to say, "This inevitableness of destiny can only be illustrated in terms of human life by incidents which in fact involve unhappiness. For it is only by them that the futility of escape can be made evident in the drama."

The tragedy of the commons develops in this way. Picture a pasture open to all. It is to be expected that each herdsman will try to keep as many cattle as possible on the commons. Such an arrangement may work reasonably satisfactorily for centuries because tribal wars, poaching, and disease keep the numbers of both man and beast well below the carrying capacity of the land. Finally, however, comes the day of reckoning, that is, the day when the long-desired goal of social stability becomes a reality.

At this point, the inherent logic of the commons remorselessly generates tragedy.

As a rational being, each herdsman seeks to maximize his gain. Explicitly or implicitly, more or less consciously, he asks, "What is the utility *to me* of adding one more animal to my herd?" This utility has one negative and one positive component.

1. The positive component is a function of the increment of one animal. Since the herdsman receives all the proceeds from the sale of the additional animal, the positive utility is nearly + 1.
2. The negative component is a function of the additional overgrazing created by one more animal. Since, however, the effects of overgrazing are shared by all the herdsmen, the negative utility for any particular decisionmaking herdsman is only a fraction of -1.

Adding together the component partial utilities, the rational herdsman concludes that the only sensible course for him to pursue is to add another animal to his herd. And another . . . . But this is the conclusion reached by each and every rational herdsman sharing a commons. Therein is the tragedy. Each man is locked into a system that compels him to increase his herd without limit—in a world that is limited. Ruin is the destination toward which all men rush, each pursuing his own best interest in a society that believes in the freedom of the commons. Freedom in a commons brings ruin to all.

Some would say that this is a platitude. Would that it were! In a sense, it was learned thousands of years ago, but natural selection favors the forces of psychological denial. [8] The individual benefits as an individual from his ability to deny the truth even though society as a whole, of which he is a part, suffers. Education can counteract the natural tendency to do the wrong thing, but the inexorable succession of generations requires that the basis for this knowledge be constantly refreshed.

A simple incident that occurred a few years ago in Leominster, Massachusetts shows how perishable the knowledge is. During the Christmas shopping season the parking meters downtown were covered with plastic bags that bore tags reading: "Do not open until after Christmas. Free parking courtesy of the mayor and city council." In other words, facing the prospect of an increased demand for already scarce space, the city fathers reinstituted the system of the commons.

(Cynically, we suspect that they gained more votes than they lost by this retrogressive act.)

In an approximate way, the logic of the commons has been understood for a long time, perhaps since the discovery of agriculture or the invention of private property in real estate. But it is understood mostly only in special cases which are not sufficiently generalized. Even at this late date, cattlemen leasing national land on the Western ranges demonstrate no more than an ambivalent understanding, in constantly pressuring federal authorities to increase the head count to the point where overgrazing produces erosion and weed-dominance. Likewise, the oceans of the world continue to suffer from the survival of the philosophy of the commons. Maritime nations still respond automatically to the shibboleth of the "freedom of the seas." Professing to believe in the "inexhaustible resources of the oceans," they bring species after species of fish and whales closer to extinction. [9]

The National Parks present another instance of the working out of the tragedy of the commons. At present, they are open to all, without limit. The parks themselves are limited in extent—there is only one Yosemite Valley—whereas population seems to grow without limit. The values that visitors seek in the parks are steadily eroded. Plainly, we must soon cease to treat the parks as commons or they will be of no value to anyone.

What shall we do? We have several options. We might sell them off as private property. We might keep them as public property, but allocate the right to enter them. The allocation might be on the basis of wealth, by the use of an auction system. It might be on the basis of merit, as defined by some agreed-upon standards. It might be by lottery. Or it might be on a first-come, first-served basis, administered to long queues. These, I think, are all objectionable. But we must choose—or acquiesce in the destruction of the commons that we call our National Parks.

Pollution

In a reverse way, the tragedy of the commons reappears in problems of pollution. Here it is not a question of taking something out of the commons, but of putting something in—sewage, or chemical, radioactive, and heat wastes into water; noxious and dangerous fumes into the air; and distracting and unpleasant advertising signs into the line of sight. The calculations of utility are much the same as before. The rational man finds that his share of the cost of the wastes he discharges into the commons is less than the cost of purifying his wastes before releasing them. Since this is true for everyone, we are locked into a system of "fouling our own nest," so long as we behave only as independent, rational, free enterprisers.

The tragedy of the commons as a food basket is averted by private property, or something formally like it. But the air and waters surrounding us cannot readily be fenced, and so the tragedy of the commons as a cesspool must be prevented by different means, by coercive laws or taxing devices that make it cheaper for the polluter to treat his pollutants than to discharge them untreated. We have not progressed as far with the solution of this problem as we have with the first. Indeed, our particular concept of private property, which deters us from exhausting the positive resources of the earth, favors pollution. The owner of a factory on the bank of a stream—whose property extends to the middle of the stream—often has difficulty seeing why it is not his natural right to muddy the waters flowing past his door. The law, always behind the times, requires elaborate stitching and fitting to adapt it to this newly perceived aspect of the commons.

The pollution problem is a consequence of population. It did not much matter how a lonely American frontiersman disposed of his waste. "Flowing water purifies itself every ten miles," my grandfather used to say, and the myth was near enough to the truth when he was a boy, for there were not too many people. But as population became denser, the natural chemical and biological recycling processes became overloaded, calling for a redefinition of property rights.

How to Legislate Temperance?

Analysis of the pollution problem as a function of population density uncovers a not generally recognized principle of morality, namely: *the morality of an act is a function of the state of the system at the time it is performed.* [10] Using the commons as a cesspool does not harm the general public under frontier conditions, because there is no public; the same behavior in a metropolis is unbearable. A hundred and fifty years ago a plainsman could kill an American bison, cut out only the tongue for his dinner, and discard the rest of the animal. He was not in any important sense being wasteful. Today, with only a few thousand bison left, we would be appalled at such behavior.

In passing, it is worth noting that the morality of an act cannot be determined from a photograph. One does not know whether a man killing an elephant or setting fire to the grassland is harming others until one knows the total system in which his act appears. "One picture is worth a thousand words," said an ancient Chinese; but it may take ten thousand words to validate it. It is as tempting to ecologists as it is to reformers in general to try to persuade others by way of the photographic shortcut. But the essence of an argument cannot be photographed: it must be presented rationally—in words.

That morality is system-sensitive escaped the attention of most codifiers of ethics in the past. "Thou shalt not . . . " is the form of traditional ethical directives which make no allowance for particular circumstances. The laws of our society follow the pattern of ancient ethics, and therefore are poorly suited to governing a complex, crowded, changeable world. Our epicyclic solution is to augment statutory law with administrative law. Since it is practically impossible to spell out all the conditions under which it is safe to bum trash in the back yard or to run an automobile without smog control, by law we delegate the details to bureaus. The result is administrative law, which is rightly feared for an ancient reason—*Quis custodies ipsos custodes*?—Who shall watch the watchers themselves? John Adams said that we must have a "government of laws and not men." Bureau administrators, trying to evaluate the morality of acts in the total system, are singularly liable to corruption, producing a government by men, not laws.

Prohibition is easy to legislate (though not necessarily to enforce); but how do we legislate temperance? Experience indicates that it can be accomplished best through the mediation of administrative law. We limit possibilities unnecessarily if we suppose that the sentiment of *Quis custodiet* denies us the use of administrative law. We should rather retain the phrase as a perpetual reminder of fearful dangers we cannot avoid. The great challenge facing us now is to invent the corrective feedbacks that are needed to keep custodians honest. We must find ways to legitimate the needed authority of both the custodians and the corrective feedbacks.

Freedom to Breed Is Intolerable

The tragedy of the commons is involved in population problems in another way. In a world governed solely by the principle of "dog eat dog"—if indeed there ever was such a world—how many children a family had would not be a matter of public concern. Parents who bred too exuberantly would leave fewer descendants, not more, because they would be unable to care adequately for their children. David Lack and others have found that such a negative feedback demonstrably controls the fecundity of birds. [11] But men are not birds, and have not acted like them for millenniums, at least.

If each human family were dependent only on its own resources; *if* the children of improvident parents starved to death; *if* thus, over breeding brought its own "punishment" to the germ line—*then* there would be no public interest in controlling the breeding of families. But our society is deeply committed to the welfare state, [12] and hence is confronted with another aspect of the tragedy of the commons.

In a welfare state, how shall we deal with the family, the religion, the race, or the class (or indeed any distinguishable and cohesive group) that adopts over breeding as a policy to secure its own aggrandizement? [13] To couple the concept of freedom to breed with the belief that everyone born has an equal right to the commons is to lock the world into a tragic course of action.

Unfortunately this is just the course of action that is being pursued by the United Nations. In late 1967, some thirty nations agreed to the following: "The Universal Declaration of Human Rights describes the family as the natural and fundamental unit of society. It follows that any choice and decision with regard to the size of the family must irrevocably rest with the family itself, and cannot be made by anyone else." [14]

It is painful to have to deny categorically the validity of this right; denying it, one feels as uncomfortable as a resident of Salem, Massachusetts, who denied the reality of witches in the seventeenth century. At the present time, in liberal quarters, something like a taboo acts to inhibit criticism of the United Nations. There is a feeling that the United Nations is "our last and best hope," that we shouldn't find fault with it; we shouldn't play into the hands of the archconservatives. However, let us not forget what Robert Louis Stevenson said: "The truth that is suppressed by friends is the readiest weapon of the enemy." If we love the truth we must openly deny the validity of the Universal Declaration of Human Rights, even though it is promoted by the United Nations. We should also join with Kingsley Davis [15] in attempting to get Planned Parenthood-World Population to see the error of its ways in embracing the same tragic ideal.

Conscience Is Self-Eliminating

It is a mistake to think that we can control the breeding of mankind in the long run by an appeal to conscience. Charles Galton Darwin made this point when he spoke on the centennial of the publication of his grandfather's great book. The argument is straightforward and Darwinian.

People vary. Confronted with appeals to limit breeding, some people will undoubtedly respond to the plea more than others. Those who have more children will produce a larger fraction of the next generation than those with more susceptible consciences. The differences will be accentuated, generation by generation.

In C. G. Darwin's words: "It may well be that it would take hundreds of generations for the progenitive instinct to develop in this way, but if it should do so, nature would have taken her revenge, and the variety *Homo contracipiens* would become extinct and would be replaced by the variety *Homo progenitivus.*" [16]

The argument assumes that conscience or the desire for children (no matter which) is hereditary—but hereditary only in the most general formal sense. The result will be the same whether the attitude is transmitted through germ cells, or exosomatically, to use A. J. Lotka's term. (If one denies the latter possibility as well as the former, then what's the point of education?) The argument has here been stated in the context of the population problem, but it applies equally well to any instance in which society appeals to an individual exploiting a commons to restrain himself for the general good—by means of his conscience. To make such an appeal is to set up a selective system that works toward the elimination of conscience from the race.

Pathogenic Effects of Conscience

The long-term disadvantage of an appeal to conscience should be enough to condemn it; but it has serious short-term disadvantages as well. If we ask a man who is exploiting a commons to desist "in the name of conscience," what are we saying to him? What does he hear?—not only at the moment but also in the wee small hours of the night when, half asleep, he remembers not merely the words we used but also the nonverbal communication cues we gave him unawares? Sooner or later, consciously or subconsciously, he senses that he has received two communications, and that they are contradictory: 1. (intended communication) "If you don't do as we ask, we will openly condemn you for not acting like a responsible citizen"; 2. (the unintended communication) "If you *do* behave as we ask, we will secretly condemn you for a simpleton who can be shamed into standing aside while the rest of us exploit the commons."

Every man then is caught in what Bateson has called a "double bind." Bateson and his co-workers have made a plausible case for viewing the double bind as an important causative factor in the genesis of schizophrenia. [17] The double bind may not always be so damaging, but it always endangers the mental health of anyone to whom it is applied. "A bad conscience," said Nietzsche, "is a kind of illness."

To conjure up a conscience in others is tempting to anyone who wishes to extend his control beyond the legal limits. Leaders at the highest level succumb to this temptation. Has any president during the past generation failed to call on labor unions to moderate voluntarily their demands for higher wages, or to steel companies to honor voluntary guidelines on prices? I can recall none. The rhetoric used on such occasions is designed to produce feelings of guilt in noncooperators.

For centuries it was assumed without proof that guilt was a valuable, perhaps even an indispensable, ingredient of the civilized life. Now, in this post-Freudian world, we doubt it.

Paul Goodman speaks from the modern point of view when he says: "No good has ever come from feeling guilty, neither intelligence, policy, nor compassion. The guilty do not pay attention to the object but only to themselves, and not even to their own interests, which might make sense, but to their anxieties." [18]

One does not have to be a professional psychiatrist to see the consequences of anxiety. We in the Western world are just emerging from a dreadful two centuries-long Dark Ages of Eros that was sustained partly by prohibition laws, but perhaps more effectively by the anxiety-generating mechanisms of education. Alex Comfort has told the story well in *The Anxiety Makers*; [19] it is not a pretty one.

Since proof is difficult, we may even concede that the results of anxiety may sometimes, from certain points of view, be desirable. The larger question we should ask is whether, as a matter of policy, we should ever encourage the use of a technique the tendency (if not the intention) of which is psychologically pathogenic. We hear much talk these days of responsible parenthood; the coupled words are incorporated into the titles of some organizations devoted to birth control. Some people have proposed massive propaganda campaigns to instill responsibility into the nation's (or the world's) breeders. But what is the meaning of the word conscience? When we use the word responsibility in the absence of substantial sanctions are we not trying to browbeat a free man in a commons into acting against his own interest? Responsibility is a verbal counterfeit for a substantial quid pro quo. It is an attempt to get something for nothing.

If the word responsibility is to be used at all, I suggest that it be in the sense Charles Frankel uses it. [20] "Responsibility," says this philosopher, "is the product of definite social arrangements." Notice that Frankel calls for social arrangements—not propaganda.

Mutual Coercion Mutually Agreed Upon

The social arrangements that produce responsibility are arrangements that create coercion, of some sort. Consider bank robbing. The man who takes money from a bank acts as if the bank were a commons. How do we prevent such action? Certainly not by trying to control his behavior solely by a verbal appeal to his sense of responsibility. Rather than rely on propaganda we follow Frankel's lead and insist that a bank is not a commons; we seek the definite social arrangements that will keep it from becoming a commons. That we thereby infringe on the freedom of would-be robbers we neither deny nor regret.

The morality of bank robbing is particularly easy to understand because we accept complete prohibition of this activity. We are willing to say "Thou shalt not rob banks," without providing for exceptions. But temperance also can be created by coercion. Taxing is a good coercive device. To keep downtown shoppers temperate in their use of parking space we introduce parking meters for short periods, and traffic fines for longer ones. We need not actually forbid a citizen to park as long as he wants to; we need merely make it increasingly expensive for him to do so. Not prohibition, but carefully biased options are what we offer him. A Madison Avenue man might call this persuasion; I prefer the greater candor of the word coercion.

Coercion is a dirty word to most liberals now, but it need not forever be so. As with the four-letter words, its dirtiness can be cleansed away by exposure to the light, by saying it over and over without apology or embarrassment. To many, the word coercion implies arbitrary decisions of distant and irresponsible bureaucrats; but this is not a necessary part of its meaning. The only kind of coercion I recommend is mutual coercion, mutually agreed upon by the majority of the people affected.

To say that we mutually agree to coercion is not to say that we are required to enjoy it, or even to pretend we enjoy it. Who enjoys taxes?

We all grumble about them. But we accept compulsory taxes because we recognize that voluntary taxes would favor the conscienceless. We institute and (grumblingly) support taxes and other coercive devices to escape the horror of the commons.

An alternative to the commons need not be perfectly just to be preferable. With real estate and other material goods, the alternative we have chosen is the institution of private property coupled with legal inheritance. Is this system perfectly just? As a genetically trained biologist I deny that it is. It seems to me that, if there are to be differences in individual inheritance, legal possession should be perfectly correlated with biological inheritance—that those who are biologically more fit to be the custodians of property and power should legally inherit more. But genetic recombination continually makes a mockery of the doctrine of "like father, like son" implicit in our laws of legal inheritance. An idiot can inherit millions, and a trust fund can keep his estate intact. We must admit that our legal system of private property plus inheritance is unjust—but we put up with it because we are not convinced, at the moment, that anyone has invented a better system. The alternative of the commons is too horrifying to contemplate. Injustice is preferable to total ruin.

It is one of the peculiarities of the warfare between reform and the status quo that it is thoughtlessly governed by a double standard. Whenever a reform measure is proposed it is often defeated when its opponents triumphantly discover a flaw in it. As Kingsley Davis has pointed out, [21] worshipers of the status quo sometimes imply that no reform is possible without unanimous agreement, an implication contrary to historical fact. As nearly as I can make out, automatic rejection of proposed reforms is based on one of two unconscious assumptions: (1) that the status quo is perfect; or (2) that the choice we face is between reform and no action; if the proposed reform is imperfect, we presumably should take no action at all, while we wait for a perfect proposal.

But we can never do nothing. That which we have done for thousands of years is also action. It also produces evils. Once we are aware that the status quo is action, we can then compare its discoverable advantages and disadvantages with the predicted advantages and disadvantages of the proposed reform, discounting as best we can for our lack of experience. On the basis of such a comparison, we can make a rational decision which will not involve the unworkable assumption that only perfect systems are tolerable.

Recognition of Necessity

Perhaps the simplest summary of this analysis of man's population problems is this: the commons, if justifiable at all, is justifiable only under conditions of low-population density. As the human population has increased, the commons has had to be abandoned in one aspect after another.

First we abandoned the commons in food gathering, enclosing farm land and restricting pastures and hunting and fishing areas. These restrictions are still not complete throughout the world.

Somewhat later we saw that the commons as a place for waste disposal would also have to be abandoned. Restrictions on the disposal of domestic sewage are widely accepted in the Western world; we are still struggling to close the commons to pollution by automobiles, factories, insecticide sprayers, fertilizing operations, and atomic energy installations.

In a still more embryonic state is our recognition of the evils of the commons in matters of pleasure. There is almost no restriction on the propagation of sound waves in the public medium. The shopping public is assaulted with mindless music, without its consent. Our government has paid out billions of dollars to create a supersonic transport which would disturb 50,000 people for every one person whisked from coast to coast 3 hours faster. Advertisers muddy the airwaves of radio and television and pollute the view of travelers. We are a long way from outlawing the commons in matters of pleasure. Is this because our Puritan inheritance makes us view pleasure as something of a sin, and pain (that is, the pollution of advertising) as the sign of virtue?

Every new enclosure of the commons involves the infringement of somebody's personal liberty. Infringements made in the distant past are accepted because no contemporary complains of a loss. It is the newly proposed infringements that we vigorously oppose; cries of "rights" and "freedom" fill the air. But what does "freedom" mean? When men mutually agreed to pass laws against robbing, mankind became more free, not less so. Individuals locked into the logic of the commons are free only to bring on universal ruin; once they see the necessity of mutual coercion, they become free to pursue other goals. I believe it was Hegel who said, "Freedom is the recognition of necessity."

The most important aspect of necessity that we must now recognize, is the necessity of abandoning the commons in breeding. No technical solution can rescue us from the misery of overpopulation. Freedom to breed will bring ruin to all. At the moment, to avoid hard decisions many of us are tempted to propagandize for conscience and responsible parenthood. The temptation must be resisted, because an appeal to independently acting consciences selects for the disappearance of all conscience in the long run, and an increase in anxiety in the short.

The only way we can preserve and nurture other and more precious freedoms is by relinquishing the freedom to breed, and that very soon. "Freedom is the recognition of necessity"—and it is the role of education to reveal to all the necessity of abandoning the freedom to breed. Only so, can we put an end to this aspect of the tragedy of the commons.

Notes:

1. J. B. Wiesner and H. F. York, *Scientific American* 211 (No. 4), 27 (1964).
2. G. Hardin, *Journal of Heredity* 50, 68 (1959), S. von Hoernor, Science 137, 18, (1962).
3. J. von Neumann and O. Morgenstern, *Theory of Games and Economic Behavior* (Princeton University Press, Princeton, N.J., 1947), p. 11.
4. J. H. Fremlin, *New Scientist*, No. 415 (1964), p. 285.
5. A. Smith, *The Wealth of Nations* (Modern Library, New York, 1937), p. 423.
6. W. F. Lloyd, *Two Lectures on the Checks to Population* (Oxford University Press, Oxford, England, 1833).
7. A. N. Whitehead, *Science and the Modern World* (Mentor, New York, 1948), p. 17.
8. G. Hardin, Ed., *Population, Evolution, and Birth Control* (Freeman, San Francisco, 1964), p. 56.
9. S. McVay, *Scientific American* 216 (No. 8), 13 (1966).
10. J. Fletcher, *Situation Ethics* (Westminster, Philadelphia, 1966).
11. D. Lack, *The Natural Regulation of Animal Numbers* (Clarendon Press, Oxford, England, 1954).
12. H. Girvetz, *From Wealth to Welfare* (Stanford University Press, Stanford, Calif, 1950).
13. G. Hardin, *Perspectives in Biology and Medicine* 6, 366 (1963).
14. U Thant, *International Planned Parenthood News*, No. 168 (February 1968), p. 3.
15. K. Davis, *Science* 158, 730 (1967).
16. S. Tax, Ed., *Evolution After Darwin* (University of Chicago Press, Chicago, 1960), vol. 2, p. 469.
17. G. Bateson, D. D. Jackson, J. Haley, J. Weakland, *Behavioral Science* 1, 251 (1956).
18. P. Goodman, *New York Review of Books* 10 (8), 22 (23 May 1968).
19. A. Comfort, *The Anxiety Makers* (Nelson, London, 1967).
20. C. Frankel, *The Case for Modern Man* (Harper & Row, New York, 1955), p. 203.
21. J. D. Roslansky, *Genetics and the Future of Man* (Appleton-Century-Crofts, New York, 1966), p.177.

THE TRAGEDY OF THE COMMON REVISITED

by Beryl Crowe

1969[2]

"There has developed in the contemporary natural sciences a recognition that there is a subset of problems, such as population, atomic war, and environmental corruption, for which there are no technical solutions.

"There is also an increasing recognition among contemporary social scientists that there is a subset of problems, such as population, atomic war, environmental corruption, and the recovery of a livable urban environment, for which there are no current political solutions. The thesis of this article is that the common area shared by these two subsets contains most of the critical problems that threaten the very existence of contemporary man." [p. 53]

ASSUMPTIONS NECESSARY TO AVOID THE TRAGEDY

"In passing the technically insoluble problems over to the political and social realm for solution, Hardin made three critical assumptions:

(1) that there exists, or can be developed, a 'criterion of judgment and system of weighting . . . ' that will 'render the incommensurables . . . commensurable . . . ' in real life;
(2) that, possessing this criterion of judgment, 'coercion can be mutually agreed upon,' and that the application of coercion to effect a solution to problems will be effective in modern society; and
(3) that the administrative system, supported by the criterion of judgment and access to coercion, can and will protect the commons from further desecration."[p. 55]

ERODING MYTH OF THE COMMON VALUE SYSTEM

"In America there existed, until very recently, a set of conditions which perhaps made the solution to Hardin's subset possible; we lived with the myth that we were 'one people, indivisible . . . . ' This myth postulated

---

2 reprinted in MANAGING THE COMMONS by Garrett Hardin and John Baden W.H. Freeman, 1977; ISBN 0-7167-0476-5

that we were the great 'melting pot' of the world wherein the diverse cultural ores of Europe were poured into the crucible of the frontier experience to produce a new alloy—an American civilization. This new civilization was presumably united by a common value system that was democratic, equalitarian, and existing under universally enforceable rules contained in the Constitution and the Bill of Rights.

"In the United States today, however, there is emerging a new set of behavior patterns which suggest that the myth is either dead or dying. Instead of believing and behaving in accordance with the myth, large sectors of the population are developing life-styles and value hierarchies that give contemporary Americans an appearance more closely analogous to the particularistic, primitive forms of 'tribal' organizations in geographic proximity than to that shining new alloy, the American civilization." [p. 56]

"Looking at a more recent analysis of the sickness of the core city, Wallace F. Smith has argued that the productive model of the city is no longer viable for the purposes of economic analysis. Instead, he develops a model of the city as a site for leisure consumption, and then seems to suggest that the nature of this model is such is such that the city cannot regain its health because the leisure demands are value-based and, hence do not admit to compromise and accommodation; consequently there is no way of deciding among these value-oriented demands that are being made on the core city.

"In looking for the cause of the erosion of the myth of a common value system, it seems to me that so long as our perceptions and knowledge of other groups were formed largely through the written media of communication, the American myth that we were a giant melting pot of equalitarians could be sustained. In such a perceptual field it is tenable, if not obvious, that men are motivated by interests. Interests can always be compromised and accommodated without undermining our very being by sacrificing values. Under the impact of electronic media, however, this psychological distance has broken down and now we discover that these people with whom we could formerly compromise on interests are not, after all, really motivated by interests but by values. Their behavior in our very living room betrays a set of values, moreover, that are incompatible with our own, and consequently the compromises that we make are not those of contract but of culture. While the former are acceptable, any form of compromise on the latter is not a form of rational behavior but is rather a clear case of either apostasy or heresy. Thus we have arrived not at an age of accommodation but one of confrontation. In such an age 'incommensurables' remain 'incommensurable' in real life." [p. 59]

EROSION OF THE MYTH OF THE MONOPOLY OF COERCIVE FORCE

"In the past, those who no longer subscribed to the values of the dominant culture were held in check by the myth that the state possessed a monopoly on coercive force. This myth has undergone continual erosion since the end of World War II owing to the success of the strategy of guerrilla warfare, as first revealed to the French in Indochina, and later conclusively demonstrated in Algeria. Suffering as we do from what Senator Fulbright has called 'the arrogance of power,' we have been extremely slow to learn the lesson in Vietnam, although we now realize that war is political and cannot be won by military means. It is apparent that the myth of the monopoly of coercive force as it was first qualified in the civil rights conflict in the South, then in our urban ghettos, next on the streets of Chicago, and now on our college campuses has lost its hold over the minds of Americans. The technology of guerrilla warfare has made it evident that, while the state can win battles, it cannot win wars of values. Coercive force which is centered in the modern state cannot be sustained in the face of the active resistance of some 10 percent of the population unless the state is willing to embark on a deliberate policy of genocide directed against the value dissident groups. The factor that sustained the myth of coercive force in the past was the acceptance of a common value system. Whether the latter exists is questionable in the modern nation-state." [p.p. 59-60]

EROSION OF THE MYTH OF ADMINISTRATORS OF THE COMMONS

"Indeed, the process has been so widely commented upon that one writer postulated a common life cycle for all of the attempts to develop regulatory policies. The life cycle is launched by an outcry so widespread and demanding that it generates enough political force to bring about establishment of a regulatory agency to insure the equitable, just, and rational distribution of the advantages among all holders of interest in the commons. This phase is followed by the symbolic reassurance of the offended as the agency goes into operation, developing a period of political quiescence among the great majority of those who hold a general but unorganized interest in the commons. Once this political quiescence has developed, the highly organized and specifically interested groups who wish to make incursions into the commons bring sufficient pressure to bear through other political processes to convert the agency to the protection and furthering of their interests. In the last phase even staffing of the regulating agency is accomplished by drawing the agency administrators from the ranks of the regulated." [p.p. 60-61]

E.F. Schumacher

1911-1977

Small is Beautiful
Economics as if People Mattered

1973

E.F. Schumacher was one of the most notable economists in history, a man far beyond his times. Born in Bonn, Germany to a traditional academic family, he was an avid learner. In 1930, he was chosen to represent Germany as a Rhodes Scholar at New College, Oxford. During this time he made his first trip to America and discovered an intellectual freedom he had not previously known existed. However, he was aware of the rise of National Socialism in his homeland and returned to Germany in 1934. The situation was much as he had feared, with few individuals speaking against the evils being done around them. In 1936, he moved with his new wife to England, the country he would call home until his death in 1977.

During World War II when anti-German feelings were high, he was relegated to the role of farm laborer in rural England, where he remained until the war's end. He became an English citizen in 1946, and was subsequently selected as a member of the British Control Commission for post-war Germany. As he studied Germany, the critical position of energy became apparent to him and began a focus that was maintained throughout his life and career. In 1949 he was asked to become an economic advisor to the National Coal Board of Britain; he accepted the position and remained as Chief Economic Advisor for the next 20 years.

His influences include the economist Leopold Kohr, a little-known economist who believed that many economic ills can be attributed to the largeness of the system. Also a voracious reader, he studied Buddhism and Taoism and was deeply moved by the nonviolent teachings of Mahatma Gandhi. These lifelong interests in energy, economics, and eastern philosophy were combined in his seminal work *Small is Beautiful*. The selections below represent just a portion of the breadth of his introspective analysis of western economic thought. According to *The London Times Literary Supplement*, this work is considered to be one of the 100 most significant works of the twentieth century. A thorough reading of this text will leave readers with new thoughts and ideas on economics and the importance of size. Maybe bigger is not always better . . .

SOURCE:

Todd, N. J. (2008). Accessed March 22, 2008 from http://www.schumachersociety.org/about/biographies/schumacher_full_bio.html.

SELECTION FROM:

Schumacher, E. F. (1973). *Small is Beautiful: Economics as if People Mattered*. Harper & Row Publishers. New York: 1973. 12-20, 50-58, 95-109.

Part I
The Modern World

I. The Problem of Production

One of the most fateful errors of our age is the belief that 'the problem of production' has been solved. Not only is this belief firmly held by people remote from production and therefore professionally unacquainted with the facts—it is held by virtually all the experts, the captains of industry, the economic managers in the governments of the world, the academic and not-so-academic economists, not to mention the economic journalists. They may disagree on many things but they all agree that the problem of production has been solved; that mankind has at last come of age. For the rich countries, they say, the most important task now is 'education for leisure' and, for the poor countries, the 'transfer of technology'.

That things are not going as well as they ought to be going must be due to human wickedness. We must therefore construct a political system so perfect that human wickedness disappears and everybody behaves well, no matter how much wickedness there may be in him or her. In fact, it is widely held that everybody is born good; if one turns into a criminal or an exploiter, this is the fault of 'the system'. No doubt 'the system' is in many ways bad and must be changed. One of the main reasons why it is bad and why it can still survive in spite of its badness, is this erroneous view that the 'problem of production' has been solved. As this error pervades all present-day systems there is at present not much to choose between them.

The arising of this error, so egregious and so firmly rooted, is closely connected with the philosophical, not to say religious, changes during the last three or four centuries in man's attitude to nature. I should perhaps say: *western* man's attitude to nature, but since the whole world is now in a process of westernisation, can this be corrected? the more generalised statement appears to be justified. Modern man does not experience himself as a part of nature but as an outside force destined to dominate and conquer it. He even talks of a battle with nature, forgetting that, if he won the battle, he would find himself on the losing side. Until quite recently, the battle seemed to go well enough to give him the illusion of unlimited powers, but not so well as to bring the possibility of total victory into view. This has now come into view, and many people, albeit only a minority, are beginning to realise what this means for the continued existence of humanity.

The illusion of unlimited powers, nourished by astonishing scientific and technological achievements, has produced the concurrent illusion of having solved the problem of production. The latter illusion is based on the failure to distinguish between income and capital where this distinction matters most. Every economist and businessman is familiar with the distinction, and applies it conscientiously and with considerable subtlety to all economic affairs—except where it really matters; namely, the irreplaceable capital which man has not made, but simply found, and without which he can do nothing.

A businessman would not consider a firm to have solved its problems of production and to have achieved viability if he saw that it was rapidly consuming its capital. How, then, could we overlook this vital fact when it comes to that very big firm, the economy of Spaceship Earth and, in particular the economics of its rich passengers?

One reason for overlooking this vital fact is that we are estranged from reality and inclined to treat as valueless everything that we have not made ourselves. Even the great Dr. Marx fell into this devastating error when he formulated the so-called 'labour theory of value'. Now, we have indeed laboured to make some of the capital which today helps us to produce—a large fund of scientific, technological, and other knowledge; an elaborate physical infrastructure; innumerable types of sophisticated capital equipment, etc—but all this is but a small part of the total capital we are using. Far larger is the capital provided by nature and not by man—and we do not even recognise it as such. This larger part is now being used up at an alarming rate, and that is why it is an absurd and suicidal error to believe and act on the belief, that the problem of production has been solved.

Let us take a closer look at this 'natural capital'. First of all, and most obviously, there are the fossil fuels. No one, I am sure, will deny that we are treating them as income items although they are undeniably capital items. If we treated them as capital items, we should be concerned with conservation; we should do everything in our power to try and minimise their current rate of use; we might he saying, for instance, that the money obtained from the realisation of these assets—these irreplaceable assets—must be placed into a special fund to be devoted exclusively to the evolution of production methods and patterns of living which do *not* depend on fossil fuels at all or depend on them only to a very slight extent. These and many other things we should be doing if we treated fossil fuels as capital and not as income. And we do not do any of them, but the exact contrary of every one of them: we are not in the least concerned with conservation; we are maximising, instead of minimising, the current rates of use; and, far from being interested in studying the possibilities of alternative methods of production and patterns of living—so as to get off the collision course on which we are moving with ever-increasing speed—we happily talk of unlimited progress along the beaten track, of 'education for leisure, in the rich countries, and of 'the transfer of technology' to the poor countries.

The liquidation of these capital assets is proceeding so rapidly that even in the allegedly richest county in the world, the United States of America, there are many worried men, right up to the White House, calling for the massive conversion of coal into oil and gas, demanding ever more gigantic efforts to search for and exploit the remaining treasures of the earth. Look at the figures that are being put forward under the heading 'World Fuel Requirements in the Year 2000'. If we are now using something like 7000 million tons of coal equivalent, the need in twenty-eight years' time will be three times as large-around 20,000 million tons! What are twenty-eight years? Looking backwards, they take us roughly to the end of World War II, and, of course, since then fuel consumption has trebled; but the trebling involved an increase of less than 5000 million tons of coal equivalent. Now we are calmly talking about an increase three times as large.

People ask: Can it be done? And the answer comes back: It must be done and therefore it shall be done. One might say (with apologies to John Kenneth Galbraith) that it is a case of the bland leading the blind. But why cast aspersions? The question itself is wrong-headed, because it carries the implicit assumption that we are dealing with income and not with capital. What is so special about the year 2000? What about the year 2028, when little children running about today will be planning for their retirement? Another trebling by then? All these questions and answers are seen to be absurd the moment we realise that we are dealing with capital and not with income: fossil fuels are not made by men; they cannot be recycled. Once they are gone they are gone for ever.

But what—it will be asked—about the income fuels? Yes, indeed, what about them? Currently, they contribute (reckoned in calories) less than four per cent to the world total. In the foreseeable future they will have to contribute seventy, eighty, ninety per cent. To do something on a small scale is one thing: to do it on a gigantic scale is quite another, and to make an impact on the world fuel problem, contributions have to be truly gigantic. Who will say that the problem of production has been solved when it comes to income fuels required on a truly gigantic scale?

Fossil fuels are merely a part of the 'natural capital' which we steadfastly insist on treating as expendable, as if it were income, and by no means the most important part. If we squander our fossil fuels, we threaten civilisation; but if we squander the capital represented by living nature around us, we threaten life itself. People are waking up to this threat, and they demand that pollution must stop. They think of pollution as a rather nasty habit indulged in by careless or greedy people who, as it were, throw their rubbish over the fence into the neighbour's garden. A more civilised behaviour, they realise, would incur some extra cost, and therefore we need a faster rate of economic growth to be able to pay for it. From now on, they say, we should use at least some of the fruits of our ever-increasing productivity to improve 'the quality of life' and not merely to increase the quantity of consumption. All this is fair enough, but it touches only the outer fringe of the problem.

To get to the crux of the matter, we do well to ask why it is that all these terms—pollution, environment, ecology, etc.—have *so suddenly* come into prominence. After all, we have had an industrial system for quite some time, yet only five or ten years ago these words were virtually unknown. Is this a sudden fad, a silly fashion, or perhaps a sudden failure of nerve?

The explanation is not difficult to find. As with fossil fuels, we have indeed been living on the capital of living nature for some time, but at a fairly modest rate. It is only since the end of World War II that we have succeeded in increasing this rate to alarming proportions. In comparison with what is going on now and what has been going on, progressively, during the last quarter of a century, all the industrial activities of mankind up to, and including, World War II are as nothing. The next four or five years are likely to see more industrial production, taking the world as a whole, than all of mankind accomplished up to 1945. In other words, quite recently—so recently that most of us have hardly yet become conscious of it—there has been a unique quantitative jump in industrial production.

Partly as a cause and also as an effect, there has also been a unique qualitative jump. Our scientists and technologists have learned to compound substances unknown to nature. Against many of them, nature is virtually defenceless. There are no natural agents to attack and break them down. It is as if aborigines were suddenly attacked with machine-gun fire: their bows and arrows are of no avail. These substances, unknown to nature, owe their almost magical effectiveness precisely to nature's defencelessness—and that accounts also for their dangerous ecological impact. It is only in the last twenty years or so that they have made their appearance *in bulk*. Because they have no natural enemies, they tend to accumulate, and the long-term consequences of this accumulation are in many cases known to be extremely dangerous and in other cases totally unpredictable.

In other words, the changes of the last twenty-five years, both in the quantity and in the quality of man's industrial processes, have produced an entirely new situation—a situation resulting not from our failures but from what we thought were our greatest successes. And this has come so suddenly that we hardly noticed the fact that we were very rapidly using up a certain kind of irreplaceable capital asset, namely the *tolerance margins* which benign nature always provides.

Now let me return to the question of 'income fuels' with which I had previously dealt in a somewhat cavalier manner. No one is suggesting that the world-wide industrial system which is being envisaged to operate in the year 2000, a generation ahead, would be sustained primarily by water or wind power. No, we are told that we are moving rapidly into the nuclear age. Of course, this has been the story for quite some time, for over twenty years, and yet, the contribution of nuclear energy to man's total fuel and energy requirements is still minute. In 1970, it amounted to 2.7 per cent in Britain; 0.6 per cent in the European Community; and 0.3 per cent in the United States, to mention only the countries that have gone the furthest. Perhaps we can assume that nature's tolerance margins will be able to cope with such small impositions, although there are many people even today who are deeply worried, and Dr. Edward D. David, President Nixon's Science Adviser, talking about the storage of radioactive wastes, says that "one has a queasy feeling about something that has to stay underground and be pretty well sealed off for 25,000 years before it is harmless".

However that may be, the point I am making is a very simple one: the proposition to replace thousands of millions of tons of fossil fuels, every year, by nuclear energy means to 'solve' the fuel problem by creating an environmental and ecological problem of such a monstrous magnitude that Dr. David will not be the only one to have 'a queasy feeling'. It means solving one problem by shifting it to another sphere—there to create an infinitely bigger problem.

Having said this, I am sure that I shall he confronted with another, even more daring proposition: namely, that future scientists and technologists will be able to devise safety rules and precautions of such perfection that the using, transporting, processing and storing of radioactive materials in ever-increasing quantities will be made entirely safe; also that it will be the task of politicians and social scientists to create a world society in which wars or civil disturbances can never happen. Again, it is a proposition to solve one problem simply by shifting it to another sphere, the sphere of everyday human behaviour. And this takes us to the third category of 'natural capital' which we are recklessly squandering because we treat it as if it were income: as if it were something we had made ourselves and could easily replace out of our much-vaunted and rapidly rising productivity.

Is it not evident that our current methods of production are already eating into the very substance of industrial man? To many people this is not at all evident. Now that we have solved the problem of production, they say, have we ever had it so good? Are we not better fed, better clothed, and better housed than ever before—and better educated? Of course we are: most, but by no means all, of us: in the rich countries. But this is not what I mean by 'substance'. The substance of man cannot be measured by Gross National Product. Perhaps it cannot be measured at all, except for certain symptoms of loss. However, this is not the place to go into the statistics of these symptoms, such as crime, drug addiction, vandalism, mental breakdown, rebellion, and so forth. Statistics never prove anything.

I started by saying that one of the most fateful errors of our age is the belief that the problem of production has been solved. This illusion, I suggested, is mainly due to our inability to recognise that the modern industrial system, with all its intellectual sophistication, consumes the very basis on which it has been erected. To use the language of the economist, it lives on irreplaceable capital which it cheerfully treats as income. I specified three categories of such capital: fossil fuels, the tolerance margins of nature, and the human substance. Even if some readers should refuse to accept all three parts of my argument, I suggest that any one of them suffices to make my case.

And what is my case? Simply that our most important task is to get off our present collision course. And who is there to tackle such a task? I think every one of us, whether old or young, powerful or powerless, rich or poor, influential or uninfluential. To talk about the future is useful only if it leads to action *now*. And what can we do *now*, while we are still in the position of 'never having had it so good'? To say the least—which is already very much—we must thoroughly understand the problem and begin to see the possibility of evolving a new life-style, with new methods of production and new patterns of consumption: a lifestyle designed for permanence. To give only three preliminary examples: in agriculture and horticulture, we can interest ourselves in the perfection of production methods which are biologically sound, build up soil fertility, and produce health, beauty and permanence. Productivity will then look after itself. In industry, we can interest ourselves in the evolution of small-scale technology, relatively nonviolent technology, 'technology with a human face', so that people have a chance to enjoy themselves while they are working, instead of working solely for their pay packet and hoping, usually forlornly, for enjoyment solely during their leisure time. In industry, again—and, surely, industry is the pace-setter of modern life—we can interest ourselves in new forms of partnership between management and men, even forms of common ownership.

We often hear it said that we are entering the era of 'the Learning Society'. Let us hope this is true. We still have to learn how to live peacefully, not only with our fellow men but also with nature and, above all, with those Higher Powers which have made nature and have made us; for, assuredly, we have not come about by accident and certainly have not made ourselves.

The themes which have been merely touched upon in this chapter will have to be further elaborated as we go along. Few people will be easily convinced that the challenge to man's future cannot be met by making marginal adjustments here or there, or, possibly, by changing the political system.

The following chapter is an attempt to look at the whole situation again, from the angle of peace and permanence. Now that man has acquired the physical means of self-obliteration, the question of peace obviously looms larger than ever before in human history. And how could peace be built without some assurance of permanence with regard to our economic life?

IV. Buddhist Economics

'Right Livelihood' is one of the requirements of the Buddha's Nobile Eightfold Path. It is clear, therefore, that there must be such it thing as Buddhist economics.

Buddhist countries have often stated that they wish to remain faithful to their heritage. So Burma: "The New Burma sees no conflict between religious values and economic progress. Spiritual health and material wellbeing are not enemies: they are natural allies."[1] Or: "We can blend successfully the religious and spiritual values of our heritage with the benefits of modern technology."[2] Or: "We Burmans have a sacred duty to conform both our dreams and our acts to our faith. This we shall ever do."[3]

All the same, such countries invariably assume that they can model their economic development plans in accordance with modern economics, and they call upon modern economists from so-called advanced countries to advise them, to formulate the policies to be pursued, and to construct the grand design for development, the Five-Year Plan or whatever it may be called. No one seems to think that a Buddhist way of life would call for Buddhist economics, just as the modern materialist way of life has brought forth modern economics.

---

1 *The New Burma* (Economic and Social Boar, Government of the Union of Burma, 1954)

2 *Ibid*

3 *Ibid*

Economics themselves, like most specialists, normally suffer from a kind of metaphysical blindness, assuming that theirs is a science of absolute and invariable truths, without any presuppositions. Some go as far as to claim that economic laws are as free from 'metaphysics' or 'values' as the law of gravitation. We need not, however, get involved in arguments of methodology. Instead, let us take some fundamentals and see what they look like when viewed by a modem economist and a Buddhist economist.

There is universal agreement that a fundamental source of wealth is human labour. Now, the modern economist has been brought up to consider 'labour' or work as little more than necessary evil. From the point of view of the employer, it is in any case simply an item of cost, to be reduced to a minimum if it cannot be eliminated altogether, say, by automation. From the point of view of the workman, it is a 'disutility'; to work is to make a sacrifice of one's leisure and comfort, and wages are a kind of compensation for the sacrifice. Hence the ideal from the point of view of the employer is to have output without employees, and the ideal from the point of view of the employee is to have income without employment.

The consequences of these attitudes both in theory and in practice are, of course, extremely far-reaching. If the ideal with regard to work is to get rid of it, every method that 'reduces the work load' is a good thing. The most potent method, short of automation, is the so-called 'division of labour' and the classical example is the pin factory eulogised in Ad*am Smith's Wealth of Nations.*[4] Here it is not a matter of ordinary specialisation, which mankind has practised from time immemorial, but of dividing up every complete process of production into minute parts, so that the final product can he produced at great speed without anyone having had to contribute more than a totally insignificant and, in most cases, unskilled movement of his limbs.

The Buddhist point of view takes the function of work to be at least threefold: to give a man a chance to utilise and develop his faculties; to enable him to overcome his egocentredness by joining with other people in a common task; and to bring forth the goods and services needed for a becoming existence. Again, the consequences that flow from this view are endless. To organise work in such a manner that it becomes meaningless, boring, stultifying, or nerve-racking for the worker would be little short of criminal; it would indicate a greater concern with goods than with people,

---

4 *Wealth of Nations* by Adam Smith

an evil lack of compassion and a soul-destroying degree of attachment to the most primitive side of this worldly existence. Equally, to strive for leisure as an alternative to work would he considered a complete misunderstanding of one of the basic truths of human existence, namely that work and leisure are complementary parts of the same living process and cannot be separated without destroying the joy of work and the bliss of leisure.

From the Buddhist point of view, there are therefore two types of mechanisation which must be clearly distinguished: one that enhances a man's skill and power and one that turns the work of man over to a mechanical slave, leaving man in a position of having to serve the slave. How to tell the one from the other? "The craftsman himself," says Amanda Coomaraswamy, a man equally competent to talk about the modern west as the ancient east, "can always, if allowed to, draw the delicate distinction between the machine and the tool. The carpet loom is a tool, a contrivance for holding warp threads at a stretch for the pile to be woven round them by the craftsmen's fingers; but the power loom is a machine, and its significance as a destroyer of culture lies in the fact that it does the essentially human part of the work."[5] It is clear, therefore, that Buddhist economics must be very different from the economics of modern materialism, since the Buddhist sees the essence of civilisation not in a multiplication of wants but in the purification of human character. Character, at the same time, is formed primarily by a man's work. And work, properly conducted in conditions of human dignity and freedom, blesses those who do it and equally their products. The Indian philosopher and economist J. C. Kumarappa sums the matter up as follows:

"If the nature of the work is properly appreciated and applied, it will stand in the same relation to the higher faculties as food is to the physical body. It nourishes and enlivens the higher man and urges him to produce the best he is capable of. It directs his free will along the proper course and disciplines the animal in him into progressive channels. It furnishes an excellent background for man to display his scale of values and develop his personality."[6]

If a man has no chance of obtaining work he is in a desperate position, not simply because he lacks an income but because he lacks this nourishing and enlivening factor of disciplined work which nothing

---

5 *Art and Swadeshi* by Ananda K. Coomaraswamy (Ganesh & Co., Madras)

6 *Economy of Permanence* by J.C. Kumarappa (Sarva-Seva Sangh Publication, Rajghat, Kashi, 4th edn.,1958)

can replace. A modern economist may engage in highly sophisticated calculations on whether full employment 'pays' or whether it might be more 'economic' to run an economy at less than full employment so as to ensure a greater mobility of labour, a better stability of wages, and so forth. His fundamental criterion of success is simply the total quantity of goods produced during a given period of time. "If the marginal urgency of goods is low," says Professor Galbraith in *The Affluent Society*, "then so is the urgency of employing the last man or the last million men in the labour force."[7] And again: "If we can afford some unemployment in the interest of stability—proposition, incidentally, of impeccably conservative antecedents—then we can afford to give those who are unemployed the goods that enable them to sustain their accustomed standard of living."

From a Buddhist point of view, this is standing the truth on its head by considering goods as more important than people and consumption as more important than creative activity. It means shifting the emphasis from the worker to the product of work, that is, from the human to the subhuman, a surrender to the forces of evil. The very start of Buddhist economic planning would be a planning for full employment, and the primary purpose of this would in fact be employment for everyone who needs an 'outside' job: it would not be the maximisation of employment nor the maximisation of production. Women, on the whole, do not need an 'outside' job, and the large-scale employment of women in offices or factories would be considered a sign of serious economic failure. In particular, to let mothers of young children work in factories while the children run wild would be as uneconomic in the eyes of a Buddhist economist as the employment of a skilled worker as a soldier in the eyes of a modern economist.

While the materialist is mainly interested in goods, the Buddhist is mainly interested in liberation. But Buddhism is 'The Middle Way' and therefore in no way antagonistic to physical well-being. It is not wealth that stands in the way of liberation but the attachment to wealth; not the enjoyment of pleasurable things but the craving for them.

The keynote of Buddhist economics, therefore, is simplicity and non-violence. From an economist's point of view, the marvel of the Buddhist way of life is the utter rationality of its pattern—amazingly small means leading to extraordinarily satisfactory results.

For the modern economist this is very difficult to understand. He is used to measuring the 'standard of living' by the amount of annual

---

7 *The Affluent Society* by John Kenneth Galbraith (Penguin Books Ltd., 1962)

consumption, assuming all the time that a man who consumes more is 'better off' than a man who consumes less. A Buddhist economist would consider this approach excessively irrational: since consumption is merely a means to human well-being, the aim should be to obtain the maximum of well-being with the minimum of consumption. Thus, if the purpose of clothing is a certain amount of temperature comfort and an attractive appearance, the task is to attain this purpose with the smallest possible effort, that is, with the smallest annual destruction of cloth and with the help of designs that involve the smallest possible input of toil. The less toil there is, the more time and strength is left for artistic creativity. It would be highly uneconomic, for instance, to go in for complicated tailoring, like the modern west, when a much more beautiful effect can be achieved by the skilful draping of uncut material. It would be the height of folly to make material so that it should wear out quickly and the height of barbarity to make anything ugly, shabby or mean. What has just been said about clothing applies equally to all other human requirements. The ownership and the consumption of goods is a means to an end, and Buddhist economics is the systematic study of how to attain given ends with the minimum means.

Modern economics, on the other hand, considers consumption to be the sole end and purpose of all economic activity, taking the factors of production—land, labour, and capital—as the means. The former, in short, tries to maximise human satisfactions by the optimal pattern of consumption, while the latter tries to maximise consumption by the optimal pattern of productive effort. It is easy to see that the effort needed to sustain a way of life which seeks to attain the optimal pattern of consumption is likely to be much smaller than the effort needed to sustain a drive for maximum consumption. We need not be surprised, therefore, that the pressure and strain of living is very much less in, say, Burma than it is in the United States, in spite of the fact that the amount of labour-saving machinery used in the former country is only a minute fraction of the amount used in the latter.

Simplicity and non-violence are obviously closely related. The optimal pattern of consumption, producing a high degree of human satisfaction by means of a relatively low rate of consumption, allows people to live without great pressure and strain and to fulfil the primary injunction of Buddhist teaching: 'Cease to do evil; try to do good.' As physical resources are everywhere limited, people satisfying their needs by means of a modest use of resources are obviously less likely to be at each other's throats than people depending upon a high rate of use. Equally, people who live in highly self-sufficient local communities are less likely to get involved in large-scale violence than people whose existence depends on world-wide systems of trade.

From the point of view of Buddhist economics, therefore, production from local resources for local needs is the most rational way of economic life, while dependence on imports from afar and the consequent need to produce for export to unknown and distant peoples is highly uneconomic and justifiable only in exceptional cases and on a small scale. Just as the modern economist would admit that a high rate of consumption of transport services between a man's home and his place of work signifies a misfortune and not a high standard of life, so the Buddhist economist would hold that to satisfy human wants from faraway sources rather than from sources nearby signifies failure rather than success. The former tends to take statistics showing an increase in the number of ton/miles per head of the population carried by a country's transport system as proof of economic progress, while to the latter—the Buddhist economist—the same statistics would indicate a highly undesirable deterioration in the *pattern* of consumption.

Another striking difference between modern economics and Buddhist economics arises over the rise of natural resources. Bertrand de Jouvenel, the eminent French political philosopher, has characterised 'western man' in words which may be taken as a fair description of the modern economist:

"He tends to count nothing as an expenditure, other than human effort; he does not seem to mind how much mineral matter he wastes and, far worse, how much living matter he destroys. He does not seem to realise at all that human life is a dependent part of an ecosystem of many different forms of life. As the world is ruled from towns where men are cut off from any form of life other than human, the feeling of belonging to an ecosystem is not revived. This results in a harsh and improvident treatment of things upon which we ultimately depend, such as water and trees."[8]

The teaching of the Buddha, on the other hand, enjoins a reverent and non-violent attitude not only to all sentient beings but also, with great emphasis, to trees. Every follower of the Buddha ought to plant a tree every few years and look after it until it is safely established, and the Buddhist economist can demonstrate without difficulty that the

---

8 *A Philosophy of Indian Economic Development* by Richard B. Gregg (Navajivan Publishing House, Ahmedabad, 1958)

universal observation of this rule would result in a high rate of genuine economic development independent of any foreign aid. Much of the economic decay of south-east Asia (as of many other parts of the world) is undoubtedly due to a heedless and shameful neglect of trees.

Modern economics does not distinguish between renewable and non-renewable materials, as its very method is to equalise and quantify everything by means of a money price. Thus, taking various alternative fuels, like coal, oil, wood, or water-power: the only difference between them recognised by modern economics is relative cost per equivalent unit. The cheapest is automatically the one to be preferred, as to do otherwise would be irrational and 'uneconomic'. From a Buddhist point of view, of course, this will not do; the essential difference between non-renewable fuels like coal and oil on the one hand and renewable fuels like wood and water-power on the other cannot be simply overlooked. Non-renewable goods must be used only if they are indispensable, and then only with the greatest care and the most meticulous concern for conservation. To use them heedlessly or extravagantly is an act of violence, and while complete non-violence may not be attainable on this earth, there is nonetheless an ineluctable duty on man to aim at the ideal of non-violence in all he does.

Just as a modern European economist would not consider it a great economic achievement if all European art treasures were sold to America at attractive prices, so the Buddhist economist would insist that a population basing its economic life on non-renewable fuels is living parasitically, on capital instead of income. Such a way of life could have no permanence and could therefore be justified only as a purely temporary expedient. As the world's resources of non-renewable fuels—coal, oil and natural gas—are exceedingly unevenly distributed over the globe and undoubtedly limited in quantity, it is clear that their exploitation at an ever-increasing rate is an act of violence against nature which must almost inevitably lead to violence between men.

This fact alone might give food for thought even to those people in Buddhist countries who care nothing for the religious and spiritual values of their heritage and ardently desire to embrace the materialism of modern economics at the fastest possible speed. Before they dismiss Buddhist economics as nothing better than a nostalgic dream, they might  wish to consider whether the path of economic development outlined by modern economics is likely to lead them to places where they really want to be. Towards the end of his courageous book *The Challenge of Man's Future*, Professor Harrison Brown of the California Institute of Technology gives the following appraisal:

"Thus we see that, just as industrial society is fundamentally unstable and subject to reversion to agrarian existence, so within it the conditions which offer individual freedom are unstable in their ability to avoid the conditions which impose rigid organisation and totalitarian control. Indeed, when we examine all of the foreseeable difficulties which threaten the survival of industrial civilisation, it is difficult to see how the achievement of stability and the maintenance of individual liberty can be made compatible."[9]

Even if this were dismissed as a long-term view there is the immediate question of whether 'modernisation', as currently practised without regard to religious and spiritual values, is actually producing agreeable results. As far as the masses are concerned, the results appear to be disastrous—a collapse of the rural economy, a rising tide of unemployment in town and country, and the growth of a city proletariat without nourishment for either body or soul.

It is in the light of both immediate experience and long-term prospects that the study of Buddhist economics could be recommended even to those who believe that economic growth is more important than any spiritual or religious values. For it is not a question of choosing between 'modern growth' and 'traditional stagnation'. It is a question of finding the right path of development, the Middle Way between materialist heedlessness and traditionalist immobility, in short, of finding 'Right Livelihood'.

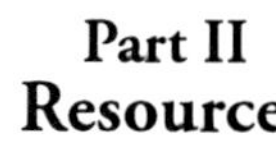

Part II
Resources

II

II. The Proper Use of Land

Among material resources, the greatest, unquestionably, is the land. Study how a society uses its land, and you can come to pretty reliable conclusions as to what its future will be.

The land carries the topsoil, and the topsoil carries an immense variety of living beings including man. In 1955, Tom Dale and Vernon Gill Carter, both highly experienced ecologists, published a book called

---

9 *The Challenge of Man's Future* by Harrison Brown (The Viking Press, New York, 1954)

Topsoil and Civilisation. I cannot do better, for the purposes of this chapter, than quote some of their opening paragraphs:

> "Civilised man was nearly always able to become master of his environment temporarily. His chief troubles came from his delusions that his temporary mastership was permanent. He thought of himself as 'master of the world', while failing to understand fully the laws of nature.
>
> "Man, whether civilised or savage, is a child of nature—he is not the master of nature. He must conform his actions to certain natural laws if he is to maintain his dominance over his environment. When he tries to circumvent the laws of nature, he usually destroys the natural environment that sustains him. And when his environment deteriorates rapidly, his civilisation declines.
>
> "One man has given a brief outline of history by saying that 'civilised man has marched across the face of the earth and left a desert in his footprints'. This statement may be somewhat of an exaggeration, but it is not without foundation. Civilised man has despoiled most of the lands on which he has lived for long. This is the main reason why his progressive civilisations have flawed from place to place. It has been the chief cause for the decline of his civilisations in older settled regions. It has been the dominant factor in determining all trends of history.
>
> "The writers of history have seldom noted the importance of land use. They seem not to have recognised that the destinies of most of man's empires and civilisations were determined largely by the way the land was used. While recognising the influence of environment on history, they fail to note that man usually changed or despoiled his environment.
>
> "How did civilised man despoil this favourable environment? He did it mainly by depleting or destroying the natural resources. He cut down or burned most of the usable timber from forested hillsides and valleys. He overgrazed and denuded the grasslands that fed his livestock. He killed most of the wildlife and much of the fish and other water life. He permitted erosion to rob his farm land of its productive topsoil. He allowed eroded soil to clog the streams and fill his

reservoirs, irrigation canals, and harbours with silt. In many cases, he used and wasted most of the easily mined metals or other needed minerals. Then his civilisation declined amidst the despoliation of his own creation or he moved to new land. There have been from ten to thirty different civilisations that have followed this road to ruin (the number depending on who classifies the civilisations)."[10]

The 'ecological problem', it seems, is not as new as it is frequently made out to be. Yet there are two decisive differences: the earth is now much more densely populated than it was in earlier times and there are, generally speaking, no new lands to move to; and the rate of change has enormously accelerated, particularly during the last quarter of a century.

All the same, it is still the dominant belief today that, whatever may have happened with earlier civilisations, our own modern, western civilisation has emancipated itself from dependence upon nature. A representative voice is that of Eugene Rabinowitch, editor-in-chief of the *Bulletin of Atomic Scientists.*

"The only animals", he says (in *The Times* of 29 April, 1972), "whose disappearance may threaten the biological viability of man on earth are the bacteria normally inhabiting our bodies. For the rest there is no convincing proof that mankind could not survive even as the only animal species on earth! If economical ways could be developed for synthesising food from inorganic raw materials—which is likely to happen sooner or later—man may even be able to become independent of plants, on which he now depends as sources of his food . . . .

"I personally—and, I suspect, a vast majority of mankind—would shudder at the idea (of a habitat without animals and plants). But millions of inhabitants of 'city jungles' of New York, Chicago, London or Tokyo have grown up and spent their whole lives in a practically 'azoic' habitat (leaving out rats, mice, cockroaches and other such obnoxious species) and have survived."

---

[10] *Topsoil and Civilisation* by Tom Dale and Vernon Gill Carter (University of Oklahoma Press, USA, 1955)

Eugene Rabinowitch obviously considers the above a 'rationally justifiable' statement. He deplores that "many rationally unjustifiable things have been written in recent years—some by very reputable scientists—about the sacredness of natural ecological systems, their inherent stability and the danger of human interference with them".

What is 'rational' and what is 'sacred'? Is man the master of nature or its child? If it becomes 'economical' to synthesise food from inorganic materials—'which is likely to happen sooner or later'—if we become independent of plants, the connection between topsoil and civilisation will be broken. Or will it? These questions suggest that 'The Proper Use of Land' poses, not a technical nor an economic, but primarily a metaphysical problem. The problem obviously belongs to a higher level of rational thinking than that represented by the last two quotations.

There are always some things which we do for their own sakes, and there are other things which we do for some other purpose. One of the most important tasks for any society is to distinguish between ends and means-to-ends, and to have some sort of cohesive view and agreement about this. Is the land merely a means of production or is it something more, something that is an end in itself? And when I say 'land', I include the creatures upon it.

Anything we do just for the sake of doing it does not lend itself to utilitarian calculation. For instance, most of us try to keep ourselves reasonably clean. Why? Simply for hygienic reasons? No, the hygienic aspect is secondary; we recognise cleanliness as a value in itself. We do not calculate its value; the economic calculus simply does not come in. It could be argued that to wash is uneconomic: it costs time and money and produces nothing—except cleanliness. There are many activities which are totally uneconomic, but they are carried on for their own sakes. The economists have an easy way of dealing with them: they divide all human activities between 'production' and 'consumption'. Anything we do under the heading of 'production' is subject to the economic calculus, and anything we do under the heading of 'consumption' is not. But real life is very refractory to such classifications, because man-as-producer and man-as-consumer is in fact the same man, who is always producing and consuming *at the same time*. Even a worker in his factory consumes certain 'amenities', commonly referred to as 'working conditions', and when insufficient 'amenities' are provided he cannot—or refuses to—carry on. And even the man who consumes water and soap may be said to be producing cleanliness.

We produce in order to be able to afford certain amenities and comforts as 'consumers'. If, however somebody demanded these same amenities and comforts while he was engaged in 'production', he would be told that this would be uneconomic, that it would be inefficient, and that society could not afford such inefficiency. In other words, everything depends on whether it is done by man-as-producer or by man-as-consumer. If man-as-producer travels first-class or uses a luxurious car, this is called a waste of money; but if the same man in his other incarnation of man-as-consumer does the same, this is called a sign of a high standard of life.

Nowhere is this dichotomy more noticeable than in connection with the use of the land. The farmer is considered simply as a producer who must cut his costs and raise his efficiency by every possible device, even if he thereby destroys—for man as-consumer—the health of the soil and the beauty of the landscape, and even if the end effect is the depopulation of the land and the overcrowding of cities. There are large-scale farmers, horticulturists, food manufacturers and fruit growers today who would never think of consuming any of their own products. 'Luckily,' they say, 'we have enough money to be able to afford to buy products which have been organically grown, without the use of poisons.' When they are asked why they themselves do not adhere to organic methods and avoid the use of poisonous substances, they reply that they could not afford to do so. What man-as-producer can afford is one thing; what man-as-consumer can afford is quite another thing. But since the two are the same man, the question of what man—or society—can really afford gives rise to endless confusion.

There is no escape from this confusion as long as the land and the creatures upon it are looked upon as *nothing but* 'factors of production'. They are, of course, factors of production, that is to say, means-to-ends, but this is their secondary, not their primary, nature. Before everything else, they are ends-in-themselves; they are meta-economic, and it is therefore rationally justifiable to say, as a statement of fact, that they are in a certain sense sacred. Man has not made them, and it is irrational for him to treat things that he has not made and cannot make and cannot recreate once he has spoilt them, in the same manner and spirit as he is entitled to treat things of his own making.

The higher animals have an economic value because of their utility; but they have a meta-economic value in themselves. If I have a car, a man-made thing, I might quite legitimately argue that the best way to use it is never to bother about maintenance and simply run it to ruin.

I may indeed have calculated that this is the most economical method of use. If the calculation is correct, nobody can criticise me for acting accordingly, for there is nothing sacred about a man-made thing like a car. But if I have an animal—be it only a calf or a hen—a living, sensitive creature, am I allowed to treat it as nothing but a utility? Am I allowed to run it to ruin?

It is no use trying to answer such questions scientifically. They are metaphysical, not scientific, questions. It is a metaphysical error, likely to produce the gravest practical consequences, to equate 'car' and 'animal' on account of their utility, while failing to recognise the most fundamental difference between them, that of 'level of being'. An irreligious age looks with amused contempt upon the hallowed statements by which religion helped our forbears to appreciate metaphysical truths. 'And the Lord God took man and put him in the Garden of Eden'—not to be idle, but 'to dress it and keep it. 'And he also gave man dominion over the fish in the sea and the fowl in the air, and over every living being that moves upon the earth.' When he had made 'the beast of the earth after his kind, and cattle after their kind, and everything that creepeth upon the earth after his kind', he saw that it was 'good'. But when he saw everything he had made, the entire biosphere, as we say today, 'behold, it was *very* good'. Man, the highest of his creatures, was given 'dominion', not the right to tyrannise, to ruin and exterminate. It is no use talking about the dignity of man without accepting that *noblesse oblige*. For man to put himself into a wrongful relationship with animals, and particularly those long domesticated by him, has always, in all traditions, been considered a horrible and infinitely dangerous thing to do. There have been no sages or holy men in our or in anybody else's history who were cruel to animals or who looked upon them as *nothing but* utilities, and innumerable are the legends and stories which link sanctity as well as happiness with a loving kindness towards lower creation.

It is interesting to note that modern man is being told, in the name of science, that he is really *nothing but* a naked ape or even an accidental collocation of atoms. "Now we can define man," says Professor Joshua Lederberg. "Genotypically at least, he is six feet of a particular molecular sequence of carbon, hydrogen, oxygen, nitrogen and phosphorous atoms."[11] As modern man thinks so 'humbly' of himself, he thinks even more 'humbly' of the animals which serve his needs: and treats them as if they

---

11 *Man and His Future,* edited by Gordon Wolstenholme (A Ciba Foundation Volume, J. & A. Churchill Ltd.;London, 1963)

were machines. Other, less sophisticated—or is it less depraved?—people take a different attitude. As H. Fielding Hall reported from Burma:

> "To him (the Burmese) men are men, and animals are animals, and men are far the higher. But he does not deduce from this that man's superiority gives him permission to ill treat or kill animals. It is just the reverse. It is because man is so much higher than the animal that he can and must observe towards animals the very greatest care, feel for them the very greatest compassion, be good to them in every way he can. The Burmese's motto should be *noblesse oblige*. He knows the meaning, if he knows not the words."[12]

In *Proverbs* we read that the just man takes care of his beast, but the heart of the wicked is merciless, and St. Thomas Aquinas wrote: "It is evident that if a man practises a compassionate affection for animals, he is all the more disposed to feel compassion for his fellowmen." No one ever raised the question of whether they could *afford* to live in accordance with these convictions. At the level of values, of ends-in-themselves, there is no question of 'affording'.

What applies to the animals upon the land applies equally, and without any suspicion of sentimentality, to the land itself. Although ignorance and greed have again and again destroyed the fertility of the soil to such an extent that whole civilisations foundered, there have been no traditional teachings which failed to recognise the meta-economic value and significance of 'the generous earth'. And where these teachings were heeded, not only agriculture but also all other factors of civilisation achieved health and wholeness. Conversely, where people imagined that they could not 'afford' to care for the soil and work with nature, instead of against it, the resultant sickness of the soil has invariably imparted sickness to all the other factors of civilisation.

In our time, the main danger to the soil, and therewith not only to agriculture but to civilisation as a whole, stems from the townsman's determination to apply to agriculture the principles of industry. No more typical representative of this tendency could he found than Dr. Sicco L. Mansholt, who, as Vice-President of the European Economic Community, launched the Mansholt Plan for European Agriculture. He believes that the farmers are "a group that has still not grasped the

12 *The Soul of a People* by H. Fielding Hall (Macmillan & Co., Ltd., London, 1920)

rapid changes in society". Most of them ought to get out of farming and become industrial labourers in the cities, because "factory workers, men on building sites and those in administrative jobs—have a five-day week and two weeks' annual holiday already. Soon they may have a four-day week and four weeks' holiday per year. And the farmer: *he is condemned to working a seven-day week because the five-day cow has not yet been invented, and he gets no holiday at all.*"[13] The Mansholt Plan, accordingly, is designed to achieve, as quickly as humanely possible, the amalgamation of many small family farms into large agricultural units operated as if they were factories, and the maximum rate of reduction in the community's agricultural population. Aid is to be given "which would enable the older as well as the younger farmers to leave agriculture".[14]

In the discussion of the Mansholt Plan, agriculture is generally referred to as one of Europe's 'industries'. The question arises of whether agriculture is, in fact, all industry, or whether it might be something *essentially* different. Not surprisingly, as this is a metaphysical—or metaeconomic—question, it is never raised by economists.

Now, the fundamental 'principle' of agriculture is that it deals with life, that is to say, with living substances. Its products are the results of processes of life and its means of production is the living soil. A cubic centimetre of fertile soil contains milliards of living organisms, the full exploration of which is far beyond the capacities of man. The fundamental 'principle' of modern industry, on the other hand, is that it deals with man-devised processes which work reliably only when applied to man-devised, non-living materials. The ideal of industry is the elimination of living substances. Man-made materials are preferable to natural materials, because we can make them to measure and apply perfect quality control. Man-made machines work more reliably and more predictably than do such living substances as men. The ideal of industry is to eliminate the living factor, even including the human factor, and to turn the productive process over to machines. As Alfred North Whitehead defined life as "an offensive directed against the repetitious mechanism of the universe", so we may define modern industry as "an offensive against

13 *Our Accelerating Century* by Dr. S.L. Mansholt (The Royal Dutch/Shell Lectures on Industry and Society, London, 1967)

14 *A Future for European Agriculture* by D. Bergmann, M. Rossi-Doria, N. Kaldor, J.A. Schnittker, H.B. Krohn, C. Thomsen, J. S. March, H. Wilbrandt, Pierre Uri (The Atlantic Institute, Paris, 1970)

the unpredictability, unpunctuality, general waywardness and cussedness of living nature, including man".

In other words, there can be no doubt that the fundamental 'principles' of agriculture and of industry, far from being compatible with each other, are in opposition. Real life consists of the tensions produced by the incompatibility of opposites, each of which is needed, and just as life would be meaningless without death, so agriculture would be meaningless without industry. It remains true, however, that agriculture is primary, whereas industry is secondary, which means that human life can continue without industry, whereas it cannot continue without agriculture. Human life at the level of civilization, however, demands, the *balance* of the two principles, and this balance is ineluctably destroyed when people fail to appreciate the *essential* difference between agriculture and industry—a difference as great as that between life and death-and attempt to treat agriculture as just another industry.

The argument is, of course, a familiar one. It was put succinctly by a group of internationally recognised experts in *A Future for European Agriculture*:

> "Different parts of the world possess widely differing advantages for the production of particular products, depending on differences in climate, the quality of the soil and the cost of labour. All countries would gain from a division of labour which enabled them to concentrate production on their most highly productive agricultural operations. This would result both in higher income for agriculture and lower costs for the entire economy, particularly for industry. No fundamental justification can be found for agricultural protectionism."[15]

If this were so it would be totally incomprehensible that agricultural protectionism, throughout history, has been the rule rather than the exception. Why are most countries, most of the time, unwilling to gain these splendid rewards from so simple a prescription? Precisely because there is more involved in 'agricultural operations' than the production of incomes and the lowering of costs: what is involved is the whole relationship between man and nature, the whole life-style of a society, the health, happiness and harmony of man, as well as the beauty of his

---

15 *Ibid*

habitat. If all these things are left out of the experts' considerations, man himself is left out—even if our experts try to bring him in, as it were, after the event, by pleading that the community should pay for the 'social consequences' of their policies. The Mansholt Plan, say the experts, "represents a bold initiative. It is based on the acceptance of a fundamental principle: agricultural income can only he maintained if the reduction in the agricultural population is accelerated, and if farms rapidly reach an economically viable size."[16] Or again: "Agriculture, in Europe at least, is essentially directed towards food-production . . . . It is well known that the demand for food increases relatively slowly with increases in real income. This causes the total incomes earned in agriculture to rise more slowly in comparison with the incomes earned in industry; to maintain the same rate of growth of incomes per head is only possible if there is an adequate rate of decline in the numbers engaged in agriculture."[17] . . . The conclusions seem inescapable: under circumstances which are normal in other advanced countries, the community would be able to satisfy its own needs with only one-third as many farmers as now."[18]

No serious exception can be taken to these statements if we adopt—as the experts have adopted—the metaphysical position of the crudest materialism, for which money costs and money incomes are the ultimate criteria and determinants of human action, *and the living world has no significance beyond that of a quarry for exploitation.*

On a wider view, however, the land is seen as a priceless asset which it is man's task and happiness 'to dress and to keep'. We can say that man's management of the land must be primarily orientated towards three goals—health, beauty, and permanence. The fourth goal-the only one accepted by the experts—productivity, will then be attained almost as a by-product. The crude materialist view sees agriculture as 'essentially directed towards food-production'. A wider view sees agriculture as having to fulfil at least three tasks:

- to keep man in touch with living nature, of which he is and remains a highly vulnerable part;
- to humanize and ennoble man's wider habitat; and
- to bring forth the foodstuffs and other materials which are needed for a becoming life.

---

16 *Ibid*

17 *Ibid*

18 *Ibid*

I do not believe that a civilisation which recognises only the third of these tasks, and which pursues it with such ruthlessness and violence that the other two tasks are not merely neglected but systematically counteracted, has any chance of long-term survival.

Today, we take pride in the fact that the proportion of people engaged in agriculture has fallen to very low levels and continues to fall. Great Britain produces some sixty per cent of its food requirements while only three per cent of its working population are working on farms. In the United States, there were still twenty-seven per cent of the nation's workers in agriculture at the end of World War I, and fourteen per cent at the end of World War II; the estimate for 1971 shows only 4.4 per cent. These declines in the proportion of workers engaged in agriculture arc generally associated with a massive flight from the land and a burgeoning of cities. At the same time, however, to quote Lewis Herber:

> "Metropolitan life is breaking down, psychologically, economically and biologically. Millions of people have acknowledged this breakdown by voting with their feet, they have picked up their belongings and left. If they have not been able to sever their connections with the metropolis, at least they have tried. As a social symptom the effort is significant."[19]

In the vast modern towns, says Mr. Herber, the urban dweller is more isolated than his ancestors were in the countryside: "The city man in a modern metropolis has reached a degree of anonymity, social atomisation and spiritual isolation that is virtually unprecedented in human history."[20]

So what does he do? He tries to get into the suburbs and becomes a commuter. Because rural culture has broken down, the rural people are fleeing from the land; and because metropolitan life is breaking down, urban people are fleeing from the cities. "Nobody," according to Dr. Mansholt, "can afford the luxury of not acting economically",[21] with the result that everywhere life tends to become intolerable for anyone except the very rich.

---

19 *Our Synthetic Environment* by Lewis Herbert (Jonathan Cape Ltd., London, 1963)

20 *Ibid*

21 *Op. cit.*

I agree with Mr. Herber's assertion that "reconciliation of man with the natural world is no longer merely desirable, it has become a necessity". And this cannot be achieved by tourism, sightseeing, or other leisure-time activities, but only by changing the structure of agriculture in a direction exactly opposite to that proposed by Dr. Mansholt and supported by the experts quoted above: instead of searching for means to accelerate the drift out of agriculture, we should he searching for policies to reconstruct rural culture, to open the land for the gainful occupation to larger numbers of people, whether it be on a full-time or a part-time basis, and to orientate all our actions on the land towards the threefold ideal of health, beauty, and permanence.

The social structure of agriculture, which has been produced by—and is generally held to obtain its justification from—large-scale mechanisation and heavy chemicalisation, makes it impossible to keep man in real touch with living nature; in fact, it supports all the most dangerous modern tendencies of violence, alienation, and environmental destruction. Health, beauty, and permanence are hardly even respectable subjects for discussion, and this is yet another example of the disregard of human values—and this means a disregard of man—which inevitably results from the idolatry of economism.

If 'beauty is the splendour of truth', agriculture cannot fulfil its second task, which is to humanise and ennoble man's wider habitat, unless it clings faithfully and assiduously to the truths revealed by nature's living processes. One of them is the law of return; another is diversification—as against any kind of monoculture; another is decentralisation, so that some use can be found for even quite inferior resources which it would never be rational to transport over long distances. Here again, both the trend of things and the advice of the experts is in the exactly opposite direction—towards the industrialisation and depersonalisation of agriculture, towards concentration, specialisation, and any kind of material waste that promises to save labour. As a result, the wider human habitat, far from being humanised and ennobled by man's agricultural activities, becomes standardised to dreariness or even degraded to ugliness.

All this is being done because man-as-producer cannot afford 'the luxury of not acting economically', and therefore cannot produce the very necessary 'luxuries'—like health, beauty, and permanence—which man-as-consumer desires more than anything else. It would cost too much; and the richer we become, the less we can 'afford'. The aforementioned experts calculate that the 'burden' of agricultural support within the

Community of the Six amounts to 'nearly three per cent of Gross National Product', an amount they consider 'far from negligible'. With an annual growth rate of over three per cent of Gross National Product, one might have thought that such a 'burden' could be carried without difficulty; but the experts point out that "national resources are largely committed to personal consumption, investment and public services . . . By using so large a proportion of resources to prop up declining enterprises, whether in agriculture or in industry, the Community foregoes the opportunity to undertake . . . necessary improvements"[22] in these other fields.

Nothing could be clearer. If agriculture does not pay, it is just a 'declining enterprise'. Why prop it up? There are no 'necessary improvements' as regards the land, but only as regards farmers' incomes, and these can be made if there are fewer farmers. This is the philosophy of the townsman, alienated from living nature, who promotes his own scale of priorities by arguing in economic terms that we cannot 'afford' any other. In fact, any society can afford to look after its land and keep it healthy and beautiful in perpetuity. There are no technical difficulties and there is no lack of relevant knowledge. 'There is no need to consult economic experts when the question is one of priorities. We know too much about ecology today to have any excuse for the many abuses that are currently going on in the management of the land, in the management of animals, in food storage, food processing, and in heedless urbanisation. If we permit them, this is not due to poverty, as if we could not afford to stop them: it is due to the fact that, as a society, we have no firm basis of belief in any meta-economic values, and when there is no such belief the economic calculus takes over. This is quite inevitable. How could it be otherwise? Nature, it has been said, abhors a vacuum, and when the available 'spiritual space' is not filled by some higher motivation, then it will necessarily be filled by something lower—by the small, mean, calculating attitude to life which is rationalised in the economic calculus.

I have no doubt that a callous attitude to the land and to the animals thereon is connected with, and symptomatic of, a great many other attitudes, such as those producing a fanaticism of rapid change and a fascination with novelties—technical. organisational, chemical, biological, and so forth—which insists on their application long before their long-term consequences are even remotely understood. In the simple question of how we treat the land, next to people our precious

---

22 *Op. cit.*

resource, our entire way of life is involved, and before our policies with regard to the land will really be changed, there will have to be a great deal of philosophical, not to say religious, change. It is not a question of what we can afford but of what we choose to spend our money on. If we could return to a generous recognition of meta-economic values, our landscapes, would become healthy and beautiful again and our people would regain the dignity of man, who knows himself as higher than the animal hut never forgets that *noblesse oblige*.

James F. Childress

1940-

Priorities in Biomedical Ethics

1981

James F. Childress is currently the John Allen Hollingsworth Professor of Ethics in the department of Religious Studies at the University of Virginia (UVA). His area of specialty is biomedical ethics and he holds a parallel appointment as Professor of Medical Education, where he directs the Institute for Practical Ethics. He earned his BA from Guilford College, and a BD from Yale Divinity School, followed by a MA and PhD from Yale University.

Selections from his published works in the area of biomedical ethics include; *Principles of Bioethics, Practical Reasoning in Bioethics,* and *Priorities in Biomedical Ethics, Who Should Decide?* As a member of the Board of the United Network for Organ Sharing (UNOS), he has served with various groups including the Recombinant DNA Advisory Committee and the Human Gene Therapy subcommittee. He also served as the vice chair of the national Task Force on Organ Transplantation. In 2002 he received the highest honor given to faculty at UVA, The Thomas Jefferson Award.

The selection which follows is Chapter 5 from his 1981 work *Priorities in Biomedical Ethics.* His thoughtful and critical discussion bridges the views of scientists and technologists, with the morals, ethics, and values of religion and philosophy.

1. What are the connections between technology and ideology?
2. Choose a significant current technology. Give a brief risk-benefit analysis. How does Childress affect how you approach this analysis?
3. Can an individual have both a rational and an emotional view of the same issue? Why or why not?

Source:

Center for Biomedical Ethics & Humanities. Accessed April 12, 2008 from http://www.healthsystem.virginia.edu/internet/bio-ethics/childress.cfm.

Selection from:

Childress, J. F. (1981). *Priorities in Biomedical Ethics.* Philadelphia: The Westminster Press. 98-118.

Chapter 5

THE ART OF TECHNOLOGY ASSESSMENT

Technology, Assessment, and Control

"It was the best of times, it was the worst of times, it was the age of wisdom, it was the age of foolishness." These words, which Charles Dickens uses for the French Revolution in *A Tale of Two Cities,* could easily apply to our discourse about technology. Positive and negative superlatives abound. We are quick to applaud or to disapprove. Rarely do we grasp the ambiguity of technology and the necessity of subtle and nuanced evaluations. Our public policies will not be responsible until we grasp this ambiguity and deal with it in relation to moral principles and values.

In the late 1950s and early 1960s, many commentators declared that the modern world had lost interest in, or the capacity to answer, big questions such as the meaning of life and the goals of our institutions. Social scientists such as Daniel Bell announced the "end of ideology," philosophers such as Peter Laslett observed that "political philosophy is dead," and theologians such as Harvey Cox noted the decline of religion. According to Cox, the secular city was emerging, and its inhabitants would be pragmatic and profane, interested only in what will work in this world. All these interpretations converged: individuals and communities are no longer interested in, or able to deal with, ideology, metaphysics, and mystery.[1]

Some interpreters even went so far as to say that the important issues are merely technical and can be handled by the technicians or experts. President Kennedy expressed this viewpoint in the early '60s, when he held that the real issue today is the management of industrial society—a problem of ways and means, not of ideology. As he put it, "the fact of the matter is that most of the problems, or at least many of them, that we now face are technical problems, are administrative problems [requiring] . . . very sophisticated judgments which do not lend themselves to the great sort of 'passionate movements' which have stirred this country so often in the past."[2]

The obituaries for ideology, social and political philosophy, and religion were premature—as the events of the last twenty years have demonstrated. In the rapid growth of various religious communities and in the conflicts over civil rights, the war in Vietnam, abortion, and technology, it became clear that interest in the big questions was only dormant or overlooked in the rush to embrace new trends.

For the most part, those who wrote the obituaries for meaning and value in the modern world were quite sanguine about technological society and the technocrats who would run it without worrying about larger perspectives. But while they praised technological man, others such as Jacques Ellul, viewed him with distrust and disdain.[3] However, their debates lacked subtlety and discrimination largely because the protechnologists and the antitechnologists tended to agree that the issue was technology as

---

1 See Harvey Cox, The Secular City (MacMillan Co. 1965); Daniel Bell, The End of Ideology (Free Press of Glencoe, 1960), especially "An Epilogue: The End of Ideology in the West"; and Peter Laslett (ed.), Philosophy, Politics and Society. First Series (Oxford: Basil Blackwell, Publisher, 1957), "Introduction."

2 Arthur Schlesinger, Jr., A Thousand Days (Houghton Mifflin Co., 1965), p. 644. See also William Lee Miller, Of Thee, Nevertheless, I Sing (Harcourt Brace Jovanovich, 1975, pp. 78-95. The themes were prominent in President Kennedy's commencement speech at Yale University in 1962.

3 Jacques Ellul, The Technological Society, tr. from the French by John Wilkinson (Vintage Books, 1964).

such (or at least modern technology as such}. As a result, they obscured the importance of assessing and controlling particular technologies.

Unfortunately, these global perspectives endure. Two examples can be found in recent books. In *The Republic of Technology: Reflections on Our Future Community*, Daniel Boorstin, the Librarian of Congress, connects the growth of technology with the (alleged) decline of ideology: "Technology dilutes and dissolves ideology . . . More than any other modern people we have been free of the curse of ideology."[4] Holding that we are most human when we are making and using tools, Boorstin is enthusiastic about technology as such.

An example of a global perspective that is negative toward technology (at least within one area of medicine) is Stanley Reiser's *Medicine and the Reign of Technology*. Reiser, a historian of medicine, traces the development of various diagnostic technologies such as the stethoscope and concludes that they have increasingly alienated physicians from patients. Because they provide external, objective signs, the physician no longer relies on his own personal contact with the patient for diagnosis. Thus, the physician concentrates on the measurable aspects of illness rather than on human factors. "Accuracy, efficiency, and security are purchased at a high price," Reiser contends, "when that price is impersonal medical care and undermining the physician's belief in his own medical powers." The physician, he says, must rebel against this "reign of technology."[5]

It is interesting that both Boorstin and Reiser choose "political" metaphors and images when they discuss technology: "republic," "reign," and "rebellion." And despite their different responses to technology, both appear to hold a form of technological determinism, either hard or soft. Technology determines social relationships, for example, between patient and physician. Not only are there problems with this determinism which makes technology an independent variable, but it is not accurate or helpful to approach technology as such, to offer global praise or blame. More precise and discriminate judgments are required if we are to reap the benefits and avoid the evils of particular technologies. One attempt in the last fifteen years to provide a way to control technologies through public policy is *technology assessment*. I want to examine the art of technology assessment, its possibilities and its limitations.

---

4 Daniel J. Boorstin, The Republic of Technology: Reflections on Our Future Community (Harper & Row, 1978).

5 Stanley Joel Reiser, Medicine and the Reign of Technology (Cambridge University Press, 1978).

For our purposes, "technology" can be defined as the "systematic application of scientific knowledge and technical skills for the control of matter, energy, etc., for practical purposes."[6] I shall concentrate on biomedical technologies: the technologies, (techniques, drugs, equipment, and procedures) used by professionals in delivering medical care. Examples include insulin, the totally implantable artificial heart, kidney dialysis, CAT scanners, and in vitro fertilization.

We assess technologies in order to be able to "control" them responsibly through our public policies.[7] Public policy is a purposive course or pattern of action or inaction by government officials. Public policies designed to "control" technologies may operate in many different ways. The most typical and common controls are the allocation of funds (e.g., the decision to give research on cancer priority) and regulation or prohibition (e.g., the prohibition of the use of Laetrile). But it is also possible to permit and even to fund a technology while trying to control its side effects through other measures.

Control cannot be properly directed without an assessment of technology. The phrase "technology assessment" was apparently first used in 1966 by Philip Yeager, counsel for the House Committee on Science and Astronautics, in a report by the House Subcommittee on Science, Research and Development, chaired by Congressman Emilio Q. Dadderio (D-Conn.), later the first head of the Office of Technology Assessment. Basically, technology assessment is a comprehensive approach, considering all the possible or probable consequences, intended and unintended effects, of a technology on society. It is thus multidisciplinary and interdisciplinary.

Against some interpreters and practitioners of technology assessment, I would argue that it is "an art form," not a science.[8] As an art form, it is basically

---

6 This definition is a modification of the definition offered in Assessing Biomedical Technologies: An Inquiry Into the Nature of the Process, by the Committee on the Life Sciences and Social Policy, National Research Council (Washington, D.C.: National Academy of Sciences, 1975), p. 1.

7 The term "control" is anathema to many critics of contemporary society and technology, perhaps especially in religious contexts; some critics have retreated into the private sphere because technology appears to be out of control or because the issues are thought to be cultural rather than political. For a valuable discussion of "autonomous technology," see Langdon Winner, Autonomous Technology: Technics-out-of-Control as a Theme in Political Thought (MIT Press, 1977).

8 Joseph F. Coates, "The Identification and Selection of Candidates and Priorities for Technology Assessment," Technology Assessment, Vol. 2, No. 2

the work of imagination which is indispensable for judgment-making. All sorts of methods can be used, and technology assessment should not be identified with any particular methods. Before policy-makers had access to systems analysts, and the like, they consulted astrologers, and, on the whole, Hannah Arendt once suggested it would be better if they still consulted astrologers! I want to show that technology assessment can be more than a narrow technique and that, as a broad approach, drawing on several different methods it is an indispensable art.

Theological Convictions

Technology assessments will draw on theological (or quasi-theological) convictions as well as on moral principles and values. Before turning to the latter, I want to indicate how general theological convictions provide perspectives on and engender attitudes toward technology, often through perspectives on and attitudes toward nature.[9] It should be noted that Christian (and Jewish) convictions reflect certain tensions which may be creative or destructive.

On the one hand, the Christian tradition affirms the goodness of creation, holding that nature is not an enemy to be assaulted. On the other hand, it also leads to what Max Weber called "the disenchantment of the world" or "the rationalization of the world."[10] Its stress on God's transcendence tends to exclude spirits in nature who need to be approached with awe, and it thus frees nature for man's dominion.

(1974), p. 78. For an overview of technology assessment, see LeRoy Walters, "Technology Assessment," in Reich (ed.), Encyclopedia of Bioethics, Vol. 4, pp. 1650-1654.

9 See James M. Gustafson, The Contributions of Theology to Medical Ethics, The 1975 Pere Marquette Theology Lecture (Marquette University Press, 1975). In a critique of most, if not all, theological approaches to technology and the life sciences, Gustafson castigates casuists and moralists for their myopia and prophetic theologians for their inability to deal with specifics. See James M. Gustafson, "Theology Confronts Technology and the Life Sciences," Commonweal, June 16, 1978, pp. 386-392.

10 Weber drew the phrase "disenchantment of the world" (Entzauberung der Welt) from Friedrich Schiller. See Max Weber, The Protestant Ethic and the Spirit of Capitalism, tr. by Talcott Parsons (Charles Scribner's Sons, 1958), esp. pp. 105 and 221-222, fn. 19, and H. H. Gerth and C. Wright Mills (eds.), From Max Weber: Essays in Sociology (Oxford University Press, 1958), p. 51.

Another tension can be seen in the distinction between sovereignty over nature and stewardship of nature. Although the Christian tradition has sometimes engendered (or at least supported) attitudes of human sovereignty over nature,[11] its dominant theme is human stewardship, deputyship, or trusteeship. While the sovereign is not accountable, the trustee is accountable to God and for what happens to nature. Human action takes place within a context in which humans are ultimately responsible to God as the sovereign Lord of life, Creator, Preserver, and Redeemer. Within this perspective of trusteeship, we cannot be satisfied with a short-term view of responsibility. For example, there is penultimate responsibility to and for future generations: it is not legitimate to slight this responsibility by asking, What has posterity ever done for us? And there is penultimate responsibility to and for nonhuman nature, not only because "nature bats last"!

Some theological critics reject the image of stewardship or trusteeship because it involves *dominium terrae*. But it is irresponsible to neglect or to repudiate human control over nature. The issue is not control (technology) but, rather, the ends, effects, and means of control (technology). This control is not total or unlimited: it is not absolute dominion. It is limited and constrained by nature itself, by moral principles and rules, and by ultimate loyalty and responsibility to God. It is not necessary or desirable to conceive these limits and constraints in terms of "rights" (e.g., rights of trees) as though we can imagine moral requirements only when we can invoke rights. However important rights are—and they are very important—we can conceive moral limits on our control of nature without appealing to them.

The ends of *dominium terrae* are also subject to criticism. If there is a hierarchy of interests, and if human interests are dominant, they should not be construed narrowly—for example, in terms of material goods. Nor should they exclude the goods of nature which are not reducible to human interests. Theologically, the propensity of human beings to construe their interests narrowly and to exclude nonhuman interests or goods is explained in terms of sin. Because humanity is fallen, its control over nature will frequently be misdirected and even destructive. In addition, as we will see when we discuss process later, procedures and mechanisms for reducing the effects of sin are indispensable; even though they cannot eradicate sin, they can lessen its destructiveness.

---

11 Lynn White, Jr., "The Historical Roots of Our Ecologic Crisis," Science, March 10, 1967.

According to some theological critics, the image of stewardship or trusteeship is also suspect because it appears to separate human beings and nonhuman nature. To be sure, this image depends on a distinction between humanity and nature, but it does not imply an invidious separation. Humanity is part of nature. But, created in the image of God, it is a distinctive, even unique, part of nature. In addition, there may be a hierarchy of value with humanity at the apex. However much we need to emphasize the continuity between humanity and nature, discontinuity, at least as distinction, is still evident and important. Even as part of nature, humanity can still be a steward and trustee for nature.

Furthermore, to distinguish humanity and nature is not to deny their interdependence. Humanity should recognize its solidarity, its community of interests, with nature, because what affects nonhuman nature also affects humanity. It is not necessary or desirable, however, to focus on oneness or organic harmony or to develop a process theology in order to support an adequate ethic. It is possible, for example, to develop adequate limits on human control over nature from a perspective of conflict between humanity and nature in a fallen world. As Gerhard Liedke argues, such a perspective would hold that nonhuman nature is more than material, for, at the very least, it is a rival partner in a conflict. And it needs protection to ensure its participation as an equal in this conflict.[12] Furthermore, recognizing nature in this way is compatible with an attitude of awe and wonder that supports limits on human control over nature.

Although general theological (or quasi-theological) convictions provide perspectives and engender attitudes, they are not by themselves sufficient for the assessment of technologies. For such a task, we need an ethical bridgework or framework to connect these convictions, perspectives, and attitudes with judgments about technologies. Such a bridgework or framework will consist, in part, of general principles and values. But theological convictions, along with the perspectives they provide and the attitudes they engender, do not merely serve as warrants for moral principles and values. They also shape interpretations of

12 Gerhard Liedke, "Solidarity in Conflict," in Faith and Science in an Unjust World: Report of the World Council of Churches' Conference on Faith, Science and the Future, Vol. 1, Plenary Presentations, ed. by Roger Shinn (Fortress Press, 1980), pp. 73-80. In contrast, Charles Birch's presentation in the same volume stresses oneness and harmony and calls for a process theology ("Nature, Humanity and God in Ecological Perspective," pp. 62-73).

situations to which we apply principles and values. Consider, for example, beliefs about death in debates about technologies to prolong and extend life. If a society views death as an enemy, always to be opposed, it will be inclined to provide funds to develop life-prolonging and life-extending technologies and to use them even when the expected quality of life is poor. An adequate critique would thus include convictions, perspectives, and attitudes that shape interpretations of situations, as well as moral principles and values.

Because it is not possible here to establish all the important connections between theological convictions, moral principles and values, and interpretations of situations, I shall assume several principles and values in order to trace their implications for the assessment of technologies.[13] Unless a single principle or value is accepted as overriding, conflicts and dilemmas are inevitable. As Guido Calabresi and Philip Bobbitt emphasize in *Tragic Choices*, tragedy is largely a cultural phenomenon: it depends on the principles and values of the individual or the society.[14] This point was underlined during a 1979 visit to the People's Republic of China with an interdisciplinary and interprofessional delegation interested in ethics, public policy, and health care. Frequently members of our delegation asked Chinese policy makers, health care professionals, and others how they handle some of our "problems" such as refusal of treatment. The most common response was: "That's not a problem here. It doesn't exist here." Sometimes this response reflected the state of technological development: often, however, it reflected the unimportance of some Western principles and values such as autonomy, privacy, (for which there is no Chinese word), and other ingredients of individualism.[15]

Principles and Values in Technology Assessment

I now want to indicate how technology assessment might proceed and, in particular, what principles and values it ought to consider. Nothing in its logic requires that it be as narrow as it sometimes is. Its

---

13 For some of these principles, see Beauchamp and Childress, Principles of Biomedical Ethics.

14 Calabresi and Bobbitt, Tragic Choices.

15 See James F. Childress, "Reflections on Socialist Ethics," and H. Tristram Engelhardt, Jr., "Bioethical Issues in Contemporary China," The Kennedy Institute Quarterly Report, Fall 1979, pp. 11-14 and 4-6.

practitioners need not be what John Stuart Mill called "one-eyed men" attending only to the "business" side of life.[16]

1. Any technology assessment depends to a great extent on the principle of proportionality—proportion between the probable good and bad effects of technologies. This principle is expressed in various methods used to assess technologies, for example, cost-benefit analysis and risk-benefit analysis, which are only "new names for very old ways of thinking" (as William James said of pragmatism). They represent attempts to systematize, formalize, and frequently to quantify what we ordinarily do. For example, outside Canton, patients in a commune hospital formed their own risk-benefit analysis of traditional Chinese herbal medicine and Western medicine, both of which were available. They said, "Chinese medicine might not help you, but it won't hurt you: Western medicine might help you, but it also might hurt you."

I shall concentrate on *risk* and *benefit*, viewing risk as one sort of cost, i.e., cost as threat to safety, health, and life. The terms "risk" and "benefit" are perhaps not the best. Risk includes both amount or magnitude of harm and probability of harm. When we juxtapose benefit and risk, we are likewise interested in the magnitude and probability of benefit. It would be more accurate then to say that we need to balance the probability and magnitude of harm and the probability and magnitude of benefit. But since that expression is too cumbersome. I will use the common formulation of *risk-benefit analysis.*

Risk-benefit analysis involves what has been called "statistical morality."[17] Risks are everywhere, and one major question is how far we are willing to go in order to reduce the risks of premature mortality, morbidity, and trauma. Let us concentrate on mortality and ask the troubling question: How much is it worth to save a life (really to postpone death, since lives are never really saved)? Or what is the value of a life? Consider the controversy over the Pinto. Apparently in 1973

---

16 Mill, "Bentham," in Warnock (ed.), Utilitarianism, On Liberty, Essay on Bentham, pp. 92 and 105.

17 Warren Weaver, "Statistical Morality," Christianity and Crisis, Jan. 23, 1961, pp. 210-215. In the last chapter, I introduced Thomas Schelling's idea of "statistical lives." For a fuller analysis of risk, see James F. Childress, "Risk," in Reich (ed.), Encyclopedia of Bioethics, Vol. 4, pp. 1516-1522.

Ford officials decided not to install a safety device that would prevent damage to the Pinto's gasoline tank in rear-end collisions. According to some reports, this device would have cost eleven dollars per vehicle or 137 million dollars for the whole production run. It is not accurate to say that Ford valued human life at eleven dollars. Rather, using a figure of approximately $200,000 per life, it concluded that the safety device should not be used because its costs outweighed its benefits.[18]

Economists propose two different ways to determine the value of life.[19] First, discounted future earnings. This approach tends to give priority to young adult white males. Thus a program to encourage motorcyclists to wear helmets would be selected over a cervical cancer program. Second, a willingness to pay. The question is not how much we would be willing to pay in order to avoid certain death, but how much we would be willing to pay to reduce the risk of death. How is willingness to pay determined? By finding out how much all those who are affected would be willing to pay, summing up the individual amounts and then dividing by the anticipated number of deaths prevented. While it might be possible to study actual behavior (e.g., in the workplace), one promising approach uses opinion polls to determine, for example, how much a community would be willing to pay in taxes for a technology that would reduce the chances of death after a heart attack.

Although it may be impossible to avoid valuing lives (at least implicitly} in technology assessment, criticisms abound. Religious critics contend that life has infinite or absolute value. But their criticism is not serious insofar as it is directed against policies that do not do everything possible to reduce the risk of death. Judaism and Christianity, to take two examples, do not hold that life is an absolute value superior to all other values. Both traditions honor martyrs who refuse to value life more highly than other goods such as obedience to the divine will. Furthermore, there is a difference between negative and positive duties, and the duty not to kill is more stringent than the duty to save lives.

---

18 For a discussion, see George I. Mavrodes, "The Morality of Chances: Weighing the Cost of Auto Safety," The Reformed Journal, March 1980, pp. 12-15.

19 See Steven E. Rhoads (ed.), Valuing Life: Public Policy Dilemmas (Westview Press, 1980), especially his chapter "How Much Should We Spend to Save a Life?" pp. 285-311. His formulations have shaped this paragraph.

Other critics hold that it is immoral to put a value on life. But we all have life plans and risk budgets.[20] Our life plans consist of aims, ends, and values, and our risk budgets indicate the risks to our health and survival we are willing to accept in order to realize some other goods. Health and survival are conditional, not final, values. A society might justly choose to put more of its budget into goods other than health and survival, as I argued in *Priorities in Biomedical Ethics.* Such a choice may be more political, i.e., to be resolved through the political process in terms of the community's values, or even aesthetic. One way to make this choice is to determine a community's willingness to pay for different goods.

An extension of these religious and moral objections opposes the calculation of consequences. Utilitarianism has sometimes been depicted as "ethics in cold blood." But, as I will argue later, consequences are always morally relevant even if they are not always morally decisive. This objection to calculation of consequences may simply be an objection to doing self-consciously and openly what we have to do. For example, Steven Rhoads argues that we should do a little dissembling since to put a public value on life would shock the community and perhaps lead to callousness.[21] In effect, he offers consequentialist grounds for not openly pursuing consequentialism.

These various objections to valuing lives do not hold. For the most part, they are not even aimed at the right targets. And it would be useful for us as individuals and members of a community to ask how much we are willing to spend to reduce the risk of death (in brief, to put a value on life).

It is obvious that value considerations determine what counts as benefit and what counts as harm. They also determine how much particular benefits and harms count, how much weight they should have in the calculation. An adequate risk-benefit analysis needs to keep in play a wide range of values to identify, weigh, and balance benefits and harms. Analysts tend to prefer the hard, quantifiable variables, rather than the soft variables that are less susceptible to quantification. But a "narrow" cost or risk-benefit analysis fails to convey the richness of our moral values and principles.

2. Value considerations not only shape our perceptions of benefits and harms, they also "dictate the manner in which uncertainty as to the potential adverse consequences will be resolved."[22] To

---

20 These are Charles Fried's terms as introduced in the previous chapter.

21 Rhoads, "How Much Should We Spend to Save a Life?" pp. 305-306.

22 Harold P. Green, "The Risk-Benefit Calculus in Safety Determinations," George Washington Law Review, Vol. 43 (1975), p. 799.

> some analysts, the absence of evidence that harm will result is taken as evidence that the harm will not result, and so forth. The resolution of uncertainty, then, will reflect the value judgments of the analyst, whether he uses his own values or reflects the society's values. Description and evaluation cannot be separated even in the determination of the probability of harm because of "opposing dispositions or outlooks toward the future" such as confidence and hope or fear and anxiety.[23]

In the face of uncertainty, a procedural suggestion seems justified.[24] In the past, technology has been presumed innocent until proven guilty. ("Guilt" and "innocence" are used metaphorically to refer to risk-benefit analysis.) But in the light of our experiences in the last twenty years, we cannot be satisfied with this approach: we should, perhaps, presume that technology is guilty until proven innocent. The burden of proof and of going forward should be placed on the advocates of a technology who hold that its benefits will outweigh its harms. Such a shift in the *onus probandi* would not signal opposition to technological development. It would only indicate that we have not been sufficiently attentive to the harmful side effects and second-order consequences in technological development and that we intend to correct this deficiency.

A version of this procedure is mandated for the Food and Drug Administration, which cannot approve drugs for use outside research until they have been shown to be safe and efficacious. In effect, research may go forward (within the limits sketched in Chapter 3 of my *Priorities in Biomedical Ethics* [Philadelphia: Westminster, 1981], "Human Subjects in Research"), research may even be funded (in accord with priorities sketched in Chapter 4 of the same book, "Allocating Health Care Resources"), but let's not introduce a technology until we have determined with a reasonable degree of assurance that its probable benefits outweigh its probable harms. This procedure will not harass or arrest technology.

---

23 James M. Gustafson, "Basic Ethical Issues in the Biomedical Fields," Soundings, Summer 1970, p. 153.

24 National Academy of Sciences, Panel on Technology Assessment, Technology: Processes of Assessment and Choice. Report to the Committee on Science and Astronautics, U.S. House of Representatives, July 1969 (Washington, D.C.: Government Printing Office, 1969), pp. 33-39.

3. It is not sufficient for a technology to have a favorable risk-benefit ratio; its proponents should also show that its risk-benefit ratio is more favorable than alternative technologies or even no technology at all. For example, if both X and Y have favorable risk-benefit ratios, they may not be equally acceptable if Y's ratio is more favorable. Many critics of technology call on society to consider alternative technologies, particularly technologies that emphasize the values of smallness and the integrity of person, community, and nature.[25] To a great extent, the issue is again the range of values that should be invoked for risk-benefit analysis.
4. We should seek to minimize risks even by *some* reduction in the probability and amount of the benefit we seek, if that is the only way to minimize the risks. Because we have duties to do no harm and to benefit others, we are responsible for balancing harms and benefits in an imperfect world. But, *ceteris paribus,* the principle of not harming others (including imposing risks) takes priority over the principle of benefiting others: thus, we should minimize risks even at some reduction in the magnitude and/or probability of the benefit. Although this principle is sound, it is difficult to specify how far we should go to minimize risks short of making it impossible to realize the benefit we seek.
5. In the long run, "the reversibility of an action should . . . be counted as a major benefit; its irreversibility a major cost."[26] Thus, reversibility of a technology and its effects should be preferred over irreversibility. Why should reversibility have this privileged position? Surely, if we could realize the ideal social order on earth, we would prefer that it be irreversible and imperishable. But precisely because of the *uncertainties* about probabilities and magnitudes of benefits and harms, we should be particularly cautious about technologies with apparently irreversible effects. The "preservation of future options" IS an important goal, and

---

25 For a defense of "intermediate technologies," see E. F. Schumacher, Small Is Beautiful (Harper & Row, 1973); for a defense of "alternative technology," see David Dickson, The Politics of Alternative Technology (Universe Books, 1975). For a critique of these movements, see Witold Rybczynski, Paper Heroes: A Review of Appropriate Technology (Doubleday & Co., 1980).

26 National Academy of Sciences, Technology: Processes of Assessment and Choice, p. 32.

it requires, for example, special concern about the destruction of an animal species and about nuclear waste.

Let me summarize these points about the principle of proportionality, the first consideration in technology assessment. We should balance the probabilities and amounts of benefits and harms. Value considerations will influence all aspects of the balance, including what counts as benefits and harms, how much they count, and how uncertainty is to be resolved. If lives are valued in public policy by determining how much people are willing to pay, the process of valuing lives is not inherently objectionable and may even be illuminating. Procedurally, the advocates of a technology should demonstrate its innocence before it is implemented and should show that its risk-benefit ratio is more favorable than any alternative technologies. We should minimize risks when we reduce (within limits) the probability and amount of benefit. Finally, reversibility is a benefit, irreversibility a cost.

LIMITING PRINCIPLES

Many flaws in contemporary technology assessments can be traced to the perspective of utilitarianism—the moral, social, and political doctrine that acts and policies are to be judged by their consequences and effects. It is an end-result view of life. After my praise for the principle of proportionality, the reader may wonder whether I am not at least a "closet utilitarian." After all, isn't the principle of proportionality roughly what the utilitarians mean by the principle of utility—maximizing net benefit relative to harm? Any adequate moral, social, or political theory must include the principle of proportionality or the principle of utility. In a world that is not ideal, it is impossible always to do good and to avoid harm. Often doing good produces at least the risk of harm. The principle of proportionality or utility requires that we weigh and balance these benefits and harms when they come into conflict and that we try to produce a net benefit (or, when considering only bad states of affairs, the best of the alternatives). Whatever we call this principle it is required by any adequate morality.

But we can accept the principle of proportionality or utility without accepting utilitarianism, which may be stated more sharply as the doctrine that right and wrong are determined *only* by the consequences of acts or policies. It makes the utility the only principle (act-utilitarianism) or the *primary* principle (rule-utilitarianism). And it distorts many technology assessments by restricting the range of relevant moral considerations. In particular, it concentrates on aggregative rather than distributive matters and it ignores other moral limits such as "rights" (which it frequently translates into "interests").

Utilitarian assessors sum up the interests of various individuals and groups to be affected by the technology, and they use this summation to determine our policy toward that technology. Although they may take account of wider and wider ranges of impacts and interests, they frequently overlook how burdens and harms are distributed. "Acceptable level of risk" of a technology, for example, should not be considered only in terms of the summed-up interests of the society. Principles of justice require that we consider the distribution of risks and benefits.

This issue can be sharpened by an examination of four possible patterns of distribution of risks and benefits. (1) The risks and benefits may fall on the same party. For example, in most therapy, the patient bears the major risks and stands to gain the major benefits. (2) One party may bear the risks, while another party gains the benefits. For example, in non-therapeutic research, the subject bears risks, while others in the future will gain the benefits. Or we may gain the benefits of some technologies that will adversely affect future generations. (3) Both parties may bear the risks, while only one party gains the benefits. For example, a nuclear-powered artificial heart would benefit the user but would impose risks on other parties as well as on the user. (4) Both parties may gain the benefits, while only one party bears the risks. For example, persons in the vicinity of a nuclear power plant may bear significantly greater risks than other persons who also benefit from the plant. These patterns suggest the importance of considerations of distributive justice. As an Advisory Committee on the Biological Effects of Ionizing Radiations reports:

For medical radiation, as well as for certain uses of radiation in energy production, the problem of balancing benefits and costs is complicated by issues of ethics and discrimination. As an example, increased years of life expectation or increased economic productivity can be a useful measure of health benefit in some contexts. If, however, these parameters are used to balance the benefit-cost equation against the elderly with limited life expectancy or those with limited productivity, important values of society will have been overlooked.[27]

---

[27] Advisory Committee on the Biological Effects of Ionizing Radiations, National Research Council, Considerations of Health Benefit-cost Analysis for Activities Involving Ionizing Radiation Exposure and Alternatives (Washington, DC: National Academy of Sciences, 1977), p. 150.

Utilitarianism in technology assessment often fails to take account of other limits because of its particular view of rationality. Max Weber drew classic distinctions between types of social action: "goal-rational" (*zweckrational*), "value-rational" (*wertrational*), affective, and traditional types of action. For our purposes the first two, which I introduced in Chapter 4 of *Priorities in Biomedical Ethics,* are the most important. Value-rational conduct involves "a conscious belief in the absolute value of some ethical, aesthetic, religious, or other form of behavior, entirely for its own sake and independently of any prospects of external success."[28] Goal-rational conduct involves reasoning about means to ends. It is a form of "instrumental rationality," involving the choice of effective (and efficient) means to given ends. It has been dominant not only in technology but also in technology assessment. By stressing limits, I have tried to include another type of rationality that may modify instrumental rationality by setting boundaries and constraints on the pursuit of goals.

Instrumental rationality tends to exclude value-rational considerations because they do not fit easily into the schema of means and ends. Just as I suggested about policies of the allocation of resources, we might choose policies toward technologies not because they *achieve* certain goals, but because they *express* certain values. They are expressive, symbolic, or representative. This range of considerations frequently involves *gestures,* not only *tasks.* For example, we might approach nature to make it serve our needs, or to express a certain attitude toward or relationship with it. As Laurence Tribe indicates, technology assessors typically ask what are society's current values regarding nature and they treat nonhuman life merely in relation to those values. But suppose society asked seriously, How should we value nature, including wildlife? And suppose the society came to the conclusion that it should treat nature with respect. Although this conclusion would not necessarily imply that the society would never give human interests priority over nature, "the very process of according nature a fraternal rather than an exploited role would shape the community's identity and at least arguably alter its moral character."

---

28 Weber, Max Weber on Law in Economy and Society, p. 1. It should also be obvious from my argument that I believe that it is both possible and desirable to have rational deliberation about the ends that are chosen. They are not merely arbitrary. Yet, as I suggested in Chapter 4, the selection of some ends is mainly political or even aesthetic.

As Tribe suggests, the decision maker's own identity might be at stake, for in choosing policies toward technologies, "the decision-maker chooses not merely how to achieve his ends but what they are to be and who he is to become."[29] Who are we and who shall we be? These are considerations of agent-morality that do and should influence our technology assessments.

PROCESS

One critical issue in technology assessment is often overlooked: process. Process is largely a matter of who should decide—that is, who should make the assessment, and how. It is possible to argue that technology assessors do not overlook process. Rather, they judge processes by their results. They ask whether particular processes "pay off" in producing the best possible outcomes—that is, the best possible predictions, evaluations, and controls of technology. When this judgment of processes by their results is combined with the view that we should judge technologies by their predicted consequences for human interests as measured by preferences, there is one obvious conclusion: the *experts* should make the assessment. This viewpoint simply perpetuates the myth of the end of ideology even while trying to control technology.

Its critics are numerous and vocal. Many of them are concerned with processes of evaluation and decision-making in some independence of their results. In technology assessment, the demand for public participation has become widespread and has encouraged the language of "participatory technology."[30] The World Council of Churches Church and Society Conference on "Faith, Science and the Future" at

---

29 Laurence Tribe, "Technology Assessment and the Fourth Discontinuity. The Limits of Instrumental Rationality," Southern California Law Review, June 1973, pp. 657, 631-635. See also Laurence Tribe, "Polity Science: Analysis or Ideology, Philosophy and Public Affairs, Fall 1972, pp. 66-110. Tribe's discussion has been important for this chapter, especially for this paragraph and the previous one. For another critique of the assumptions of much technology assessment, see Carroll Pursell, "Belling the Cat, Critique of Technology Assessment," Lex et Scientia, Oct-Dec. 1974, pp. 130-145.

30 See James D. Carroll, "Participatory Technology," Science. Vol. 171 (1971), pp-647-653.

the Massachusetts Institute of Technology in July 1979 emphasized a just, participatory and sustainable society. As the general secretary of the WCC, Philip Potter, put it in his address at the MIT conference, "a just and sustainable society is impossible without a society which is participatory." He continued:

In the present situation of science and technology, they are not really participatory, or rather they are forced to be biased on the side of those who wield economic and political power. There is little sign that they are on the side of the oppressed, the deprived and the marginalized, or simply the people.[31]

It is no exaggeration to claim that "the central issue in technology assessment concerns democratic theory."[32] Involving the public, and especially the individuals and groups affected by the technology, expresses the value of equal concern and respect. It should be built not so much on anticipated results as on the right to treatment as an equal.[33] Processes of public participation in technology assessment are essential to embody this right to treatment as an equal, as one whose wishes, choices, and actions count. In addition, fairness, a principle derived from the principle of equal concern and respect applies to specific procedures that may be used for public participation (e.g., adversary hearings and public forums). These values and principles are independent of the results of the procedures and processes.

Emphasizing that technology requires a "new ethics of long-range responsibility," Hans Jonas notes the "insufficiency of representative government to meet the new demands on its normal principles and by

---

[31] Philip Potter, "Science and Technology: Why Are the Churches Concerned?" in Faith and Science in an Unjust World, Vol. 1, Plenary Presentations, pp. 26-27. For the reports and Recommendations, see Faith and Science in an Unjust World, Vol. 2,ed. by Paul Abrecht (Fortress Press, 1980). For a critical analysis of the conference, see Alan Geyer, "The EST Complex at MIT: The Ecumenical-Scientific-Technological Complex," Ecumenical Review, October 1979, pp. 372-380, and other essays in that issue (e.g., those by Ian Barbour and Ole Jensen).

[32] Harold P. Green, "Cost Risk-Benefit Assessment and the Law: Introduction and Perspective, George Washington Law Review, August 1977, p 908.

[33] For the principle of equal concern and respect, see Ronald Dworkin, Taking Rights Seriously.

its normal mechanics."[34] In a lighter vein, H. L. Mencken once said, "I do not believe in democracy, but I admit that it provides the only really amusing form of government ever endured by mankind." He went on to describe democracy as "government by orgy, an orgy of public opinion." Obviously, it is necessary to devise procedures and mechanisms that can both satisfy independent principles and values and sustain effective and disciplined public participation in technology assessment. The creation of such procedures and mechanisms may presuppose that we transcend interest-group liberalism.

TEMPORAL PERSPECTIVE

As currently practiced, technology assessment tends to "find opportunities for making judgments and taking action only at those points in which a new development in technology occurs."[35] Why? Perhaps because the utilitarianism back of much technology assessment is forward-looking, or because many assessors believe that what we now have is good, or because they believe that we cannot undo what has already been done. Whatever the reason, technology assessment for the most part predicts and evaluates for the future and is less interested in the evaluation of technologies already developed. Langdon Winner argues that we need not only technology assessment, but also "technology criticism," which can look at the past and the present as well as the future, which can look at long-term trends of technological development as well as at particular technologies, and which can look at the society as well as at the technologies it produces.[36]

Winner's concerns are legitimate, but technology assessment, properly understood, can encompass them. It should be an ongoing process, dealing not only with the introduction of a technology but also with its impact as it is implemented. For example, there was no systematic assessment of the technology of renal dialysis in the 1950s and 1960s, but it has received careful scrutiny since its introduction,

---

34 Hans Jonas, "Technology and Responsibility: Reflections on the New Tasks of Ethics," Philosophical Essays: From Ancient Creed to Technological Man (Prentice-Hall, 1974), pp. 18-19

35 Langdon Winner, "On Criticizing Technology," in Albert H. Teich (ed.), Technology and Man's Future, 2d ed. (St. Martin's Press, 1977).

36 Ibid.

widespread use, and funding by the Government. While it is difficult to make adjustments once societal momentum has reached a certain point, we have learned, and are continuing to learn from the experience with dialysis, and our experience may improve our policies in other areas. Among the numerous questions that remain about dialysis are whether it is worth the cost (already over one billion dollars a year), whether the money could have spent better elsewhere, and whether we are able to cope with the successes of technologies (e.g., prolongation of life vs. quality of life of dialysis patients).

Nevertheless, our struggle with these questions, and others may illuminate present and future technology assessments.

Another point needs to be made about temporal orientation. Historical perspective may bring a cautionary tone to discussions of technology assessment. In a fine essay, entitled "Technology Assessment from the Stance of a Medieval Historian," Lynn White, Jr., directs our attention away from the easily measured factors to what he calls the "imponderables" and insists that technology assessment requires "cultural analysis" since the impact of a technology is filtered through the culture and the society.[37] Among his several case studies is alcohol, which was distilled from wine as a pharmaceutical at Salerno, the site of Europe's most famous medical school. How, he asks, could anyone have offered an assessment of alcohol in the twelfth century? Alcohol was praised in medieval literature as a pharmaceutical with beneficial effects for chronic headaches, stomach trouble, cancer, arthritis, sterility, falling or graying hair, and bad breath. It was supposed to be good for people who had a "cold temperament." But then widespread drunkenness and disorder became problems. To shorten the history, we have problems of traffic deaths and cirrhosis of the liver. White observes, "a study group eight centuries ago, equipped with entire foresight, would have failed at an assessment of alcohol as we today fail."

Although White's point is not always clear, it appears to be that technologies touch on many aspects of life (e.g., psychological and sociological factors) that cannot be determined with great precision. What will happen in the interactions between technologies and society, culture, and psyches is an "imponderable." His lesson is salutary. History is ironic,

---

[37] Lynn White, Jr., "Technology Assessment from the Stance of a Medieval Historian," Medieval Religion and Technology: Collected Essays (University of California Press, 1978), pp. 261-276.

and we can only be modest about (a) our ability to *predict* effects, (b) our ability to *assess* effects, and (c) our ability to *control* effects. It is true, as a character in *Death Trap* puts it, that "nothing recedes like success." While modesty is in order because our abilities are indeed limited, we have no choice but to try to predict, to assess, and to control in the light of moral principles and values.[38]

---

[38] This chapter originated in a lecture for a Conference on the Technological Society and the Individual sponsored by the Program on Social and Political Thought at the University of Virginia in 1978. It was subsequently delivered in modified form at Whitworth College (1979), at a symposium on Religious Belief in the Age of Science and Technology sponsored by the Religion Club of the University of Virginia (1980), at Earlman School of Religion as one of the 1980 Willson Lectures, and at Miami University (Ohio) as one of the 1980 Wickenden Lectures. It has been strengthened by various comments and suggestions I received in these settings. I am particularly grateful to Dante Germino who, alas, will not be satisfied that I have answered his criticisms.

Index